This volume of essays is intended as a tribute to the distinguished medieval historian Christopher Brooke. It addresses new questions in areas of medieval history which Professor Brooke has made his own: urban life and religious life.

The fourteen essays explore the coexistence of religious ideas and ecclesiastical institutions with urban practices and townspeople. They span five hundred years of the history of western Christendom, ranging from Magdeburg to Majorca, and from Cambridge to Cluny. The essays break new ground in a number of areas in medieval history: in economic history, the history of ideas, and the history of religious institutions. The contributors have been attuned throughout to the complex interactions of groups and ideas within urban space. The book also contains a bibliography of Christopher Brooke's writings and an appreciation of his work.

Contributors: Anna Sapir Abulafia, David Abulafia, Paul Binski, Brenda Bolton, Martin Brett, Marjorie Chibnall, Giles Constable, Barrie Dobson, Michael Franklin, Rosalind Hill, Peter Linehan, David Luscombe, Robert Markus, Henry Mayr-Harting, Miri Rubin, Elisabeth Van Houts, J. A. Watt.

Church and city, 1000–1500

Christopher Brooke

CHURCH
AND CITY
1000–1500

Essays in honour of
Christopher Brooke

Edited by
DAVID ABULAFIA
MICHAEL FRANKLIN
and
MIRI RUBIN

CAMBRIDGE
UNIVERSITY PRESS

Published by the Press Syndicate of the University of Cambridge
The Pitt Building, Trumpington Street, Cambridge CB2 1RP
40 West 20th Street, New York, NY 10011-4211, USA
10 Stamford Road, Oakleigh, Victoria 3166, Australia

© Cambridge University Press 1992

First published 1992

Printed in Great Britain at the University Press, Cambridge

A catalogue record for this book is available from the British Library

Library of Congress cataloguing in publication data

Church and city, 1000–1500: essays in honour of Christopher Brooke/
edited by David Abulafia, Michael Franklin, and Miri Rubin.
p. cm.
Includes bibliographical references and index.
ISBN 0-521-35611-3
1. Church history – Middle Ages, 1000–1500.   2. Cities and towns, Medieval – Europe –
History.   3. Cities and towns – Europe – Religious
aspects.   4. Europe – Church history – Middle Ages, 1000–1500.
I. Brooke, Christopher Nugent Lawrence.   II. Abulafia, David.
III. Franklin, M. J. (Michael J.)   IV. Rubin, Miri.
BR252.C538   1992
274′.04 – dc20   91-20487 CIP

ISBN 0 521 35611 3 hardback

Contents

Contents

Illustrations

Contributors

ANNA SAPIR ABULAFIA Fellow and College Lecturer in History at Lucy Cavendish College, Cambridge

DAVID ABULAFIA Reader in Mediterranean History in the University of Cambridge and Fellow of Gonville and Caius College, Cambridge

PAUL BINSKI Lecturer in the History of Art, University of Manchester

BRENDA BOLTON Senior Lecturer in Medieval History, Queen Mary and Westfield College, University of London

MARTIN BRETT Fellow of Robinson College, Cambridge

MARJORIE CHIBNALL Emeritus Fellow of Clare Hall, Cambridge

GILES CONSTABLE Professor and Permanent Member at the Institute for Advanced Study, Princeton, New Jersey, USA

BARRIE DOBSON Professor of Medieval History, University of Cambridge and Fellow of Christ's College, Cambridge

MICHAEL FRANKLIN Fellow and Tutor of Wolfson College, Cambridge

ROSALIND HILL Emeritus Professor of History, Queen Mary and Westfield College, University of London

PETER LINEHAN Fellow and Tutor of St John's College, Cambridge

DAVID LUSCOMBE Professor of Medieval History, University of Sheffield

List of contributors

ROBERT MARKUS Emeritus Professor of Medieval History, University of Nottingham

HENRY MAYR-HARTING Fellow and Tutor in History at St Peter's College, Oxford

MIRI RUBIN Fellow and Tutor in History at Pembroke College, Oxford

ELISABETH VAN HOUTS Fellow and Tutor of Newnham College, Cambridge

J. A. WATT Emeritus Professor of Medieval History, University of Newcastle-upon-Tyne

Preface

Christopher Brooke's years as a young professor, and in particular the 1960s and the 1970s, in Liverpool and in London, coincided with dramatic changes in the intellectual climate and the institutional and political underpinnings of historical work. His expansive and generous intellectual tenor can only be understood against the background of a world of optimistic growth in which universities, departments, research centres were mushrooming, where posts and numbers of students were multiplying, and where a variety of historical approaches and idioms was emerging in historians' circles. Christopher responded to these changes as a lively head of department, as a supervisor of research, as a commentator and colleague. In his vision history could be done in many ways: as history teachers, as university lecturers, as archivists, local historians, and part-time enthusiasts. While family tradition and an upbringing in Cambridge grounded Christopher in a venerable school of ecclesiastical history, the world around him was at flux, and offered new challenges. Some of the new trends in history significantly oriented Christopher's mature work: the new urban history and the new religious history. The adjective 'new' here points to an orientation in study which is sensitive to the wide range of practices and experiences of a wide range of historical actors, to a variety of ways of living in the past. Christopher's study of London, his long standing observation of the rhythm of life in Italian towns (influenced no doubt by the work of Rosalind Brooke), his scrutiny of parish churches and their communities, of colleges, of the living sacrament of marriage boldly expanded the contours of traditional history. The engagement with the detail of town life and of religious practice would have also appealed to Christopher's practical nature, his love for solving riddles and getting things right. The work in London offered an occasion to mark an affection and loyalty to a new home; it was also an exciting early venture which was to be followed (and still is followed) by myriad monographs on towns. In studying popular religion, Christian marriage, liturgical practice, parochial foundation, Christopher responded to a trend which elsewhere animated colleagues such as Raoul Manselli, Georges Duby and Jacques Le Goff.

The church and the town thus offered themselves to us as fitting and exciting topics for study in this volume which is also an offering. It is a tribute to Christopher that this choice can in no way even hint at the breadth of his interests and the range of his influence. Yet it captures a preoccupation which was constant in his life, from boyhood when he studied St Paul's Cathedral in his father's company, till this very day. The period broadly spanned by the volume is also a mark of Christopher's interest in the central Middle Ages over many years, and his eventual entry into the later Middle Ages, an entry which coincided with his work on the university and colleges of Cambridge in recent years. These decisions on period and subject have forced upon us an inevitable exclusion of subjects and of potential contributors who should have been part of a tribute for Christopher Brooke, and who would have undoubtedly wished to contribute to such a venture.

DAVID ABULAFIA
MICHAEL FRANKLIN
MIRI RUBIN

Abbreviations

AC	Capitular or cathedral archive
ASRSP	*Archivio della Societa Romana di Storia Patria*
BL	British Library, London
CS	*Councils and Synods* I, D. Whitelock, M. Brett and C. N. L. Brooke, eds. (Oxford, 1982); II, F. M. Powicke and C. R. Cheney, eds. (Oxford, 1964).
CUL	Cambridge University Library
EHR	*English Historical Review*
LE	*Liber Eliensis*
MGH	Monumenta Germaniae Historica
PL	*Patrologiae cursus completus. Series Latina*, J.-P. Migne, ed., 221 vols., (Paris, 1841–64).
PRS	Pipe Roll Society
RH	*Rotuli Hundredorum*
RS	Chronicles and memorials of Great Britain and Ireland during the Middle Ages, published under the direction of the Master of the Rolls (Rolls Series)
VCH	The Victoria History of the Counties of England
YCA	York City Archives

Christopher Brooke
... at Cambridge

MARJORIE CHIBNALL

Christopher Brooke has held chairs in three universities, but Cambridge, with Caius College at its heart, is his home. The son of a Fellow and librarian of the college, who became the second Professor of Medieval History in the university, he grew up with the college and its traditions in his blood. Schooling at Winchester added another city and college to his loyalties, but he returned naturally to Caius as a scholar. There he came under the influence of David Knowles, and added to the meticulous accuracy required in a university that had produced the original Cambridge medieval and modern histories, and to the early training of his father in church history, the warm humanity and ecumenical interests of Knowles himself. There he remained for a few years as college Fellow, university lecturer, and a *praelector rhetoricus* who gave dignity to his office, before being tempted away to a chair in medieval history. Appropriately it was in Cambridge that he met and married Rosalind, and began the happy family life, shortly to be shared with Francis, Philip and Patrick. For some twenty years Liverpool and London claimed him; but finally he has come home once again, to the delight of his friends, as Dixie Professor of Ecclesiastical History and Professorial Fellow of Caius.

Colleges, as he himself has written, are pieces of living history, and their dons and undergraduates exponents of traditions equally alive. So he has learnt from both the Caius and the Cambridge traditions, and given them new life. He has respected his father's belief enshrined in the older Cambridge Tripos, that a Teaching Fellow should try to teach the whole of history, but in a more professional way. His inaugural as Dixie Professor (later to be expanded into a book) carried the theme of marriage far beyond the Middle Ages in time, and from history into art, literature and theology. His Birkbeck Lectures handled the theme of religion in the University of Cambridge from the nineteenth century to 1960 and beyond with learning, eloquence and wit. The range is wide, the subject matter kept within those disciplines where he enjoys true mastery – and at the same time it honours the theological tradition he found in Caius, which stretched from Cosin and Jeremy Taylor to Geoffrey Lampe. Similarly he may be reckoned heir to the antiquarian tradition of such men as Brady and Blomefield; he has graced the office of President of the Society of Antiquaries of London, and carried his duties there into a wide field by leading the struggle to preserve and continue the work at Sutton Hoo.

Love of Cambridge, its buildings, its learning, even its more engaging eccentricities has been at the heart of much of his most recent writing and teaching. Through his collaboration with the photographer Wim Swann, which began before his return to Cambridge when they worked together on medieval monasteries, he has been able to show the changing face of colleges and universities, in both his history of Caius College and the history of Oxford and Cambridge, which he published with Roger High-field. And now, while actively at work on the more detailed history of Cambridge University, he is himself adding a new chapter to that history in his writing and teaching, his encouragement of research, his participation in scholarly activities wherever history is studied, and above all in his warm and generous friendships. As he himself wrote in his history of his college, its fortunes had to be shown 'in the wider perspective of the University and the world of education and culture and religion, and even of politics, without which it makes no sense'. Only his own graceful pen could do justice to all his achievements; but surely they show the fulfilment of the gifts for which, through the centuries, Caians have asked in the prayer written by their founder: 'the power of learning, the desire of wisdom, and the grace to do good'.

... at Liverpool

ROBERT MARKUS

Christopher Brooke succeeded Geoffrey Barraclough in the Chair of Medieval History at Liverpool, as one of the youngest professors ever appointed in that university, in 1956. His appointment there, almost simultaneously with a new occupant of the Chair of Modern History, had one immediate consequence: the plan of two staircases rather than a single one for the School of History – to enable the two professors to avoid unnecessary encounters with each other – could now be abandoned. One would, and in the event did, suffice. On the foundations secured by their predecessors, Christopher Brooke and his colleague in the Chair of Modern History (David Quinn) rapidly built up one of the most lively and distinguished schools of history in the country. In 1956 the Professor of Medieval History had four colleagues in his department; in 1967 there were seven.

Growth secured range and variety; and Christopher took care to encourage a rare sense of working together, and indeed, in the school's civilised Georgian premises, of living together. He was firmly committed to the view that a happy team of colleagues makes for a successful school. Daily coffee and tea taken in the relaxed life of the common room were almost as important to the department's work as were individual or paired tutorials, or the special subjects taught in tiny groups. He was a perfect taker of seminars, creating an atmosphere in which students felt free and stimulated to speak. In his special subject classes on the friars they stubbed out cigarettes irreverently into a Friar Tuck ash-tray. The warm friendships in the school crossed the two floors between the senior and the students' common rooms. The residential reading-weeks that were introduced in the Liverpool History School in Christopher's time were to enhance this easy informal trust and friendship; they were also to serve as the occasion for revealing in Christopher an unsuspected and dangerous talent for football. His breezy informality did not stop him being a formidably effective member of university committees and official bodies; indeed, his severe rationing of the serious attention he was prepared to give to carefully selected committees made him all the more effective.

In his inaugural lecture, 'The dullness of the past' (1957),[1] Christopher spoke of the convictions that underlay both his own scholarly work and his teaching. He concluded his lecture with words quoted from Jacob Burckhardt: 'An artist must be a master or nothing ... In learning, on the other hand, a man can only be a master in one particular field, namely as a specialist, and in some field he *should* be a specialist. But if he is not to forfeit his capacity for taking general views or even his respect for general views, he should be an amateur at as many points as possible ...' Both the amateur of widely ranging curiosity and the expert in half a dozen specialised disciplines, from Palaeography and Diplomatic (he regularly lectured on diplomatic to those taking the postgraduate Archives Diploma) to architectural history and archeology, are clearly to be seen in the work of these years. This was also why it was a delight to be either a colleague or a pupil of Christopher's. The distinction between these two categories never ran very deep – no deeper than did the distinction between teaching and research, activities that he liked to conflate under the heading of 'learning', something we are all equally engaged in; and a 'place of learning' was his favoured definition of a university. The school grew quickly into a true intellectual community.

Two highly successful text-books, *From Alfred to Henry III* (vol. 2 in the Nelson History of England, 1961) and *Europe in the central Middle Ages, 962–1154* (in Longman's General History of Europe, 1964), and books addressed to a wider public, *The Saxon and the Norman kings* (1963) and *The twelfth century Renaissance* (1969), published only a little later, grew from his teaching and reflected its broad humanity, its concern to keep students and readers always close to the sources, and its inclusion of the visual and tangible remains of the past. Work was proceeding at the same time on his editions (with different collaborators) of the letters and charters of Gilbert Foliot and the letters of John of Salisbury. The essays gathered in *Medieval church and society* (1971) are a fair indication of the themes which began to exercise Christopher's mind during these years, many of which remained lasting preoccupations and were to lead to major works on their subjects: Christian marriage in the Middle Ages, popular religion, religion

---

[1] Published by Liverpool University Press, 1957; reprinted in his *Medieval church and society* (London, 1971), pp. 23–38.

and urban society, the mendicant orders. Some of these interests he shared with his wife and collaborator, Rosalind.

Although he once quoted Albert Schweitzer on hatred as sharpening historical insight, Christopher lacked the streak of icy hatred that could give so sharp an edge, for instance, to the way his loved and revered mentor David Knowles wrote of Gilbert Foliot. What is much more characteristic of his work is broad imaginative sympathy, elegance of expression, and the ability to enter the emotional and spiritual world of characters as widely varied as Hildebrand, Héloïse, Wolfram von Eschenbach, Francesco di Marco Datini, and, among the moderns, Paul Sabatier or Edmund Bishop. These last two he often used to epitomise the essentials of what makes a historian: Sabatier's 'romantic faith' – 'we must see things from the inside, see them as individual expressions of the things which make the world what it is' – combined with the critical study of the sources; or Bishop's 'rare combination of breadth and depth of vision, with a style... which reveals a philosopher's precision'. These are not the worst models for a historian to adopt. Once he praised Sabatier for helping historical studies to avoid 'a divorce between romantic journalism and learned dust'. To have upheld and encouraged such a model of historical study might well be seen as Christopher Brooke's most characteristic achievement in his tenure of the Liverpool chair.

... at London

ROSALIND HILL

When Christopher Brooke accepted the Chair of History at Westfield College his future department knew, from reliable rumours, that he had already refused the offer of other posts which might appear to have conferred greater prestige. Here, we realised, was a man of discernment. When he arrived, looking extremely young for a professor of some years' standing, wearing a bright blue anorak and accompanied by a large dog, we quickly learned three other things about him. First, that here was a man of deep and perceptive learning, carried without any trace of conceit or pomposity. Next, that he would treat anyone, from the Principal to the youngest candidate, with the same graceful and instinctive courtesy, and, finally, that he had a turn of speed, shown in his meteoric travels round the college's buildings and gardens, which would not have disgraced an Olympic sprinter.

Others have paid tribute to his many learned writings and to his brilliant lectures. We remember particularly his power of relating history to the visual image, in painting, architecture and music. From this, and from his collaboration with two colleagues, Nicolai Rubinstein and Neil Stratford, there grew up the Westfield school of history combined with history of art, a new venture in the blending of two traditions which has produced some excellent scholars and has been the model for subsequent experiments in other places. Christopher's guidance, whether at the excavation of a monastic building, in the picture-gallery of a great house, or in those 'London walks' which became a very good institution, illuminated history for us in ways which we could not have imagined, and which we shall always remember.

In our departmental meetings of staff and students he held the chair with great good-humour and extreme clear-headedness. One of his colleagues recalled his power of sitting quietly through a long discussion, taking a few notes, and producing at the end a short, masterly summary which was exactly right. Those of us who sat with him on the Board of Studies noticed the same quality of clear, deep simplicity, which enabled him to unravel tangled arguments, and to arrive at a conclusion which should have been obvious, but which had been in danger of being buried under the endless irrelevances which beset committees.

He worked extremely hard, usually getting up at five o'clock in the morning in order to put in a spell of his own research before starting his day's activities in college. (One of his friends remembered also how he used to serve the household with breakfast.) He had, said one who had collaborated with him as a writer, an unusual capacity for bringing together the right person and the right project. This meant that not only did he produce good work himself, he also inspired it in others. He would give to his first-year students the same meticulous and single-minded care which he bestowed on the many distinguished scholars who came, often from far-off places, in order to consult him. To him, all historians were members of one craft, equally in need of the best help he could give, and never, I think, did they go away without having acquired some new and lasting insight into their work.

Westfield has always possessed a strong tradition of personal friendship among its people, and into this Christopher entered most fully. His department was a place of lively impromptu parties, of scholarship mixed with sheer fun, of expeditions and experiments. 'Looking back', said one of his colleagues, 'I wonder how he found time for so many pleasant touches – walking the dog in Highgate Woods while discussing my forthcoming visit to the Italian archives, or exploring Canterbury before a conference of the Ecclesiastical History Society.' His dogs became something of a departmental legend. One – a most gentle creature so far as we were concerned – frustrated a would-be mugger on Hampstead Heath (an event which clearly caused Christopher a good deal of amusement). Another, a spotted Dalmatian called Dubrovnik, used to lie at his feet during tutorials, and occasionally, at the conclusion of a particularly wordy essay, she would utter a heartfelt groan ('after which', said Christopher, 'there wasn't much which I could add').

Any account of Christopher's work in Westfield would be incomplete without a tribute to the influence which flowed, quite unconsciously, from his strong Christian faith and from his extremely happy marriage. He never pontificated, but the whole tenor of his work was suffused with his trust in God and his reliance on earthly affection. This made him a very satisfying person to be with. A student much given to proselytising once asked him when he was converted to Christianity. 'I don't know', was the reply, 'it has never occurred to me to believe in anything else.' In a moment of irritation with some rather tiresome theologian, he was heard to remark that, because the Gospels were not biographies in the modern sense, it was ridiculous to contend that they were not biographies at all. I remember his once preaching a most moving sermon in the college chapel, taking as his text the story of the appearance of Christ to Mary Magdalene on the first Easter Day, – 'that strange scene, unlike anything else in history'.

All good times come to an end, and we knew that we should eventually lose him to Cambridge, which by tradition and achievement was his rightful place. His departure was marked, in typical style, by his giving to all his colleagues in the department a perfectly splendid party. Like that of some of the twelfth-century teachers whom he rather resembled, 'his memory with us is pleasantness and blessing'.

Urban life and the language of religion

———◆◇◆———

Religious culture in town and country: reflections on a great divide

MIRI RUBIN

Christopher Brooke's work has been informed by two of the most fruitful areas of exploration of the medieval world: the study of town life and the study of religious practice.[1] The intersection of these interests produced notions of distinctive urban culture and urban religion, some of the most enduring ideas about medieval life: that it was experienced differently in town and countryside. This view emerged from prevailing materialist conceptions of culture which seek a strong grounding for ideas in the rhythms of work and in institutional determination, which unambiguously embed identity and experience in the physical expectations of work and leisure. This paper will question the degree to which medieval villagers and townspeople were separated in the realms of culture. It will do so through two approaches: one which will consider medieval religious culture as partly transcending or effacing such a divide; the other which will present urban and rural life as sharing some important characteristics rather than being divided, say, by the nexus of the market. Throughout the term 'urban' will become increasingly difficult to settle and define, as we move between 'town' as legal definition, as economic function, as a mystical fantasy, as the 'other'.

In urban history, the studies of the past within the framework of towns, economic history, cultural history, religious history, legal history, and recently women's history, have interacted more fruitfully than in any other area. The river-harbours, cross-roads and ancient markets which brought forth medieval towns have

---

[1] On trends in the study of medieval religion see discussion in J. Van Enghen, 'The Christian Middle Ages as a historiographical problem', *American Historical Review* 91 (1986), 519–52.

also provided a meeting point for a wide range of disciplines and approaches to the past. As the project of urban history developed towns emerged as vibrant and intense places, where ideas travelled quickly, intrigues flared up and sometimes grew into civic wars, where frequent discussion prompted scepticism and rational scrutiny, where men's minds worked quickly: calculating the value of a keg of wine, of a length of cloth, of a slave, eyeing the sheen of a fur, seizing the most opportune moment for intervention in the deliberations of the town-council. To the modern imagination and the theorists of progress (and modernisation) which produced the urban history of the 1960s and 1970s, towns embodied the very essence of civilisation cast in the shape of modern values. Town life was rational, entrepreneurial, innovative, manipulative of its countryside and of its less adept partners and competitors. It was also the place where the finest institutions of human interaction were said to flourish; councils and guilds, fraternities and committees, in a brotherhood that was chosen, deliberated, rational, controlled and supervised. Town life was not a natural order, but a cultivated one, an effort of mind and intellect, not the legacy of soil and blood. The town which urban history set out to study was forward looking and future-orientated. Away from the atavism of kinship and the hold of tradition, away from the injustices of servility, it was seen as transporting men and women into the order of rationality, the freedom of the market (which Adam Smith called 'calm'). Towns have been deemed to be as progressive, as energetic and as free as western historians hoped their own cities and states would become or remain. Medieval towns were particularly attractive since they existed before the advent of factory chimneys, pollution or drug abuse; they were thus irresistible.[2]

Towns soon came to fill a mediating function between the historian and a host of new themes in social history: crime in Ghent, learning in York, prostitution in the towns of Languedoc, charity in Cambridge. An array of activities in towns was thus discovered, areas of study that even the prophetic Frederick Maitland, Henri Pirenne or Helen Cam would hardly have anticipated, far transcending the legal and economic confines

[2] On the uses of the medieval past in conceptualisation of the present see L. Patterson, *Negotiating the past: the historical understanding of medieval literature* (Madison, WI, 1987), pp. 3–39.

within which towns were traditionally observed. Worlds of rich human and group experiences unfolded, in which the routines of family life, workshop, market, ritual and ceremony could be closely observed. Besides merchants, royal officials, bishops, canons, and sometimes rebellious artisans, we gradually came to learn of craftsmen and the labourers in their employ, servants, and travellers, the poor, the studious, and women at all these levels, at work, love and play. Outside the guild–halls and stone houses of merchants a world was being revealed, of friendship and competition, charity, poverty, crime, education and exchange, in parishes, in craft-guilds, in prisons, in workshops, in poor tenements, in hospitals and in taverns; a complex world ridden with tensions and conflict, violence and pageantry.

Now the study of urban communities has produced in the last two decades some illuminating knowledge, an acquaintance with religious practices which had hitherto remained out of sight. Attention to towns and to the lives of their humbler folk focused attention on groupings in which townspeople habitually took initiatives and assembled for social and religious action. An institution which cried out for attention was the religious fraternity (or religious guild),[3] a corporation of members combined in efforts for the increase of social and religious opportunity, which offered mutual help, maintained an elaborate system of commemoration of dead members, pooled resources and merit in a wide range of commercial, religious and political activities. Fraternities varied enormously in almost every aspect: some were town-wide, others limited to a parish, some were strongly associated with certain crafts, others were not; they varied in the degree of integration offered to wives of members, and to family in general. They differed in the level of payments required from members and in their social complexions: thus Venice had the *scuole grandi* as well as *arti minori*,[4] and a city like Norwich had the

---

[3] Following problems laid out in the classic article of G. Le Bras, 'Les Confréries chrétiennes: problèmes et propositions', *Revue du droit français et étranger*, ser. 4, 10–20 (1940–1), 310–63. On early guilds and the question of continuity throughout the Middle Ages see G. Rosser, 'The Anglo-Saxon gilds', in *Minsters and parish churches: the local church in transition, 950–1200*, ed. J. Blair, Oxford University Commission for Archaeology Monograph 17 (Oxford, 1988), 31–4.

[4] The former studied in B. Pullan, *Rich and poor in Renaissance Venice: the social institutions of a city state, to 1620* (Oxford, 1971), and the latter in R. C. MacKenney, *Tradesmen and traders: the world of the guilds* (London, 1986).

patrician fraternity of St George, as well as humble parish bodies like St Augustine's fraternity 'for the poor of the parish'.[5] Some fraternities recruited regionally and even nationally: famous fraternities like Corpus Christi of York attracted members from all over England, and some merchant fraternities offered membership and the related benefits to substantial merchants from other towns.[6] Fraternities invested communal funds in the maintenance of liturgy and celebration, and sometimes participated as a group in large urban ceremonial affairs; they commissioned and received works of art: altar-pieces, fine chalices and drinking vessels, monstrances for the eucharist, hangings and canopies given to them by well-to-do members for eternal memory. Fraternities appeared quintessentially urban, embodying the urban spirit of cooperation, the habits of extended trust learned in business, the discerning eye for organisational forms developed in the administratively complex towns.

Fraternities have thus revealed areas of town life which could only have been discovered once the close attention to urban social life was under way. They raise important questions about the contours of popular religion, since they often transcended parochial obligation and were thus able to reflect fashion, taste and religious sensibility. Yet once our acquaintance with fraternities is turned in a comparative mode to the rural sphere, we find striking similarities. Rural fraternities provided all the services that urban ones did, albeit on a smaller scale: they commemorated, buried, celebrated feast-day masses, offered help in poverty, and recognised the prerogative of kin in offering relief. Rural fraternities just like urban ones attempted to identify a certain respectable and capable element in a village, as shown in Charles de la Roncière's work on the fraternities of the Florentine *contado*; like urban ones they tended to include the 'effective' parish, what Gabriel Le Bras called 'la paroisse consensuelle'.[7] Not all male parishioners were fraternity members, but only those who were effective, respectable, productive: usually men of between thirty

---

[5] M. Rubin, 'Fraternities and lay piety in the later Middle Ages', *Städteforschungen* (1992), 1–14: 5.
[6] G. Rosser, 'The town and guild of Lichfield in the late Middle Ages', *Transactions of the South Staffordshire Archaeological and Historical Society* 27 (1987), 39–47.
[7] Le Bras, 'Les Confréries chrétiennes', 35.

and fifty-five years of age. Dedications of rural fraternities did not differ widely in the spread of patron saints or devotional motives: they had their predominance of dedications to the Virgin and to the Trinity, and a noticeable preference for Corpus Christi in the fourteenth century.[8] The comparative gaze confirms Susan Reynolds' claim that 'guilds were originally religious and social associations with no particular urban connotations'.[9] Indeed, why should the discriminating and knowing cooperation with neighbours – or even with strangers become brothers and sisters – for the extension of sociability, for provision of intercession, in the hope of relief, be an urban prerogative?

Finding that even small rural parishes contained within them a multiplicity of extremely small and rudimentary fraternities or groupings, humble affairs where people with a shared interest congregated around an altar, a light, an image of a saint, makes the point even more emphatically. Thus the churchwardens' accounts of Ashburton (Devon) show that there were discreet if humble groups of the 'wives' – married women of the parish; of bachelors – young unmarried men; and of 'maidens' – young unmarried women;[10] in other parishes there may be groups of 'upland' and 'lowland' bachelors. The impulse to socialise was constructed along numerous lines of identity: stage in life-cycle, age, gender, important distinctions in lives lived in towns or in villages.[11] The scope of such action clearly depended on the availability of resources and of leisure, on institutional constraints, but it cannot be analysed, in any useful way, as being *either* urban *or* rural. An institution found in urban life, has led us to discover similar formations in rural society, and perhaps ultimately to the dissipation of any necessary difference between the rural and urban types of perception and aspiration which fraternities might betoken in the members.

---

[8] J. Chiffoleau, *La Comptabilite de l'au-delà: les hommes, la mort et la religion dans la région d'Avignon à la fin du moyen-âge (vers 1320-vers 1480)*, Collection de l'Ecole française de Rome 47 (Rome, 1980), 448–53; M. Rubin, *Corpus Christi: the eucharist in late medieval culture* (Cambridge, 1991), pp. 232–43.

[9] S. Reynolds, 'Medieval urban history and the history of political thought', *Urban History Yearbook* (1982), 14–23, at 19.

[10] M. Rubin, 'Small groups: identity and solidarity in the later Middle Ages', in *Enterprise and individualism in the fifteenth century*, ed. J. Kermode (Gloucester, 1991), p. 141.

[11] For 'maidens' gatherings' in the late medieval parish of St Margaret, Westminster see G. Rosser, *Medieval Westminster, 1200–1540* (Oxford, 1989), p. 272.

Another area of religious/cultural activity brought to our attention through closer scrutiny of urban social life is the institution of chantries. In England these were popular forms for the endowment of what were rather optimistically designed to be perpetual commemorative arrangements for the souls of founders and their relatives and friends.[12] The impulse towards commemoration after death is familiar from the multiplication of provisions in late medieval wills. This mode of provision was flexible and responsive: they could be the great chantries of bishops in cathedrals, magnificent edifices in stone and marble, serviced by an army of chantry priests, or they could be humbler affairs, founded by merchants or members of the gentry; even collective efforts, as a group of people pooled resources for the maintenance in perpetuity of an income for the support of a chantry priest. It has been suggested that this form of provision for the soul in the later Middle Ages betokens a type of new 'rationality', reason, which for so many writers is the essence of the urban mentality.[13] Only a decade ago Jacques Le Goff suggested that there was something particularly urban about the type of preoccupation with settling the debts of the soul which induced the elaboration and refinement of the idea of purgatory in the twelfth century. The multiplication of intercession, that hard-headed calculation of sums and numbers and frequencies of prayer and masses, enshrined into chantry formation, the shrewdest investment of all, has been firmly located by historians in notions of rationality. Yet when we look into the countryside, the practice of the gentry, or the funerary provisions of the rural parish, we find the same sort of impulses, the provision of commemorative prayer, the distribution of food on anniversaries, and the attempt to multiply, diversify and secure as far into the future as possible routines of commemoration even for the soul of the peasant man or woman. Rural folk were as adept as town-dwellers in arranging and computing the welfare of their souls.

But it is above all in the creativity and precocity of cultural

12 On chantries see C. Burgess, '"For the increase of divine service": chantries in the parish in late medieval Bristol', *Journal of Ecclesiastical History* 36 (1985), 46–65; Burgess '"By quick and by dead": wills and pious provision in late medieval Bristol', *English Historical Review* 102 (1987), 837–58; B. Dobson, 'The formation of perpetual chantries by the citizens of medieval York', *Studies in Church History* 4 (1967), 22–38.
13 Chiffoleau, *La comptabilité*, pp. 344–56, 429–35.

forms, in their pageantry, ceremonial, drama and art, that towns
have championed as the conduits of civilisation, as seats of new
learning which emerged in Europe from the eleventh century.[14]
Townsmen, and sometimes townswomen, have been seen as
having enabled the creation of new modes of thought and new
forms of representation and self–understanding. Eager to display
their wealth and subtle distinctions in status, they also relished self-
display in ritual and ceremonial. Historians have followed this
rich vein of urban life: Richard Trexler examined the ceremonial
and processional life of late medieval Florence, Edward Muir
studied Venetian civic ritual, and in England Charles Phythian-
Adams' pioneering studies introduced us to the rhythm of civic
ceremonial in Coventry.[15] The latter is a classic study of urban
life, one which wove together men's experience in the spheres of
work, public life, sociability, mutual help; a striking study of the
reaction of such a community to economic change, and ultimately
to the decline in the trades which had previously sustained its
prosperity. In Phythian-Adams' analysis of ceremonial life, civic
and religious rituals inhabited different spheres of the citizen's
year. Crafts and fraternities were shown to be deeply embedded
in the political institutions of the town and displayed and reflected
these links through ritual and sociability. The town was thus
discovered to be constantly ritualising and representing itself, in
ideal-types which expressed the wishes of the patrician élite to
establish an understanding of its rôle as the head and leader of a
healthy town which comprised many interdependent parts. In this
view, ceremonial had a vital rôle in town-life, bringing the
different parts together, and it was experienced by multitudes in
the enclosed spaces of streets and market-places, bounded by
town-houses from the windows of which fine cloths and tapestries
hung on ceremonial occasions, and from which flowers were
strewn onto the processing bodies. Towns were thus set, in the

[14] See for example the analysis offered in E. Werner, *Stadt und Geistesleben im Hochmittelalter, 11.
bis 13. Jahrhundert* (Weimar, 1980).
[15] R. C. Trexler, 'Ritual in Florence: adolescence and salvation in the Renaissance', in *The pursuit
of holiness in late medieval and Renaissance religion*, ed. H. Oberman and C. Trinkaus (Leiden,
1974), pp. 200–64; E. Muir, *Civic ritual in Renaissance Venice* (Princeton, NJ, 1982); C.
Phythian-Adams, 'Ceremony and the citizen: the communal year at Coventry, 1450–1550',
in *Crisis and order in English towns, 1500–1700*, ed. P. Clark and P. Slack (London, 1972), pp.
57–85; Phythian-Adams, *Desolation of a city: Coventry and the urban crisis of the late Middle Ages*
(Cambridge, 1979).

works of Mervyn James as of Jacques Heers,[16] as natural ceremonial spaces: the artificial nature of town-life coincided well with the dissimulations of mimes, *tableaux vivants*, vernacular drama, of processional portrayal. Towns were thus seen as fitting sites for the playing out of a reality which was richer and more intense than anything experienced in the mundane rural time and space.

We can now challenge such claims about urban specificity and compare processes of symbolisation which developed in towns and villages. The underlying assumption of much of the work on religion and culture in towns, much of which was conceived in the wake of explorations into popular culture, imputes to town-dwellers a certain urban mentality, or a *structure mentale*. This is supposed to be a world-view which prefers gradation to dichotomy, variety to uniformity, cooperation to isolation, perhaps even change to continuity, a culture where chances are assessed and solutions to problems are willingly devised. Yet when we look closely at villages some of these very activities are encountered: in self-government, sociability, political action, and cultural creativity.[17] Let us examine the possibilities of cultural action around a new late-medieval religious feast, Corpus Christi, in towns and villages.

Corpus Christi was founded as a universal feast in 1264 by pope Urban IV who had been in earlier life an archdeacon in the diocese of Liège; he became involved in the foundation of a eucharistic feast in that diocese in the 1240s. He died very soon after the publication of his bull *Transiturus* and the feast thus remained practically unknown except in Liège and its surrounding area, and in a small number of religious houses and towns. The feast was refounded by John XXII, and published in the new collection of canon law, the *Clementines*, which was dispatched from Avignon all over Christendom in 1317.[18] From the following year we have evidence of celebration of Corpus Christi

---

[16] J. Heers, *Espaces publiques et espaces privés dans la ville: le Liber Terminorum de Bologne (1294)* (Paris, 1985); M. James, 'Ritual, drama and the social body in the late medieval town', *Past and Present* 98 (1983), 3–29.

[17] See the activities of self-government and regulation in Havering (Essex), M. K. McIntosh, *Autonomy and community: the royal manor of Havering, 1200–1500*, Cambridge Studies in Medieval Life and Thought Fourth Series 5 (Cambridge, 1986).

[18] Rubin, *Corpus Christi*, pp. 164–212.

in southern England, and by 1322 in the province of York. Although the bull explained the meaning of the feast, a joyful celebration of the eucharist as a source of hope of redemption, a thanks-giving through veneration of Christ's body in the eucharist, it did not prescribe a particular form of celebration. Yet rapidly all over Europe, in town and countryside, processions with the eucharist developed. Throughout the twelfth and thirteenth centuries the processional mode had been adopted in the context of eucharistic practice, as a suitable form for its veneration: processions brought the eucharist to the sick, and in some English dioceses a eucharistic procession recreated the moment of Christ's entry to Jerusalem in the drama of Palm Sunday.

Now, Corpus Christi's liturgy for mass and office was dis-seminated from Avignon, but its celebrations were devised locally, in the form of processions which displayed and exalted the eucharist, kept in a monstrance and carried in the hands of the clergy. Very soon, by the second half of the fourteenth century, we find that urban processions had evolved in which the clergy surrounded and carried the eucharist, but corporations and town officials, as well as religious orders, friars and fraternities also ordered themselves around the eucharist. The processions became increasingly elaborate and in towns they gradually came to be controlled by town-officials. These out-door summer events (Corpus Christi could then occur between early June and early July) offered a clear ordering logic: proximity to the eucharist betokened privilege and power. Thus mayors and members of town councils came to process in the positions closest to the eucharist and the clergy, and although they were never allowed to handle the eucharist, the iconography of Corpus Christi soon developed an element which looks almost as if it had been invented for them: the canopy over the eucharist, that symbol of royal majesty, which was usually carried by select members of the town patriciate. The processional route of Corpus Christi often marked important relations between the town parishes, and demarcated its boundaries: thus in Marseille, Aix-en-Provence and Avignon, studied recently by Nicole Coulet, town walls and ancient ramparts provided the processional trajectory, moments in collective memory of the town history which were here ritually recreated.[19] Processions often started at the cathedral, passing through parishes and returning to the cathedral, sewing the whole town together with a processional thread. They created an important sacred trail in the urban space, and it was often heralded by the pure voices and bodies of children, sometimes dressed up as angels, who sometimes strewed flowers on their path. What then followed in most towns was an ordered hierarchy of corporations, mostly by single craft, or – as in Ipswich – in groups of crafts, carrying a distinctive banner or symbols of their trade. Along the processional route stood those who were outsiders in one of many possible senses: women, foreigners, youngsters, journeymen, visitors from the countryside, and on the Continent Jews, all those who did not and could not take part in the display of political might and spiritual privilege.[20] When considering the claims of the urban élite which organised and designed these celebrations – that such events displayed the whole body of the town – one must bear in mind the exclusive nature of such processions and the adversarial feelings they might inspire in some of those observing from the sidelines.

Corpus Christi has been studied almost exclusively as an urban phenomenon, and it offers a good example of the tendency to take as given the specificity of certain ceremonial and cultural forms to the urban milieu. The examination of churchwardens' accounts from the late fourteenth and fifteenth centuries, many of them from rural parishes, shows that almost all the elements which were found in urban accounts, ordinances and descriptions of the feast, existed in the rural settings, too, albeit on a smaller scale. Children were used to announce the beginning of the processions, walking at the front, cross-bearers and bell-ringers were paid to excite the processing crowd, the monstrance was a grand and beautiful object, the costliest vessel owned by many parishes in towns and villages. Rural parishes possessed and often repaired their processional canopies, and like their urban counterparts often chose to sit and eat together at the end of a hectic ceremonial day. Village processions do not seem to display the formal hierarchy of a town full of corporations, but the symbols of power were never far off: the monstrance was often the gift of a local gentry family, and

---

[19] N. Coulet, 'Processions, espace urbain, communauté civique', *Cahiers de Fanjeaux* 17 (1982), 381–97.   [20] On procession see Rubin, *Corpus Christi*, pp. 243–71.

people often observed the great processions of monastic houses in their vicinities. Corpus Christi fraternities abounded in the countryside. The eucharist was a symbol of power and authority and similarly to urban usage, its itinerary marked boundaries and sanctioned their legality. Thus the common route for a rural Corpus Christi procession was along the hedges surrounding the village fields. In towns and villages alike we find the eucharist brought out at moments of crisis and misfortune: during a visitation of the plague, or war, to ward off crop failure, storms or drought, the eucharist was used as a focus for supplication, as protection against evil. It seems that the eucharist's message prompted some extremely similar usages in town and countryside, responses which varied in scale or elaboration, but which do not lead us to consider the urban person and the rural person as apprehending authority and the sacred in fundamentally different ways.

Many English towns had by the later fourteenth century famous town-wide processions: York, Chester, Beverley. A number also produced the quintessential art form for Corpus Christi, the Corpus Christi cyclical drama, of which four whole versions have survived, and many sections of others.[21] These cycles were vernacular renditions of the Christian story from Creation to the Last Judgement in separate episodes which could range from the comic to the farcical, from the high drama of Crucifixion to the boisterous mass scenes of the Resurrection. For a long time they were seen, following the lead of V. A. Kolve, perhaps their most inspired and influential interpreter, as important reflections of the impulse provided by the new eucharistic feast.[22] The view prevailed that the eucharistic feast possessed an inherent drive towards wholeness and universality, beginning and end, multiplicity under the structure of the narrative of salvation. Kolve distinguished between what he took to be the basic components of the dramatic tale, scenes which would be told in every Corpus Christi drama, and those scenes which towns could choose according to their wish, need and most importantly – size. The drama was understood to be a product of

---

[21] For a summary of surviving material on Corpus Christi drama in English towns see A. H. Nelson, *The medieval stage; Corpus Christi pageants and plays* (Chicago, IL, 1974).
[22] V. A. Kolve, *The play called Corpus Christi* (London, 1966).

a particular urban structure, which tends to create cultural products reflective of variety and of cooperation. This was an analysis of great beauty and force. Local research into the context of production has now revealed that the picture was far from being so simple.

Recent attention to the materials surrounding the context of dramatic production shows a variety in practice and a flexibility in financing and performance of the plays that was scarcely suspected by Kolve.[23] It showed that not all towns which staged drama on Corpus Christi displayed the drive towards universal Christian cycles, not all towns which produced cycles performed them wholly every year, and many towns chose one great extravaganza, or even to have no drama at all, or to have a traditional play of some other form.[24] Moreover, looking into the countryside, we encounter very familiar dramatic responses to Corpus Christi and its celebration. Whereas in towns guilds came together to produce a play or a cycle of plays, villages, like a number of Cambridgeshire villages around Bassingbourn, came together to commission the composition of a cycle of biblical tales which were to be performed intermittently when funds allowed, and often by companies of players who travelled the region.[25] Cambridge with its many fraternities chose to perform the story 'of the Children of Israel', while Norwich, only fifty miles away, chose a short cycle as more fitting. The reason for the different decisions may well have to do with the size of communities and the degree of guild autonomy within them; close examination will reveal some telling patterns. Great schemes which separate the urban experience collapse under comparative scrutiny.

A number of similarities in response and interpretations of religious impulses lead us to believe that urban/rural, like literate/illiterate, like élite/popular, is a dichotomy which illuminated early research but which now encumbers rather than

---

[23] The Toronto based project of publication of archival material related to the production of early English drama, *Records in Early English Drama* (REED), has produced regionally based volumes of transcripts accompanied by introductions since 1979.

[24] See H.-J. Diller, 'Städtegeschichte und dramatische Formgeschichte: Die *Records of Early English Drama* und ihre Bedeutung für die Erforschung der mittelenglischen Fronleichnamszyklen', in *Zusammenhänge, Einflüße, Wirkungen*, ed. J. O. Fichte, K. H. Göller and B. Schimmelpfennig (Berlin and New York, 1986), pp. 145–53.

[25] H. R. L. Beadle, 'The medieval drama of East Anglia: studies in dialect, documentary record and stagecraft', 2 vols. (York University Ph.D. thesis, 1977).

liberates our understanding of the past.[26] And there are good reasons for us to believe that the best way to approach towns is by observing them as sites for interaction whose people and streets are hosts to a wide range of economic and cultural activities.

More than ever before we are now aware of the economic and political interdependence between towns and their surrounding countryside.[27] English urban historians such as Susan Reynolds, Gervase Rosser and Steven Rigby have re-examined the salient character of town-growth, the development of urban institutions and of a nexus of exchange and manufacture, and have re-evaluated the degree to which these depended on borough status.[28] Urban institutions and commercial spheres could develop under the eye of Westminster abbey or of the bishop of Winchester. Rodney Hilton has reminded us in recent work that the very commercial imperatives of large land-holding and life in the 'feudal' mode encouraged the development of markets which facilitated, besides distribution and marketing of agricultural produce, the movement of raw materials to towns for manufacture.[29] One must recognise therefore that a variety of factors of necessity met in the towns, where leading townsmen often came from well-connected rural families in the service of feudal lords or from families of humble knightly status. Such were the Blangernons of Cambridge, studied by Arthur Hibbert, who lived between town and country and who were reduced to financial ruin due to the demands of the two spheres upon their resources.[30] Neither at their inception nor in their subsequent lives were towns distinct from the scrutiny of, and contact with, those who operated most of the time in manors, castles and fields.

---

[26] See an attempt to rethink these terms in a study of late medieval literature, U. Peters, *Literatur in der Stadt. Studien zu den sozialen Voraussetzungen und kulturellen Organisationsformen städtischer Literatur im 13. und 14. Jahrhundert* (Tübingen, 1983).

[27] For a powerful analysis of the economic relations between towns and countryside in late medieval Tuscany and Sicily see S. R. Epstein, 'Cities, regions and the late medieval crisis: Sicily and Tuscany compared', *Past and Present* 130 (1991), 3–50.

[28] Reynolds, 'Medieval urban history', 16–17. On the development of Hungarian towns there was initially little specificity in legal status, E. Fügedi, 'La Formation des villes et les ordres mendiants en Hongrie', *Annales* 25 (1970), 966–87; 977. S. Rigby, 'Boston and Grimsby in the Middle Ages: an administrative contrast?', *Journal of Medieval History* 10 (1984), 51–66.

[29] R. H. Hilton, 'Small town society in England before the Black Death', *Past and Present* 105 (1984), 53–78; Hilton, 'Towns in societies – medieval England', *Urban History Yearbook* (1982), 7–13.

[30] A. B. Hibbert, 'The origins of the medieval town patriciate', *Past and Present* 3 (1953), 15–27.

A large number of important figures in trade and in town
government moved between both spheres out of necessity as well
as out of choice. One can even talk, by the late fourteenth century,
of an urban gentry, a class of person who had progressed through
profession or service into close social and professional interaction
with the gentry, often as servants of the crown or of the high
aristocracy, and yet whose business kept them frequently in
towns.[31] The lives of townspeople were as dependent on the
rhythm of the seasons as were those of village dwellers. They
hoarded food in cellars and granaries to provide for winter
needs, and as summer came many rushed out into the countryside,
offering their hands for the harvest, or indulging their bodies in
the cleaner air and more salubrious water. Everything we know
about the economic relations between the town and its hinterland
points at important structural interdependence between the
people whose lives made up the relationship. In Adam Smith's
simple words: 'The inhabitants of the town and those of the
country are mutually the servants of one another.'[32] These
'servants' met and interacted in localities ranging from villages to
rural markets, from industrialised villages to larger towns, and on
roads and rivers. These sites were points along a continuous line of
possibilities, their characteristics were *clusters* of functions, of
topographical features, and each town's cluster was a unique
combination.[33]

Looking at the divide from the other end, from the perspective
of the rural population, this was at all levels moving in and out of
spheres of exchange, in and out of the nexus of the market.
Richard Britnell's and more recently Rodney Hilton's work on
small towns and rural markets have revealed a whole area of
activity where peasants turned buyers and traders, at markets
which were only a few miles away from their villages, and in
small towns, which their sons and daughters moved in and out of

[31] R. Horrox, 'The urban gentry', in *Towns and townspeople in the fifteenth century*, ed. J. A. F.
Thomson (Gloucester, 1988), pp. 22–44.

[32] Adam Smith, *The wealth of nations*, ed. E. Cannan (Chicago, 1976), p. 403.

[33] On problems of neat classification of central Italian towns in the fourteenth century see P.
Jansen, 'Les Constitutions Egidiennes de 1357: l'idée du fait urbain et sa classification au
moyen-âge', in *Les Petites villes du moyen-âge à nos jours*, ed. J.-P. Poussou and P. Loupès (Paris,
1987), pp. 15–28. On the mismatch between demographic and administrative hierarchies of
French towns see F. Beriac, 'Petites villes ou bourgs? Le cas du Gers', ibid., pp. 29–39; p. 33.

with startling frequency.[34] This was true before the Black Death
when the imperative to produce coin for payment of dues meant
that even very meagre surplus had to be exchanged, and even
more so after the Black Death, when movement was prompted
by the greater opportunities in agricultural work, service or
craft.[35] Even the life of the serf, the villein whose existence was so
closely determined by customary obligations, was not devoid of
travel, perhaps especially in regions like Norfolk, criss-crossed
by a network of waterways, where Mark Bailey has found
in court rolls frequent mention of young men and women
moving livestock, travelling up and down the river to markets
in the Fenland.[36] The villeins on the manors of the bishop
of Ely were part of a complex system of provisioning the
episcopal table through extensive inter-manorial marketing and
distribution.[37] Moving southwards, at Great Waltham (Suffolk)
men and women inhabited service tenancies in return for postage;
they delivered letters to London, some thirty-five to forty miles
away.[38] These rural people: gentry, peasants, priests, feudal
officials, moved, bought and sold and thus came across a much
greater variety of experiences than has usually been appreciated.
Were they of the market or of the field? To ask this question
seems now to be a *question malposée*.

The difference between urban and rural life can also be
approached through the concept of culture. The study of urban
religion, the religion of the urban laity has been related to a
general interest in popular religion, the religion experienced by
the majority of lay people. In the search for popular religious
culture historians have tended to classify certain practices as
popular: practices which were vernacular, carnivalesque, folk-
loric, criticised by the church, were popular; those which were

[34] On density of markets see R. H. Britnell, 'The proliferation of markets in England 1200–1349', *Economic History Review* 34 (1981), 209–21; Hilton, 'Towns in societies'. See also discussion of East Anglia in L. R. Poos, 'Population and resources in two fourteenth-century Essex communities: Great Waltham and High Easter, 1327–1389' (Cambridge University Ph.D., 1984), pp. 36–7.
[35] A. F. Butcher, 'The origins of Romney freemen, 1453–1523', *Economic History Review* 27 (1974), 16–27.   [36] By personal communication.
[37] E. Miller, *The abbey and bishopric of Ely*, Cambridge studies in medieval life and thought, new ser. 1 (Cambridge, 1951), pp. 84–6. See also customary services for the transport of food from High Easter (Suffolk) to Plechey Castle; Poos, 'Population and resources', pp. 33–4.
[38] See Poos, 'Population and resources', pp. 198–9.

literate, bookish, indoors, controlled by the clergy, were learned or formal. Despite the great inspiration of Mikhail Bakhtin and his insightful influence on our reading of popular culture of late medieval and early modern Europe, we soon come across difficulties in using his classificatory taxonomy of high and low for some medieval phenomena: what would Corpus Christi drama be? It was biblical tale, on a feast day, directed by friars, comic and often irreverent, played out by lay people in the vernacular, attended by multitudes from the town and the countryside – so was it high or low? It was this type of difficulty in the classification of cultural artifacts that prompted Roger Chartier to explore in a number of seminal articles what makes something popular or not; and he developed the notion of cultural *use*.[39] According to Chartier, a book, a play, a prayer, a procession only receive their cultural meaning from the person or group using, consuming them. The meaning does not inhere in the artifact, the cultural object, but in the process of its cultural use. The possibilities of this inversion are great; it dissolves the need to classify objects but traces uses and cultural practices. Thus we can take a Corpus Christi drama, and need not call it inherently urban or not, but see it in the multiplicity of contexts which defined its use. The costly Book of Hours is a good example; falling into the hands of a humble peasant woman, its images of Christ as a Man of Sorrows would be decipherable, and if its Latin prayers were read out to her, they would have struck an evocative chord.[40] If we are to talk of lay culture; we must talk of contexts of cultural practice, and these are not always usefully captured by the urban/rural divide.

Furthermore, thinking of our consumers, townsfolk and villagers, their identities were neither uniform nor monolithic. An artisan's life was, no doubt, determined in important ways by craft affiliation, by the status of his guild, by the rhythm of workshop life, which was family-based just as agricultural

[39] R. Chartier, 'Culture as appropriation: popular cultural uses in early modern France', in *Understanding popular culture: Europe from the Middle Ages to the nineteenth century*, ed. S. L. Kaplan (Berlin, 1984), pp. 229–53; Chartier, *Cultural history: between practices and representations* (Cambridge, 1988).

[40] See for example the images reproduced in A. Bennett, 'A book designed for a noblewoman: an illustrated *Manuel des pêches* of the thirteenth century', in *Medieval book production: assessing the evidence*, ed. L. L. Brownrigg (Los Altos Hills, CA, 1990), pp. 163–81.

husbandry was. But the life of his household would have also been significantly determined by the rhythm of agricultural seasons. The supply of food depended on it, and the availability of labour, as the summer drew multitudes out of the towns for work in the harvest.[41] And there are spheres which are never wholly captured by professional and economic circumstances: family, and neighbourhood, fantasy and sexuality, areas which culture both defines and expresses. The importance of age and gender in the creation of people's identities, tastes and needs, would surely create patterns of use which transcended or traversed the division of town/country in meaningful ways. In seeking the components of personal and group identities we must allow a place for all of these: for the variety of situations in each town and each village, for a diversity in capabilities and expectations, for varying routines of work and of leisure, for the graduation in access to power, relief and security.[42]

Meaning and experience are constructed in context, and many areas of medieval life were influenced by the over-arching sacramental–sacerdotal world-view. The religious culture provided strong universalising drives: it designed rituals which were to be executed similarly in town or country, its messages and salient symbols were powerful and ubiquitous. Inasmuch as it strove for uniformity of practice in liturgy and devotion, it attempted (most effectively from the central Middle Ages) to substitute local, regional tendencies in the cult of saints, in liturgy and in ecclesiastical law. People participated in the orthodox milieu of ideas and explanations of the world in a similar manner in town and in countryside: they examined them, doubted some, accepted others, and created new formulations. Although preachers such as Honorius 'Augustodinensis' or Jacques de Vitry wrote clever Latin sermons *ad status* which distinguished spiritually between the sins which imperilled townsmen and villagers, they none the less offered the same remedies to the identical

---

[41] On these seasonal elements which left towns empty in the summer see B. Chevalier, *Les Bonnes villes de France du XIVe au XVIe siècle* (Paris, 1982), pp. 180–1.

[42] On unemployment and attitudes to refusal of work see B. Geremek, 'Le Refus du travail dans la société urbaine du bas moyen âge', in *Le Travail au moyen âge: une approche interdisciplinaire*, ed. J. Hamesse and C. Muraille-Samaran (Louvain-la-Neuve, 1990), pp. 379–94. For presentation of the distribution of the tax burden in Welsh towns see I. Soulsby, *The towns of medieval Wales* (Chichester, 1983), pp. 19–24.

underlying vices, which simply took different manifestations in town and countryside. In a town it might be the use of unlawful weights and measures; in the countryside defrauding the bailiff of a bushel or two. Yet it was avarice in both cases, and the Church's treatment of it was one and the same.[43] When this is borne in mind it is perhaps less surprising to read David d'Avray's assessment that there was only very little specificity in the urban orientation of the sermons of friars in the thirteenth century,[44] much less specificity than the existing orthodoxy on the urban preoccupations of the friars would lead us to expect.[45] The frequency of preaching would have been, no doubt, greater in towns, but there it was also available to people passing through the towns, and on their travels friars inevitably passed through and depended upon the hospitality of rural communities.[46]

Moving from orthodoxy to dissent: the more we know about dissent in late medieval England, the more we discover that the established assumption about Lollardy, that it was a heresy of some members of the gentry, but mainly of poor urban workers, must be discarded. The networks of Lollard book-production and patronage show that it reached deep into respectable middling peasant society, as well as into the urban merchant class. Lollard texts drew from a wide range of sources, and were produced in urban centres to be marketed in them as well as in the deepest countryside.[47]

Inasmuch as piety, religion, culture, relate so often to the imaginary, the spiritual, to people's yearnings and strivings, as well as to the mundane, they will of necessity have a strong element which cannot and ought not to be attached too strongly to any *function*, such as the town/countryside dichotomy implies. This distinction was not always a clear one in the minds of our subjects. Elements of exchange and craft were important to

[43] On representations of avarice which transcend the urban/rural division see R. Newhauser, 'The love of money as deadly sin and deadly disease', in *Zusammenhänge, Einflüße, Wirkungen*, pp. 315–26. [44] D. L. d'Avray, *The preaching of the friars* (Oxford, 1985).
[45] A view powerfully formulated by J. Le Goff and underpinning a project under his supervision which studied the correlation between urbanisation and mendicant presence in French towns; see J. Le Goff, 'Apostolat mendiant et fait urbain dans la France', *Annales* 23 (1968), 335–52. For a critique based on the Hungarian experience see Fügedi, 'La Formation des villes', pp. 966–87.
[46] On the hire of preachers by town authorities in late medieval France see H. Martin, 'La Prédication comme travail reconnu et retribué à la fin du moyen âge', in *Le Travail au moyen*, pp. 395–412. [47] A. Hudson, *The premature Reformation* (Oxford, 1988).

village life, towns came in many shapes and sizes, and within them people inhabited differing positions and situations lived widely divergent experiences: as merchants, journeymen, mistresses of workshops, prostitutes, beggars, lawyers, mayors. A distinction in *mentality* crumbles in the face of our growing understanding of networks of work, migration, distribution and exchange, the complicated webs tying town and countryside.[48] Perhaps the history to be undertaken next is one which examines the nature of the interdependence, the historically variable nature of this relationship in different European regions, and in different periods.[49]

None of this is meant to suggest that town life and village life are one and the same. Rather, it is to say that the difference has been seen as one of specific *function* and of a fixed and necessary *nature*. To talk about structural difference between them is to ignore gradation and change over time in the nature of the relation between town and countryside. Even those differences we would wish to acknowledge should, perhaps, be seen rather as differing horizons and experiences which were not exclusively tied down to patterns of production and consumption (especially as consumption aspirations seem to have converged in the later Middle Ages).[50] Perhaps that which made life different in town and in country was not so much the market, but the circumstance captured by the fact that the sex ratio of late medieval towns and villages meant that women outnumbered men in towns and were outnumbered by men in villages.[51] Similarly, perhaps the variety and array of crafts and occupations is more significant in constructing experience than is the 'simple' fact of working in a craft; after all, many carpenters, tailors, smiths obviously did so in medieval villages.[52] Perhaps the size of family and the number

---

[48] See for example a study of the involvement of great urban corporations in the development of northern Flanders, J. Renes, 'Urban influences in rural areas: peat-digging in the northern part of the Dutch province of North Brabant from the thirteenth to the eighteenth century', in *The medieval and early modern rural lands of Europe under the impact of the commercial economy*, ed. H.-J. Nitz (Göttingen, 1987), pp. 49–60.

[49] A major contribution in this area will be made by the project currently conducted by Bruce Campbell and Derek Keene at the Centre for Metropolitan History of the Institute of Historical Research of London University. This project examines the impact of London's consumption demands in the Middle Ages on the agrarian economy of southern England; see *Centre for Metropolitan History Annual Report, 1989–90* (London, 1990), 6–10.

[50] C. Dyer, *Standards of living in the Middle Ages* (Cambridge, 1989), pp. 188–210, 211–33.

[51] P. J. P. Goldberg, 'Urban identity and the poll taxes of 1377, 1379 and 1381', *Economic History Review* 43 (1990), 212–13, see sex-ratios in table 2, p. 200.   [52] Ibid., 213.

of servants around the household is similarly important in influencing outlook. Life worlds are constructed in contexts which are shifting, and such shifting political and economic factors can make a town sometimes seem safer and sometimes more dangerous, more promising or forbidding.

So images of towns must also be considered, not as mirrors of a lived reality, but as imaginary constructions embedded in certain contexts, as ideals, as fantasies, as symbols which can be referred to by many. Towns can represent freedom and opportunity, they can also seem close and hostile. Some preferred to represent the town as a whole, others, like Chaucer in his *Cook's Tale*, as a complex field of loyalties and conflicts, rather than as a community. In the literature of romance they often appear as nurturing, maternal and protective,[53] in homilies and mystical visions, they are golden.[54] The most powerful image of the town, the town walls, were never so impregnable as they seem in the fine miniatures which decorated the calendars of Books of Hours. But even when walls and laws were in place, surely very recent history has taught us that they need not, and cannot, limit and contain the reaches of the human experience and the vistas of the human mind.[55]

[53] As in the thirteenth-century work of Jean Renart, see M. Struyf, 'Symbolique des villes dans les romans de Jean Renart', *Cahiers de civilisation médiévale* 30 (1987), 245–61.
[54] P. Vallin, 'Genèse médiévale des villes de l'Occident: points de vue d'histoire sociale et de théologie', in *L'Idée de la ville*, ed. P. Guery (Seyssel, 1984), pp. 65–84. On 'holy' cities see A. Haverkamp, '"Heilige Städte" im hohen Mittelalter', in *Mentalitäten im Mittelalter: methodische und inhaltliche Probleme*, ed. F. Graus (Sigmaringen, 1987), pp. 119–56.
[55] On the symbolism of town walls see Chevalier, *Les Bonnes villes de France*, pp. 192–3.

Theology and the commercial revolution: Guibert of Nogent, St Anselm and the Jews of northern France

ANNA SAPIR ABULAFIA

I

Anselm of Canterbury's famous maxims 'credo ut intelligam' and 'fides querens intellectum' have given rise to a great deal of discussion about Anselm's use of reason and his ideas concerning the relationship between it and faith and his definition of faith itself.[1] This discussion has not limited itself to Anselm; scholars have cast their nets to include the men he taught and those who showed affinity to his works.[2]

For students of the medieval Jewish–Christian debate the most important work of Anselm is his *Cur Deus Homo*. There are those who see it as a polemic addressed to the Jews;[3] others read in it the denial of collective Jewish guilt for the crucifixion.[4] These scholars, but also many scholars who disagree with them,[5]

---

[1] *Proslogion, Prooemium*, 1; S 1. 94, 100. Examples of the discussion: K. Barth, *Fides quaerens intellectum. Anselms Beweis der Existens Gottes im Zusammentrag seines theologischen Programms* (Zurich, 1981; first appeared in 1931); R. Campbell, 'Anselm's theological method', *Scottish Journal of Theology* 32 (1979), 541–62; J. McIntyre, *St Anselm and his critics* (Edinburgh/London, 1954).

[2] E.g. R. W. Southern, 'St Anselm and his English pupils', *Mediaeval and Renaissance Studies* 1 (1941–3), 3–34.

[3] E.g. G. van der Plaas, 'Des hl. Anselm *Cur Deus Homo* auf dem Boden der jüdisch-christlichen Polemik des Mittelalters', *Divus Thomas*, 7 (Freiburg, Switzerland, 1929), 446–67 and 8 (1930), 18–32; J. Gauss, 'Anselmus von Canterbury zur Begegnung und Auseinandersetzung der Religionen', *Saeculum* 17 (1966), 277–363; R. Roques, *Pourquoi Dieu s'est fait homme, Sources Chrétiennes*, 91 (Paris, 1963), pp. 70–4. Gauss and Roques argue that it is also a polemic against the Muslims.

[4] A. Funkenstein, 'Basic types of Christian anti-Jewish polemics', *Viator* 2 (1971), 378; G. Dahan, 'S. Anselme, les Juifs, le judaïsme', *Les Mutations socio-culturelles au tournant des XIe–XIIe siècles. Etudes Anselmiennes (IVe Session). Colloque organisé par le CNRS, Abbaye Notre-Dame du Bec, Le Bec-Hellouin 11–16 juillet 1982* (Paris, 1984), p. 522.

[5] See for example my 'St Anselm and those outside the Church', in *Faith and identity: Christian political experience*, ed. D. Loades and K. Walsh, *Studies in Church History, Subsidia* 6 (Oxford, 1990), 11–37.

recognise the impact of Anselm's rational thought on subsequent anti-Jewish polemics. In the *Cur Deus Homo* Anselm argues that the Incarnation was both possible and necessary. Gilbert Crispin borrowed these ideas for his *Disputatio Iudei et Christiani* even before Anselm had a chance to complete his work.[6] Odo of Cambrai, Guibert of Nogent, Pseudo-William of Champeaux and others all selected arguments from the *Cur Deus Homo* in their attempts to refute the Jews.[7]

In Odo of Cambrai's *Disputatio contra Iudeum Leonem nomine de adventu Christi* (1106–13) it is relatively easy to ascertain how Anselm's notions were adapted to serve as weapons against the Jews.[8] Odo uses the first part of his disputation to argue the Anselmian case for the necessity of the Incarnation.[9] The Jew of the disputation, who may or may not have been fashioned after a real Jew,[10] admits that he cannot think of any rational arguments which could refute those of Odo.[11] But this does not mean that he is prepared to accept Christianity. On the contrary, he proceeds to deride the Virgin Birth as being not only irrational but unpalatable. Odo's reply is to argue that man can judge things either by employing his reason or by relying on his senses. Although according to the senses, the birth of Christ might seem incompatible with the divine nature of God, reason knows that it was a glorious event. Christians use their reason as men should; Jews think with their senses and as such resemble animals who lack reason. It is the Jews' own fault that they do not believe in Jesus Christ and the Virgin Mary. They insist on interpreting their law in a literal sense and notwithstanding all the rational arguments they are offered concerning the Incarnation they continue to refuse to exercise their reason.[12]

It is plain that Odo found Anselm's rational explanations of the

---

[6] R. W. Southern, 'St Anselm and Gilbert Crispin, abbot of Westminster', *Mediaeval and Renaissance Studies* 3 (1954), 78–115.

[7] G. Dahan, 'S. Anselme, les Juifs, le judaïsme'; A. Sapir Abulafia, 'The Jewish–Christian debate and the twelfth-century Renaissance', *Journal of Medieval History* 15 (1989), 105–25; 'Christian imagery of Jews in the twelfth century: a look at Odo of Cambrai and Guibert of Nogent', *Historiography and Theory/Theoretische Geschiedenis* 16 (1989), 383–91.

[8] PL 160. 1103–12.   [9] PL 160. 1103–9.

[10] It is difficult to assess the plausibility of Odo's claim that Leo is a Jew with whom he discussed the Incarnation in Senlis (PL 160. 1103A–B). We do not know of any Jews residing in Senlis at this time and very much of what Leo says is un-Jewish. See, however, n. 24 on Laon and see my comments in 'Christian imagery of Jews in the twelfth century', 385.

[11] PL 160. 1109C.   [12] PL 160. 1110–12; see my 'Christian imagery of the Jews' 386.

Incarnation so valid that he felt that their force should compel Jews to adopt Christianity. This implies that unlike Anselm, Odo seems to have believed that understanding could somehow lead to faith.[13] The fact that Anselm's reasons did not move the Jews could only frustrate him. Anselm's ingenious arguments, which Odo had assimilated into his own thinking, were naturally enough not considered to be at fault. Instead it was the Jews who received the blame. If reason could not convince them, they must lack the capacity to think rationally.

Perhaps it is hardly surprising that Odo of Cambrai's use of the *Cur Deus Homo* is as unequivocal as it is. Odo was an expert dialectician; he taught the subject for many years at the schools in Tournai before he converted to the religious life.[14] And all his theological writings betray how much store he set by ratiocination.

The nature of the dependence of other twelfth-century Renaissance scholars on St Anselm is, however, usually much more difficult to ascertain. I have argued elsewhere that Gilbert Crispin, for example, did not share Anselm's optimism about man's potential to delve into the mysteries of God through the use of his reason. This, I think, determined the limited use he made of reason in his polemics against the Jews.[15] The milieu of Pseudo-William of Champeaux seems to have been the School at Laon. Although he did make use of the *Cur Deus Homo* and a number of Anselm's other treatises to write his *Dialogus inter Christianum et Iudeum de fide Catholica* (1123–48), his conception of the usefulness of rational arguments would stand nearer to those of Anselm of Laon than to those of Anselm of Canterbury.[16]

In all our efforts to discover how twelfth-century thinkers did or did not follow in Anselm's footsteps it is essential to take into

---

[13] See PL 160. 1106D, where he says to Leo that he hopes that he will become a Christian when he has explained to him that man had to achieve blessedness even though man could not save himself, and PL 160. 1112, where he asks why Leo will not believe once he has admitted that he had been unaware of all the reasons supporting the Christian doctrine of the Virgin Birth. This does not, I think, contradict Odo's closing remarks in his work on Original Sin where he says that he uses philosophical arguments not to strengthen or to defend the Catholic faith but to teach it (PL 160. 1102B–C). At this point he is speaking to fellow Christians.

[14] C. Dereine, 'Odo de Tournai et la crise du cénobetisme au xie siècle', *Revue du Moyen Age Latin* 4 (1948), 140–1.

[15] See my 'Christians disputing disbelief: St Anselm, Gilbert Crispin and Pseudo-Anselm', Conference proceedings of 25. *Wolfenbütteler Symposion, 11. bis 15. Juni 1989*, forthcoming.

[16] My 'Jewish–Christian disputations', 121–3.

account how complicated terms such as reason and faith are. *Ratio* does not always indicate rational arguments; faith does not only mean 'correct' belief. And nowhere are we reminded of this more vigorously than when we try to analyse the use Guibert of Nogent made of the *Cur Deus Homo*. The complexity of Guibert's mind is proverbial, and his views on the Jews and his approach to their denial of Christianity are as convoluted as one might expect. What I propose to do in this article is to analyse what Guibert says about the Jews in his autobiography and in his *Tractatus de Incarnatione contra Iudeos*. First I hope to discover what impulses Guibert might have received from St Anselm to think about the Jews as he did. Then I hope to correlate this information with Guibert's perception of the rôle played by the Jews in twelfth-century northern French society. What I hope will emerge is a more precise understanding of Guibert's enmity towards the Jews and an appraisal of how representative his attitudes are for his period.

II

What does Guibert have to say about the Jews? The first Jew he mentions in his *De Vita Sua* is the doctor who introduces a monk to the Devil in order to learn the secrets of black magic. The Jew has to be pressed hard before he consents to mediate between his charge and Satan. The Devil will only agree to teach the monk if he denies his Christian faith and tastes his semen, which he must pour out before the Devil as a libation offering. Eventually, the monk confesses what he has done. His judgement is referred to Anselm, who is abbot of Bec at the time. Anselm rules that the man might never again celebrate the sacraments. He dies a few years later in a confused state of mind.[17] The emphasis of the tale is very much on the abhorrent behaviour of the priest involved. Very little is said about the Jew. Guibert would have him present when the monk makes his weird offering to the Devil, but he does not tell us whether the Jew had made a similar sacrifice when he received his knowledge of magic. Nor does he say that the Jew has

---

[17] *De Vita Sua*, 1.26, ed. E.-R. Labande, *Les Classiques de l'Histoire de France au Moyen Age* 34 (Paris, 1981), 202–7; *Self and society in medieval France. The memoirs of Abbot Guibert of Nogent*, trans. J. F. Benton (New York etc., 1970), 115–16.

corrupted the Christian. It is the Christian who is curious about magic and, in a sense, compels the Jew to help him gain access to the fountain of magic, that is to say, the Devil.

In book two of his autobiography, Guibert tells of the persecution of the Jews in Rouen in 1096. According to Guibert, those who had taken the cross decided that it was absurd to go to fight the Muslims in the East while ignoring the Jews at home *quibus inimicior existat gens nulla Dei*. A small Jewish boy is saved by William, the brother of Count Henry I of Eu. He is baptised and becomes a monk at Fly, where Guibert must have known him. He is given the name of the man who saved his life.[18] Guibert gives no indication of his feelings about the persecution the Jews suffered in Rouen. Nor does he expand on his report of the crusaders' view that there exist no people who are more hostile to God than the Jews. The boy consents to be baptised only because he fears for his life. Guibert is rather surprised that he turns out to be such an exemplary Christian and monk. He says that this rarely happens to someone of a Jewish background. This background is denoted as *nequam natura*. William overcomes his Jewishness, resisting his family's efforts to win him back. William stayed at Fly after Guibert had left the monastery to become abbot of Nogent. When the abbot completed his treatise on the Incarnation, he sent it to William to 'increase the strength of his unbroken faith'. In his turn William wrote a number of sermons and a commentary on the book of Judges.[19]

Following his graphic description of the commune of Laon, Guibert turns his attention to Count John of Soissons whom he accuses of favouring the Jews to the extent that he himself says things about Jesus Christ that Jews would not dare utter.[20] We know that there was a Jewish community in Soissons by the end of the eleventh or beginning of the twelfth century. Many of these

[18] II.5, ed. Labande, 246–53; ed. Benton, 134–7.

[19] II.5, ed. Labande, 252–3; ed. Benton, 136–7. For William's works see J. Leclercq, 'Prédicateurs bénédictins aux XIᵉ et XIIᵉ siècles', *Revue Mabillon* 33 (1943), 59–65. In book one of his autobiography (I.23; ed. Labande, 186–7; ed. Benton, 109) Guibert relates that two boys, one of whom was a Jewish convert, were flung through the church of Fly by lightning during a storm one morning. It is unclear whether this boy, who is described as profoundly religious, is William or another Jew who converted and became a monk at Fly.

[20] III.16, ed. Labande, 422–9; ed. Benton, 209–11.

Jews were probably merchants who were involved in money-lending. They may have been Count John's financial agents.[21]

Guibert loathes John of Soissons and his entire family. His mother is said to have poisoned her brother with the help of a Jew and John himself commits adultery with an old hag in a Jew's house. His father's and grandfather's bad deeds are said to have been ruinous for the Church.[22] It is to combat the blasphemous utterings of John of Soissons that Guibert writes his *Tractatus de Incarnatione contra Iudeos*.[23] Guibert attacks John and the Jews whose criticism of Christianity he is said to have adopted in one and the same breath. Two things seem to concern Guibert most. First, he is intent to quell any doubts about the Christian faith to which the continued Jewish rejection of the Incarnation might give rise. Secondly, he wants to put his finger on what it is that prevents the Jews from accepting the doctrine that God became man.

Guibert concludes his composition by giving an account of a reported conversation between a clerk and a Jew in Laon. According to Guibert's informant, the Jew in question refused to convert to Christianity even after the clerk had held a piece of burning wood in his hand to prove that Christ is God. To Guibert this occurrence is more telling than all the words he has used in his treatise, for it shows up the abyss of Jewish deceit.[24] It is indeed his appraisal of Jewish behaviour that informs him why it is that no arguments can be found which will convince Jews to become Christians.

As far as Guibert is concerned, it is endemic to the Jewish race

---

[21] F. Vercauteren, *Etude sur les civitates de la Belgique seconde. Contribution à l'histoire urbaine du nord de la France de la fin du IIIe à la fin du XIe siècle. Académie royale de Belgique, classe des lettres et des sciences morales et politiques. Mémoires, deuxième série* 33 (Brussels, 1934), 124–34; R. I. Moore, *The formation of a persecuting society* (Oxford, 1987), p. 117. Vercauteren (131–2) thinks that the merchant of Soissons in *De Vita Sua*, III.15 (ed. Labande, 418–19), to whom a thief of Laon offers stolen goods from a church, is probably a Jew. Guibert does not say he is. Perhaps he was unwilling to because the merchant very properly reports the theft to the pertinent authorities in Laon.   [22] III.16, ed. Labande, 422–3, 426–7; ed. Benton, 209, 211.

[23] PL 156. 489–528.

[24] III.11; PL 156. 528. Robert Chazan does not indicate that there is any documentary evidence for Jewish settlement in Laon in Guibert's day. This does not mean that no Jews were living there then. Chazan argues for widespread Jewish settlement in the towns of northern France, noting that evidence for existing communities is not always available (*Medieval Jewry in northern France. A political and social history* (Baltimore and London, 1973), pp. 207–12, 215). On the other hand, Guibert does not say that the Jew in question lived in Laon; he could have been there on business.

to murmur against the Virgin Birth and, by implication, against the Incarnation too.[25] Guibert finds two matters especially jarring in his interpretation of the content of these murmurings: the idea that a woman's body would have been too impure to house God before he was born and the idea that it would have been unseemly for God to take on a human body. Whatever view one adopts of Guibert's personality, there can be little doubt that his concern with sexuality and bodily functions influences the way he interprets Jewish rejection of Christianity and the way he goes about identifying its causes.[26]

Guibert hotly defends the purity of the bodies of Mary and her son. Bodies are pure if sin is absent.[27] It was easier for Jesus to put up with the trials of his body than for God to bear the wicked murmurings of the Jews in the desert.[28] The mouths of the Virgin's enemies (i.e. John of Soissons and the Jews) are not as clean as her privy parts. And what is it that fouls these mouths? The sins of *fraus* and *luxuria*.[29]

Jews are only interested in material things because the literal interpretation of the Law of Moses, to which they stubbornly adhere, offers them no other rewards than material ones. They continue to wallow in legal minutiae while ignoring what really matters: love of God and loving one's neighbour as oneself. Jews are thieves piling up interest on the necks of the needy.[30]

The words of the *Cur Deus Homo* echo in much of what Guibert has to say about the necessity and possibility of the Incarnation,[31] although it should be noted that the Devil plays a greater rôle in his account than in Anselm's. He seems much closer to Anselm than Odo of Cambrai when he states that it is the aversion of the Jews to the Passion that prevents them from grasping the reasons why Jesus Christ had to die. Only faith

---

[25] I.1; PL 156. 489.
[26] One does not have to be a psycho-historian in order to be convinced that Guibert was concerned with, if not obsessed by, these subjects. To what extent he was peculiar in this in his own time is a matter of opinion. See J. Kantor, 'A psychological source: the memoirs of Abbot Guibert of Nogent', *Journal of Medieval History* 2 (1976), 281–304 and M. D. Coupe, 'The personality of Guibert of Nogent reconsidered', *Journal of Medieval History* 9 (1983), 317–29. See also my 'Christian imagery of the Jews', 385–7.　　　[27] II.1; PL 156. 499.
[28] III.1; PL 156. 506.　　　[29] I.6; PL 156. 497.　　　[30] III.6–8; PL 156. 519–24.
[31] J. Pelikan lists the relevant passages in 'A first-generation Anselmian, Guibert of Nogent', in: *Continuity and discontinuity in Church history. Essays presented to G. H. Williams*, ed. F. Forrester Church and T. George (Leiden, 1979), pp. 75–6.

would be able to remove this hatred and open the way to understanding.[32] But faith cannot enter the hearts of the Jews because their hearts are impure, filled as they are with mundane things as long as they adhere to the law literally. They cannot see God because their filthy customs shut them off from any perception of matters spiritual. And because they cannot see God, they denigrate him.[33]

Adherence to a literal interpretation of the Hebrew Bible prevents Jews from understanding the christological passages Guibert thinks it contains. Thus they are deaf to scriptural arguments construing the Incarnation.[34] Because Jews cannot see beyond material things they argue that the Virgin Birth did not take place because it would be unnatural. Yet they refuse to listen to arguments taken from nature too. According to Guibert, certain insects and animals reproduce themselves without coition. But Jews will not accept the obvious implications this contains for the divine generation of Jesus Christ.[35] Nor will they accept 'scientific' arguments which prove that God would not have contracted any impurity from the womb of the Virgin and that his assumed humanity would not have interfered with his divinity in the person of Jesus: the rays of the sun remain pure notwithstanding the filth of the substances they shine upon; oil does not mix with the water in which it is poured.[36] In any case, what does nature matter when God can do as he pleases? But how can Jews, whose hearts are bogged down in theft and usury, have any idea of the mysteries of God's sacraments?[37]

III

Guibert's view that the Jews will not understand the workings of the Virgin Birth and the Incarnation before they believe in Jesus as God and man seems to be an obvious application of Anselm's 'fides querens intellectum'. If, however, we take into account

[32] III.3; PL 156. 509–10.   [33] I.1, II.5; PL 156. 491, 496.
[34] II.1; PL 156. 499. Guibert quotes here Isaiah 7:9 according to the Septuagint. I am interpreting his use of it according to Jerome's understanding of Isaiah's words (*Comm. in Es.* III, vii.9; *Corpus Christianorum, Series latina*, 73. 99).   [35] II.2; PL 156. 499–500.
[36] I.6; PL 156. 498.   [37] II.5; PL 156. 506.

how much more Anselm meant by faith than correct belief, we can, I think, gain more insight into Guibert's perception that it is the Jews' appalling behaviour that lies at the root of their rejection of Christianity.

Faith for Anselm was not something static and it was not limited to a state of mind. Correct behaviour and living under total obedience to God were important elements of faith. If a man lives a full Christian life and if he manages to achieve some understanding of his Christian beliefs, his faith can be deepened. Intensified faith can then advance to even more cognisance of God. Proper moral conduct, however, is by no means easily come by.[38] Guibert tells us in his autobiography how Anselm helped him to learn how to behave and how to set about his reading of the Bible. The fourteen-year-old was told how he must conduct his inner self by applying the law of reason to control the natural impulses of his adolescent body. These words are reminiscent of the language used in chapter seven of Paul's Letter to the Romans.[39] There man's mind is seen to be struggling to overcome his unruly members ever since the Fall. The succour which man needs so badly to win this battle is not thought available in the law of the Old Testament, because it is seen simply to forbid what the flesh is doing. A law of the spirit, not the flesh, is what is considered necessary; Christ's law is seen to fit the bill.[40]

Turning to Guibert's mind, 'Anselm taught [me] to subdivide it into three or four categories, desire, will, reason and intellect, in order to understand the working of the whole interior mystery [of the mind?]. And he showed that the first two [i.e. desire and will], which many, myself included, thought were one, are not identical, separated as they are by certain divisions, even though it is plainly evident that they are almost the same in comparison to

---

[38] See McIntyre, *St Anselm and his critics*, pp. 38–55.
[39] I.17; ed. Labande, 138–41; ed. Benton, 89–90; Labande, 'Guibert de Nogent disciple et témoin de Saint-Anselme au Bec', *Les Mutations socio-culturelles*, 229–32.
[40] Romans 7. Guibert had referred to Romans 7 in his tract on the Incarnation to explain why it is that men have to cover up their privy parts. After the Fall a man's penis often becomes active against his wish. This is what makes the male organ unclean and this is why it must be hidden from view; in itself the organ is pure. The fact that Jesus wore breeches implies nothing unseemly about his body; his body was without sin. He simply dressed as other men did. *Tract. de Inc.* 1.5; PL 156. 496–7. (The relevance of the passage on clothes in 1.5 to the treatise is not immediately obvious. I have linked it to the passage in 1.2 (PL 156. 492) concerning Jesus' body and its functions.)

the other two.' Guibert goes on to say that Anselm showed him how to expound some chapters of the Gospels using these principles. Guibert then continued to apply them on his own.[41]

Anselm would seem to be teaching Guibert two things at once here. On the one hand he is explaining how the mind works in a philosophical framework. He is adapting here Augustine's tripartite soul consisting of will, memory and intelligence. To will is added desire, reason taking the place of memory. And we can guess from Anselm's sayings how important the distinction between will and appetite (or desire) was for his judgement of human behaviour. According to Anselm the element of reason in man's soul allies him to the angels; appetite connects him with the animals; will he has in common with both.

Will lies between appetite and reason. When his will turns to reason, man is said to be rational and spiritual because he knows the things which are rational and spiritual; when his will addresses itself to appetite, man is said to be carnal or animal-like because he knows matters which are carnal and irrational. Whence it is written: 'the sensual man does not perceive what belongs to God for it is foolishness to him'; 'but the spiritual man judges all things, and he himself is judged of no man'.[42]

Beyond reason, however, there is intellect or understanding. And this is where hermeneutics would seem to come in. For Anselm is not interested in the workings of man's mind for its own sake; he wants to discover how man can use his mind to come closer to God. Guibert's statement that Anselm used his principles about the mind to expound the Gospels, vindicates Klaus Guth in relating Anselm's components of the mind to the traditional four-tiered method of interpreting Scripture.[43] Indeed,

---

[41] 1.17; ed. Labande, 140–1; ed. Benton, 89–90. The infuriatingly difficult passage reads: *Is itaque tripartito aut quadripartito mentem modo distinguere docens, sub affectu, sub voluntate, sub ratione, sub intellectu commercia totius interni mysterii tractare, et quae una a plerisque et a me ipso putabantur certis divisionibus resoluta, non idem duo prima fore monstrabat, quae tamen accendentibus quarto vel tertio eadem mox esse promptis assertionibus constat.* My translation lies closest to that in Benton's edition which in turn is influenced by R. W. Southern's interpretation (*Saint Anselm and his biographer* (Cambridge, 1966), p. 225).

[42] Labande, 'Guibert de Nogent', 233; *Dicta Anselmi*, XVII, ed. R. W. Southern and F. S. Schmitt, *Memorials of St Anselm. Auctores Britannici Medii Aevi,* I (London, 1969), p. 174. I Cor. 2:14ff.

[43] K. Guth, 'Zum Verhältnis von Exegese und Philosophie im Zeitalter der Frühscholastik (Anmerkungen zu Guibert von Nogent, *Vita* I, 17)' *Recherches de Théologie ancienne et médiévale* 38 (1971), 121–36. Labande, 'Guibert de Nogent', 233, asserts that no reference is made here to exegesis.

when Guibert first mentions that he began to study the Bible he lists the three levels of interpretation which lie beyond the literal one: allegoric, moral and anagogic. And he tells us that it was Anselm who helped him find his way in this field of study.[44]

If one follows Guth's analysis, the mental component 'appetite' corresponds to a literal understanding of the Bible and 'will' to an allegorical one, while 'reason' governs tropology and 'intellect' anagogy. In other words, to enter the sphere of faith, a man's will must lean towards reason for him to perceive the existence of a spiritual meaning lying beyond the plain meaning of the text. The combined efforts of man's will, reason and intellect will open to him the realm of moral teachings; intellect is the vehicle to a mystical union with God.[45]

How does all this tie in with what Guibert has to say about the Jews? Jews argue in favour of the literal meaning of the ceremonial parts of the Hebrew Bible as opposed to the figurative meaning Christians have assigned to them. The Jewish approach to the Bible is not only described as *literaliter* but *carnaliter*. And what does Guibert associate with the so-called carnal law of Moses? For him this is the law that governs but does not control the impulses of the body. And what do Jews find impossible to believe? They refuse to accept the virginity of Mary with all its implications of sexual purity. What type of people cannot proceed beyond a carnal understanding of childbirth? Those whose will leans towards appetite away from reason. It is little wonder then that Guibert says of Jews: 'Shut up, you stubborn ones, all your words must be empty because reason is completely neglected. How can you, who involve your hearts in theft and usury, perceive the causes of God's sacraments and the mysteries of those causes?[46] The circle is complete. Jews are evil because they will not rise above a literal understanding of the Bible; it is precisely because they engage in evil activities that they are stuck in the rut of carnality.

---

[44] 1.17; ed. Labande, 138–9; ed. Benton, 89. In this context Guibert does not mention literal interpretation.

[45] I am incorporating in Guth's analysis (133–6) my understanding of Anselm's ideas about the four parts of the mind.

[46] *Tract. de Inc.*, II. 5; PL 156. 506: *Desistite, pertinaces, verbositas vestra vacet, quia ratio tota jacet. Qui furtis aut fenoribus corda convolvitis, causas Dei sacramentorum, et sacramenta causarum quomodo pervidetis?*

Guibert's specific accusations against the Jews of being thieves and usurers and his assumption that Jews are only interested in material things now need further examination in the light of what we actually know about the Jews who lived in northern France in the beginning of the twelfth century. And we need to place Guibert's intense dislike of Jews in the context of his *Weltanschauung*.

IV

There is a difference between the way that Guibert speaks about the Jews in his autobiography and the way he talks about them in his treatise on the Incarnation. In the first they are the accomplices of evil Christians and sometimes they even mediate between them and the Devil. In the second they are before anything else usurers. To complicate matters even further, the usurers who feature in Guibert's *De Vita Sua* are not Jews but Christians. One of his usurers operates in Laon, the other in Arras; both end up by going to the Devil.[47]

Usury had existed in some form or other at all times since antiquity. What was changeable was the measure in which usury took place and the way usury was judged by secular and above all ecclesiastical institutions.

Before 1050 thoughts on usury were rather undeveloped. It was, of course, proscribed as a serious sin, but it was described rather loosely as a form of shameful gain (*turpe lucrum*). As such it was regarded as a form of avarice or uncharitableness. It was the commercial revolution of the eleventh and twelfth centuries that made new considerations on usury necessary, and before long usury was treated as a sharply defined sin against justice.

Anselm of Lucca (1035–87), who may have studied under Lanfranc at Bec, is regarded as the first medieval author to define usury as theft. He is also the first to demand from usurers restitution for stolen goods. Ivo of Chartres (d. 1116) points out in his collection of canons that usuries may not be given as charity because they are stolen goods. He defines usury as anything that is taken beyond the principle, distinguishing between the loans in which usury occurs and contracts of lawful partnership. The classification of usury as a form of theft is taken up by Hugh of

[47] III.19; ed. Labande, 450–3; ed. Benton, 221–2.

Saint-Victor, Peter Comestor and Peter Lombard.[48] The twelfth and thirteenth centuries saw a proliferation of canon law legislation aimed at stamping out usury.[49]

Although some continued to regard usury as shameful gain rather than distinctly as theft,[50] Guibert of Nogent clearly adopted the view that exacting interest was tantamount to stealing. Each time he calls Jews usurers he says they are thieves as well, specifying in one instance that they take interest off the necks of the needy.[51] His usurer in Laon takes the very last penny from a poor woman in interest even though she had repaid the sum that she had originally borrowed. Both he and his counterpart in Arras are described by Guibert as devourers of the poor.[52] The fact that Guibert equates usury to theft may not, however, simply reflect his concern with the plight of the poor at the mercy of usurers. It is possible that it reflects the growing concern among twelfth-century moralists about the phenomenon of the possibility of making a living without perceptibly doing any work. A usurer did not produce any goods as such. His gain was directly related to the time it took for his client to repay him. In a sense then, time was the commodity he was trading in. But time was thought to belong to God; it was not the usurer's to sell. As a result a usurer was considered a thief of time.[53]

Developing ideas about usury in the twelfth-century Renaissance tie in with the fundamental economic and social changes that took place in northern Europe at this time. New techniques in farming substantially increased the production of food. A

---

[48] J. Lestocquoy, 'Les Usuriers du début du Moyen Age', in: *Studi in onore di Gino Luzzatto*, vol. I (Milan, 1949), pp. 67–77; J. T. Noonan, *The scholastic analysis of usury* (Cambridge, MA, 1957), pp. 16–18; J. Gilchrist, *The Church and economic activity in the Middle Ages* (London, 1969), p. 278 n. 1; *Lexikon des Mittelalters* I, 679–80. Noonan (p. 17) asserts that Anselm of Canterbury was the first medieval author to suggest a similarity between usury and theft, but the text he refers to (PL 158.659) is not by Anselm. It is a homily written by Hervé de Bourgdieu who was born *c.* 1080 in Le Mans. He writes that no alms may be given from what is earned from pillage, usury and theft.

[49] J. Le Goff, 'The usurer and purgatory', in *The dawn of modern banking* (New Haven and London, 1979), pp. 27ff.; B. Nelson, *The idea of usury. From tribal brotherhood to universal otherhood*, 2nd enlarged edition (Chicago and London, 1969), pp. 9ff.; Noonan, pp. 18–20.

[50] Noonan, p. 17 n. 22.

[51] *Tract. de Inc.*, II.5, III.3 and 8; PL 156. 506, 513, 524. Reference to the poor is in III.8.

[52] *De Vita Sua*, III.19; ed. Labande, 450–3; ed. Benton, 221–2. Lestocquoy ('Les Usuriers', 71–2) points out that the Arras man seems to operate on a much grander scale than the usurer in Laon.

[53] J. Le Goff, 'The Usurer', pp. 31–3. Peter the Chanter writes at the end of the twelfth century that a usurer *vendit tempora Dei* (J. W. Baldwin, *Master, princes and merchants. The social views of Peter the Chanter and his circle*, vol. 2 (Princeton, NJ, 1970), p. 191, n. 13).

significant growth in population followed. New villages absorbed the growing number of people as did the towns. Both in town and countryside different types of industries developed. Local markets multiplied and fairs were arranged to facilitate the exchange of goods. These developments went hand in hand with the increased use of money. Money, as a commodity, was experienced by more and more people every day of their lives. This was especially true in the growing cities where familial bonds or ties of provenance were often replaced by more impersonal connections between strangers. Money was often the operational force in those connections. Those who lacked money wanted and needed to obtain it; those who had it wanted more. It was only natural that lending and borrowing money at interest was widespread.[54]

The Jews of northern France played a significant rôle in this economic boom. Although we lack documentary sources for the history of northern French Jewry of the tenth and eleventh centuries, we can deduce from the responsa literature and from some other sources that by the eleventh century French Jews were supporting themselves primarily through their commercial activities. It is in the course of that century that moneylending seems to have become an increasingly important part of their livelihood. Thus Jews contributed to and benefited from the growth of urban centres in the twelfth century.[55]

The increase in usury was not the only thing that Christian theologians found worrying about the monetary economy they saw developing around them.[56] They were concerned about money itself. Was it right for a Christian to want to earn it? Was not material gain very much inferior to spiritual achievements? As Lester Little has so aptly put it, the eleventh and twelfth centuries experienced a gap between a nascent social and economic ethos and traditional concepts of Christian morality. These concepts had been formulated in the early Christian period when the economic benefits of an urban economy had passed by the

[54] L. K. Little, *Religious poverty and the profit economy in medieval Europe* (London, 1978), pp. 19–34; Little, 'Pride goes before avarice: social change and the vices in Latin Christendom', *American Historical Review* 76 (1971), 27–30; J. Le Goff, *Your money or your life. Economy and religion in the Middle Ages*, trans. P. Ranum (New York, 1988), pp. 23–7.

[55] Chazan, *Medieval Jewry*, pp. 10–34.

[56] For the concern about usury among the Rabbis of this period see H. Soloveitchik, 'Pawnbroking: a study in *Ribbit* and of the Halakhah in exile', *Proceedings of the American Academy for Jewish Research* 38–9 (1970–1), 203–68.

Church and in the patristic period when urban economies were in disarray. In the eleventh century a thoroughly Christian society was beginning to experience the effects of a monetary economy. And many moralists were opposed to the fundamental changes which were taking place. These moralists often expressed their opposition in repeated denunciations of what they saw as the greed of modern men and women.[57]

Guibert of Nogent's autobiography exudes a deep-rooted hostility to change; he was firmly attached to the established social order as he perceived it. One need only examine his treatment of the commune of Laon to be convinced of that. But the whole of his history is jam-packed with greedy and lecherous people who bring havoc upon themselves and others. Anselm of Canterbury and Anselm of Laon are among the very few who are spared the viciousness of Guibert's tongue.[58] Guibert's aversion to modernity must have contributed to his enmity towards the Jews. Jews played a visible part in the new economic realities of his day. Hatred for that reality could only deepen his hatred for Jews. Thus, notwithstanding his knowledge that usury was by no means a profession reserved for Jews, the disbelieving Jews of his tract on the Incarnation become usurers *par excellence*. Jews emerge as people who by their very nature are obsessed by the love of money and the lures of material gain. When Guibert writes such words about Jews it is as if for a moment he is ascribing to them what he hates so much not only in Jews but in everyone else too.[59]

V

The *Tractatus de Incarnatione adversus Iudeos* makes it plain that Guibert of Nogent had no illusions about converting Jews. Guibert knew of Jewish converts to Christianity, but the conversions of which he gives details in his autobiography are

---

[57] Little, 'Pride goes before avarice', 30–1, 20–7; Little, *Religious poverty*, pp. 35–41.

[58] R. I. Moore, 'Guibert of Nogent and his world', *Studies in medieval history presented to R. H. C. Davis*, ed. H. Mayr-Harting and R. I. Moore (London, 1985), pp. 109ff.; A. Vermeesch, *Essai sur les origines et la signification de la commune dans le nord de la France (XIe et XIIe siècles)* (Heule, 1966), pp. 108–13.

[59] On attitudes to Jews in this period see L. K. Little, 'The function of the Jews in the commercial revolution', *Povertà e ricchezza nella spiritualità dei secoli XI e XII. Atti dell'VIII convegno storico internazionale del Centro di studi sulla spiritualità medievale* (Todi, 1969), pp. 271–87 and his *Religious poverty*, pp. 42–57.

conversions by force not persuasion.[60] What exercised Guibert's mind was the question why Jews did not convert notwithstanding all the evidence being offered to them supporting the truth of the Christian faith. Indeed, it is the nature of this evidence and the continued rejection by Jews of it that helps account for some of Guibert's bitter hatred for Jews.

The Incarnation was a favourite topic in the monastic and cathedral schools of the twelfth-century Renaissance. The subject of the human nature of Jesus Christ attracted the greatest thinkers of the period. The nature of human beings was drawing interest in its own right. What was man's rôle in nature? What made man different from animals? What was the meaning of man's speech? And what was man's relationship to God? All these questions were questions which engaged twelfth-century scholars.

The important point for the purposes of our investigation is that the thought of the twelfth-century Renaissance was conducted within the parameters of Christianity. We are in the period when after many years of insecurity northwestern Europe was slowly but surely coming into its own. But this Europe was a Christian one; the God twelfth-century Renaissance scholars were seeking to understand was the Christian Trinity. The concept of man that they were pondering was essentially a Christian one. This is not to say that they were unaware of non-Christians. On the contrary, most of the impetus for their researches came from the Pagan world of antiquity. But the whole purpose of their work was to incorporate what they were learning from the liberal arts into their Christian outlook on God and man.

The position of the Jews in the midst of this activity was in the nature of things tricky. On the one hand, their sustained queries about the basic tenets of the Christian faith stimulated further inquiry into those doctrines by Christians. On the other, they could help Christian scholars in their endeavours. Renewed interest in grammar and the semantics of language encouraged Christian scholars to take a greater interest in the Hebrew of the Old Testament. The expertise of rabbis would indeed be drawn on by the Victorines and others in their quest to understand better the language of the Hebrew Bible. These rabbis hailed from the

---

[60] The Jewish boy who is saved from the massacre at Rouen, converts because he thinks he will be killed if he refuses to be baptised (*De Vita Sua*, II.5, ed. Labande, 248–9; ed. Benton, 135).

numerous flourishing Jewish academies of northern France.[61] But in the long run none of this could bode well for the Jews. Christians studied the Old Testament for their own purposes, not out of love or tolerance for Jews. They needed to improve their literal understanding of Scripture in order to be able to refine their figurative interpretation of it. Christian figurative exegesis of the Bible was by definition unacceptable to Jews. And the harder Christians worked at answering questions about Christianity, the more they resented the fact that Jews would never accept the answers. It was, I think, inevitable that Christian scholars should begin to formulate ideas about the reasons for Jewish disbelief and at the same time blame Jews for their incredulity.[62]

The intellectual endeavours of the twelfth-century Renaissance did not take place in a vacuum. The economy was expanding; existing cities were growing, new towns were founded; all sorts of social changes were taking place. In all of this Jews played a visible part, and it is natural that when Christian thinkers pondered these changes, they should think about Jews too. As in the intellectual sphere, these changes were not beneficial to Jews as time went by. Apart from anything else Jews were permanently associated with the ills of an urbanising society. They never lost the epithets with which they were dubbed in this period: money-grubbing thieves and usurers.

Guibert of Nogent's fruitful links with Saint Anselm assured him of his own niche in the intellectual movement of his day. His work clearly betrays his interest in the Incarnation, the human nature of Christ and especially the Virgin Mary. The book he wrote about himself shows his interest in his own psyche and that of others. The changes he witnessed in his lifetime impressed him deeply.

All these elements played their separate rôles when Guibert thought about Jews. In this way arguments, which on the surface would seem traditional enough, on closer examination take on new meaning. Jews had been attacked by Christians for centuries for being guided by their literal understanding of the Law of Moses and for refusing to accept the christological interpretation

---

[61] A. Grabois, 'The *Hebraica Veritas* and Jewish–Christian intellectual relations in the twelfth century', *Speculum* 50 (1975), 613–34; B. Smalley, *The study of the Bible in the Middle Ages* (Notre Dame, Indiana, 1964), pp. 83–195. [62] See n. 15.

of the Old Testament. Guibert uses the existing arsenal of anti-Jewish arguments, but in his hands the attack is much more comprehensive. The supposed literalness of the Jews becomes actual carnal behaviour. This behaviour aligns Jews with animals and excludes them from any spiritual aspirations. The Pentateuch offers Jews nothing but material gain; thus to Guibert the Law of Moses exemplifies the usurious rôle of Jews in the expanding northern French economy. In short, Jews are evil in mind and body. As such they are the natural accomplices of evil Christians. Guibert seems to associate all evil with the Devil; the Jews are no exception to the rule.[63]

To sum up: Guibert's hatred of Jews must be seen in the context of his hostility to the changes he witnessed in northern French society of his day.[64] His assessment of Jewish disbelief and its causes has much to do with what he learned from St Anselm about man and how man should try to come closer to God. To be sure, the virulence of Guibert's language concerning Jews is more indicative of his character and the way he was wont to express himself about his fellow man than of anything else. But the various elements which constitute the core of his enmity to Jews are not eccentric. They reflect the intellectual, economic and social realities of Guibert's time and will go on to play their part in determining Christian attitudes towards Jews in the course of the twelfth century and beyond.[65]

[63] J. Trachtenberg, *The Devil and the Jews. The medieval conception of the Jew and its relation to modern antisemitism* (New Haven, 1943), pp. 66–7, 213, mentions Guibert's story about the Jewish doctor mediating between a Christian and the Devil. More work, I think, needs to be done on Guibert's demonology and the Jews.

[64] Moore, 'Guibert of Nogent', 108–9.

[65] Research for this article was conducted during my tenure of the Laura Ashley Research Fellowship at Lucy Cavendish College, Cambridge, and I wish to thank the Laura Ashley Foundation and Lucy Cavendish for their support.

—◦◦—

City and politics before the coming of the Politics: some illustrations

DAVID LUSCOMBE

The unavailability of Aristotle's *Politics* in the West before the thirteenth century may be a remote consequence of the development of autocracies in which the *polis* seemed insignificant, just as the availability of the *Politics* from the thirteenth century may be associated with the development of civic and communitarian bodies – like the Italian city republics. But it would be difficult to turn this broad observation into an explanation. Aristotle's *Politics* was unavailable in the West until the thirteenth century and most of his *Ethics* until the twelfth. Throughout the same period (and beyond) the political speculations of Plato – Aristotle's master – were also unavailable, with the exception of a part of his *Timaeus*. Losses had occurred.

The Carlyles in their great *History of mediaeval political theory in the West* found 'a real break' in the history of political theory between Aristotle and the Roman lawyers.[1] They began their work with a study of the Roman lawyers from the second to the sixth century, and of the Christian Fathers. These were the foundations of the political theory of the Middle Ages.[2]

The Carlyles also examined earlier Latin writers such as Cicero and Seneca who share some of the characteristic conceptions of the lawyers and of the Fathers,[3] but who also present a startlingly complete change from the political theory of Aristotle. For they upheld the natural equality of human nature, the sharing by all men, in spite of their actual differences, of a universal capacity both to reason and to attain to virtue. Aristotle, on the other hand,

---

[1] R. W. Carlyle and A. J. Carlyle, *A history of mediaeval political theory in the West*, I (3rd edition, Edinburgh, 1930), p. 2.   [2] R. W. and A. J. Carlyle, *History*, I, p. 3.   [3] Ibid., p. 3.

had held to the *natural* inequality of men, to the necessity of slavery as a natural and necessary condition of a civilised social order.[4] Cicero followed in the line of Aristotle in so far as he defined the goal of the state as the promotion of the well being of all, through justice and law, and in defining the state or commonwealth as a natural association.[5] In his *De officiis* Cicero portrayed man as a naturally social and civic being: man's possession of reason and speech leads naturally to a kind of association or community (I.xvi). So human association is in accordance with nature (III.v). Although not every human association constitutes a people, where there is consent to law and an agreement as to the advantages of association, a people (*populus*) is constituted (*De republica* I.xxv). Such ideas were known in later centuries not least because Augustine and Isidore discussed them.[6]

So the Carlyles began with a demonstration that Aristotle's political thought had ceased to command allegiance by the time of Cicero and Seneca, although important traces survived and could be found.

In their fifth volume the Carlyles gave an account of the political theory of the thirteenth century. While giving Thomas Aquinas no undue prominence they carefully showed how he crossed and modified the prevalent traditions of political theory deriving from the Stoics, the Roman lawyers and the Fathers with the newly rediscovered work of Aristotle, including the *Politics*

---

[4] Ibid., pp. 7–8.

[5] Ibid., pp. 14–17. And see W. L. Newman, *The Politics of Aristotle*, II (Oxford, 1887), pp. xiv–xvi for suggestions that Cicero had some knowledge of the *Politics* which may underlie *De republica*, IV.iii.3, V.vi.8 (on the goal of the state), I.xxv.39 (on its origin), and IV.iv.4 (criticisms of Plato's communism). Scattered passages from Pliny, Plutarch and other Roman writers who seem to have had some acquaintance with Aristotle's *Politics* are collected here, pp. xviii–xx. Newman thought that the establishment of the Roman empire made Aristotle's *Politics* redundant as a work of guidance.

[6] Augustine, *De civitate Dei*, II.xxi, also XIX.xxi. Isidore of Seville, *Etymologiae*, IX.iv.5–6, ed. W. M. Lindsay (Oxford, 1911). Isidore (ibid.) defines the *populus* as *tota civitas* or *universi cives*. In *Etymologiae* XV.ii.1 Isidore links *civitas* to *urbs*: 'civitas est hominum multitudo societatis vinculo adunata, dicta a civibus, id est, ab ipsis incolis urbis...Nam urbs ipsa moenia sunt, civitas autem non saxa, sed habitatores vocantur.' (The *civitas* is a multitude of men united by a bond of association, so-called from the citizens. For although the *urbs* itself is made by its walls, the *civitas* gets its name not from stones but from the inhabitants.) Compare also *Etymologiae*, IX.ii.1: 'Gens est multitudo ab uno principio orta sive ab alia natione secundum propriam collectionem distincta, ut Graeciae, Asiae'; and *Etymologiae* IX.iv.2: 'Cives vocati, quod in unum coeuntes vivant, ut vita communis et ornatior fiat et tutior.'

and the *Ethics*.[7] When Aristotle's teaching on the naturalness of the *polis* became available in the West in the thirteenth century it served to reinforce positions already familiar through Cicero and the Roman law. The Augustinian tradition that viewed the state of original innocence as the only really natural state was counterbalanced by the surviving Stoic insistence that men and things continue to be regulated by natural law.

It is notorious that medieval political vocabulary lacked precision. Social groups and political communities in the medieval West developed in many different ways, being governed by blood-relationships, historical traditions, laws and customs, in many varying amalgamations.[8] Medieval writers had no word equivalent to that of the state. Yet words closely associated with the noun *polis* were known through surviving Roman texts. *Politia*, meaning the state or its government as well as the title of Plato's *Republic*, was found in Cicero, Ambrose and Cassiodorus. The adjective *politicus* was likewise known through Cicero and others and the *politicae virtutes* – those virtues which man promotes because he is a social animal living in a commonwealth or city – were enumerated by Macrobius in his *Commentary on the Dream of Scipio*, I.viii.[9] Medieval writers also had a choice of terms – found in Cicero, in Roman law, in St Augustine and elsewhere – which have in common the notion of men united in pursuit at least of some common aim (if not justice). Such were *res publica*, *populus*, *regnum* and *civitas*. The word *communitas* also came to be applied to what we might call a political community with a recognised juridical status.[10] And *communitas* or *communio* or *commune* might also denote the community found in a town, whether or not it was constituted into a commune and bound together on the basis of an oath.[11]

When William of Moerbeke started to translate the *Politics*

---

[7] R. W. and A. J. Carlyle, *History*, v (2nd edition, Edinburgh, 1938), pp. 10–24 and elsewhere.

[8] Susan Reynolds, *Kingdoms and communities in western Europe 900–1300* (Oxford, 1984).

[9] For references see e.g. Forcellini's *Lexikon*, IV (Prati, 1868); *Oxford Latin Dictionary*, ed. P. G. W. Glare (Oxford, 1982); A. Souter, *A glossary of later Latin to 600 A.D.* (Oxford, 1949). Notable occurrences of *politia* are in Cicero, *De divinatione*, I.xxix.60; II.xxvii.59, Ambrose, *Hexaemeron*, v.xv (PL 14. 227B, 228A) and Cassiodorus, *Variae*, IX.ii, ed. Å. J. Fridh, *Corpus Christianorum. Series Latina*, 96 (Turnhout, 1973), p. 348.

[10] P. Michaud-Quantin, *Universitas: Expressions du mouvement communautaire dans le moyen-âge latin*, L'Eglise et l'Etat au Moyen Age, 15 (Paris, 1970), chapter 6, pp. 147–66.

[11] Ibid.; Reynolds, *Kingdoms and communities*, pp. 170–83.

c. 1260[12] he chose the word *communitas* to represent the Greek *koinonia*, i.e. the civil community of which the *polis* is an example: 'every city exists as a kind of community ... every community has been established for the sake of some good'.[13] William of Moerbeke used the word *communitas* more frequently in his earlier translation (*translatio prior*) than in his later translation (*translatio vetus*) of Aristotle's *Politics*: in the latter, *civitas* appears more regularly. For the *civitas* (under Aristotle's insistence) means the *communitas perfecta*, not any kind of community with a common interest or activity, but the ultimate natural community.[14]

The word *civitas* had a long pedigree. Cicero defined *civitas* as *constitutio populi*, an organised people subject to government or *consilium* (*De republica*, i.xxvi); and probably in the medieval centuries *civitas* never lost its general sense of body politic and was never reduced to meaning simply the space occupied by an urban nucleus.[15]

In late antiquity the *civitas* commonly stood for an administrative district with a capital city which was generally identical to a bishopric and to its seat. The *civitas* might mean either this chief town itself or the bishop's seat or the entire 'city state'. But it was more than an *oppidum* for the *civitas* was a wider community and was not really thinkable apart from the rural hinterland. In time these Roman city-communities gave way to other units of rule; they lost their senates as well as their public baths, theatres

---

[12] For this date see M. Grabmann, *Guglielmo di Moerbeke, O.P., il traduttore delle opere di Aristotele*, Miscellanea Historiae Pontificiae, xi (Rome, 1946), p. 112 and G. v. Hertling, 'Zur Geschichte der Politik im Mittelalter', *Rheinischer Museum*, 1884, 446ff. (reprinted in G. v. Hertling, *Historische Beiträge zur Philosophie*, ed. I. A. Endres (Kempten, 1914)). Also, B. G. Dod, 'Aristoteles Latinus', *The Cambridge history of later medieval philosophy*, ed. N. Kretzmann, A. Kenny and J. Pinborg (Cambridge, 1982), pp. 62–7, 78.

[13] 'Quoniam autem omnem civitatem videmus communitatem quandam existentem, et omnem communitatem boni alicuius gratia institutam ... ipsa autem est que vocatur civitas et omnis communitas politica', Aristotle, *Politica, translatio prior imperfecta interprete Guillelmo de Moerbeka*(?), ed. P. Michaud-Quantin, 'Aristoteles Latinus', 29, 1 (Bruges–Paris, 1961), p. 3.

[14] The earlier translation was edited by Michaud-Quantin (cited above), the later by F. Susemihl, *Aristotelis Politicorum libri octo, cum vetusta translatione Guilelmi de Moerbeke* (Leipzig, 1872). See on this J. Quillet, 'Community, I. Community, counsel and representation', *The Cambridge history of medieval political thought, c. 350 to c. 1450*, ed. J. H. Burns (Cambridge, 1988), pp. 526–7 with reference to *Politics* I, 1252 b 9 and the *translatio prior* ed. Michaud-Quantin, p. 4 (52 b 7); *Politics* 1252 b 16 and *translatio prior*, ed. Michaud-Quantin, p. 4 (52 b 10, 13); 1252 b 29 and *translatio prior*, ed. Michaud-Quantin, p. 5 (52 b 28): 'communitas perfecta civitas, iam omnis habens terminum per se sufficientiae'.

[15] For a fascinating discussion of the words used in the Middle Ages to designate cities and towns see chapter 4 of P. Michaud-Quantin, *Universitas*, pp. 111–27.

and temples, and in some cases declined into mere castles or into communities with a largely clerical composition. The functions of towns also changed over the centuries of Germanic invasion and settlement and the *civitas* community often evolved into an ecclesiastical diocese.

But *civitas*-related terms abounded and new ones were coined – and by no means only in the later part of the medieval period. Indeed, they proliferated and older words were refreshed, as may be seen in the various dictionaries of medieval Latin words. Here we find: *civilitas* meaning the body of citizens, citizenship, the city or the city state;[16] *civiliter* meaning – as in antiquity – sociably or peacefully or according to civil law; *civitatensis*, both an adjective meaning 'of the city' and a noun meaning townsman or city-dweller;[17] *civitonicus*, a noun found in the late eighth century and meaning city-dweller; *civiloquium*, from the end of the Middle Ages, meaning city council;[18] *civissa* or *civinis*, a female citizen;[19] *civitatula* or *civitatella* or *civitella*, meaning a small *civitas* such as Cambridge[20] and *civitare*, meaning to make (or to live in) a city.[21]

The *civitas* concept had also entered theology. It could mean the wider community of all the faithful or of all the faithless, God's city or the devil's. Of the wider city Otto of Freising wrote (1143–6) to express the view that all human power was coming to an end and that the Empire of his own day was a final manifestation before the coming of Antichrist.[22] Otto reproduces

[16] For most of the following see Du Cange, *Glossarium Mediae et Infimae Latinitatis* and J. F. Niermeyer and C. Van de Kieft, *Mediae Latinitatis Lexicon Minus* (Leiden, 1976). See too for *civilitas* A. Souter, *A glossary of later Latin to 600 A.D.* (Oxford, 1949) and *Thesaurus Linguae Latinae*, III (Leipzig, 1906–12). Other meanings are *benignitas*, *humanitas* and *urbanitas*, cf. *Lexicon Latinitatis Nederlandicae Medii Aevi*, II C, composuerunt J. W. Fuchs, O. Weijers, M. Gumbert (Leiden, 1981); *Dictionary of medieval Latin from British sources*, fasc. II C prepared by R. E. Latham (London, 1981).
[17] *Glossarium till medeltidslatinet i sverige*, ed. V. Westerbergh, fasc. I (Stockholm, 1969) e.g. *civitatensis communitatensis stokholmensis* (AD 1312); *Dictionary of medieval Latin from British sources* fasc. II C. One mention (AD 538) in the *Thesaurus Linguae Latinae*, III.
[18] *Lexicon Latinitatis Nederlandicae Medii Aevi*, II C. (AD 1458).   [19] Ibid.
[20] Ibid.; *Dictionary of medieval Latin from British sources*, fasc. II C. *Civitatula* is listed in the *Thesaurus Linguae Latinae*, III.
[21] *Lexicon Latinitatis Nederlandicae Medii Aevi*, II C; *Thesaurus Linguae Latinae*, III.
[22] *Chronica sive Historia de Duabus Civitatibus*, ed. A. Hofmeister. MGH SS rerum Germanicarum in usum scholarum, 45 (1912). English translation by C. C. Mierow, *The two cities. A chronicle of universal history to the year 1146 AD by Otto, Bishop of Freising*. Records of Civilisation, Sources and Studies (New York, 1928). Revised edition by W. Lammers with a translation into German by A. Schmidt, *Otto Bischof von Freising, Chronik oder Die Geschichte der zwei Staaten* (Darmstadt, 1960). On the *civitas dei* and *civitas terrena* see Lammers, here pp. xliv–liv. On Otto's thought

Augustine's distinction between two kinds of city in the Prologue to the first book of his *Historia de duabus civitatibus*: one city is temporal and worldly and belongs to the devil; the other is eternal and heavenly and belongs to Christ. But in the prologue to his fifth book Otto declares that once the peoples of the Roman empire, along with their rulers, had mostly become Catholics, the two cities were almost replaced by one, which is the church. This single city, since it is composed of both the elect and the damned – or of wheat and chaff – is a mixed city, *civitas permixta*. In the prologue to Book eight, Otto writes that at the end of time only the elect will remain in the church.

To the theologian *civitas* might also denote the solitary community of the single human person. One twelfth-century writer, perhaps Alcher of Clairvaux, could write thus of a personal community which is a human soul, counselled by its intellective faculties, defenced by reason as by military knights fighting in the cause of justice, supported by sensual faculties just as labourers and countrymen support a city community.[23] Another religious use of the image of the city was made by William of Auvergne, bishop of Paris from 1228 to 1249. He dreamed of a spiritual city administered by the priests of the King of Kings and populated by the recipients of the seven sacraments.[24]

on the city see further H. M. Klinkenberg, 'Der Sinn der Chronik Ottos von Freising' in *Aus Mittelalter und Neuzeit. Festschrift für Gerhard Kallen* (Bonn, 1957), pp. 63ff.; J. Spörl, 'Die Civitas Dei im Geschichtsdenken Ottos von Freising', *La Ciudad de Dios. Revista de cultura e investigación*, 167 (1955); W. Lammers, *Weltgeschichte und Zeitgeschichte bei Otto von Freising*, Sitzungsberichte der Wissenschaftlichen Gesellschaft an der Johann Wolfgang Goethe-Universität Frankfurt am Main, 14, 3 (Wiesbaden, 1977).

[23] (*Inter Augustinianos*), *De spiritu et anima*, PL 40, 779–832, here 807–8. Doubts about the attribution of the work to Alcher have been expressed by G. Raciti, 'L'autore del *De Spiritu et anima*', *Rivista di filosofia neo-scolastica*, 53 (1961), 385–401 and by M.-T. d'Alverny, *Alain de Lille: textes inédits avec une introduction sur sa vie et ses oeuvres*. Etudes de philosophie médiévale, 52 (Paris, 1965), pp. 177–8.

[24] See J. Le Goff, 'Une Métaphore urbaine de Guillaume d'Auvergne', *L'Imaginaire médiéval* (Editions Gallimard, 1985), pp. 242–7; English translation by A. Goldhammer under the title *The medieval imagination* (Chicago and London, 1988), pp. 177–80. Le Goff refers to William's *summa, Opera omnia* (Orleans and Paris, 1674), pp. 407–16. In the Venice edition (1591) of William's *Magisterium divinale* one of the chapter titles uses the term *politia clericalis* to refer to the ecclesiastical hierarchy: 'Quod ordines angelorum, officia & dignitates se habent modo, quo debet se habere politia clericalis', *De universo*, ii.ii, c.113 in *Guilielmi Alverni episcopi Parisiensis ...Opera omnia ...per Iohannem Dominicum Traianum Neapolitanum*, p. 909. I am not sure that William himself provided the chapter title; the earliest MS of the work, Paris, Bibliothèque nationale, latin 15756, contains some chapter titles but lacks this one. William was writing between 1231 and 1236 according to J. Kramp, 'Des Wilhelm von Auvergne *Magisterium divinale*', *Gregorianum* 2 (1921), 42–103. *De universo*, ii presents detailed tableaux

These spiritualised concepts, ultimately derived from Augustine and the Bible, witness, however imprecisely, to the continuing power of an urban ideology.

Calcidius had summarised Plato's idea of the city state in the prologue to his Latin translation of the *Timaeus* and in the twelfth century at least it attracted regular attention from readers and commentators.[25] Of especial interest to them – to William of Conches, for example, as well as to Bernard Silvestris and Alan of Lille and several anonymous writers – was the analogy drawn between the structure of the human body (head, heart, members, etc.) and that of the *civitas* (rulers, soldiers, workers).[26]

In the twelfth century too many writers felt the attractions of classical ways of life and thought. Peter Abelard, in particular, claimed that the ancient philosophers' teaching about the *rei publicae status* and about the lives led by the citizens within it, was, like the philosophers' moral teaching, almost completely in accord with the Gospel. Their teaching on the active life and on the right way of ruling and of living in cities, was as wholesome as their teaching on the virtuous life. Cities are 'convents' for married people and their rulers should live lives of continence and abstinence as monks and clerks now do. Cities, too, are convents bound together by charity. Every city is a fraternity (*nihil civitas nisi fraternitas*). Abelard believed that the philosophers had enjoined the rulers of cities to establish the communal life and communal sharing of goods in the manner extolled in the *Acts of the Apostles* 4.32, and followed now by Christian monks. Socrates

with the parallel hierarchies which constitute the earthly kingdom, the church and heaven. See B. Vallentin, 'Der Engelstaat. Zur mittelalterlichen Anschauung vom Staate (bis auf Thomas von Aquino)', *Grundrisse und Bausteine zur Staat und zur Geschichtslehre zusammengetragen zu den Ehren Gustav Schmollers*, ed. K. Breysig, F. Wolters, B. Vallentin, F. Andreae (Berlin, 1908), pp. 41–120.

[25] *Timaeus a Calcidio translatus commentarioque instructus.* 2nd edition. *Plato Latinus*, 4 (London, 1975). See *Timaeus*, 17C–26E (pp. 8–19) and Calcidius' *Commentary*, V–VI, pp. 59–60; also CCXXXI–CCXXXIII, pp. 245–7. P. E. Dutton, '*Illustre civitatis et populi exemplum.* Plato's *Timaeus* and the transmission from Calcidius to the end of the twelfth century of a tripartite scheme of society', *Mediaeval Studies* 45 (1983), 79–119.

[26] For a full discussion see Dutton, '*Illustre civitatis*'. Of particular interest are the following instances: William of Conches, *Glosae super Macrobium*, cited by E. Jeauneau, ed., *Guillaume de Conches, Glosae super Platonem*, Textes philosophiques du Moyen Age 13 (Paris, 1965), p. 75 n.e., and *Glosae super Platonem*, 15, ed. Jeauneau, p. 74; Bernard Silvestris, Commentary on the *Aeneid*, ed. J. W. Jones and E. F. Jones, *The Commentary on the first six books of the 'Aeneid' of Vergil commonly attributed to Bernardus Silvestris. A new critical edition* (Lincoln, Nebraska, 1977), pp. 15, 109; Alan of Lille, *The plaint of nature*, ed. N. Häring, 'Alan of Lille, *De planctu naturae*', *Studi medievali*, 3rd series, 19 (1978), 827–8.

in the *Timaeus* (18c–d) extended the communal life to embrace the sharing of wives and children; and Abelard compares this favourably with the adulterous and lustful tendencies, condemned by Jerome (*Adversus Iovinianum*, 1.49), that arise where wives are viewed as objects of personal pleasure. So government in a *res publica* should foster the *communis utilitas*; the rulers and *concives* of a true *civitas* should follow the law of love. Christian convents also are properly called *civitates*. Abelard cites Cicero on *civitates* as *concilia coetusque hominum iure sociati*. He looked back to Plato as well as to the Bible and Augustine to find encouragement for rulers to love and to serve their people.[27] Thus civic life was the object of some original reflection before the re-entry of Aristotle. Abelard brings together the classical and Judaeo-Christian elements and, in basing his concept of *civitas* on charity and fraternity, effectively, if implicitly, repairs the Augustinian rupture between the city and justice.

Shortly before or after 1270 Aquinas gave varying definitions of *civitas* in his *Super Politicam*. He was of course expounding Aristotle's text but his sympathy may be presumed. *Civitas* is – in terms of self-sufficiency in this human life – the ultimate community, the most complete of all human communities.[28] Its study is called politics or civil science, a branch of practical philosophy which excels all others since it deals with the most perfect means of procuring goodness in human affairs through the use of human reason.[29]

Aquinas distinguishes *civitas* into two kinds according to their regimen – which is *politicum* if government is according to the laws of the *civitas* or *regale* if the ruler has full power.[30]

[27] Peter Abelard, *Theologia christiana*, II.43–56, ed. E. M. Buytaert, *Petri Abaelardi opera theologica*, II. Corpus Christianorum. Continuatio mediaeualis, XII (Turnhout, 1969), pp. 149–55. Cf. Cicero, *De republica*, VI.xiii. On medieval attitudes to the *Timaeus* and to marital communism see S. Kuttner, 'Gratian and Plato', *Church and government in the Middle Ages. Essays presented to C. R. Cheney*, ed. C. N. L. Brooke, D. E. Luscombe, G. H. Martin and D. Owen (Cambridge, 1976), pp. 93–118.

[28] 'Quarum quidem communitatum cum diuersi sint gradus et ordines, ultima est communitas civitatis ordinata ad per se sufficientia uite humane: unde inter omnes communitates humana ipsa est perfectissima … necesse est quod hoc totum quod est civitas sit principalius omnibus totis que ratione humana cognosci et constitui possunt', *Sententia Libri Politicorum*, Sancti Thomae de Aquino opera omnia iussu Leonis XIII P.M. edita, XLVIII (Rome, 1971), *Prologus*, A 69. To my great regret I have not been able to consult the nearly contemporary (and probably slightly earlier) commentary on the *Politics* written by Albert the Great, ed. Borgnet, *Opera omnia*, vol. 8 (Paris, 1891). [29] *Sententia Libri Politicorum, Prologus*, A 69–A 70.

[30] *Sententia Libri Politicorum*, I.i/a, A 72.

It is of course a natural community[31] but one in which different social as well as political structures are possible e.g. for the family, property and law (*politica conversatio, ordinationes civitatis, conversatio civitatis, politie civitatum*).[32] One polity (*politia*, which is the *ordinatio regiminis civitatis* or *regimen civitatis*) will not be like another.[33] *Politia* is nothing else but the *ordo* to be found among the inhabitants of a *civitas*,[34] and the *civitas* is nothing other than the multitude of those who live in a self-sufficient community.[35]

Only with William of Moerbeke's translation of the *Politics* had such precision become possible. The perfect community – the end of all comunities – is the self-sufficient community which is not the household, not the village – and not the Greek *polis*. Its study is a practical science, because communities of differing kinds have to be maintained. And it is a moral science, not a mechanical one, because the differences between the different types of human communities are measured by reference to the good for which each community is established.

The notion of politics as a science or as a branch of philosophy was not lost in the early Middle Ages. But it faced regular competition from another classification of the sciences, derived from Stoic teaching and presented by Isidore, which divides philosophy into physics, ethics and logic. In this scheme ethics comprises the four virtues – prudence, justice, fortitude and temperance.[36] Only in the classifications inspired by Boethius and Cassiodorus did philosophy retain a civil branch.

Cassiodorus presents in book two of his *Institutions* (written *c.* 544–5) a division of philosophy into two parts, *inspectiva* and

---

[31] *Sententia*, I.i/b, A 77–80.   [32] *Sententia*, II. i, A 120–1.

[33] *Sententia*, II. xvii, A 180. Cf. *Sententia*, III. v, A 200–5.

[34] 'politia nichil aliud est quam ordo inhabitantium civitatem', *Sententia*, III.i, A 186.

[35] 'civitas nichil est aliud quam multitudo talium qui sic dicuntur cives sufficiens ad autarkiam, id est per se sufficientiam uite, ut potest absolute dici. Est enim civitas communitas per se sufficiens', *Sententia*, III.i, A 188. For Aquinas' *theological* conception of a universal *communitas* or *respublica humana*, destined for beatitude and subject to the divine law given by God, see the remarks and references in I. Th. Eschmann, 'Studies on the Notion of Society in St Thomas Aquinas, II. Thomistic social philosophy and the theology of original sin', *Mediaeval Studies* 9 (1947), 19–55, here 46–50. This *totus orbis* encloses the full variety of human communities (*regna, provinciae, civitates, domus*). But, *pace* Eschmann, it does not seem to be called a *civitas*.

[36] J. A. Weisheipl, 'Classification of the sciences in medieval thought', *Mediaeval Studies* 27 (1965), 54–90. See Isidore, *Etymologiae*, II.xxiv.

actualis. The former, theoretical part of philosophy consists of three divisions: natural (the nature of things), doctrinal (arithmetic, music, geometry and astronomy) and divine (nature of God and of spiritual creatures). The latter, practical part of philosophy has three divisions: moral, dispensative or domestic and civil. It is called 'actual' because it explains the operations of things. The moral part of actual philosophy deals with life according to virtue and honesty. The dispensative part concerns the wise ordering of domestic affairs. The civil part concerns the promotion of the welfare of the whole *civitas*. Cassiodorus' classification of the sciences, which follows that of Boethius, was widely available during the Middle Ages. Moreover, it was reproduced unchanged by Isidore in the early seventh century in his *Etymologies*.[37] Cassiodorus related rhetoric closely to the handling of civil questions (*civilibus quaestionibus*). To this a supply of eloquence is both necessary and honourable, and he defines civil questions as those which arise when anyone enquires into what is good and fair.[38] This close link between rhetoric and civic life was kept alive. For example, Adelard of Bath, in the course of writing (*c.* 1105–10) about the peaceful benefits procured by rhetoric, observed that men by their own good sense had put aside the life led without the support of law and were drawn to the life of the *civitas* and to acceptance of communal justice. Civil consents, as Adelard terms them, underlie the practice of the honest life, while the unreasonableness of modern tyrants is checked by the impulse of men to combine in humane society.[39]

Alcuin in his *Dialectica*, c.1, presented both the physics/ethics/logic division of philosophy and the *inspectiva/actualis*

[37] 'Moralis dicitur, per quam mos vivendi honestus appetitur, et instituta ad virtutem tendentia praeparantur. dispensativa dicitur domesticarum rerum sapienter ordo dispositus. civilis dicitur, per quam totius civitatis amministratur utilitas', Cassiodorus, *Institutiones*, lib.II, c.III, 4–7, here 7, ed. R. A. B. Mynors (Oxford, 1937), pp. 110–12, here p. 112. This is reproduced by Isidore, *Etymologiae*, II.xxiv.

[38] *Institutiones*, lib.II, *Praefatio*, 4 and lib.II, c.II, ed. Mynors, pp. 91, 97.

[39] '...ut illi, qui prius indiscrete et sine legali iure vivebant, in civitatem communemque iustitiam tam potenti admonitione tracti sint. Quare quicquid universae honestatis ex civilibus consensibus ortum est, huic ascribendum esse diiudico. Deinde cui dubium est, qua vi modernos tyrannos ab irrationabili impetu adhibita refrenet, cum primo mortales omni feritate rigidos in humanitatem coetumque compulerit?' Adelard of Bath, *De eodem et diverso*, ed. H. Willner, *Des Adelard von Bath Traktat De eodem et diverso*. Beiträge zur Geschichte der Philosophie des Mittelalters, IV.1 (Münster, 1903), p. 19. Adelard invokes Cicero (*De officiis*, 1.22, 77, *In Pisonem* c. 29–30, §72–74): 'Cedant arma togae, concedi, laurea, linguae' (*De eodem*, p. 20).

division. *Inspectiva* consists of the contemplation of divine and heavenly objects; *actualis* concerns what is necessary in mortal life, especially for the promotion of the life according to virtue.[40] In the twelfth century, the well known *Didascalicon* of Hugh of St Victor, which contains a remarkable rearrangement of earlier classifications of knowledge, includes ethics, economics and politics – or moral, managerial and civil science – within the moral/practical/active branch of philosophy, one of four branches of which the other three are the theoretical, the mechanical and the linguistic. Public, political and civil knowledge comprise a single science, for the civil science, politics, derives its name from *polis*, the Greek word for *civitas*.[41] As Martin Grabmann noted, Hugh was much followed by Ralph 'Ardens' in the late twelfth century. In his *Speculum universale* and in other treatises of similar date Grabmann (writing in 1911) found clear traces of a summary knowledge of the Aristotelian distinction of practical philosophy into ethics, economics and politics.[42]

But without text books in the subject, politics – unlike the seven liberal arts – could hardly be taught or learned.[43] As readers in the early Middle Ages had no access to Aristotle's *Politics* or *Ethics*, knowledge of the Boethian classification of the sciences was of limited value. Only with new translations of Greek and Arabic writings did new approaches become possible.

The Muslim *Falāsifa* or philosophers possessed a wide range of the works of Aristotle and of his commentators, all in Arabic versions. Their knowledge cannot be overlooked in an account of

---

[40] Alcuin, *De dialectica*, c.1 (*PL* 101.952): 'Actualis est, quae in operationibus huic vitae mortali necessariis consistit. Per hanc igitur modus honestus vivendi appetitur et instituta ad virtutes tendentia exercentur.' For the physics/ethics/logic division see both here and Alcuin *Dialogus de rhetorica et virtutibus*, *PL* 101.947–50. Philosophy requires *contemptus saeculi*; Alcuin, *De dialectica*, c.1 (*PL* 101.952A).

[41] Hugh of St Victor, *Didascalicon*, II, 1; II, 19, trans. J. Taylor, *The Didascalicon of Hugh of St. Victor*. Records of Civilization. Sources and Studies (New York, 1961), pp. 62, 74. Cf. Clarembald of Arras, *Der Kommentar des Clarenbaldus von Arras zu Boethius De Trinitate*, ed. W. Jansen (Breslau, 1926), 26*–27*. Also, Radulfus de Longo Campo, Commentary (*c.* 1216) on the *Anticlaudianus* of Alan of Lille, on which see M. Grabmann, *Die Geschichte der Scholastischen Methode* (Freiburg im Breisgau, 1911; reprinted Darmstadt, 1957), vol. II, pp. 48–52. Radulfus placed ethics, politics and economics within the practical (as distinct from the theoretical) branch of philosophy, philosophy being one of four branches of *scientia* (*eloquentia, philosophia, poesis* and *mechanica*). [42] M. Grabmann, *Geschichte*, I, pp. 246–57, here p. 253.

[43] Of this difficulty some medieval writers were aware; see Michaud-Quantin, *Universitas*, p. 5, n. 4.

medieval western thought about politics and the city, not least because in Andalusia in the twelfth century, especially under the leadership of Ibn Rushd, a revival of Aristotelianism took place. And earlier than this, especially in Spain, Latin scholars developed an interest in Arabic thought and learning.

It is possible that Aristotle's *Politics* was never translated into Arabic. But by the tenth century full Arabic translations of Plato's *Timaeus, Republic*, and *Laws* had been made. The Muslims turned to Plato for guidance on human society and law, to Aristotle on ethics. Al-Fārābi (d. 950) wrote a commentary upon Plato's *Republic* and possibly also upon the *Laws*. After *c.* 1150 Dominicus Gundissalinus (Gondisalvi), perhaps in collaboration with Ibn Dawud (Iohannes Avendauth), translated about half of Al-Fārābi's *Enumeration of the sciences.*[44]

Dominic reviewed the different sciences found in earlier Arabic and Latin sources in his *De divisione philosophiae.*[45] This work has the character of a compilation and is largely Aristotelian in its sympathies. Political science appears among the practical sciences and consists of a knowledge of government and law or (to be more precise) of such knowledge in relation to *civitates* and to *cives.*[46] Here Dominic follows Algazel.[47] At the end of his work is found a short *Summa Avicenae* which closely follows Al-Fārābi and which includes a few pages of excerpts from Avicenna on the content of political science. This consists in the study of voluntary actions and customs as well as of the habits, *mores* and deeds which give rise to those actions and customs. It also consists in the study of their ends and how they may or may not promote happiness in the future life. Politics therefore studies the actions and customs to

[44] Ed. M. A. Alonso, *Domingo Gundisalvo, De Scientiis* (Madrid, 1954). A complete translation was made by Gerard of Cremona in Toledo *c.* 1175, ed. A. Palencia, *Alfarabi, Catalogo de las Ciencias* (Madrid, 1932). An earlier edition of this was made by Camerarius in *Alpharabii opera* (Paris, 1638). See too C. Baeumker, ed., *Alfarabi, Ueber den Ursprung der Wissenschaften (De ortu scientiarum)*. Beiträge zur Geschichte der Philosophie des Mittelalters (Münster, 1916).

[45] Ed. L. Baur, *Dominicus Gundissalinus, De divisione philosophiae.* Beiträge zur Geschichte der Philosophie des Mittelalters, IV 2–3 (Münster, 1903). He was followed by Michael Scot, *Divisio philosophiae*; see Baur, *Dominicus Gundissalinus*, pp. 364–7, 399.

[46] '…practica…dividitur in tres partes. Quarum una est sciencia disponendi conversacionem suam cum omnibus hominibus. cui necessaria est gramatica, poëtica, rhetorica et sciencia legum secularium, in quibus est sciencia regendi civitates et sciencia cognoscendi iura civium, et hec dicitur politica sciencia et a Tullio "civilis racio" vocatur', ed. Baur, *Dominicus Gundissalinus*, p. 16. The other two practical sciences are economics (*ordinacio familiaris*) and ethics. Theoretical philosophy consists of physics, mathematics and theology.

[47] Baur, *Dominicus Gundissalinus*, pp. 202–3.

be adopted between fellow citizens, between different peoples, by
rulers towards their subjects, and by subjects towards their rulers.
The good customs observed by subjects follow upon their just
government by those set over them. *Civitates* and *populi* can be
differentiated by the goals they follow. Just *civitates* and *populi*
strive for happiness. A kingdom rent by divisions (*regnatus
stolidus*) may be pursuing illusory goals such as wealth (*regnatus
congregacionis*) or glory (*regnatus glorie*). Kingship requires the
support of virtue, *virtus regia* which is both a knowledge of the
rules which have universal value and an ability to apply them in
practice. Such knowledge is found in Aristotle's book called the
Politics.[48] As for law (*sciencia legis*), this comprises two parts –
statutes (*sentencie*) and their applications (*actiones* or *operationes*).
Laws should be made so that the *civitas* is administered with
special regard for its *dispositores*, *ministri* and *legisperiti*. And in each
of these orders (*ordo*) everyone – whatever his rank – should have
a useful and praiseworthy position (*status*) or else should be
expelled from the *civitas*.[49]

The strongest single Muslim influence upon the ways in which
Aristotle was studied in the Latin West after the twelfth century
was to be Ibn Rushd of Córdoba (Averroes, 1126–98) who lived
for most of his life in Spain, under the Almohads, and in
Marrakesh. His commentaries on Aristotle became an important
part of medieval Judaeo–Christian culture. But, like Maimonides,
Ibn Rushd was himself a follower of Plato in political thought. He
studied Plato's ideal state with the qualification that for him the
ideal state was Islamic and originated with the prophet–lawgiver.
He wrote a commentary on Plato's *Republic c.* 1177.[50] Although
Aristotle's *Politics* was not available to him, the *Nicomachean Ethics*
was and he commented upon it, his 'middle' commentary
becoming available in a Latin version in 1240.

Aristotle's *Politics* was not translated into Latin until *c.* 1260.[51]
However, his *Nicomachean Ethics* began to circulate in Latin in the

---

[48] 'Et hec quidem sciencia continetur in libro Aristotelis qui politica dicitur, et est pars ethice in
quo etiam docet, quas condiciones et disposiciones naturales oportet observare in filiis regum
et in aliis ad hoc, ut ille in quo invente fuerint eligatur ad regnum, deinde illum in quo fuerint,
qualiter oportet morigerari, quousque perficiatur in eo uirtus regia et fiat rex perfectus,' ed.
Baur, *Dominicus Gundissalinus*, pp. 134–6, here p. 136. For the influence of Al-Fārābī here see
Baur, *Dominicus*, p. 309. [49] Ed. Baur, *Dominicus Gundissalinus*, pp. 136–9.

[50] Ibn Rushd's commentary on the *Republic* was first translated into Hebrew in the early
fourteenth century and into Latin in 1491. [51] See above, n. 12.

twelfth century, at first in partial versions. The version made by
Robert Grosseteste shortly before 1250 and its anonymous revision
(1250–60) became the prevalent ones.[52] Grosseteste found in the
Ethics a large part of the inspiration for his wide-ranging and
devastating statement to the pope and cardinals on 13 May 1250
concerning the principles that should prevail in the government
of the church.[53] Shortly afterwards (1250–2) Albert the Great
composed his first commentary and his questions on the *Ethics*:
they are filled with interest (*inter alia*) in the nature of political or
civil science as well as in ethics. Albert duly notes that man is a
political animal by nature:[54] a good citizen is one whose deeds and
prudent actions are public and civil, not only private.[55] Political
science is subordinate to moral science.[56] But it is an operational
science which is best practised by those who are expert and
knowledgeable in it (*politici*; *experti in civilibus*).[57] It is closely
linked to rhetoric.[58] The statesman practises politics: *politicus est
operativus quidam*.[59]

The perception of political science as a practical discipline and
as a distinct category of skilful human activity was obviously
boosted by the rediscovery of the *Politics* and *Ethics*. The new
emphases are found in Brunetto Latini's *Li livres dou tresor*
(completed in the 1260s)[60] and in the earliest commentaries on
William of Moerbeke's translation of the *Politics*: those of Albertus
Magnus (*c.* 1265),[61] Thomas Aquinas (on Books I–III, 6, *c.* 1269–

[52] B. G. Dod, 'Aristoteles latinus', pp. 47, 49, 52, 61, 63–4, 77 following *Aristoteles latinus*, XXVI.1–3; *Ethica Nicomachae*, ed. R. A. Gauthier (Leiden, 1972–4). See too A. Pelzer, 'Les versions latines des ouvrages de morale conservés sous le nom d'Aristote', *Revue néoscolastique de Philosophie* 23 (1921), 316–41, 378–412 and G. Wieland, 'The reception and interpretation of Aristotle's *Ethics*' in *Cambridge history of later medieval philosophy* (Cambridge, 1982), pp. 657–72.

[53] See S. Gieben, 'Robert Grosseteste at the papal curia, Lyons 1250: edition of the documents', *Collectanea Franciscana* 41 (1971), 340–93; R. W. Southern, *Robert Grosseteste* (Oxford, 1986), pp. 276–91. Grosseteste also published a Latin translation of Greek commentaries on the *Ethics*, H. P. F. Mercken (ed.), *The Greek commentaries on the Nicomachean ethics in the Latin translation of Robert Grosseteste, Bishop of Lincoln* (†1253), I–. Corpus Latinum Commentariorum in Aristotelem Graecorum, VI, 1 (Leiden, 1973–).

[54] *Super Ethica commentum et quaestiones, Alberti Magni Opera omnia*, XIV (Münster 1969–87), p. 326, lines 88–9, p. 468, lines 11–12.   [55] Ibid., p. 327, lines 16–41. Cf. p. 634.

[56] Ibid., p. 789, lines 85–8.

[57] Ibid., p. 467, lines 78–86; p. 789, lines 19–31; p. 791, line 82–p. 792, line 7.

[58] Ibid., p. 791, lines 29–32.   [59] Ibid., p. 791, line 90–p. 792, line 1.

[60] Brunetto Latini, *Li livres dou Tresor*. University of California Publications: Modern Philology, 22 (Berkeley, 1948).

[61] *Politicorum Aristotelis commentarii*, ed. A. Borgnet, VIII (Paris, 1891). This has unfortunately not been available to me in the course of preparing this study.

72)[62] and his continuator Peter of Auvergne (*c.* 1274–90).[63] These middle and later decades of the thirteenth century undeniably mark a clear turning point in the understanding and development of the subject. Earlier generations had had much less to reflect upon. Yet reflect they did. The notion of politics had been preserved. Concepts of the city had clearly persisted from antiquity and had occasionally provoked fresh thought and observation.

[62] See above, n. 28.

[63] Edited by R. M. Spiazzi in Aquinas, *In octo libris Politicorum Aristotelis expositio* (Marietti, 1951). G. M. Grech (ed.), *The commentary of Peter of Auvergne on Aristotle's* Politics. *The inedited part: Book III, lesson i–vi* (Toronto, 1967). For general assessments of the earliest commentaries on the *Politics*, beginning with Albert, see C. Martin, 'Some medieval commentaries on Aristotle's *Politics*', *History* 36 (1951), 29–44 and J. Dunbabin, 'The reception and interpretation of Aristotle's *Politics*', *The Cambridge history of later medieval philosophy*, pp. 723–37.

New arrivals

57

—◆—

Nuns and goldsmiths: the foundation and early benefactors of St Radegund's priory at Cambridge

ELISABETH VAN HOUTS

...many more monasteries of servants and handmaids of God are known to have been founded in England during the brief period when Stephen reigned – or rather, held the title of king – than in the hundred years previously.[1]

One of the monastic institutions which was founded during the reign of King Stephen (1135–54) was the Benedictine nunnery at Cambridge known as St Radegund's priory. The site where once it stood is nowadays occupied by Jesus College, and its surviving charters are in the college archive.[2] Arthur Gray published an admirable account of the priory in 1898.[3] No new documents have come to light since that date, but recent research means that we know more than Gray did about background material, i.e. about the history of Cambridge and of the diocese of Ely.[4] This

---

[1] *William of Newburgh, the history of English affairs, Book I*, ed. and trans. by P. G. Walsh and M. J. Kennedy (Warminster, 1988), pp. 78–9; for this particular remark, see D. Knowles, *The monastic order in England* (Cambridge, 1963), pp. 296–8.

[2] I should like to thank the Master and Fellows of Jesus College Cambridge for their kind permission to use and quote the archives of St Radegund's priory, and in particular the present Fellow Archivist John Mills, whose advice and assistance has been invaluable. Mary Cheney, Tom Faber, Simon Keynes and John Mills have read a first draft of this article; I am deeply grateful for their corrections and comments. The final version was written during my stay at the Huntington Library (San Marino, California) as a Fletcher Jones Visiting Fellow, April–August 1990.

[3] A. Gray, *The priory of Saint Radegund Cambridge*, Cambridge Antiquarian Society (CAS), 8°, 31 (Cambridge, 1898). For short up-to-date accounts, see The Victoria History of the Counties of England (VCH), *Cambridgeshire (Cambs.)*, II (1948), 218–19; *An inventory of the historical monuments in the city of Cambridge* (London, 1959), I, pp. 81–98; S. Thompson, *Women religious: the founding of English nunneries after the Norman Conquest* (Oxford, 1991), pp. 72, 200–1, 219, 235.

[4] W. Farrer, *Feudal Cambridgeshire* (Cambridge, 1920); H. M. Cam, 'The origin of the borough of Cambridge: a consideration of Professor Carl Stephenson's theories', *Proceedings of the CAS* 35 (1935), 33–53; E. Miller, *The Abbey and Bishopric of Ely* (Cambridge, 1951); *Liber Eliensis* (*LE*), ed. E. O. Blake, Camden, 3rd series, 92 (London, 1962); *Atlas of historic towns*, II, ed. M. D. Lobel and W. H. Johns (London, 1974) fascicle on Cambridge; *The west fields of*

later work justifies a fresh study of the charters – a study which I was stimulated to embark on by Christopher Brooke's work on the churches of Cambridge.[5] In the analysis that follows I shall concentrate mainly on the priory's early benefactors, because they left traces in the historical record in a way that the nuns themselves did not. It is an indirect approach which inevitably leaves many important questions unanswered, but the glimpses which it offers of the processes whereby the priory became established are nevertheless intriguing.

In late 1143 or early 1144 the town of Cambridge was attacked by Geoffrey de Mandeville and partly devastated, and it seems to have been shortly after that event that a group of women came together to form a cell outside the vill.[6] Presumably they were local people, from the borough itself or from the surrounding county, who preferred to join a nunnery close to their homes than to take the veil at Chatteris near Ramsey.[7] They settled on a plot of land beyond, but not immediately adjacent to, the defensive moat surrounding the vill known as the King's Ditch.[8] How they acquired this land we do not know, though later in this article I shall make some suggestions. It would have formed part of the East Fields of Cambridge, fields east of the river Cam, which like the West Fields on the other side were mostly common land of the borough but were not exclusively so.[9] They included areas of waste land as well as pasture and arable, and after Geoffrey de Mandeville's attack a substantial amount of the land was waste. Perhaps it was some of this that was made available to the nuns. If the plot had a name of its own, the name is now forgotten. By the end of the twelfth century, the community was being referred to as the nuns of Grenecroft, that being the name for what is now Midsummer Common.[10]

  Cambridge, ed. C. P. Hall and J. R. Ravensdale (Cambridge, 1976); M. Rubin, *Charity and community in medieval Cambridge* (Cambridge, 1986).

  [5] C. N. L. Brooke, 'The churches of medieval Cambridge', *History, society and the churches. Essays in honour of Owen Chadwick*, ed. D. Beales and G. Best (Cambridge, 1985), pp. 49–76.

  [6] *Gesta Stephani*, ed. K. R. Potter and R. H. C. Davis (Oxford, 1976), p. 164 and VCH, *Cambs.*, III, 5 (where the attack is dated 1142). For the date of the first settlement of the nuns, see below note 11.

  [7] Founded 1006 × 16 by Ednoth, abbot of Ramsey and his sister Aelwen, wife of Athelstan ruler of East Anglia (VCH, *Cambs.*, II, 220–3). Other later nunneries are Ickleton and Swaffham Bulbeck (VCH, *Cambs.*, II, 223–6, 226).

  [8] Gray, p. 78; Cam, 'The origin', p. 50 and Lobel, p. 5 who dates the ditch after 921.

  [9] *The west fields*, ed. Hall and Ravensdale.   [10] See n. 20.

By the beginning of the thirteenth century the original site, probably small, had expanded. Four acres were added to it before *c.* 1144–5 by Bishop Nigel of Ely (1133–69)[11]; ten more acres were added towards the end of the 1150s by Malcolm IV, king of Scotland (1153–65) and earl of Huntingdon (1157–65);[12] and another five by Bishop Eustace of Ely (1198–1215).[13] By the time of the Hundred Rolls of 1279 the nuns owned land in the Cambridge fields on both sides of the river, amounting to about seventy-seven acres in all.[14] To go with this land they had acquired various rights. Countess Constance, widow of Count Eustace, son of King Stephen, granted them in perpetual alms

---

[11] Bishop Nigel's first charter is the earliest known reference to the nuns and contains the earliest grant. He gave 'quandam terram sanctimonialibus cellule extra uillam Cantebruge nouiter institute prope terram eiusdem cellule iacentem' for the annual rent of 12d (Jesus Col. Caryl A. 3 = Gray, no. 1, p. 74). This gift is probably the same as the one mentioned in the Hundred Rolls of 1279 where it is said that Bishop Nigel gave four acres free of alms which grant was confirmed by Prior B and the Convent of Ely (*Rotuli Hundredorum*, ed. W. Illingworth, 2 vols., Record Commissioners, 1812–19 (*RH*)), II, p. 358). If so, he later acquitted the nuns of their rent. Bishop Nigel's charter is witnessed by Radulf Olaf (*LE*, pp. 322, 325, 334, 337, 364, 386, 388 and Miller, pp. 180, 196 and 287), Peter the clerk (*LE*, p. 335) and Gilbert, chaplain of Horningsea (*LE*, p. 335; Horningsea was a manor of the bishop of Ely, see Miller, p. 80 note 6). All three witnesses occur in the *Liber Eliensis* (pp. 334–7) at an occasion dated *c.* 1144–5 where Radulf is mentioned first as steward and then as chamberlain, offices which he probably combined. The fact that Radulf here occurs without a title presumably means that he was not yet active in either of these offices. Bishop Nigel's charter therefore dates from before *c.* 1144–5; see also below n. 29.

[12] There are two charters of King Malcolm both issued at Huntingdon (Jesus Col. Caryl A. 2 = Gray, nos. 4a and 4b, pp. 76–7 = *Regesta Regum Scotorum*, I, ed. G. W. S. Barrow (Edinburgh, 1960), nos. 147 and 207). The first one, dated between 1157–8 or 1159 (Barrow, pp. 105–6), says that the king granted the nuns ten acres of land beside Grenecroft in order to build their church. He also ordered his servant, who receives a rent of 2 s., to offer it at the altar of their church. In the summer of 1163, the date of the second charter, King Malcolm confirmed the first one and freed the nuns from their rent (Barrow, p. 106). King Malcolm's grants are the first ones listed in the Hundred Rolls, where they have been conflated into one (*RH*, II, p. 358). The first grant was also confirmed by Archbishop Theobald of Canterbury (1139–61), see A. Saltman, *Theobald, archbishop of Canterbury* (London, 1956), no. 296, p. 522) which is known only from the confirmation charter of Stephen Langton, archbishop of Canterbury (1213–28) (Jesus Col. Caryl A. 5 = Gray, no. 4d, p. 77 = *Acta Stephani Langton Cantuariensis archiepiscopi*, ed. K. Major (Oxford, 1950), no. 138, pp. 152–3). Archbishop Thomas Becket (June 1162–70), too, confirmed this grant, referring only to one charter of King Malcolm. His confirmation therefore dates from the period June 1162 × Summer of 1163 (Jesus Col. Caryl A.2 = Gray, no. 4c, p. 77 = *English Episcopal Acta*, vol. ii (Canterbury), ed. C. R. Cheney and B. Jones (London, 1986), no. 3, pp. 2–3 and facs. pl. 1).

[13] This grant is only known from a confirmation by his successor John de Fontibus (1220–25) (Jesus Col. Caryl A.8 = Gray, no. 7a, p. 78) where it is stated that the grant was confirmed by the prior and monks of Ely.

[14] F. M. Maitland, *Township and borough* (Cambridge, 1898), p. 150 and map between pp. 54–55. For a breakdown of the nuns' possessions in the West Fields, see *The west fields*, ed. Hall and Ravensdale, *passim*. The priory's charters relating to the fields are listed in Gray, nos. 302–61, pp. 133–40.

exemption from hagable and landgable for all their lands, within
and without the borough, whether already acquired or to be
acquired, and also fishing rights belonging to the borough.[15] Since
these probably formed part of the countess's dower, her grant of
them can be linked with her departure from England to marry
Count Raymond V of Toulouse at an unknown date in 1154, and
since it was confirmed by her father-in-law, King Stephen, the
grant can be dated to the short period between Eustace's death on
17 August 1153 and Stephen's own death in October 1154.[16] King
Stephen confirmed the grant when he visited Cambridge late in
1153 or in 1154,[17] and it was presumably on the same occasion that
he granted the nuns the right to hold a fair for two days during the
vigil and the feast of the Assumption of the Blessed Virgin Mary,
on 14 and 15 August.[18] Bishop Nigel also confirmed the
countess's grant.[19] Finally, in or shortly before November 1180
the nuns acquired the advowson, followed by the rectory, of All
Saints in the Jewry from Sturm, and about forty years later they
acquired the advowson of St Clement's from Hugh fitz Absolon.
Both these benefactors were Cambridge burghers.[20]

   This recital of early benefactions pertaining to the borough

[15] Jesus Col. Caryl A.1 = Gray, no. 3a, p. 75. The witnesses are Bishop Nigel of Ely (see below),
William Monachus I of Shelford (see below), Alexander pincerna (*LE*, pp. 322, 364, 386),
Geoffrey de Waterville, son-in-law of Pain Peverel refounder of Barnwell Priory (*Regesta
Regum Anglo-Normannorum* vol. III, ed. H. A. Cronne, R. H. C. Davis, H. W. C. Davis
(Oxford, 1968), nos. 58, 68; E. King, *Peterborough Abbey 1086–1310* (Cambridge, 1973), p. 39
and K. Stringer, *Earl David of Huntingdon 1152–1219* (Cambridge, 1985), pp. 19, 278),
Ralph the Sheriff (only known reference, see *Regesta*, III, p. xxiv) and the burghers of
Cambridge: Eustace de Bans, Robert Grim, Gilbert son of Dunning, Herbert and Herveus son
of Warin.   [16] See below, p. 77.
[17] Jesus Col. Caryl A.1 = Gray, no. 3b, pp. 75–6 = *Regesta*, III, no. 139; T. A. M. Bishop, 'Two
charters of Stephen in Jesus College', *Proceedings of the CAS* 45 (1951), 1–5, facs. pl. 1.
[18] *RH*, II, p. 359 where it is said that King Stephen confirmed his gift by a charter. This is now
lost, see Gray, p. 7.
[19] Jesus Col. Caryl A.1 = Gray, no. 3c, p. 76. Refers to King Stephen's charter. No witnesses.
[20] Sturm of Cambridge occurs in the Pipe Roll 23 Henry II (1176–7) (Pipe Roll Society (PRS),
26, p. 181). His charter is Jesus Col. Caryl D.11 = Gray, no. 79a, p. 90. Bishop Geoffrey Ridel
of Ely (1174–89) confirmed his charter and instituted the nuns to the rectory (Jesus Col. Caryl
D.11 = Gray, no. 79b, pp. 90–1). The prior and convent of Ely also confirmed this (Jesus Col.
Caryl D.11 = Gray, no. 79c, p. 91; see also pp. 24–6). Hugh fitz Absolon's charter is Jesus Col.
Caryl M.2 = Gray, no. 239a, p. 121 and pp. 26–8. The grant and the advowson date from after
1215, the year of the death of Bishop Eustace of Ely, and 1218, the date of a plea of
'Estrilda fil.[ia] Scobic' versus the prioress of St Radegund about the advowson of St Clement's
(*Pedes Finium or Fines relating to the county of Cambridge*, ed. W. Rye (Cambridge, 1891), p. 9).
Sturm's charter was witnessed by a Robert of St Clement's who presumably was chaplain
there, if so, this is the earliest known reference to St Clement's (cf. Brooke, 'The churches',
pp. 58, 71). For other grants of Hugh fitz Absolon to the nuns, see Gray, nos. 211a–c, 212a–b
(p. 115) and 337a–b (p. 137).

prompts one immediate question: by what right did the bishops of Ely and King Malcolm IV of Scotland grant land in the East Fields neighbouring the original plot? Cambridge was a royal town, in the sense that the farm was paid to the king via his sheriff, and perhaps because of this the king of England undoubtedly had the right to transfer land from the fields of Cambridge to religious foundations. Evidence is provided by Henry I's grant of thirteen acres near the sources of Barnwell for the foundation of Barnwell Priory, *c.* 1110.[21] The foundation sometime in the middle of the twelfth century, slightly to the east of Barnwell Priory, of the leper hospital of Mary Magdalene may be another relevant example, though in this case the burghers of Cambridge may have been responsible rather than the king.[22] But there is no evidence whatever of royal involvement in the foundation of St Radegund's priory.

Cambridge formed part of the earldom of Huntingdon, and the earls were entitled to the third penny of the borough.[23] It is no surprise, therefore, that the earls held possessions in and around Cambridge: apart from the ten acres near Grenecroft which King Malcolm IV granted to the nuns, two acres of land within the borough, between the church of St Giles and the river Cam, were given by Countess Maud to the canons of St Giles shortly before 1112,[24] and early thirteenth-century references show that tenements in Cambridge, Newnham and Barnwell belonged to King Malcolm's grandson, Earl David.[25] If this land was old comital land, it is quite likely that the fields near Grenecroft were fields on which the Cambridge burghers exercised pasture rights.[26] Perhaps King Malcolm encroached upon such rights by his gift to the nuns, but we have no evidence that he did so. The jurors of 1279 on whose testimonies the Hundred Rolls were based recorded no dissent; they merely stated that they did not know how King Malcolm had acquired the land.[27]

The position with regard to the grants made by the bishops of

---

[21] *Liber Memorandorum ecclesie de Bernewelle*, ed. J. W. Clark (Cambridge, 1907), pp. 43–4, 46; *Regesta*, II, no. 939; VCH, *Cambs.*, II, 234, 249.   [22] *RH*, II, p. 359; Rubin, pp. 111–14.
[23] VCH, *Cambs.*, III, 30–1 and VCH, *Hunts.*, II, 7–8.
[24] *Liber Memorandorum*, ed. Clark, pp. 98–9, 168; *Regesta regum Scotorum*, I, no. 52.
[25] *The west fields*, ed. Hall and Ravensdale, p. 144; VCH, *Cambs.*, III, 31; Stringer, p. 167.
[26] F. M. Maitland, *Domesday Book and beyond* (Cambridge, 1921), pp. 197, 200–2.
[27] *RH*, II, p. 358.

Ely is more complicated and more interesting. The bishopric was created in 1109, when the monastery of St Etheldreda of Ely became one of the English monastic cathedrals and a bishop replaced an abbot. Its estates were then split between the convent, that is the prior and the monks, and the bishop, a process which lasted many years; Edward Miller has shown that it was not completed until the beginning of the reign of King Henry II (1154–87), while Nigel was bishop.[28] During the first decades of Nigel's office many conflicts arose between him and the monks, because he used the convent's revenues for himself and his *familia*, and he had several documents drawn up stating precisely what belonged to each party. Rather surprisingly, none of these documents refers to holdings in Cambridge, but there is ample other evidence that such holdings existed, and since the abbey had held land and houses within the borough we can safely assume that the holdings included land in the Cambridge fields as well.[29] Now according to the Hundred Rolls, Bishop Nigel's grant to the nuns was confirmed by the prior and monks of Ely, a statement which is also to be found in King Edward's *inspeximus* of the nuns' charters, dated 13 October 1313.[30] This evidence, though late in date, strongly suggests that the land which Bishop Nigel granted formed part of the convent's estates rather than the bishop's, since only in such circumstances would confirmation have been necessary. But what induced Bishop Nigel to dispose of land belonging to the monks, in order to support a recently founded nunnery? The answer lies, I suggest, in his relationship with another early benefactor, William Monachus the Goldsmith.

William Monachus I (the numeral distinguishes him from a

[28] Miller, pp. 75–6.
[29] *LE*, pp. 288–305. For Ely holdings in Cambridge, see *Inquisitio Eliensis*, ed. N. Hamilton, (London, 1876), p. 121 = VCH, *Cambs.*, I, 359 note 1). The monks held 1 mill, 2 dwellings in the first ward, 3 dwellings in the second ward ('Bridgeward'), 2 dwellings in the third ward of which 1 unoccupied, 1 dwelling and a church and 2 unoccupied houses in the fourth ward, 1 dwelling in the fifth ward, 1 unoccupied dwelling in the ninth ward, 3 gardens and 1 unoccupied garden in the tenth ward. For comments on the wards, see VCH, *Cambs.*, III, 4. I am grateful to Simon Keynes, who is preparing a book on the pre-conquest possessions of the abbey of Ely, for discussing this material with me. For references to post-conquest Ely possessions in Cambridge, see F. Chapman, *Sacrist rolls of Ely* (Cambridge, 1907), I, pp. 120–1; *RH*, II, pp. 385, 387 and Lobel, p. 9.
[30] *RH*, II, p. 358 where a prior B of Ely is mentioned. No prior whose name begins with a B is known, and the letter B is probably a misprint for A. Alexander was prior from 1144 × 51 – *c.* 1163 (*LE*, p. 316, note 1). The *inspeximus* of King Edward II is Jesus Col. Caryl A.11 = Gray, no. 8, p. 78 = *Calendar of charter rolls*, vol. III (1300–26) (London, 1903), pp. 223–4.

grandson of the same name) was one of two principal benefactors who gave land outside the borough; the other was Stephen de Scaler, to whom I shall turn in due course. William granted the nuns 'two virgates of land and six acres of pasture and four cottars with their holdings' at (Great) Shelford, in free alms for the soul of King Henry I and God's faithful. William's own charter has not survived, but the grant is known from King Stephen's confirmation charter, issued during the siege of Meppershall in 1149 or 1150,[31] and from Bishop Nigel's confirmation, which can be dated to before 1158 because that was the last year in which William de Lavington, one of the witnesses, was archdeacon of Ely.[32] William's grant was presumably made, therefore, in the late 1140s, after the grant of Bishop Nigel but nevertheless within five or six years of the founding of the priory.

The land at Great Shelford is still owned by Jesus College, and its ownership can be traced back to Domesday Book. For it is commonly assumed that the estate of three hides and forty-six acres at Shelford which in 1086 was held by Peter de Valognes, sheriff of Essex and Hertfordshire,[33] is the same as that which was described in 1210–12 as the three hides held by William Monachus II by goldsmith's serjeanty.[34] The area granted to the nuns seems to have been about $57\frac{1}{2}$ acres, to judge by the charter in which

[31] Jesus Col. Caryl s.10 = Gray, no. 2a, pp. 74–5 = *Regesta*, III, no. 138 and Bishop 'Two charters of Stephen', facs. pl. 1. For the date, see Appendix A.

[32] Jesus Col. Caryl s.10, Gray, no. 2b, p. 75. The last occurrence of William de Lavington, archdeacon of Ely, is in 1156 and *c.* 1158. His successor Richard, son of (Bishop) Nigel, first occurs in *c.* 1158, by which date William was dead (John le Neve, *Fasti Ecclesiae Anglicanae 1066–1300*, compiled by D. E. Greenway, vol. II, p. 50). Several of the witnesses are members of Bishop Nigel's *familia*: Richard of St Paul's (*LE*, pp. 289, 364, 386; still active *c.* 1159), Richard fitz Gilbert (*LE*, pp. 188, 190, 194, 198, 204, 225, 420), Magister Ernulfus is the same as Ernulfus medicus (*LE*, p. 335), John of St Albans (*LE*, p. 364), Radulfus the steward (above n. 11), Alexander pincerna (above n. 15), Henricus peregrinus (*LE*, pp. 286, 297, 325, 335, 386). Two witnesses are more obscure. Richard de Pontechardon is mentioned in the *Liber Eliensis* (p. 333 and note 2) as one of King Stephen's clerks who acted on an embassy to Bishop Nigel in *c.* 1144–5. (*Regesta*, III, no. 267). On this basis Blake, the editor of the *LE*, dates the present charter for the nuns to those years. (*LE*, pp. 333 note 2 and 335 note 9). Gilbert the clerk is otherwise unknown.

[33] *Inquisitio Comitatus Cantabrigiensis*, ed. N. Hamilton (London, 1876), p. 49 = VCH, *Cambs.*, I, 413 and Domesday Book (VCH, *Cambs.*, I, 362). For Peter de Valognes, see J. Green, 'The sheriffs of William the Conqueror', *Anglo-Norman studies*, 5, ed. R. Allen Brown (Woodbridge, 1983), 134, 140–1. He died after 13 June 1109 and was succeeded by his son Roger (*Regesta*, II, no. 1396 note). For the family, see Farrer, p. 165. For the present ownership of land at Shelford by Jesus College, see VCH, *Cambs.*, VIII, 211, n. 93–4.

[34] *The red book of the exchequer*, ed. H. Hall (London, 1896), II, p. 530. VCH, *Cambs.*, VIII, 210 and n. 55 refer to William Monachus holding 100 acres at Shelford in 1198.

Nicholas, son and heir of William Monachus I, confirmed the gift at his father's request.[35] Considering how uncertain the measurement of area clearly was, it could correspond to the area by which Peter de Valognes's estate seems to have shrunk before it reached William Monachus II. The Valognes land at Shelford was used before and after 1066 to reward royal servants.[36] Why and when it was taken away from the Valognes family is unknown, but William Monachus I served the king as royal goldsmith and it may have formed part of his emolument in that capacity.

Our most informative, though biased, source for William's career is the *Liber Eliensis*, the chronicle and cartulary composed at Ely in *c.* 1169. There he is described as one of the *familiares* of Bishop Nigel, who had helped him to raise money for his journey to Rome in late 1143 and early 1144, and who had pledged twenty marks as surety for the sum of 200 marks which Bishop Nigel needed to buy peace with King Stephen a year or two later.[37] The author of the *Liber*, himself a monk of Ely, describes with some bitterness how the bishop and his associates plundered the treasury which was part of the monks' estates.[38] The bitterness is understandable, because Prior Thembert, who should have protected the interests of the monks, sided with the bishop. He describes in particular how William Monachus used his skill as a goldsmith to attack a shrine with axes, hammers and (gold)smith's

[35] The text of the confirmation charter of Nicholas (Jesus Col. Caryl s.11) occurs abbreviated in King Edward's *inspeximus* (see above n. 30). According to Nicholas the grant consisted of fifty-five acres of land and one and a half acres of meadow and one acre of land for the building of barns and cattlesheds. Nicholas himself added another five acres which the nuns had asked for. The witnesses are Jonathan the priest (*LE*, p. 390: 'of Cambridge', *c.* 1160 × 69), Nicolas the priest (*LE*, p. 390, *c.* 1160 × 69 and p. 364, 1154 at Shelford), Joscelin the priest, Peter, clerk of Shelford (*LE*, p. 364, 1154 at Shelford), Herveus fitz Warin (also witness of Countess Constance's charter to the nuns, see above n. 15), John his son, Normannus.

[36] This land was an outlier (*berwick*) of the manor of Newport (Essex). At the time of King Edward it was held by Earl Harold, who also held the manor of Newport (VCH., *Essex*, I, 435–6), but after 1066 it was held by the king who gave it to Peter de Valognes. For the suggestion that Shelford was royal land before 1066, see A. Williams, 'Land and power in the eleventh century: the estates of Harold Godwineson', *Anglo-Norman studies*, 3, ed. R. Allen Brown (Woodbridge, 1981), 174. [37] *LE*, pp. 325, 335–7.

[38] *LE*, p. 340: 'Alius vero de concilio malignantium Willelmus supermemoratus de Sceldford, comes in universis, paratus ad scelus, cum ligonibus, cum malleis, cum fabrorum instrumentis temere processit, super feretrum secundus ipse manum inicit, es inde tulit, sed factum doluit mox amarissime. Cum enim esset dives valde et nullius egeret, casu in tantam devenit inopiam, ut nec etiam vite necessaria haberet. Consumptisque omnibus que illius erant, quid ageret, quo se verteret ignoravit. Tandem multum diu postulans vix a fratribus in Ely meruit ad monachatum suscipi, ubi in luctu et lacrimis in vigiliis et orationibus persistens reatum ingemuit, reliquum vite spatium vero penitendo explevit.'

tools and stripped off the precious metal with his own hands. He goes on to say that William paid dearly for his crime, for the man who was once rich lost his wealth and spent the last years of his life as a monk at Ely, where he died.

William seems to have been succeeded as royal goldsmith in 1154, and that is probably when he retired to Ely.[39] It seems unlikely that he retired in a state of indigence, as the author of the *Liber* would have us suppose. He was certainly in good standing with King Stephen in 1149–50, or the king would not have confirmed his grant to the nuns as he did, and the fact that he, together with Bishop Nigel and several burghers of Cambridge, acted as witness to the charter recording the grant of Countess Constance is evidence that he remained a man of substance in 1153–4. Moreover, his estate at Shelford remained in his family's hands, as we have seen.

The hypothetical date of William's retirement and the fact that he died before 1169 suggest that much of his career was already behind him in 1143, when he is recorded as having supported Bishop Nigel. It seems to me highly probable, though this cannot be more than speculation, that he had known and helped Nigel previously, while Nigel was court treasurer to King Henry I, during the years 1120–33.[40] As a goldsmith, he no doubt acted as moneylender and provider of cash, or more generally as financial adviser.[41] He would also have had valuable contacts with members of the Jewish community.[42] Thus when Nigel, as bishop of Ely, pawned a silver cross which had been given to the monks of Ely by King Edgar,[43] William Monachus could have acted as an intermediary between the bishop and the Jews of Cambridge, and perhaps he had acted in a similar capacity on earlier occasions. I therefore attribute to Nigel the patronage which led to William's appointment as royal goldsmith for coronations, the consequent

---

[39] See below, p. 72.

[40] C. Warren Hollister, 'The Origin of the English treasury', *Monarchy, magnates and institutions in the Anglo-Norman world* (London, 1986), pp. 209–23, esp. 218–19 and J. Green, *The government of England under Henry I* (Cambridge, 1986), pp. 34–5, 263.

[41] H. A. Cronne, *The reign of Stephen 1135–54* (London, 1970), pp. 236–44; P. Nightingale, 'Some London moneyers and reflections on the organisation of English mints in the eleventh and twelfth centuries', *Numismatic Chronicle* 140 (1982), 34–51. For goldsmiths, see N. Stratford, 'Metalwork', *English Romanesque Art 1066–1200* (London, 1984), pp. 232–3.

[42] H. P. Stokes, *Studies in Anglo-Jewish history* (Edinburgh–London, 1913), pp. 122–6; VCH, *Cambs.*, III, 175–6.   [43] *LE*, p. 339.

grant to him of what had once been the Valognes' manor at Shelford, and the goldsmith's serjeanty attached to that estate.[44] But the appointment and grant came from King Henry I; we know this from the terms in which William's son Nicholas confirmed his father's gift to the nuns. Thus we can date them with certainty to before December 1135, when King Henry I died, and with rather less certainty to after 1133, when Nigel became bishop of Ely and thereby lord of the manor of Shelford.

No contemporary description exists of the tasks of a royal goldsmith for coronations, but in 1275 he was expected to make, prepare or repair the king's crown, for which he received a wage of 3s per day.[45] From a writ dated 22 July 1199, shortly after the first coronation of King John, we may infer that he was responsible for other regalia besides the crown, and that besides supplying skilled labour he supplied precious materials at his own cost. This writ summons William Monachus II, who was then royal goldsmith as his grandfather had been, to acquit William fitz Otto, the keeper of the dies of the king's money, of half the cost of the king's regalia which he ought to have paid.[46]

We do not know whether or not William Monachus I was involved in the coronation of King Stephen on 22 December 1135 or later in the plans for the coronations of the Empress Matilda and Stephen's son Eustace.[47] By the time of the coronation of King Henry II on 19 December 1154 his rôle seems to have been taken over by one Solomon the Goldsmith, who is named in the returns of the sheriff of Cambridgeshire, in Pipe Roll 2 Henry II (1155–6), as having been paid eleven pounds, through the bishop (Nigel) of Ely, for work done for the king.[48] This must surely have been money spent on the regalia for Henry II's coronation. There is no entry in the next Pipe Roll, but Solomon is mentioned annually from 4 Henry II (1157–8) to 11 Henry II (1164–5) as the

[44] For the origin of serjeanties, see E. G. Kimball, *Serjeanty tenure in medieval England* (New Haven, 1936), pp. 1–16 and Green, pp. 163–94.
[45] *Calendar of inquisitions post mortem*, II (London, 1906), p. 73; *RH*, II, p. 545; Farrer, p. 211; Kimball, p. 64, note 237: the tenant of land at Grace Church (Middlesex) was to send charcoal for making the king's crown.
[46] *Pleas before the king and his justices 1198–1202*, ed. D. M. Stenton (London, 1953), pp. 18, 994–5, no. 3523. For the fitz Otto family as hereditary goldsmiths and moneyers, see Nightingale, 'Some London moneyers', passim; Green, *The government*, p. 280; Cronne, *The reign*, p. 238 and C. Clark, 'Women's names in post-Conquest England', *Speculum* 53 (1978), 227–8.
[47] See below, p. 76.
[48] *The great roll of the pipe...AD 1155, 1156, 1157, 1158*, ed. J. Hunter (London, 1844), p. 14.

king's goldsmith who receives 60s from the Cambridge mill. William's son Nicholas presumably knew enough about his father's craft to teach his own son, William Monachus II, and why we cannot find him named in the sources as a royal goldsmith is a minor mystery. Perhaps he was not quite experienced enough in 1154 to carry the responsibilities involved, though he was old enough to act as witness in that year, as we shall see below.[49]

Solomon deserves a short digression. Originally from Ely, he learned his trade at St Albans from the monk Ansketil, formerly moneyer of the Danish king, during the abbacy of Geoffrey (1116–46).[50] His tenure of the post of royal goldsmith seems to have terminated in about 1164, for there is no mention of him in the Pipe Roll for 1165–6, and although he appears in the Pipe Rolls for the following decade he is referred to simply as Solomon the Goldsmith, with no mention of any connections with the king.[51] During this decade he was goldsmith for the convent at Ely, and when he died, probably in 1177, he was succeeded in that position by his son Jordan. They were the first two in a line of hereditary goldsmiths of the prior and monks of Ely.

Solomon was rewarded by the prior and monks of Ely with a 5 mark rentcharge on the land of Brame (Braham) *que pertinet ad aurifabricacionem ecclesie*; the grant was confirmed by King Henry II in May 1177. Now, in 1211–12 William Monachus II claimed two carucates of land at Brame from Jordan the Goldsmith, on the grounds that his grandfather had held the seisin of the land, and that although this had been lost during the reign of King Henry II the title to the land had passed from William Monachus I to Nicholas Monachus and then to himself. Jordan won the case, counter-claiming successfully that the land had been given to his father Solomon; he produced as evidence of this two charters, one of the convent and the other King Henry II's confirmation.[52]

---

[49] *LE*, p. 364 and below, p. 71.

[50] Thomas Walsingham, *Gesta Abbatum Monasterii sancti Albani*, ed. H. T. Riley (London, 1867), I, pp. 83–88. For the historical circumstances, see B. Golding, 'Wealth and artistic patronage at twelfth-century St Albans', *Art and patronage in the English romanesque*, ed. S. Macready and F. H. Thompson (London, 1986), The Society of Antiquaries occasional papers, n.s. VIII, 107–17, at 109–10.   [51] In 1169–70 he only received 30s (PRS, xv, p. 92).

[52] For the grant of the Prior and convent of Ely to Solomon, see Chapman, *Sacrist rolls*, I, p. 151, note 1; King Henry II's confirmation contains a slightly different wording which implies that Solomon was given the land at Brame (Chapman, I, p. 152, note 2). For the case in 1211–12, see *Curia Regis Rolls*, VI, (London, 1932), pp. 300, 363.

William then had to pay a fine of two marks.[53] However, the claim that William Monachus I had once held the land was presumably justified, and to make sense of the Latin phrase I have quoted above we must therefore assume that William was goldsmith to the prior and monks at Ely as well as to the king. Perhaps his son Nicholas took over the first position when William retired, though not the second, and held it until Solomon replaced him about 1166. How William acquired this land at Brame in the first place is unknown. How he, or his son Nicholas after him, lost the land is even more obscure, but conceivably it was this loss which led the author of the *Liber Eliensis* to claim that William died a poor man.[54]

Twelve charters survive from the thirteenth century which relate to the nuns' land at Shelford. From these it is clear that the Monachus family had by then become tenants of the land, a situation which led to disagreement as to who held land from whom.[55] In 1246–7 a lawsuit resulted in the king's order that fifty acres which John Le Moyne (Monachus), son of Nicholas, had claimed as his own had to be returned to the nuns.[56] The charters show that as the Monachus clan multiplied, this land was gradually divided into smaller parcels, and they also reveal that much of it bordered land held by the bishop of Ely, who was lord of the Shelford manor.[57] The geographical proximity of estates held by the bishop, the Monachus family and the nuns was a constant reminder of the close contacts that had existed between these parties at the time of the priory's foundation.[58]

Another neighbour at Shelford was Stephen de Scaler, the

---

[53] PRS, n.s. xxviii, p. 98 (1211): 'Willelmus Monacus debet ii m pro habendo pone de duabus carrucatis terre in Braham' (cf. PRS, n.s. xxx, p. 80). For other references to William Monachus II, see PRS, n.s. I, p. 115 (1190), XVI, p. 5 (1203), XVIII, p. 118 (1204), XX, p. 167 (1206); *Curia Regis Rolls*, II (London, 1925), pp. 39, 75 (1201), III (London, 1926), p. 196 (1204). It is not clear whether he is the same as the William the Goldsmith of Cambridge mentioned in 1235 (*Curia Regis Rolls*, XV (London, 1972), pp. 358–9).   [54] *LE*, p. 340 quoted above in note 38.

[55] They have been registered by Mrs Freda Jones, former archivist of Jesus College, whose notes I used for the writing of this section. However, much research would be needed to establish a family tree of the Monachus family as names like William, Nicholas and John recur so frequently. One of its members was John le Moyne (Monachus), sheriff of Cambridgeshire in 1253–4 who died in 1275, see Farrer, p. 211; VCH, *Cambs.*, VIII, 210, 211, 216, 217 and Rubin, pp. 188, 224.

[56] Jesus Col. Caryl 21. This John is not necessarily the same as John the sheriff (see above n. 55).

[57] Jesus Col. Caryl s.21, Caryl s.7 and Caryl s. 1–2.

[58] The earliest reference to a member of the Monachus family owing service to the bishop of Ely dates from 1236 (*Liber Memorandorum*, ed. Clark, p. 250).

second lay benefactor to grant land to the nuns outside the borough.[59] He was a grandson of Hardwin, who acquired a substantial amount of land in Cambridgeshire after the Norman Conquest; Hardwin and the abbot of Ely were the largest landholders there. Hardwin divided his thirty fees between his two sons, Richard, the father of Stephen, and Hugh. In Cambridgeshire, (Little) Shelford was the caput of Richard's share and Whaddon that of Hugh.[60] Richard died when Stephen was still a minor, whereupon Hugh became his guardian. Stephen was a tenant in chief at (Little) Shelford, but at (Great) Shelford he was a tenant of both the bishop and the convent of Ely. Each year he and his uncle had to pay 126 quarters of grain to the monks as compensation for two and a half hides at (Great) Shelford which Hardwin had seized. This farm was paid reluctantly and sometimes only after much pressure from the king and his sheriffs.[61] Stephen also held one and a half knight's fee from the bishop.

On Palm Sunday in the year 1154 Stephen was summoned to appear before Bishop Nigel at Ely, to explain why he was yet again in arrears over payment of his farm to the monks.[62] According to Stephen, the problem was that the boundaries of the lands which he held of the monks had disappeared. The monks then agreed that if he would restore the boundaries they would allow him to continue to hold the land in return for an annual farm. It was also agreed that if there proved to be any residual land he could add that to the knight's fee held of the bishop. Shortly after Easter, Prior Alexander, for the monks, and Archdeacon William de Lavington, for the bishop, came to Shelford, where in the presence of jurors, amongst whom were William Monachus I and his son Nicholas, the boundaries were re-established and the case settled. It is of interest as an indication that by 1154 Bishop Nigel and the monks of Ely were able to cooperate in matters to do with land, to an extent that would have been inconceivable ten years previously. But the author of the *Liber Eliensis*, who incorporates an account of the case, comments tartly that Stephen committed perjury, and that the illness which led to his death (in 1168) was divine retribution.

---

[59] For this grant, see below, p. 72.   [60] Farrer, pp. 208–9.
[61] *LE*, pp. 263, 320, 323; *Regesta*, III, nos. 263–5 and Miller, pp. 40, 178.   [62] *LE*, pp. 363–4.

Stephen's grant to the nuns of St Radegund, made jointly by himself and his wife Juliana, consisted of eighty acres of land and a *managium* at West Wratting, free and quit of all service except for the Danegeld. The original charter has not survived, but it is known from a late medieval cartulary where the names of all witnesses except one, Durandus monk of Ramsey, have been left out.[63] It is not clear why a monk from Ramsey should have been involved; the land was held by Stephen in chief, and before 1066 it had belonged to the abbey of Ely rather than to Ramsey. Stephen was, however, a Ramsey tenant at Burwell, where he held one half knight's fee of the abbot.[64] Bishop Nigel confirmed the grant, and his willingness to support Stephen in this way suggests that the case at Shelford had by then been settled.[65] The thirteen witnesses to the confirmation charter included five people who were present at Ely or at Shelford in 1154, but William Monachus I was not among them, which strongly suggests that he had already retired to Ely.[66] One of the witnesses, however, was Archdeacon William de Lavington. Thus the confirmation charter can be dated to the period between the middle of 1154 and the Archdeacon's death in about 1158, which gives us some indication of the date of the West Wratting grant.[67]

At the same time as Stephen and Juliana gave land to the priory they gave also their daughter Sibilla; she is the earliest nun known to us by name. Their gift was therefore in the nature of a dowry, or to put it more crudely an entrance fee. Such an arrangement was not at all unusual; the great majority of lay benefactors who

---

[63] Jesus Col. Caryl T.25 item 4 (not listed by Gray). Durandus may be the same as Durandus cocus who attested several charters during the abbacies of Reinaldus (1114–30) and Walter (1134–60), see *Chronicon Abbatiae Rameseiensis*, ed. W. Dunn Macray (London, 1886), pp. 249–50, 251, 253, 259–60, 260–1, 262 and 271–2.

[64] *Cartularium monasterii de Rameseia*, ed. W. H. Hart (London, 1884), I, p. 141 and II (1886), p. 219. [65] Jesus Col. Caryl T.22 = Gray, no. 5, p. 77.

[66] List of witnesses in the correct order: William archdeacon of Ely (also present at Ely and Shelford), the monks August, Adam and Walter; Roger the chaplain (also present at Ely), the clerks Ernold, Peter, Robert Crestien (Miller, p. 286), John and Paien (Miller, p. 286), the deacons Martin (probably of Bottisham, *LE*, p. 388), Radulf (probably of Whaddon, *LE*, p. 388) and Richard; Radulf the steward (present at Ely, above n. 11), Alexander pincerna (present at Ely, above n. 15), Stephen and Geoffrey de Scaler, Robert de Cuninc' (undoubtedly Robertus de Cuningetuna *miles* who was present at Ely and Shelford and who probably was a vassal of the abbot of Ramsey; see *Chronicon Abbatiae Rameseiensis*, ed. Dunn Macray, pp. 260, 273, 274), Geoffrey son of Swein (vassal of Stephen and Hugh de Scaler, see *Red book of the exchequer*, ed. Hall, I, pp. 367, 369–70).

[67] This is also implied in the VCH, *Cambs.*, II, 218 where the De Scaler grant is listed before King Malcolm's grants, i.e. before 1158.

endowed nunneries did so because their mothers, sisters or daughters were to take the veil.[68] It is more than probable that William Monachus I supported the priory in the way that he did on behalf of a female relative. I am inclined to believe that she was already a member of the community at the time when his grant was made, on the grounds that her name was not attached to it in the way that Sibilla's name was attached to Stephen and Juliana's grant. William's grant to the nuns was made so soon after the priory was first established that I see him as having been a supporter almost from the start.

With a little imagination we may go further than that. In order to establish their community the nuns needed a plot of land to build upon and they also needed the wherewithall to pay for the building. Someone of substance who had influence in the borough must have helped them, first with advice and then with gifts or loans of money. A year or so later, when Bishop Nigel provided them with extra land which they no doubt needed for expansion and also, which may have been just as important for them, with official diocesan recognition, they must have had the help of someone whose requests the bishop could not lightly put aside: remember that the bishop was giving away land which probably belonged to the convent of Ely, at a time when his relations with the monks were still strained. Later still, they needed help to secure the support of the king as well as the bishop – support which finally secured their future, and which made it impossible for the prior and monks of Ely, after Bishop Nigel's death, to revoke his grant of land to them. Why should not William have been their helper? As an influential person in Cambridge, and perhaps even a burgher, as a goldsmith with financial resources and financial expertise, as an associate of Bishop Nigel to whom the bishop was indebted, and as a valued servant of the king, he was to say the least ideally placed to help.

Had the priory been founded, as many others were, on the initiative of a single benefactor, that person would very probably have become the patron of it or would have appointed someone else as patron; the patron's main right was to control the election

---

[68] E. Power, *Medieval English nunneries* (Cambridge, 1922), pp. 5–7, 21 and J. E. Burton, *The Yorkshire nunneries in the twelfth and thirteenth centuries*, Borthwick Papers, no. 56 (York, 1979), pp. 18–23; and most recently Thompson, *Women religious*.

of a new prioress.[69] The circumstances surrounding the foundation of St Radegund's, however, seem to have left it without a patron. Bishop Nigel was patron at Chatteris, and it may be that he aspired to play this rôle at Cambridge too.[70] But Arthur Gray has shown that he never possessed the patron's rights, so perhaps his ambitions were frustrated by the existence of disagreement as to whether the land which he had granted was really his to give away. Nor did William Monachus I or any of his descendants exercise the rights of patron. The nuns remained independent until shortly before the dissolution of the priory at the end of the fifteenth century.[71]

There is one aspect of the priory yet to be discussed which may provide some insight into the character of the community: its dedication to St Radegund. It was the first monastic house in England to be dedicated to this saint.[72] The earliest charters do not include her name, however, but only that of St Mary. Arthur Gray believed the earliest charter in which St Mary and St Radegund are both referred to to be the second of two recording the grants of King Malcolm IV of Scotland, and it was to Malcolm therefore that he attributed responsibility for her introduction. He linked his attribution to King Malcolm's French expedition of 1159, during which the king visited Poitiers, where St Radegund founded the nunnery of the Holy Cross in the sixth century.[73] Gray's suggestion was a plausible one, though there are no other indications that King Malcolm was a devotee of St Radegund, or that he was sufficiently interested in the nuns of

---

[69] S. Wood, *English monasteries and their patrons in the thirteenth century* (London, 1955), pp. 8–28; Power, pp. 43–5. The absence of a patron or conflicting evidence about patrons is not unusual in the history of English nunneries; see S. Thompson, 'Why English nunneries had no history: a study of the problems of the English nunneries founded after the Conquest', *Distant echoes. Medieval religious women*, ed. J. A. Nichols and L. T. Shank, I (Kalamazoo, 1984), pp. 131–49, esp. 143–4.   [70] VCH, *Cambs.*, II, 220.   [71] Gray, pp. 1–2, 39–40, 42–5.

[72] The only other monastery dedicated to St Radegund is Bradsole Abbey (Kent), founded in 1196 (A. Binns, *Dedications of monastic houses in England and Wales 1066–1216* (Woodbridge, 1989), p. 167). All other dedications to St Radegund concern churches, see Gray, p. 14 note 3 and F. Arnold Forster, *Studies in Church dedications or England's patron saints*, 3 vols. (London, 1899), II, pp. 487–91: Scruton (VCH, *York, North Riding*, I, 343), Maplebeck (Nottinghamshire) and Graylingham (Lincs.). Two churches were dedicated to both St Mary and St Radegund: Whitwell (Isle of Wight) (VCH, *Hants.*, v, 203) and Postling (Kent). Only two of the *kalendars* studied by F. Wormald refer to St Radegund: one of Chertsey (Surrey) and one of Muchelney (Somerset) (*English Benedictine Kalendars after A.D. 1100*, 2 vols., Henry Bradshaw Society, vol. 77 (London, 1939), p. 91 and vol. 81 (London, 1946), p. 99.

[73] Gray, p. 14; VCH, *Cambs.*, II, 218; Binns, p. 167.

Cambridge to wish to intervene over the dedication of their establishment; as far as we know he never even came to Cambridge. But although the suggestion has been accepted by all later scholars, it is rendered untenable by the observation that St Radegund's name appears in Bishop Nigel's confirmation charters for William Monachus I and Stephen de Scaler, as well as in Stephen's own charter, and by the evidence which shows that all of these must date before *c.* 1158.[74]

Radegund was a princess in Thuringia, who early in the sixth century was surrendered as booty to King Chlotar and was brought by him to France.[75] She grew up at Athies (arr. Peronne, cant. Ham) and married her abductor, but according to her biographers she had sworn to remain chaste and resisted the king's amorous advances. The marriage was never consummated, and shortly after it she took the veil. She may have spurned her husband, despite his sneers about her childlessness, but she did not spurn his wealth; she used it to found nunneries. The most famous of these was the one at Poitiers, but she was also associated with nearby Noyon and Saix. She died on 13 August 587. Her life was a source of inspiration for unmarried women and for married ones who remained childless, but above all for nuns.

The benefactor most likely to have known about the life of St Radegund and to have had some interest in suggesting that the nuns of Cambridge dedicate their priory to her was surely Countess Constance. She was educated in France, being the only legitimate daughter of King Louis VI and Adele of Maurienne, and while in England she was herself childless. She came to England in February 1140, when she was probably about fourteen or fifteen, much the same age as her fiancé Eustace. It is thought that the marriage was arranged by Eustace's mother, Queen

---

[74] Above nn. 31–2 and pp. 65, 72.

[75] There are three lives of St Radegund: one written shortly after her death in 587 by Venantius Fortunatus (ed. B. Krusch, *MGH Rer. Merov.* II (1888), pp. 364–77), one by the nun Baudonivia *c.* 600 (ed. Krusch, pp. 377–95) and the third by Hildebert, bishop of Le Mans and Tours (d. 1134.) *c.* 1097 (*PL.* 171.967–88). Gregory of Tours knew her well and attended her funeral, see his *Liber in gloria Confessorum* (ed. B. Krusch, *MGH Rer. Merov.*, I (1885), pp. 814–16). Fragments of the first two lives in translation can be found in *The writings of medieval women*, trans. M. Thiébaux (New York–London, 1987), pp. 25–56. The most thorough study of her life and later veneration remains E. Briand, *Sainte Radegonde reine de France et des sanctuaires et pélérinages en son honneur* (Poitiers – Paris, 1898). See also Sir M. Conway, 'St Radegund's reliquary at Poitiers', *Antiquaries Journal* 3 (1923), 1–12.

Matilda, Countess of Boulogne, and references to the young couple indicate that they were usually in her company.[76] Early in 1141 Constance was imprisoned with her mother-in-law in the Tower of London by Geoffrey de Mandeville.[77] The next year she went overseas with Queen Matilda and her husband to tour Boulogne and the neighbouring counties,[78] and we can assume that whenever King Stephen, Queen Matilda and Eustace were together in the years that followed Constance was there as well. Eustace was made count of Boulogne at Christmas 1146, this being the first step in King Stephen's campaign to have Eustace acknowledged as his heir and successor. In the early 1150s the king had plans for Eustace to be crowned,[79] and he conferred upon his son and daughter-in-law some rights which probably formed part of the fee farm of Cambridge and had been set aside for the queen's dower.[80] Count Eustace and his wife are known from the sole charter witnessed by Constance to have visited Cambridge in 1152, and the grant of rights was no doubt connected with that visit.[81] If King Stephen's plans for a coronation were in an advanced state round about Easter 1152, perhaps the couple met at Cambridge the king's goldsmith for coronations, whose task it would have been to prepare their crowns.[82] If so, perhaps we may credit William Monachus I with interesting the countess in the recently founded priory.

Shortly after that visit, of course, fate hit the royal family. The planned coronation never took place. Queen Matilda died in May, and Eustace died in August of the following year, 1153.

---

[76] R. H. C. Davis, *King Stephen 1135–1154* (London, 1967), pp. 48–9.

[77] *William of Newburgh*, ed. Walsh and Kennedy, pp. 66–8.

[78] *Regesta*, III, nos. 25–6, 196–200 and possibly 76.

[79] Henry of Huntingdon, *Historia Anglorum*, ed. T. Arnold (London, 1879), pp. 283–4; *The historical works of Gervase of Canterbury*, ed. W. Stubbs (London, 1879), I, p. 150; Cronne, p. 63; F. Barlow, *The English Church 1066–1154* (London, 1979), pp. 101–2; F. Barlow, *Thomas Becket* (London, 1986), p. 36.

[80] For the dower rights in the thirteenth century, see Gray, pp. 9–11 and VCH, III, 8, 35. Countess Constance refers to the rights as having been held by her husband and herself: 'sicut maritus Comes Eustacius et ego liberius et honorficentius habuimus'.

[81] *Regesta*, III, no. 229a. This charter is one of a group of charters (nos. 228–32) which are all related to grants by Robert de Sackville to St John Colchester. No. 229a dates from before Robert became a monk in 1152 × 3 (no. 230).

[82] An analogous situation is the case of Young Henry's coronation in 1170 for which plans existed already in 1161. In that year £38 6s. were paid for his crown, see PRS, v (1161–2), p. 43 and A. Hesdin, 'The coronation of the young king in 1170', *Studies in Church History* 2 (1965), 165–78.

Thereafter Countess Constance was left very much to herself, in the not very enviable position of a widow in her late twenties without children, and she must have contemplated entering a nunnery somewhere herself. But her brother King Louis VII of France summoned her back to her native country, to marry Count Raymond of Toulouse, then nineteen years old.[83]

Constance's last recorded act before departure was to endow the nuns of Cambridge with fishing rights. She performed it in Cambridge, and the occasion was attended by Bishop Nigel of Ely and the burghers of Cambridge, amongst whom was William Monachus I. None of the charters concerning her grant refers to St Radegund, but the saint's name appears, as we have seen, in three charters of only slightly later date. It seems likely that thoughts of St Radegund were already in the minds of several of those present.

APPENDIX: THE DATE OF THE SIEGE OF MEPPERSHALL

The siege of Meppershall is not mentioned in any chronicle and is known only from King Stephen's confirmation charter of the grant of William Monachus. When did it take place? According to Robert Howlett, the editor of the *Gesta Stephani*, Meppershall was close to Bedford and therefore the siege of Meppershall was in reality the siege of Bedford, dated 1138.[84] This date was accepted by Arthur Gray and, much later, by T. A. M. Bishop, though the latter expressed surprise that the 'Meppershall' charter was written by the scribe who wrote King Stephen's charter confirming the grant of Countess Constance, dated 1153/4.[85] Bishop's point was taken up by the editors of King Stephen's charters, who preferred a date much later than 1138, not only because of the script but also because of the witness list.[86] Among the witnesses was

---

[83] *Catalogue des Actes des Comtes de Toulouse*, III: *Raymond V (1149–94)*, ed. E. G. Leonard (Paris, 1932), pp. vi–vii, ix–xii. They had four children but the marriage broke down. In 1164 Constance left her husband and retired at the royal court. In August of the next year she stood godmother to her nephew Philip Augustus. She was still alive in 1174 (*Recueil des Historiens de France*, XVI, pp. 126–7; *Vie de Louis le Gros par Suger suivie de l'histoire du roi Louis VII*, ed. A. Molinier (Paris, 1887), pp. 176–8).

[84] *Gesta Stephani*, ed. R. Howlett, *Chronicles of the reigns of Stephen, Henry II and Richard I* (London, 1886), III, p. 31, n. 1.   [85] Bishop, 'Two charters of Stephen', pp. 1–5.

[86] *Regesta*, III. The scribe of the charter is 'scriptor xxii' responsible for a total of 24 charters, none of which dates necessarily from before 1146.

Rainald of Warenne, and Rainald did not take charge of the honour of Warenne until 1147, when his elder brother William departed for the Holy Land.[87] Can the siege have occurred after 1147?

The fifteenth-century cartulary of Biddlesden Abbey throws new light on the problem.[88] It begins with a short account of the events leading up to the abbey's foundation on 10 July 1147. According to this narrative, Biddlesden manor was held by Robert of Meppershall from Earl Robert of Leicester.[89] 'In the time of King Stephen, when warfare was at its height, the said Robert stayed at Meppershall and let Biddlesden be: neither he himself, nor anyone on his behalf, did service for it to the earl of Leicester, so the earl gave the land to his steward.' Because this steward, Arnold de Bosco, feared difficulties, so the narrative continues, he used the grant to found a Cistercian monastery, Biddlesden Abbey, and when Robert of Meppershall eventually agreed to renounce his claim to their land the monks paid him ten marks. Charter evidence shows the sequence of events as recounted in this cartulary to be correct, and makes clear that it was not until 1151 that Robert finally signed away his rights.[90]

In 1149, or at the latest in early 1150, the monks of Biddlesden reported 'disturbing intrusions from outside' and requested assistance from their bishop, Robert de Chesney of Lincoln (1149–66).[91] These intrusions were surely due to Robert of Meppershall, who was still actively trying to regain his lost lands. What happened next can only be conjecture, but presumably the bishop appealed to Earl Robert of Leicester, the man who had evicted Robert of Meppershall, and the earl appealed to the king to settle the matter once and for all. King Stephen, supported by Rainald de Warenne, who was Earl Robert's brother-in-law, came and besieged Meppershall. Its castellan was forced to submission and the king confirmed the monks of Biddlesden in their possessions.[92] Evidence for the validity of this reconstruction is provided by the fact that the 'Meppershall' charter and the charter of confirmation for Biddlesden Abbey were written by the same scribe.

Robert of Meppershall himself confirmed Arnold de Bosco's grant to Biddlesden Abbey, in a charter in which he describes *dominus meus rex Anglie Stephanus* as having already confirmed this grant at his request, and in which

---

[87] *Early Yorkshire charters*, ed. C. T. Clay, VIII (1949), pp. 26–7. Only one charter could be earlier than 1147: *Regesta* III, no. 307 (1143 × 54). The other one suggested by the editors of *Regesta* III as possibly of an early date, no. 822, should be dated 1150 × 54, see *Sibton Abbey cartularies and charters*, ed. P. Brown, 4 vols. (Woodbridge, 1985–9), III, no. 492, p. 21.

[88] *Monasticon*, v, pp. 366–7; VCH, *Beds.*, I, 356–9.

[89] *Monasticon*, v, p. 367 (based on London BL Ms Harley 4717 fo. 1r): 'Tempore vero Stephani regis, quando maxima guerra fuit sepedictus Robertus perhendinauit apud Meperteshal et dimisit Bitlesden et nec ipse nec aliquis pro eo inde seruicium fecit comiti Leycestrie sed terra illa escaeta comitis. Tunc idem comes dedit terram illam senescallo suo Ernaldo de Bosco pro seruicio suo.' For translation and commentary, see D. Crouch, *The Beaumont Twins* (Cambridge, 1986), p. 80. [90] See below, n. 94.

[91] *English Episcopal Acta*, I: *Lincoln 1067–1185*, ed. D. M. Smith (London, 1980), no. 82, p. 56.

[92] *Regesta*, III, no. 103 also written by 'scriptor XXII'.

he refers to the land of Biddlesden as *quod meis iuris erat*.[93] He further renounced all claims to his former possession in October of 1151, as I have already said.[94]

The chronology as I have sketched it here implies that the siege of Meppershall took place in 1149 or early in 1150. This date is, therefore, the most likely one for the royal confirmation of the grant to the nuns of Cambridge by William Monachus I.

[93] London BL Harley Chart. 85 G 48.
[94] *English Episcopal Acta*, I: *Lincoln*, ed. Smith, no. 83, pp. 56–7.

A tale of two cities: capitular Burgos and mendicant Burgos in the thirteenth century

PETER LINEHAN

The first century of Dominican history in St Dominic's own country still awaits its David Knowles and its Christopher Brooke. Given time no doubt they will emerge – provided they are not completely discouraged by exaggerated estimates of the damage suffered by the sources for their subject during what one of the Order's most learned modern medievalists has characterised as the 'ill-fated nineteenth century'. Beltrán de Heredia's pronouncement that 'in relation to the past the loss is already irreparable',[1] requires qualification. Certainly there have been losses, tragic losses, though not all of them are attributable to Napoleon's troops and *'esos malditos liberales'*. And things do turn up: for example, the cache of thirteenth-century bulls whose recent discovery in a cupboard under the stairs in a private house in Astorga provides at least some compensation for the (in the nature of things undocumented) loss of the *pergaminos* which the good nuns of Ciudad Rodrigo converted into sewing patterns in the early 1900s.[2]

Admittedly both those cases concern Franciscan documentation. However, the records of the Dominicans, fragmentary though they are, are capable of telling us something about that Order's early history too, given the chance. Reprehensible though the appropriation of the mendicants' materials by 'those damned

For advice and information I am indebted to Francisco Hernández, Guy Lee and Teo Ruiz.

[1] 'Examen crítico de la historiografía dominicana en las provincias de España y particularmente en Castilla', *Archivum Fratrum Praedicatorum* 35 (1965), 195, 245. The present state of knowledge is surveyed by A. Linage Conde in *Historia de la Iglesia en España*, II.ii, ed. J. Fernández Conde (Madrid, 1982), pp. 119–21, 136–42.

[2] A. Quintana Prieto, 'San Francisco de Sahagún. Primeros pasos de este convento franciscano', *Archivos Leoneses* 36 (1982), 109–11.

liberals' may have been, the nineteenth century can hardly be held responsible for the twentieth's reluctance to exploit it. I had not intended to return to the hooded man of Burgos and the saga of the stolen stones, having mentioned it in passing twenty years ago now. But since apparently no one else has done so since, the story remains to be told.[3] On this most appropriate of occasions, therefore, and with the assistance of municipal and capitular documentation published in connection with the Burgos millennium in 1984,[4] an attempt is made to do so here.

Of the ten Dominican houses within the kingdom of Castile *lato sensu* whose existence in 1250 is vouched for by the provincial chapter of that year, the Archivo Histórico Nacional possesses what little is left of the records of five, no more than some two to three hundred items.[5] Reading through these, one notices certain common features in the early history of the various communities. All ten houses were situated in cathedral cities, for example; bishops and friars came face to face from the outset. It is of course notorious that bishops everywhere regularly created difficulties for the friars and that the friars were no less regularly exhorted by their superiors to handle the ordinary gingerly, to seek his licence even if they possessed the appropriate papal privilege already, not to preach when he was preaching, and so on.[6] But in Spain, it seems, so also did rivers.

Spanish rivers (and doubtless other rivers too) were unpredictable to an almost episcopal degree. Like bishops, they had a tendency to break their banks, causing devastation all around. And when they did the friars were liable to be the first to suffer since on arrival in the city they had so often established themselves in its least favoured area, which was least favoured because experience had proved it to be uninhabitable. So the second generation of Preachers sought higher and drier ground. And that

---

[3] P. A. Linehan, *The Spanish Church and the papacy in the thirteenth century* (Cambridge, 1971), p. 317. Cf. C. Estepa Díez et al., *Burgos en la Edad Media* (Valladolid, 1984), p. 182 (T. F. Ruiz).

[4] E. González Díez, *Colección diplomática del Concejo de Burgos (884–1369)* (Burgos, 1984); F. J. Pereda Llarena, *Documentación de la catedral de Burgos (1254–1316)*, 2 vols., Fuentes medievales castellano-leonesas 16, 17, (Burgos, 1984).

[5] Burgos, Palencia, Salamanca, Toledo, Zamora (Toro). Not represented are Córdoba, León, Santiago de Compostela, Segovia, Sevilla. Cf. C. Douais, ed., *Acta capitulorum provincialium O.F.P. Première province de Provence* (Toulouse, 1894).

[6] 'Ut episcopi pauciores habeant auditores': *Litt. encyclicae*, ed. A. Frühwirth, Mon. O.F.P., 5 (Rome, 1990), 21–4.

meant moving towards the cathedral. At Salamanca the Tormes flooded them out twice – though there they were unusually fortunate in the local bishop, Pedro, who in 1256 actually facilitated their removal to the church of San Esteban which they inhabit to this day.[7] The river affected their movements at Burgos too. But at Burgos it was a different story.

The friars' earliest establishment at Burgos appears to have been situated some three hundred yards south of the bridge across the Arlanzón, to the north of which stood the cathedral church. They were probably there by 1224, though the tradition associating the foundation of their house with Dominic's visit to the city is barely less insecure than the evidence for the visit itself.[8] The earliest surviving document in their archive, an exemplar of *Quoniam abundavit*, Gregory IX's mandate to bishops requiring them to assist the friars in their preaching work, and the first of numerous general privileges with which the Burgos Dominicans prudently provided themselves during these early years, dates from 1228.[9] Later on they would have cause to be grateful for this foresight. Until the middle years of the century, however, the signs are that the Order's relationship with the cathedral was generally harmonious. When Bishop Juan of Burgos made his will in September 1246, for example, he appointed fr. Iñigo, prior of the Palencia house, one of his *fideicomissarii*.[10] There were no intimations yet of the ructions soon to come. These were confident expansive times. With Fernando III's armies sweeping through Andalucía and the prospect of the reconquest of Seville itself in view, there was still room for newcomers in Castile. In 1248 that mighty city was taken and the north of the kingdom which for a generation had borne the heavy burden of almost uninterrupted military expenditure looked to the south for relief and re-compense.

[7] Papal and episcopal indulgences for their relief, dated ?1237, ?1256, and Feb. 1265 are in Madrid, Archivo Histórico Nacional, Sección del Clero (hereafter AHN) 1893/16 (A. Potthast, *Regesta pontificum romanorum 1198–1304* (Berlin, 1874–5), 10417), 1894/5, 16. Cf. M. Villar y Macias, *Historia de Salamanca*, I (Salamanca, 1887), pp. 333–4.

[8] J. López, *Tercera parte de la historia general de S. Domingo* (Valladolid, 1613), p. 163; H. Flórez, *España Sagrada* 27 (Madrid, 1772), pp. 531–9.

[9] AHN, 181/1 (*Quoniam habundavit*, 15 Feb. 1228. Cf. Potthast, *Regesta*, 7896. Between February 1239 and October 1246 exemplars of a further twenty-five general privileges were secured, all but seven of them in October 1246: AHN, 181/2–18, 182/1–7.

[10] Capitular or cathedral archive, (hereafter AC) Burgos, vol. 46, fo. 430: L. Serrano, 'El canciller de Fernando III de Castilla', *Hispania* 15 (1941), 40.

Then the climate changed. For the Order at large it was changing already. When in 1250 Innocent IV licensed the friars to provide burial for the faithful in their churches and cemeteries, the ensuing furore fanned into flames resentments which had been smouldering for years, and the pontiff's reversal of this measure in 1254, reaffirming the integrity of parochial jurisdiction and resubmitting the mendicants to the authority of the ordinaries, failed to control the blaze. In the Parisian debates of these years secular hostility to the mendicants expressed sentiments which all Europe shared.[11] But in Castile such sentiments were expressed with particular vehemence, and not just because that is how sentiments are always expressed in Castile. The mendicants' progress created special resentment there because those at whose expense the friars continued to profit were already experiencing the disappointment of their recent expectations. In Castile the euphoria of the 1240s was in the process of being dispelled.

As late as mid-1252 it may not have seemed so as a new reign began in splendid style. But the splendour was deceptive. Alfonso X's open-handedness to ranking ecclesiastics during his first years, and in particular his exemption of sundry bishops and cathedral clergy from payment of the *moneda* tax, has recently prompted a student of the period to describe the 1250s as a 'golden age' for Castilian churchmen.[12] As the decade advanced, however, the leaden reality bore in upon both kingdom and Church. Already by 1257–8 there were stirrings of ecclesiastical discontent.[13] The ecclesiastical establishment was feeling the pinch and prepared to go onto the offensive. In July 1259 the pope heard that monks and secular clergy of the kingdoms of Castile and León were engaged in obliterating the stigmata from statues of the Poverello.[14]

It was against this sombre background that in 1257 the markedly pro-mendicant Alexander IV issued the Burgos Dom-

---

[11] Knowles, 185; Y. Congar, 'Aspects ecclésiologiques de la querelle entre mendiants et séculiers dans la seconde moitié du XIIIᵉ siècle et le début du XIVᵉ', *Archives d'histoire doctrinale et littéraire du Moyen Age* 36 (1961), 44ff.

[12] J. M. Nieto Soria, *Iglesia y poder real en Castilla. El episcopado 1250–1350* (Madrid, 1988), pp. 102–3.

[13] Linehan, *Spanish Church*, pp. 112–15, 165–70; T. F. Ruiz, 'Expansion et changement: la conquête de Séville et la société castillane (1248–1350)', *Annales* 34 (1979), 548–9.

[14] A. Vauchez, 'Les stigmates de Saint François et leurs détracteurs dans les derniers siècles du Moyen Age', *Mélanges d'archéologie et d'histoire de l'Ecole française de Rome* 80 (1968), 603, 607–8.

inicans with an indulgence designed to encourage the faithful to
visit their church, and in 1261 (just days after promulgating
Virtute conspicuos, whereby 'independence of everyone save the
pope was finally and completely attained' by the Order), that he
granted the request of Maiora Gonsalvi, wife of the prince of
Vizcaya, to be buried there together with her children and
familiares.[15]

In 1250, less than four years after Bishop Juan had engaged the
assistance of the prior of the Palencia Dominicans, Cardinal Gil
Torres had described the financial condition of the *communis mensa*
of the chapter of Burgos as 'graviter collapsa'.[16] This did not
imply that some of the canons of Burgos both then and later were
not wealthy men; some of those of them whom we are about to
encounter were very wealthy men indeed. But of what value to
the lesser lights was exemption from payment of *moneda* when
that part of their income which had not been appropriated by the
king was liable to be annexed by others, notably the friars?[17]
Moreover, corporately the church of Burgos was in dire straits.
The building of its new cathedral, consecrated in 1260, had taken
a severe toll of its resources. Some statistics assembled by T. F.
Ruiz concerning transactions of land and real estate in Burgos
between 1200 and 1350 indicate that between the first and the
second half of the thirteenth century the cathedral chapter was
reduced to economic impotence, with the proportion of transactions in which it was involved declining from 67·7 to just 4·3
per cent.[18] The chapter's rôle had been usurped by the *caballeros
villanos*, the non-noble knights of the city who, Ruiz surmises,
owed their prosperity to Alfonso X's privilege of 1255 whereby,
in return for maintaining horse and arms, they and their families

[15] AHN, 182/12, *Cum ad promerenda*, 27 Nov. 1257; 182/17, *Dilecte in Christo*, 8 Apr. 1261: ed.
I. Rodríguez de Lama, *La documentación pontificia de Alejandro IV* (Rome 1976) nos. 319, 463
(misdated to 1260). The Burgos exemplar of *Virtute conspicuos* (Potthast, *Regesta*, 18077) is
AHN, 183/1. Cf. R. F. Bennett, *The Early Dominicans* (Cambridge, 1937), p. 138.
[16] D. Mansilla, *Iglesia castellano-leonesa y curia romana en los tiempos del rey San Fernando* (Madrid,
1945), p. 361. Cf. Linehan, *Spanish Church*, pp. 270ff.
[17] For Alfonso X's commitment to rigorous tithe collection in 1255 and the reason for it (his
exaction of the *tercias*), see Linehan, *Spanish Church*, p. 123. His letter to the *concejos* of the
Burgos diocese was quite explicit: 'seruicio de los reyes e pro de si e de su tierra quando mester
es' had been one of the purposes for which Christ had instituted the tithe (Pereda Llarena, no.
24).
[18] 134/198 and 4/92 respectively: T. F. Ruiz, 'The transformation of the Castilian
municipalities: the case of Burgos 1248–1350', *Past and Present* 77 (1977), 14.

were exempted from royal taxation forever.[19] The resulting affluence of these favoured families would of course be shared by their clerical members, men such as the dean Pedro Sarracín, for example, who will figure so prominently in what follows. Pedro Sarracín, who had been a married man before becoming a cathedral dignitary, was amongst the wealthiest of Burgos's ecclesiastics. But it was not because he was an ecclesiastic that he was wealthy. It was because he was a member of one of the city's leading clans, the dynasties which both comprised the *concejo* and (as the chapter complained in 1295) bought up church property around the city and, courtesy of Alfonso X, paid no taxes on it, thereby further enriching themselves at the expense of the rural community.[20]

So much for the ecclesiastical 'golden age' conjured from royal privileges of the mid-1250s. *Qua* ecclesiastics, the chapter of Burgos was in straitened circumstances and in a new world from whose advantages it found itself excluded was more than ever intent on maintaining intact such assets as it had been bequeathed by the old. Hence the violence of its reaction when on Maiora Gonsalvi's death it found that it stood to lose what was arguably a very considerable asset. For hers was a corpse of quality; the prince of Vizcaya was Lope Díaz de Haro, a leading member of one of the kingdom's most powerful families.[21] What ensued Clement IV described in a letter sent to the bishop of Burgos, Martín González, in April 1266. First, certain canons forbad the friars to bury the dead lady, whereupon the friars appealed to Rome. However, there then appeared before them ('on your authority as he claimed') *quidam clericus*, one of the many nameless or faceless visitors who came to plague them in these years, demanding that their 'vicarius' appear before the bishop; which

---

[19] 'Que sean quitos de todo pecho': Alfonso X, Feb. 1255: González Díez, no. 26. Cf. Ruiz, 7–9, 15. Uncannily, the share of the *caballeros villanos* between 1250 and 1299 is exactly that of the chapter between 1200 and 1249.

[20] 'Otrosi, que ommes del conçeio compran los heredamientos de los logares de la eglesia e non quieren pechar por ellos, mandandolo el rey don Alfonso muchas uegadas, e por esta raçon son los logares despoblados, que non pueden cumplir los pechos': Pereda Llarena, no. 313. Cf. A. Blanco Díez, 'Dignitarios eclesiásticos burgaleses: los arcedianos de Valpuesta', *Boletín de la R. Academia de Historia* 121 (1947), 451–5.

[21] L. de Salazar y Castro, *Historia genealogica de la Casa de Haro*, ed. Archivo documental histórico 15 (Madrid, 1959), p. 314; S. de Moxó, 'De la nobleza vieja a la nobleza nueva', *Cuadernos de Historia* 3 (1969), 46ff.

he duly did and presented their documentation. Then on the following day while they were at mass they were broken in upon by Juan, a cleric, accompanied by a clerical posse, and although the 'vicarius' again read out their privileges, 'on your authority as he asserted' the said Juan forbad them to bury the body, suspended all Dominicans in the city, and had the sentence of suspension broadcast by the archdeacons.[22]

Or so the friars claimed. The *ex parte* nature of the rescript's narrative (as of the various later reports of capitular high-handedness to which we shall come) has of course to be allowed for. But it is at least apparent that since the 1240s relations between the cathedral and the priory had taken a turn for the worse. And the reason why is not far to seek. Although the precise date of the recent contretemps is unknown it can hardly have occurred much before the end of 1265. And by then the chapter must already have learned of the friars' scheme to move the priory closer to the cathedral.

In 1613 López stated that their earliest settlement at Burgos had been near the church of SS. Cosmas and Damián and that in 1267, 'because that place was unsafe', they had migrated to the site which they still occupied at the time when he was writing, the church of San Pablo. López was evidently paraphrasing what had been said on the friars' behalf in 1272, that ('in view of the danger of the place we were in') they had recently moved to a site provided for them by king and *concejo*.[23] It was a move which took them north east, to the south bank of the Arlanzón; still outside the city walls therefore, yet (as the canons in the 1260s perceived the city) *in* the city none the less.[24] Unlike their

---

[22] Which the bishop was now instructed to have relaxed: *Dilecti filii prior*, 6 Apr. 1266: AHN, 183/17.

[23] 'Videntes periculum loci in quo eramus' (AHN, 184/7: below, n. 47). Cf. López, *Tercera parte*, p. 163: 'por ser aquel sitio enfermo'. But what was López's authority for the date 1267? Alfonso X's grant was dated Aug. 1270. It comprised a group of properties some of which had been conveyed to the king by the abbess of the royal church of Las Huelgas earlier that year: AHN, 184/4bis (ed. J. M. Lizoain Garrido, *Documentación del monasterio de Las Huelgas de Burgos (1263–1283)*, Burgos 1987, no. 558), 5, 6. All were 'en el barrio de Vega a la collaçion de Sant Cosme e Damian', i.e. in the vicinity of their original settlement. However, at least two of these *huertos* gave them access to the waterways ('el calze que ua al molino de Haleua'; 'el rio que dizen Cardennuela') and thus sooner or later to the river Arlanzón itself.

[24] Below, n. 39. Sometime before 1276 Alfonso X ordered the *concejo* to have the city walls heightened: González Díez, no. 45. Cf. Ruiz in Estepa Díez et al., *Burgos en la Edad Media*, p. 107.

confrères at Salamanca who at this very time were fleeing the river, the friars of Burgos felt drawn to it. And the canons of Burgos in their new cathedral were affronted by their approach. It was not the fact that the friars would now be significantly closer to them that rankled with the canons (for actually they would not). What rankled with them was that the friars had reached the river and were installing themselves by 'the friars' bridge', the bridge across which so much hostile traffic was to pass during the coming decades.[25]

And this was not all. The friars were not merely approaching the cathedral. By laying claim to the mortal remains of Master Juan Tomé (and his estate) they had already symbolically entered it. As archdeacon of Valpuesta, Juan Tomé ranked second in Burgos's archidiaconal hierarchy.[26] So it was something of a catch for the friars when he took the Dominican habit and elected to be buried with them. No wonder the canons were so sensitive on the subject of corpses in 1266.

Master Juan Tomé had died in 1262 and was prepared for interment in the friars' church. What allegedly happened then is recounted in Urban IV's mandate of the July of that year addressed to three dignitaries of the church of Salamanca. Various *persone* and canons of the church under the command of the archdeacon of Lara (Pedro de Peñafiel) were reported to have stolen the body and buried it in the cathedral. The pope instructed the executors to deal with the matter within four months.[27] Whereupon, nothing happened. The pope had been misinformed. Those responsible had been misidentified. In view of later developments this is not surprising. The culprits may have been disguised. Six months later the pontiff issued a fresh mandate, naming different names which apparently were also wrong.[28] By

[25] What is now 'the bridge of S. Pablo' was then 'la puente de los Predicadores': *Chronicon de Cardeña*, ed. Flórez, *España Sagrada* 23 (Madrid, 1767), 375 (*s.a.* 1286).

[26] Flórez, *España Sagrada* 26 (Madrid, 1771), 313.

[27] AHN, 183/4, *Significarunt nobis*, addressed '...decano et...archidiacono de Medina et...cantori Salamantin.', 5 July 1262: ed. I. Rodríguez R. de Lama, *La documentación pontificia de Urbano IV* (Rome, 1981), no. 22 (misdated 5 March 1262. The reduplication of this mandate in the editor's collection [no. 44], dated 5 July 1262, from Reg. Vat. 26, fo. 22, no. 104, is imaginary. There is no such letter in Reg. Vat. 26. The letter emanating from the friars' complaint was not registered. The volumes of *Monumenta Hispaniae Vaticana*, though valuable in their way, have to be used with caution; cf. Linehan, *EHR* 96 [1981] 903–4 [review]).

[28] AHN, 183/5. *Dilecti filli prior*, addressed '...decano...cantori...et...archidiacono de Medina Salamantin.', 2 Jan. 1263. The amended order of the recipients apart, the identifiable raiders

now battle had been joined at the papal curia, with both parties represented by their proctors.[29]

And little good it did either of them. Further delay followed. Possibly the pope had again been misinformed. Certainly it is difficult to reconcile some of the Burgos sightings reported to him with evidence from nearer home. For example, as recently as April 1260 the delated archdeacon Pedro Pascual (accompanied by two of the chapter's senior dignitaries, Pedro Sarracín and García de Campo, archdeacon of Lara and cantor respectively) had obliged the Burgos friars by witnessing for them the text of Alexander IV's sentence of the previous October abrogating all measures hostile to their Order issued by the Spanish ordinaries.[30] Evidently capitular opinion was not solid on the mendicant issue. Corporate loyalties were divided. Burgos dinner parties in the mid-1260s must have been a nightmare. The storm was gathering. There were lawyers at work. The question had proved too difficult for the people in Salamanca. The case was now with a cardinal.[31] But even the cardinal was perplexed by the rights and wrongs of the matter. At Viterbo he was formulating various questions, no one knew how many. And alongside him the assiduous fr. Dominicus was preparing for a lengthy siege, stockpiling privileges.[32] By June 1267 he was making good the mendicants' defences in earnest. By now privileges which permitted use of the sacraments in time of interdict were at a premium. Perhaps word spread, perhaps it was news from the north that roused the ordinarily unacquisitive friars of the Toledo

---

were now listed as Master Pedro Pascual archdeacon of Treviño, Juan Gutiérrez and García de Cardeña. Cf. Pereda Llarena, no. 92 (below, p. 91).

[29] Fr. Dominicus and Gundisalvus Roderici respectively: P. Linehan, 'Proctors representing Spanish interests at the papal court, 1216–1303', *Archivum Historiae Pontificiae* 17 (1979), 106. Gundisalvus had been at Viterbo in March 1262 acting for the bishop of Burgos: T. Minguella y Arnedo, *Historia de la diócesis de Sigüenza*, i (Madrid, 1910), 590. It is to be noted that although fr. Dominicus had neither mandate registered, in Feb. 1263 *per contra* he obtained for his Burgos brethren not one but two exemplars of the latest papal privilege confirming the Order's liberties and privileges, *Cum a nobis* (Potthast, *Regesta*, 18488): AHN, 183/6, 7 (both endorsed: 'pro conuentu Burgen. fr. dominicus procurauit'). Better safe than sorry.

[30] AHN, 182/15 (Potthast, *Regesta*, 17679, *Meritis vestre religionis*).

[31] James of S. Maria in Cosmedin: AC Burgos, vol. 41.II, fo. 333.

[32] May–June 1265: AHN, 183/9 (Potthast, *Regesta*, 19137); 183/10, 11 (both with 'fr. Dominicus' inscribed at top left recto: Potthast, 19209); 183/12, 13 (Potthast, 19210); 183/14 (Potthast, 19216); 183/15 (Potthast, 19235).

priory to secure one.[33] The keepers of the Burgos capitular cartulary in the 1260s were certainly on the *qui vive*.[34]

At Valladolid in November 1267, when evidence regarding the events of 1262 was collected, the reasons for the long delay in doing so emerged.[35] It appears that it was in 1263 (the record gives no date) that Urban IV had appointed Cardinal James Savelli to hear the case at the curia. But three years later he had made no progress. Such was his perplexity that the number of questions he required answers to had risen to at least twenty-seven. So in June 1266 commissioners were appointed to interrogate witnesses in Burgos. The friars' nominee for this task was Bernardus Yspanus, archdeacon of Saldaña (Leon). This was Bernardus Compostellanus, the noted canonist and a wise man. Wise enough, certainly, to delegate his responsibilities to another. But not quick enough, for before his letter had reached its destination he died. A new team had to be appointed therefore.[36] (This was beginning to resemble *Bleak House*.) Then, in September 1267, a member of the new team ('legitimo impedimento detentus', he asserted) absented himself and appointed a proxy to act for him. It was not until that November that the witnesses to the facts of Juan Tomé's last will and testament and to the indignities to which his mortal remains had been subjected were at last assembled, by which time they must all have been aware of the gift of the site near the river which the friars either had recently received from the king and *concejo*, or were about to, for the construction of their new church.

Very little has survived of the record of the November 1267 hearing.[37] But from what has it is apparent that memories were still remarkably fresh concerning the events of five years before. The deceased's brother and co-executor, Gonzalvo Tomé, testified that while still in possession of his faculties the archdeacon had recorded the disposition of his goods 'in quadam carta'. He had intended to leave his houses to the friars. However, Gonzalvo

---

[33] AHN, 184/1 (Potthast, 20060) = AHN, 3101/7; 184/2.

[34] AC Burgos, vol. 73, fo. 164r–v: 13th-cent. Dominican privileges (detailed in D. Mansilla, 'La diócesis de Burgos vista a través de la documentación del archivo capitular en los s.XIII y XIV', *Anthologica Annua* 9 (1961) nos. 11, 17, 29, 30, 36, 38, 50) in a 14th-century cartulary, presumably reproduced from an earlier text.

[35] AC Burgos, vol. 41.ii, fo. 333 (four pieces), ed. Pereda Llarena, nos. 75, 81, 84, 87, 90–2.

[36] On 12 Dec. 1266 (Pereda Llarena, no. 81). So Bernard must have died in the autumn of that year rather than in 1267 as suggested by G. Barraclough, 'Bernard of Compostella', *EHR* 49 (1934), 491.   [37] *Rubrice* 11–14, 25–29 which stops short in mid sentence.

and another had dissuaded him, insisting that the chapter should have them, 'and so it was done'. He had indeed chosen to be buried with the friars and had asked his executors to purchase a modest property to provide oil for the lamp which was to burn above his tomb in San Pablo. But this was all hearsay. There was nothing in writing. Where was the *carta*? All very unsatisfactory, it was noted in the margin.[38] Despite the fact that they stood outside the walls on the far side of the big stone bridge (Puente de S. Pablo), the houses were described as being 'in the city'. They were situated between the residences of two senior members of the chapter, and were currently occupied by another as the chapter's tenant.[39] There was no doubt ('probatur') that the dean and chapter held and possessed the properties. What was not proved was that they had received them as a corporate bequest, and the auditor's attention was drawn to this uncertainty.[40] The commissioners similarly addressed the question of the chapter's collective responsibility for the seizure of the dead archdeacon from the bier. There had been considerable numbers present in the Dominicans' church that fateful Friday (five years on they were certain it had been a Friday.) They remembered Gonzalvo Fernández removing the body, the friars' vain attempts at resistance, and the prior calling on those present to witness what was happening. One of these, fr. Domingo (who by 1267 was prior provincial), affirmed that the violence was due to 'maior pars capituli'. He knew this because 'some canons said that the chapter of Burgos did it and others kept silent'.[41]

What the auditor made of all this we do not know. Anyway, before he can have received the answers to his questions Burgos suffered a further bereavement, the effect of which was to embroil the issue of Juan Tomé's bequest in a welter of fresh disputes between the canons and the friars of a city now without a bishop.

As late as mid-August 1267 high-ranking members of the chapter had at least been prepared to set foot on local Dominican

---

[38] 'Hec rubrica non probatur aliquomodo suficienter, licet de auditu aliquod dicere uideatur': Pereda Llarena, no. 91 (i.132–3).

[39] 'in ciuitate Burgi, ultra maiorem pontem lapideum, inter domos abbatis de Fronçea et domos Garsie de Campo cantoris': ibid. Ramón de 'Sancistes' (?Sanchester: below, p. 104) affirmed that the tenant was Gutierre Pérez, secular abbot of Cervatos.

[40] 'Hec rubrica probatur quoad capitulum set non quoad decanum. Uideat eam tamen dominus auditor': ibid., i.134.   [41] Ibid., no. 92 (i.137).

territory.[42] But in the following December, within a month of the Valladolid hearing, Bishop Martín González died, and in August 1269 his successor Juan de Villahoz died too. Both vacancies opened up capitular divisions. On the first occasion in July 1268 Clement IV appointed Juan to the see notwithstanding procedural irregularities concerning his election. But the second vacancy proved far more problematic, not least because the papacy was itself vacant until 1271 and Burgos was an exempt see subject directly to the Roman Church. So when the episcopal election was disputed between the dean and the archdeacon of Valpuesta and, although he enjoyed the support of only three of the forty-six canons, the latter took his case and himself to the curia, the issue could not be resolved. Of one consequence of the Burgos schism the new pope Gregory X was apprised in October 1272. Because vacant dignities and canonries remained unfilled, the cathedral was unmanned. (And the remedy provided by the pontiff, of inviting the dean, the archdeacon of Briviesca and other canons 'qui tunc apud sedem apostolicam morabantur' to make nominations, suggests that many of those who were not dead were at Orvieto.)[43] Burgos remained without a bishop until September 1275, and in the absence of its legitimate defenders capitular vigilantes took to the streets of the city, intent on dislodging the friars from their new place by the river.

When he made the arrangements he made in October 1272 the pope was already aware of this development. In the previous May the prior of S. Pablo had reported a further ugly incident. As instructed by certain (unnamed) judges delegate, he had been reading out in the choir of his church a public instrument concerning the friars' dispute with the dean and chapter, when a hooded layman (identity unknown) had burst in, seized the document, and escaped with it. Gregory ordered its recovery and the punishment of the culprit or culprits.[44] This was an unenviable

---

[42] On 20 August, 'Burgis, in capitulo fratrum praedicatorum', the dean Martín Gómez, the cantor García de Campo, and the archdeacon of Burgos Pedro Pascual *inter alios* had witnessed a judicial conclusion regarding the establishment of an episcopal see at Soria (Potthast, 19915): J. Loperráez Corvalán, *Descripción histórica del obispado de Osma* (Madrid, 1788), III, p. 202.

[43] *Reg. Clem. IV*, 646; *Reg. Greg. X*, 632; *Illarum ecclesiarum*, 12 Oct. 1272 ('legitimis erat servitoribus et defensoribus destituta'): AC Toledo, A.7.G.I.I.

[44] '*Querelam dilectorum*...quidam secularis cui notitiam prorsus non habent illuc uelato capite ueniens', 14 May 1272: AHN, 184/8.

task, so it is significant that the person to whom it was entrusted was the archdeacon of Valpuesta, Pedro Sarracín, currently the minority candidate for the see. The friars' choice of him, in 1272 and later, to assist them in their battles with the dean and chapter of the church of which he was an archdeacon suggests that disaccord on the mendicant question may have been one of the causes of the capitular schism itself. Judging by opposites supports the conjecture. For when Pedro's rival for the see, the dean Martín Gómez, had been angling for the archbishopric of Toledo in 1264 the delegate he had nominated to investigate his claim had been none other than the friars' principal persecutor Pedro Pascual.[45] Some such process of polarisation around S. Pablo would help to account for the dismal electoral performance of a prominent member of one of Burgos's leading families. And the existence of division of opinion on the matter at an earlier stage would explain the auditor's interest in 1267 in the question of capitular unanimity apropos the theft of Juan Tomé's corpse.[46]

However the Burgos ecclesiastics were distributed along the pro- and anti-mendicant spectrum, the most vocally hostile of them appears to have been Fernán Garcés, archdeacon of Niebla (Seville) but a Burgos man to the core. (If anyone knew the whereabouts of the friars' purloined document, it was surely Fernán Garcés.) On 10 March 1272, in the local Franciscan church the friars' proctor, fr. Domingo de Caleruega, filed a complaint with the local public *escrivano*. He protested that yet again their rights had been infringed by the archdeacon of Burgos, Master Pedro Pascual, and the chapter, regarding which infringement instruments and appeals were in the process of being prepared for transmission to Rome. He further complained that after preaching in the cathedral on Quinquagesima (four days before) Fernán Garcés had roused the rabble against the friars, provoking the people 'by words, similitudes and threats' to occupy the site which king and *concejo* had recently given them and to prevent them from building on it. The archdeacon of Niebla was

---

[45] *Reg. Urb. IV*, 664 (June 1264), on which occasion he had been threatened with deprivation of his benefices if his claim to election proved flimsy. He had previously maintained that he had been elected at Avila: ibid., 2826.

[46] For the Sarracín dynasty, see T. F. Ruiz, *Sociedad y poder real en Castilla* (Barcelona, 1981), pp. 127–37. Cf. Pereda Llarena, I, pp. 133–4, 137.

employing against the friars the friars' own most effective weapon, the power of the word.[47]

Words led to deeds. Later that same year the friars provided Gregory X with a detailed account of the harassment to which they were being subjected by 'the canons or chapter'. Arrogating to themselves legislative powers which belonged to the bishop, the latter were alleged not only to have suspended and excommunicated the friars, interdicting their church and forbidding the faithful to attend their sermons or to be buried by them, but also ('quod inhumanius est') to be intent on starving them and freezing them out of existence altogether.[48] The chapter did not deny the charges. It sought rather to justify its actions. The friars' 'new works', begun during the episcopal vacancy, had encroached on capitular property. In particular the lands which provided for the ministers of the divine office in the cathedral had been occupied. The friars were too close for comfort; there was no hiding the fact, try as they might. Accordingly eight of them and their entire workforce had been excommunicated.[49] But still they persevered, committing further trespasses under cover of appealing to Rome (the canons claimed). Gregory's letter of December 1272 reveals that the friars had complained to him before about these matters and that the pope had responded. But they had been denied assistance by the usual combination of capitular counter-claim and the grim reaper removing the judge delegate.[50] And so matters continued...for another thirty years.

In 1272 the pontiff was preoccupied with an even more vexatious Castilian problem, the resolution of Alfonso X's claim

[47] '...post publicum sermonem coram omni populo, ut nobis relatum est, uerbis suis et similitudinibus et cominationibus in ecclesia cathedrali contra nos ut potuit populum prouocauit, asserens quod in predicto fundo nos tamquam alieni uiolenter occupantes ne inde aliquid construeremus modis omnibus impedirent': AHN, 184/7. A version of the same protest in 'romanz' was also prepared. In 1277, as archdeacon of Palenzuela, Fernán Garcés was appointed one of the executors of Pedro Pascual's will: Pereda Llarena, no. 142. But was the friars' proctor in 1272 the same fr. Domingo who had acted for them at Viterbo ten years before?

[48] 'ipsos in hospitio recipere uel eis uite subsidia ministrare aut elemosinam elargiri, uictualia uendere, in ipsorum domibus aliquid operari uel ipsis ad promotionem sui operis prestare consilium aut auxilium attemptaret uitantes': Sua nobis, 21 Dec. 1272, addressed to the archdeacon of Saldaña (León): AHN, 184/9.

[49] Ibid.: '...domos et officinas ad opus eorum in ortis et aliis locis ad eandem ecclesiam Burgensem pertinentibus et nimium ecclesie ipsi uicinis...construere incepissent...et hoc esset ita notorium quod nulla poterat tergiuersatione celari'.

[50] Ibid. The text of the earlier commission, addressed to Master Gonzalvo treasurer of León, is not extant. Was it this that led to the intervention of the hooded intruder?

to the empire. While that issue remained pending, which it did until the summer of 1275, Burgos remained without a bishop and the friars had to shift for themselves. The church of Burgos was in good company: at the beginning of 1272 no fewer than ten Castilian sees (more than a third of the kingdom's total) were vacant. Meanwhile, however, the Castilian Dominicans did not lack for powerful friends: at the year's end, on the day before the pope's latest attempt to bring peace to Burgos, Alfonso took the Madrid house under his protection. And in the interim he had been at Burgos for a meeting of the Cortes which had been preceded by the appearance of his *ricos omes* on the banks of the Arlanzón, armed and turbulent, and was marked by indications of episcopal sedition to which, but for his anxiety to ingratiate himself with the pope, he would have responded by exiling the lot.[51]

When at last, in September 1275, Burgos was provided with a bishop, neither of the candidates over whom the chapter had divided six years before was preferred. The dean of Burgos, the episcopally ambitious Martín Gómez, was shunted off to Sigüenza for his sins, gazetted as a great catch for the place, and expressed his gratitude by promptly dying, while Pedro Sarracín slid into the deanery in which he remained until his death in 1290 or 1291 dividing his time between investing in the local land market and succouring the local Dominicans.[52] *Tertius gaudens* was a Toledan on the make, Gonzalo Pérez, bishop of Cuenca, one of thirteenth-century Europe's truly remarkable churchmen.[53] But notwithstanding his exceptional qualities and his intimacy with the king, Gonzalo Pérez's translation from Cuenca was a mixed blessing for the canons of Burgos since in addition to his closeness to the friars his responsibilities in the royal chancery meant that he was not very often particularly close to Burgos.[54] The friars themselves

[51] A. Ballesteros Beretta, *Alfonso X el Sabio* (Barcelona, 1963), 557, 570, 584, 1102; P. Linehan, *History and the historians of medieval Spain 589–1350* (Oxford, forthcoming), chapter 13.
[52] *Reg. Greg. X*, 608 ('virum utique probate uite, magne scientie et circumspectionis experte'); Minguella, *Hist. de Sigüenza*, i.226–7. Ruiz, *Sociedad y poder real*, 131–2, catalogues P. Sarracín's activities.
[53] *Reg. Greg. X*, 632. Francisco Hernández and the present author are preparing a study of Gonzalo Pérez.
[54] Gonzalo Pérez left little trace there. In Feb. 1276 he was unable to attend to his church's affairs 'por otras cosas que auie de uer': Pereda Llarena, no. 132. But the 12,000 maravedis he borrowed from the Burgos Dominicans far exceeded the sum total of his other Burgos debts: AC Toledo, A.7.G.1.4. In May 1282 the general chapter of the Order at Vienne established a

meanwhile were intermittently under siege. In 1276 they complained to the pope again. This time it was their building
materials, their *lapides*, that had been taken. As usual, the pope was
sympathetic.[55] Which was to be expected, for Innocent V was a
friar himself, the Order's first supreme pontiff.

In May 1280 Gonzalo Pérez was promoted to Toledo and was
replaced by bishop Fernando OFM.[56] Now here was an
interesting situation: a mendicant bishop in charge of a chapter of
secular canons locked in combat with the mendicants of the other
persuasion across the river, and the Burgos Franciscans themselves
similarly at odds with the monks of Silos. In the latter case Bishop
Fernando loyally supported his *confrères*.[57] In the other he did the
sensible thing. Like Brer Fox, he lay low. He was not much seen
in his cathedral city. In August 1291 the chapter was moved to
comment on his absence. They were hardly better off with him
than they had been with no bishop at all. It was as bad as the early
1270s. So would the bishop please empower them to impose
sentences of excommunication and the rest 'in defence of their
rights'?[58] How could the bishop refuse?

Their request was made at a meeting of the chapter summoned
to stiffen resistance to the friars. It was being suggested that some
canons were in favour of allowing them to retain 'the place which
they had again occupied by the river bank'. Each member was
therefore required to confess his allegiance. The response was
unanimous: the friars' presence there was unacceptable and it
always would be.[59] What occasioned this impressive display of
capitular solidarity was the starkness of the contrast which their
own secular circumstances presented with the pronounced
affluence of the mendicants.[60] The friars went from strength to

special relationship with him: AHN, 3021/17 (cf. Ballesteros, *Alfonso X*, 973). In April 1286 he
engaged Sancho de Ubeda OP as his proctor: AC Toledo, A.7.G.1.20.
[55] By 'nonnulli iniquitatis filii quos prorsus ignorant': Innocent V, *Sua nobis*, addressed to Pedro
Sarracín (still archdeacon of Valpuesta), 17 May 1276: AHN, 184/10, 11.
[56] *Reg. Nich. III*, 651.
[57] M. Férotin, *Recueil des chartes de l'abbaye de Silos* (Paris, 1897), pp. 312–14. The version of this
controversy remembered locally in Férotin's day included exchanges of gun fire between the
two communities!
[58] '...e porque acaeçe muchas vegadas que, por muchas priesas que el obispo avie e porque no era
en el logar, no avie qui defendiesse los bienes de la eglesia': Pereda Llarena, no. 263.
[59] Ibid.: 'et todos en vno, e cada vno por sy, respondieron que no les plazia ny les ploguiera nunca,
e que no lo otorgaban nyn lo otorgarien de su grado en ningun tiempo del mundo'.
[60] Just eleven days earlier bishop and chapter had revised its statute relating to individual
indebtedness: ibid., no. 262.

strength, reaping where others sowed, and weathering every storm. Their capacity to survive and flourish had been demonstrated in the years leading up to the Infante Sancho's rebellion against Alfonso X in 1282 and throughout the following two years of civil war, during which period royal father and son had both vied strenuously for the support of Burgos 'caput Castelle'. At the outbreak of hostilities Bishop Fernando had remained true to the king. So had the Dominicans.[61] But despite this, Sancho IV valued them as highly as his father ever had. Like Alfonso, he gave them land on which to build a church (perhaps a second church) in the city, and confirmed his father's privilege exempting them from payment of *diezmo* and *portadgo* on their books, the parchment they needed for their studies, their clothes and food and 'all other items necessary for the maintenance of their houses'. This was in November 1284, just six months into his reign.[62] A year later they were purchasing property in the street of San Lucas on the outskirts of the city, in the vicinity of the capitular hospital of that name which Pedro Sarracín (now dean) had established there; purchasing it in the full sense of the word and doing so with the express approval of king and *concejo*. For this (one of their many acquisitions in these years) they paid 2,000 maravedís, which in comparison with the sums which they had previously advanced to Gonzalo Pérez (by now archbishop of Toledo) was small change. But to the canons, whose annual allowance had been fixed at eighty maravedís in 1250, the friars' ability to complete the purchase out of petty cash must have appeared a provocation. Even in terms of the devalued state of the currency in 1285, worth perhaps not as much as a quarter of what it had represented in 1250, 2,000 maravedís was a substantial sum; possibly as much as the archdeacon of the city had been assigned

[61] González Díez, nos. 46–132. For the bishop's resistance to the Infante's efforts to secure his support in April 1282, see Pereda Llarena, no. 173; Ballesteros, *Alfonso X*, 967–9. Amongst those with him at the Dominicans' Valladolid house were the prior provincial of the Order, Munio of Zamora, and the archdeacon of Palenzuela, Fernán Garcés!

[62] '...ni de las otras cosas que ffizieren traer a ssus casas pora ssu despensa': AHN, 185/8: publ. M. Gaibrois Ballesteros, *Historia del reinado de Sancho IV*, III (Madrid, 1928), no. 28. Note the reference to 'casas' in the plural. For Sancho's gift to them of a *plaza* on which to build a church dedicated to S. Domingo, an establishment distinguishable from that of S. Pablo, see below n. 95. The text of Alfonso X's privilege (Burgos, May 1270), in favour of all houses of the Order in his kingdom, is in J. Cuervo, *Historiadores del convento de S. Esteban de Salamanca*, III (Salamanca, 1916), 939.

at that earlier date.[63] And this was only one of their recent purchases.

But though they were rich, eighteen years after Alfonso X and the *concejo* had given them the site for a new building they still had not moved from their original unsatisfactory church. Moreover, by 1285 the archdeacon of the city was Ferrán Garcés, the rabble-rouser of 1272. So when (with episcopal permission as they alleged) they resumed construction work on a plot of land given them by Mateo Pérez, there was bound to be trouble. In May 1285 they provided Honorius IV with their version of the form it had taken. 'First on the authority of the chapter, as he said, and then *motu proprio*', Ferrán Garcés had demanded the surrender of the land to him, and regardless of their appeal to Rome had excommunicated them. To Honorius IV of course all of this was very familiar. More than twenty years before, as Cardinal James Savelli, he had had the Burgos file on his desk; it was the case that had kept dying on him. He now referred its most recent development to the dean of Segovia,[64] who found for the friars on all counts. Whereupon, of course, the chapter entered an appeal on the grounds that the dean (Garcí Sánchez) was partial to the friars, which indeed he was,[65] and that he had failed to summon the dean and chapter to his hearing of the case, which indeed he had, though it was to take the dean and chapter sixteen years to prove it.

Boniface VIII's rescript of April 1301 which determined the issue partly explains why it had taken so long to settle. Although Nicholas IV and Celestine V in turn had both appointed auditors,

---

[63] Pereda Llarena, nos. 206 (Nov. 1285), 208–9. Cf. H. Casado Alonso, *La propiedad eclesiástica en la ciudad de Burgos en el s.XV: el cabildo catedralicio* (Valladolid, 1980), p. 39; Mansilla, *Iglesia castellano-leonesa*, p. 360. Regarding the wild variations in money values since 1250, see J. J. Todesca, 'The monetary history of Castile-León (c. 1100–1300) in light of the Bourgey hoard', *American Numismatic Society Museum Notes* 33 (1988), 160ff.

[64] *Significarunt nobis*, 3 May 1285: AHN, 297/4. The rescript states that a move from their former residence was necessary 'propter eius ineptitudinem et incomoditates multiplices'. (When did this S. Pablo muniment, which contains annotations in the distinctive S. Pablo hand, pass into the archive of the Benedictines of Oña? The same collection contains an exemplar of *Ex parte vestra*, Honorius's general privilege permitting the Dominicans to engage another bishop to consecrate their church if the ordinary refused to do so (Potthast, *Regesta*, 22333): AHN, 297/17).

[65] In 1289 he represented Archbishop Rodrigo González of Compostella, formerly prior provincial of the Order in Spain, in his dispute with the canons of that church, and was appointed conservator of the interests of the Dominican nuns of Madrid: *Reg. Nich. IV*, 677, Potthast, 23108.

progress had been hampered by the death of the one and the resignation of the other.[66] Meanwhile the canons had again had recourse to strong-arm tactics (stones this time), causing a fracas which ought to have led Pedro Sarracín to consider his position.[67] Tension heightened as conditions deteriorated. The serious flooding in February 1286 which raised the river level to the rooftop of the archdeacon of Valpuesta's house and caused the friars' bridge to collapse was followed after Sancho IV's death in 1295 by the collapse of public order itself.[68] These were violent times in Castile. In the will which he made at S. Pablo (where he was to be buried) in 1293, the knight Gonzalo Ruiz de Zúñiga reviewed a long career which seems to have been dedicated almost exclusively to the commission of acts of assault and battery.[69] Regrettably, the canons of Burgos followed suit. And the action they took helps to account for the failure of their affairs at the curia to prosper earlier than they did.

As has already been indicated, their style had always been robust. But in the early 1290s they overstepped the mark with what might have proved far-reaching consequences. Already beset by debt and the Dominicans, they were now visited by a further plague. In February 1289 the archdeaconry of Briviesca, and sometime before July 1291 a canonry were awarded to Italian curialists.[70] Of course, the chapter of Burgos was not unfamiliar with the system of papal provisions. But on top of their other woes these latest appointments had the effect of goading them into taking direct action. When the agents of Laurentius de Urbe arrived to take possession of yet another canonry (he had already been presented to the archdeaconry of Lara) the dean and others

---

[66] Pereda Llarena, no. 356. The complainants' *petitio* contained phrases which had been heard before in this connection, e.g. 'cum hoc esset adeo notorium quod nulla posset tergiuersatione celari' (cf. above, n. 49).

[67] 'Nonnulli iniquitatis filii quos prorsus ignorant non modicam quantitatem lapidum... asportarunt', Nicholas IV was informed by the friars, *Sua nobis*, 5 Aug. 1288. They were committed to the care of the dean whose appeal against them was pending at the curia.

[68] *Chronicon de Cardeña* (above, n. 25), 375. The 'Memorias' of the monastery of Cardeña state that *all* the Burgos bridges were broken: F. de Berganza, *Antigüedades de España*, II (Madrid, 1721), p. 179. Cf. Jofré de Loaysa's lament on the state of Castile in 1295: 'Tunc, proh dolor! mercator vel alius quivis bonus per Castellam nullatenus discurrebat... et iam non parcebatur loco sacro, sexui nec etati vel ordini': *Crónica de los reyes de Castilla*, c. 67, ed. A. García Martínez (Murcia 1982). [69] AHN, 185/7: publ. Gaibrois, III, no. 508.

[70] *Reg. Nich. IV*, 884 (Ranuccio de Murro, later 'auditor litterarum contradictarum'), 5687 (Gulielmus Accursii the Younger, the canonist).

set upon them. This was a mistake, especially since (as Boniface VIII was later informed) it was only the timely intervention of Bishop Fernando that saved them from being drowned in the Arlanzón. In October 1295 the miscreants were summoned to Rome to explain themselves.[71] Whether it was for this or for some other reason, by November 1299 when the bishop died and the chapter attempted to elect a successor they were debarred from doing so because they were all excommunicated.[72] Small wonder then that they made so little headway with their litigation in these years. (And it was not only this. Their whole approach to the matter was unprofessional. When their proctor, Iohan Ferrandez, wrote to ask them to appoint Andreas de Sezze, one of the big names of the day, to assist him, they simply failed to reply because they couldn't bear the thought of the bill. Or so Iohan Ferrandez was led to believe.)[73]

Compare their opponents. The friars were altogether better organised. Having employed the services of a professional proctor in the mid-1270s, from July 1288 they were again represented at the curia by one of their own sort, fr. Miguel Pérez of Soria, whose movements we can trace from the annotations he made on the dorse of the papal privileges and rescripts he acquired.[74] This was the practice of the Italian houses, just as it had been that of the friars of S. Pablo in the 1260s when fr. Domingo had acted for them.[75] And it certainly had its advantages. Take the case of *Dum*

---

[71] *Reg. Bon. VIII*, 537, naming the other assailants as Miguel abbot of Salas de Los Infantes, Fernán Pérez abbot of S. Millán, and Domingo Gonzálvez the bishop's vicar. Pedro Sarracín was dead by now: Blanco Díez, 'Dignitarios eclesiásticos burgaleses', 454. Cf. *Reg. Nich. IV*, 6214.

[72] 'quia decanus et canonici supradicti ejusdem electionis tempore erant excommunicationis sententia innodati': *Reg. Bon. VIII*, 3616.

[73] Pereda Llarena, no. 276 (June 1292). At about this time Andreas was described by the proctor of the dean and chapter of Tudela as a 'mighty lion': P. Linehan, 'Spanish litigants and their agents at the thirteenth-century papal curia', S. Kuttner and K. Pennington, eds., *Proc. Fifth International Congress of Medieval Canon Law, 1976*, Vatican City, 1980, 500. For his Spanish practice, Linehan, 'Proctors', 113.

[74] 'Istud priuilegium mititur priori et conuentui f. p. Burgen. per fr. Michaelem Petri Sorien': AHN, 184/15 (Potthast, 22759). On 27 June 1291 he acquired an indulgence, *Splendor paterne*, for S. Pablo, together with an 'inspeximus' of it by Bishop William of Brechin which is endorsed: 'pro quo debet soluere conuentus dicto fratri duas duplas', and had it registered: AHN, 185/4, 5; *Reg. Nich. IV*, 5480. He also secured a parallel indulgence for the Burgos Franciscans (ibid., 5562–3). Férotin believed the 'Michael Petri ... Salama (*sic*) ... procurator' whose name occurs on a Silos privilege of 1297 to have been a monk of that house: *Rec. Silos*, 303. In 1276 'Waldinus' and 'N. Waldini' had acted for the houses of Burgos and Palma: Linehan, 'Proctors', nos. 745–7a.

[75] T. Masetti, *Monumenta et antiquitates veteris disciplinae Ordinis Predicatorum*, I (Rome, 1864), p. 269; above, p. 89.

sollicite, for example, Nicholas IV's general privilege which provided the Order's churches and oratories with special protection and exempted them from all other jurisdictions. The terms of *Dum sollicite* applied precisely to the situation at Burgos. Accordingly, Miguel Pérez not only secured a chancery exemplar in July 1288. Two years later he also had a copy of it authenticated by two peninsular prelates resident at the curia.[76] This was service. This was what proctors were for.

And S. Pablo appears not to have been the only Dominican house to have profited from Miguel Pérez's professionalism. It is probably no coincidence that the reversion to earlier practice was accompanied by a resumption of the flow of general privileges to other Spanish houses of the Order, a flow which had been interrupted since the early 1270s. The evidence of the Dominican collections in the Archivo Histórico Nacional (or rather the lack of it) strongly suggests that between the death of Clement IV in 1268 and that of Martin IV in 1285 the Spanish houses other than S. Pablo were virtually out of contact with the curia. It seems that, Burgos apart, the fifteen communities whose archives are preserved there possessed not a single original papal document from these years, either mandate or privilege.[77] There is no original of *Ad fructus uberes*, Martin IV's important privilege of January 1282, for example.[78] And despite the fact that other Spanish convents had acquired originals of Honorius IV's *Meritis vestre* of September 1285 and *Religionis favor* of January 1286, it was at Paris later that year and from the cardinal-legate John of S. Cecilia that the Burgos Dominicans obtained their copies.[79] A sense of isolation and vulnerability has to be allowed for in any estimate of their activities during the 1270s and eighties, the very

---

[76] AHN, 184/17 (Potthast, 22758), 184/18 (*vidimus* by Tello of Braga and Blasius of Segovia, April 1290). The fact that they had a third copy done for them (by Blasius and Suero of Cádiz at Palencia in June 1291: AHN, 185/1) indicates the importance they attached to *Dum sollicite*.

[77] The same is true of the convent of Caleruega between 1258 and 1283: E. Martínez, *Colección diplomática del real convento de S. Domingo de Caleruega* (Vergara, 1931), pp. 250, 347–9. And the impression is confirmed by the papal registers which contain only one letter implying an appeal to Rome by either of the mendicant orders (from the Zaragoza Franciscans in May 1278: Potthast, 21322), although friars continued to be appointed as judges delegate and executors: e.g. *Reg. Greg. X*, 80, 270, 295; *Reg. John XXI*, 53; *Reg. Nich. III*, 18, 441.

[78] Potthast, 21836. The Palma, Burgos and Benavente houses received copies made by Dominican cardinals in April 1282, May 1284 and Dec. 1284 respectively: AHN, 88/5, 184/12, 3524/4.

[79] AHN, 184/13, 14 ('apud Vallem Gerardi prope Parisius'). Cf. AHN, 594/20 (Zaragoza: Potthast, 22287); 1895/10, 3572/18 (Salamanca, Toro: Potthast, 22353). (Was the Burgos exemplar of *Ex parte vestra*, Nov. 1285 (above n. 64) theirs?)

years which witnessed the beginning of the 'great building period' of the mendicants, in war-torn Castile as elsewhere throughout Europe.[80] In such circumstances the favour and protection of the king were more than ever essential.

By the early 1290s, however, the road from Burgos to Rome was open again and the efficient fr. Miguel Pérez was busily occupied on the friars' behalf. Their prospects had never appeared rosier. The parsimonious canons were loth to spend real money on a proper proctor, and in 1299 they were all excommunicated anyway.

Yet within two years the position had been completely reversed. In April 1301 judgement was finally give *in re* the chapter's appeal against the dean of Segovia's sentence. The canons were vindicated. Master Huguitio de Vercellis, Boniface VIII's auditor, found in favour of the dean and chapter and awarded them costs. The archdeacon had been right to excommunicate the friars.[81] The implication was plain: the friars had been trespassers all along. For forty years they had shared in the benefits that successive popes had lavished upon their Order and had received every ounce of assistance that the Church could provide. But now they were adjudged to have been in the wrong. How is this to be explained?

No doubt the matter had been decided in strictest accordance with the rules of law and equity. Yet it is to be observed that the friars' reverse coincided both with the chaotic minority of Fernando IV, when for the first time in their history they were deprived of effective royal protection,[82] and with the pontificate of Boniface VIII. Boniface was determined to establish a relationship between the mendicants and the diocesan and parochial authorities which would respect the Church's structural integrity. That had been the purpose of *Super cathedram*, issued in February 1300, which constituted the mendicants' first reverse since 1254.[83] Furthermore, it might also be suspected that the

---

[80] Cf. A. G. Little, *Studies in English Franciscan history* (Manchester, 1917), pp. 72–5.

[81] Pereda Llarena, no. 356.

[82] It was not until July 1302 that Fernando confirmed his father's privilege of exemption in favour of the Burgos house: AHN, 185/9.

[83] T. S. R. Boase, *Boniface VIII* (London, 1933), pp. 191ff.; G. Le Bras, 'Boniface VIII symphoniste et modérateur', *Mélanges d'histoire du Moyen Age dédiés à la mémoire de L. Halphen* (Paris, 1951), pp. 391–2; T. M. Izbicki, 'The problem of canonical portion in the later Middle

pontiff regarded the Spanish Dominicans in general with some misgivings. The murky history, not to say the seamy story of Munio of Zamora, sometime Master-General of the Order, cannot have been far from his mind. Munio had died in Rome at Easter 1300.[84] Indubitably however, the decisive consideration was the influence exercised by the new bishop of Burgos, Pedro Rodríguez.

With Pedro Rodríguez (*alias* Petrus Hispanus) all things were possible. He it was who in 1300 persuaded the pope to allow the body of Cardinal Gonzalo Pérez (sometime bishop of Burgos) to be returned to Spain; no one else had dared to ask.[85] Pedro Rodríguez was *so* discreet; his discretion almost matched his effectiveness. Not even the king of Aragon's sharp-eyed agents could catch him out, or surprise him with his hand in the till. And he was loyal. Boniface's chaplain when Boniface was still plain Benedict Caetani, he alone was with him at the end as Philip the Fair's thugs closed in.[86] Although a native of Oviedo according to the author of the *Libro del Cavallero Zifar* (who was in a position to know), he was a canon of Burgos and his Burgos credentials were impeccable. For years he had held a watching brief for the church at the curia; he it was who had advised the exasperated capitular proctor in 1292.[87] Papal referendary from 1294, he was the canons' natural choice as successor to Bishop Fernando and when in June 1300 those of them who were at Anagni were consulted by the pope they reaffirmed their view and Boniface was pleased to approve his appointment.[88]

After the friars' reverse on the matter of trespass, the substantive issue remained to be settled. This was done at Burgos in February 1302. The record of the negotiations provides the earliest indication that we have of the extent of the friars' encroachments

---

Ages: the application of *Super cathedram'*, P. Linehan, ed., *Proceedings of the Seventh International Congress of Medieval Canon Law 1984* (Vatican City, 1988), pp. 459–61.

[84] Linehan, *Spanish Church*, pp. 224–9.

[85] 'Ninguno de los otros non lo osauan al Papa demandar': *El Libro del Cauallero Zifar*, ed. C. P. Wagner (Michigan, 1929), pp. 3–4. [86] Boase, *Boniface VIII*, pp. 346ff.

[87] Pereda Llarena, no. 276 (above, n. 73). Cf. F. J. Hernández, 'Ferrán Martínez, "escrivano del rey", canónigo de Toledo, y autor del "Libro de Cavallero Zifar"', *Revista de Archivos, Bibliotecas y Museos* 81 (1978), 289–325.

[88] *Reg. Bon. VIII*, 3616. Further information in D. Mansilla, 'El cardenal Petrus Hispanus, obispo de Burgos 1300–03', *Hispania Sacra* 9 (1957), 243–80; T. Schmidt, *Der Bonifaz-Prozeß* (Cologne, 1989), pp. 150–1. He was promoted cardinal bishop of Sabina in 1302.

over the previous forty years.[89] The chapter required the return of
the houses and land where the friars were currently established
together with the other property of the church of Burgos which
they had purchased or otherwise acquired 'in New Street', the
street where they lived, as far as the houses of Juan Marín.[90] In
exchange they were to receive the house currently occupied by
Domingo Gil, canon, and compensation to be agreed by four
extimatores, two from each side. The friars were to be allowed to
build out from Juan Marín's 'small houses' (does this mean
slums?) to the 'high houses'. But on no account were they to
colonise the area towards the houses which they were now to
surrender. Nor were they to interfere with the waterway by
ditching operations or by otherwise redirecting the flow. They
might expand towards San Lucas, but on no account were they to
interfere with the waterway.[91]

That was the essence of the matter. Subsidiary to it were
various issues: the disputed ownership of the houses and garden of
Ramón dictus de Sanchester; the friars' physical removal from
their present abode within fifteen months, taking their corpses
with them ('quod... corpora sepultorum et seipsos transferant');
the chapter's undertaking not to make any new dispositions 'in
dicto uico' nor to establish any other religious order or to
construct any parish, chapel or oratory there or thereby; and the
friars', not to seek to undermine the whole agreement with the

---

[89] The following details are taken from the papal confirmation of the agreement in June 1302
(Reg. Bon. VIII, 4676, but not published in the calendar): Archivio Segreto Vaticano, Reg. Vat.
50, fos. 193v–5r.
[90] 'solum et domos quas iidem predicatores nunc inhabitant et ortos et domos et solaria alia
eiusdem ecclesie Burgensis incensata que sunt in eodem uico ubi predicatores nunc
comorantur ... has domos ubi predicatores nunc comorantur et alias domos, ortos et solaria que
predicatores emerunt uel alias habuerunt seu habent in uico dicto nouo usque ad domos
Johannis Marini' (fo. 194r).
[91] 'Et quod fratres predicatores possint easdem domos dicti Johannis Marini paruas seu depressas
cum suis ortis usque ad domos altas exclusiuere (sic), quibus altis domibus sunt contigue dicte
domui parue que consistunt in dicti uici noui limitatione, quodque predicatores habeant istum
ortum quem eis decanus et capitulum dant cum istis paramentis seu conuenientiis, uidelicet
quod predicatores a dictis domibus paruis et orto eisdem domibus paruis contiguo quo usque
ad aquam protenditur ex parte posteriori uersus domos alias quas nunc inhabitant se nullatenus
possint extendere. Item quod predicatores non possint operari per se nec per alium super aquam
illam nec effodere eiusdem aque alueum neque eandem aquam de alueo ad se discurrere uel eam
seu eius cursum solitum aliquatenus impedire nec alueum transgredi facientes ibi opus aliquod
minimum siue grande. Item quod predicatores ista ut predictum est obseruantes quantum ad
aquam non impediendam et alia huius conueniencia, quod possint se extendere uersus Sanctum
Lucam...' (fo. 194r–v).

assistance of the king or the *concejo* or any other of their smart friends.[92] The text of the agreement was then returned to Anagni where on 23 May 1302 Bishop Pedro tightened it up: 'nos addimus *nec cum aliquo alio*', he emended the clause last mentioned (Bishop Pedro knew his Dominicans), and provided a fifth *extimator* of his own choosing (the papal referendary understood about packing committees).[93] And on 8 June Boniface VIII confirmed the settlement, thus bringing to an end the strife which had begun at the archdeacon of Valpuesta's deathbed in 1262. The bishop of Calahorra was appointed to preside over the final stages of thirteenth-century Burgos's Jarndyce and Jarndyce. As was appropriate, he took his time, allowing a further fourteen months to elapse before he did so.[94]

But even that was not the end of it. As in the novel there was a final twist.

For emboldened perhaps by Bishop Pedro's promotion to the cardinalate in 1302, possibly reassured by the Dominican pope Benedict XI's revocation of *Super cathedram* in February 1304, and certainly with the encouragement of the *concejo* which had first brought them to the banks of the Arlanzón, the friars were soon on the move again. The process began as early as March 1303.[95] And over the next six years they received (and exacted) further substantial grants of land in the vicinity of their new establishment. By July 1309 they were claiming that they were short of space and the *concejo* licensed them to expand their site as far as the river.[96]

[92] 'quod...non procurent per se nec per alium cum domino rege nec cum regina nec cum proceribus nec cum concilio Burgensi nec cum aliquo istorum aliquod in preiudicium nec in grauamen aliquod Burgensis ecclesie uel capituli eiusdem' (fo. 194v).

[93] 'ut huius extimatio comodius fiat nec possit propter ipsorum extimatorum discordiam impediri' (fo. 195r). [94] AHN, 185/12 (Oct. 1304).

[95] When they surrendered to the *concejo* 'la plaza...ante las casas que fueron de Matheo Perez despensero mayor del Rey que el rey D. Sancho nos dio para fazer la nuestra eglesia de Santo Domingo', receiving in exchange 'la plaza que es a la glera cerca del rio Arlançon entre san Lucas y el rio y las casas de Juan Mar[t]in'; also defined as 'la nuestra plaza de la glera que es entre el rio de Arlançon y el solar que pasa por el molino de Tendiello que uos nos diestes para fazer la iglesia de San Pablo que nos y queremos fazer et el monasterio que nos la diestes': AHN, 185/10, 11. Cf. Ruiz, *Sociedad y poder*, p. 108. Petrus Hispanus died in 1310. Benedict XI's revocation, *Inter cunctas* (Potthast, 25370), remained in force until 1312 (Conc. Vienne, c. 10).

[96] 'desde la pared de la iglesia hasta la otra pared nueua que es ffasta el rio Arlançon...desde la dicha pared que se tiene en el rio de Arlançon hasta la que auedes labrado o labrades deaqui adelante desde Sant Lucas hasta delante las dichas casas que fueron de Ferrant Gonzales': AHN, 185/14. In the previous month D. Claris Martinez *vecino* reported to the *alcalde* that in return

All of this of course was in breach of the terms of the recent
settlement and occasioned a further confrontation in March 1311,
with the chapter protesting that the construction of the friars' new
church was interfering with a water course which drove one of
their mills,[97] and the friars insisting that they were fully within
their rights.[98]

Battle lines seemed to be being drawn again, this time along the
sluices and ditches. But remarkably they were not. Though
Avignon was nearer than Italy, this time neither party rushed off
to the papal court. And even more remarkable was the dean and
chapter's magnanimity. By all means the friars might build
towards the river and complete the church that they had begun.[99]
Dean and chapter were prepared to go further. They would
relieve the friars of their old property 'que est in uico de Vega
prope ecclesiam Sanctorum Cosme et Damiani' which was now
'useless' to them.[100] All this dean and chapter were prepared to
do, as their part of the 'amicabilis composicio', in return for an
undertaking from the friars that (as well as mending the road)
they would not obstruct the waterways which crossed their land
en route to irrigating the canons' allotments and driving their

---

for receiving his former wife and three of his daughters into the Order, the prioress of
Caleruega had demanded 'una huerta con los ffalçes que a ella pertenecian ... en Burgos a Sant
Lucas de que della son aledaños': 185/15.

[97] AHN, 185/15: 'super eo quod dicti prior et conuentus inceperunt dilatare ecclesiam prope
domos ubi nunc habitant uersus fluuium de Arlançon et cementa lapidea et parietes construere
ad opus ecclesie supradicte, propter quod decanus et capitulum asserentes fieri illud opus in
preiudicium Burgensis ecclesie et in alueo per quod pars eiusdem fluuii consueuerat decurrere ad
quoddam molendinum quod inferius in eodem fluuio iam dudum habuerant et habere eciam
intendebant, et quia ut dicebatur fiebat illud opus in quadam structura lapidea prefate ecclesie
Burgensis *presa* uulgariter nuncupata que ad opus illius molendini in solo proprio ipsius ecclesie
constructa fuerat ab antiquo, et quod inde per illud opus destruebatur funditus presa illa et
inpediebatur perpetuo usus seu utilitas molendini predicti...'. (The burden of the chapter's
complaint is not entirely clear. 'Presa' means an irrigation ditch. Was it the chapter's ditch
which had stone foundations that the friars were interfering with? Or was it that the
foundations of the stone church which they were constructing was affecting their ditch?)

[98] 'quod in illo loco iuste et licite et sine preiudicio Burgensis ecclesie poterant suam ecclesiam
ampliare': ibid.

[99] 'Et uoluerunt et consenserunt quod prior et conuentus predicti libere edificent seu edificari
faciant suam ecclesiam in illo loco ubi eam ampliare et edificare inceperunt uersus fluuium de
Arlançon et perficere opus illud quod inceperunt': ibid.

[100] Ibid. The friars were allowed to remove their building materials ('lapides tantum, ligna et
tegulas ecclesie Sancti Pauli que sunt intus in orto illo'): an arrangement which echoed the
terms of the settlement between the Franciscans and the monks of Silos in 1302 ('omnes
lapides ... et calcem, arenam et bitumen et ligna'). Similarly, the Franciscans were made
responsible for mending the road: Férotin, *Rec. Silos*, 318.

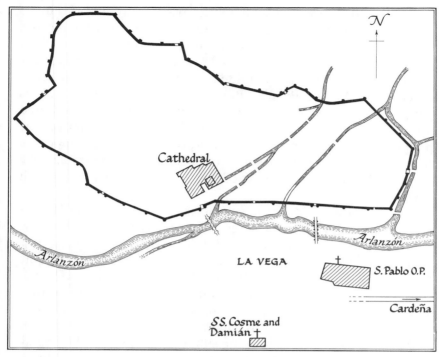

Burgos in the thirteenth century

mills.[101] In 1311 the chapter accepted the inevitable: provided the friars abided by the water rules they could have their church by the river. With the blessing of dean and chapter this time, the friars were back in the city.

The progress they had made from the suburbs over the previous eighty years had been remarkable. They were still outside the walls, they still hadn't breached the citadel. But in 1311 they were back 'in the city' (in the sense in which their presence there had been resented by the chapter in the 1260s). And just in time: in

---

[101] 'Et ultra septa monasterii suas domos et oficinas et alia sibi necessaria construere et parare ac perficere uiam publicam ante illud opus et superius et inferius sicut melius ecclesie Burgensi et suo monasterio viderint expedire, hoc saluo quod concursum cuiusdam aque que vulgariter dicitur *entrehijo* que de quodam refluuio ex alio latere defluenti a parte posteriori pro conseruacione ortorum et molendinorum ecclesie Burgensis uersus predictum fluuium de Arlançon consueuit decurrere tempore hyemali teneantur predicti prior et fratres recipere et illi concursui debitum locum dare': ibid.

1312 a royal minority began which was to prove even more anarchical than the last. Up to a point their progress parallels that of the North Italian mendicants whose movements have been described by Alexander Murray. 'The centre of gravity of our problem lies...not in the middle of the old town', Murray observes of Milan, Pistoia, Pisa and the rest, 'but round its periphery.'[102] There the various controversies that occurred involved cathedrals at the centre of the city and friars on the periphery. And so the contest in Burgos might at first appear, a contest between the canons in Santa María at the centre and the friars on the periphery, always edging in. But that was not how it really was.

For in relation to the centre, *everyone* who mattered in Burgos was on the edge. On the edge, by the river where the friars wanted to be and the chapter didn't want them. Burgos is a strange place where everything draws you to the river. Despite the competing attractions of the Plaza Mayor, its cafés and bazaars, in 1992 the river's attractions remain as powerful as they were in 1302 when the friars were shown the city gate and pointed out of town towards S. Lucas, *dirección* Cardeña. In 1302 the friars were being ushered out into the suburbs where friars belonged. But also they were being kept away from the river. This is understandable. In more senses than one the canons of Burgos depended for their livelihood on turning water into wine. They enjoyed the monopoly of the wine trade within the city, always had. And the river was the city's liveliest force. Whereas the canons, and even the friars, sometimes rested, the river never did. The mills which it drove provided Burgos with its engine, and the church was the city's major mill-owner.[103] The church was constantly complaining that the *concejo* was doing precisely what in 1302 the friars were enjoined not to do. They had complained most recently in 1295.[104] But it was not the church, nor was it the *concejo* that ruled medieval Burgos, it was the Arlanzón.

And if Burgos is a strange place (a sort of Spanish Rochester) it is also a threatening place, and a threatened one. It is threatened by

[102] 'Piety and impiety in medieval Italy', *Studies in Church History* 9 (1972), 84–6.
[103] See Ruiz, *Sociedad y poder real*, 8off. (mills), 103 (wine); H. Casado Alonso, *Señores, mercaderes y campesinos* (Valladolid, 1987), pp. 186–8.
[104] 'Las aguas, que non uan por o solien, e por esto que pierden e menoscaben mucho los herederos que an los molinos e los huertos': Pereda Llarena, no. 313 (II.36).

the presence of Santa María de Las Huelgas, the royal pantheon on the western outskirts concerning whose relationship with the city an altogether different piece might have been written. And throughout the thirteenth century it was undeniably a violent place. It was less violent at the end of it than it had been in its middle years however, and for that credit was principally due to Boniface VIII. It was Gabriel Le Bras' 'symphoniste et modérateur' whom Burgos had to thank for the unfamiliar peace that descended upon the city in 1302. In 1302 not only were the Dominicans quiescent for the time being. In the previous August the pope had also called halt to the long-running conflict between the local Franciscans and the Black Monks of Silos, and in the May of that year their differences were settled in that sanctuary of calm, the cathedral cloister. As in the case of the Dominicans, the verdict went against the mendicants and they were sent trudging down the road with their wheelbarrows of stones, sand, wood, bitumen and cement.[105] Finally, in September, Pedro Bonifaz (a relative of the Dominicanising dean) came forward and admitted responsibility for the recent sacking of the bishop's palace.[106]

So the canons could settle down again. Even read. And how better to end an essay for Christopher Brooke than in the peaceful company of canons reading in their houses by the river? Ideally of course they would be slumbering in their armchairs with Jane Austen rather than following the adventures of the *Caballero Zifar*. But never mind, there were always those rather interesting-looking legal and theological volumes on the shelf to be dipped into. Their wills describe the extent of the canons' little libraries.[107]

As they made their wills, with half an eye on the river hurrying by, they had other things to think about than books of course. In 1275 the dean, Martín Gómez, disappointed at Burgos, had moved to the see of Sigüenza. As dean, Martín Gómez seems to have been no great friend of the friars. At Sigüenza, however, he established a *hermandad* with them.[108] In the same year, 1277, Pedro Pascual prepared himself for the inevitable. It proved a lengthy business. The archdeacon of Burgos had been an archdeacon about town for many years, and the arrangements he

[105] *Reg. Bon. VIII*, 4112–13; Férotin, 315–19.   [106] Pereda Llarena, no. 372.
[107] That of García de Campo (1267 × 1274), cantor, is particularly interesting in this connection, giving very much the impression of a gentlemen accustomed to deep armchairs: ibid., no. 126.   [108] Minguella, *Hist. de Sigüenza*, 1.622.

made before his death acknowledged the multitude of obligations he had contracted. Unlike Juan Tomé, Pedro Pascual was a good chapter man. He had invested wisely. He had built houses on the chapter's lands, and these improvements he bequeathed to the chapter.[109]

In his will he settled his principal scores. The bequests he made were on the low side, pittances mostly of between fifteen and thirty maravedís. Pedro Pascual had been no friend of the friars either. Indeed just five years earlier the friars had identified him as one of their chief persecutors.[110] Yet amongst his beneficiaries there they were, the Burgos Dominicans.[111] In view of all that had gone before it may seem a quixotic gesture. But was it? We have already caught Pedro Pascual in the act of confirming for the friars the text of a papal privilege potentially prejudicial to the interests of his church.[112] Evidently the archdeacon of Burgos was capable of distinguishing corporate interests from personal salvation. Perhaps that ordinarily calculating man had got his last calculation just right then. Perhaps he had remembered in time that the two cities that mattered were not the two which in his lifetime the canons and friars of Burgos had made out of one, but the two which almost a thousand years before had been dimly perceived by a bishop even more renowned than the referendary of Pope Boniface VIII. Perhaps.

[109] Pereda Llarena, no. 143.
[111] 'E a los Predicadores, XV maravedis': ibid., no. 142.
[110] Above, p. 93.
[112] Above, p. 89.

From privilege to persecution: crown, church and synagogue in the city of Majorca, 1229–1343

DAVID ABULAFIA

In the cities of Spain, southern France and most of the Mediterranean islands that fell under Latin rule by about 1350 churches were not the only place of worship, and sizeable communities of Jews and on occasion Muslims required and obtained the right to conduct their own religious services in their own buildings. Toledo was perhaps exceptional in possessing at least ten synagogues by the middle of the fourteenth century, one of which was brand new; there were also several smaller study centres that were used for prayer.[1] A walled *judería* developed by the same period, but (as in other parts of the Mediterranean) the Jewish quarter had earlier been defined by the preference of the Jews to reside fairly close together, rather than by compulsion. In Erice (Monte San Giuliano) in Sicily the Jews lived intermingled with the Christians at the start of the fourteenth century, and a *Giudecca* probably came into existence only in the late fourteenth century. In Palermo, on the other hand, a predominantly Jewish quarter can be traced back to Norman times. In northern Europe, Jewish quarters were already being contained within walls by 1084, to judge from the example of Speyer. Here the Jews were being offered special protection by the bishop, who apparently shared their fears for safety at a time of growing hostility to the Jews of *Ashkenaz* (Germany). The precocity of this development reflects the more embattled position of the north European Jews from a much earlier time.

There was, none the less, a broad trend. Jews were gathered into defined areas of the city partly to protect them from

---

[1] F. Cantera Burgos, *Sinagogas de Toledo, Segovia y Córdoba* (Madrid, 1973), pp. 17–32.

Christian hostility, and partly because of fears that they would 'contaminate' the Christian population with their unbelief. The appearance of Jewish quarters in which only Jews may live (i.e. ghettos) is thus an interesting barometer of changing attitudes to the Jews among those possessing power over them, and also among the local Christian population. Needing security, the Jews did not necessarily resent the command to gather together, so long as they were provided with suitable facilities; what was worst about the ghettos of sixteenth-century Venice and Rome was the appalling overcrowding, but this had not always been the case in earlier times. In the newly conquered territories like medieval Majorca, the Jews may well have received an especially spacious and fairly empty area of the capital city.

What is offered here is an examination of one case where Jews were guaranteed their rights of freedom to practise their religion, but at the same time were constrained within a prescribed inner-city territory: Ciutat de Mallorca, the modern Palma, in the period from 1229, when the Catalans occupied the city, to 1435, when the Jews converted *en masse* to Catholicism. Emphasis will be placed on the period from 1276 to 1343 when (with a notable interruption during the War of the Sicilian Vespers) an autonomous kingdom of Majorca controlled the Balearic islands as well as Roussillon, Cerdagne and Montpellier on the mainland. There are a number of instructive features of the Majorcan evidence. In the first place, this was a frontier territory, an area of new settlement by the Catalans, seized from Islam, to which the Christian conquerors welcomed Jewish settlers too (but not Muslims). The conquerors valued the Jewish presence, more, it seems clear, for financial reasons that out of a spirit of *convivencia*. In the second place, the privileged position of the Jews shows striking analogies to that of other communities in Majorca and elsewhere, notably the Genoese and the Pisans.

Another good reason for singling out this community is the coherent nature of the surviving evidence. One hundred and thirteen documents containing privileges for the Majorcan Jews have been preserved in a single manuscript, the *Codice Pueyo*, and have been edited by Spanish scholars.[2] This manuscript was

---

[2] F. Fita, 'Privilegios de los Hebreos mallorquines en el Códice Pueyo', scattered throughout *Boletín de la Real Academia de la Historia* 36 (1900).

compiled between 1328 and 1387 by notaries of the kingdom of Majorca, but the earliest document it contains dates back much further, to 1247. Additional privileges, court decisions and royal mandates have also been brought to light by Yitzhak Baer, the great historian of Spanish Jewry,[3] and by Jean Régné.[4] The work of Régné focused on the Jews of Catalonia–Aragon, but he discovered a mass of material in the Barcelona archives referring to Majorca during the period from 1285 to 1298 when it was ruled by the kings of Aragon. Finally, Antonio Pons Pastor published a large selection of documents from the Majorcan archives in an eclectic series of studies of the medieval Majorcan Jews.[5] And yet, despite the good quantity and quality of the evidence, Majorca's medieval Jews have not received as much attention as their modern Christian descendants, whose separate identity even after conversion has justifiably excited much interest.[6] The Jews of medieval Majorca are mainly remembered for their important contribution to medieval cartography.[7]

The existence in the Balearics not merely of an old Jewish community but of new settlement after 1229 is striking. In fact, the Jews had welcomed James I to the city of Majorca, probably out of impatience at the ungenerous attitude of the Almohads to non–Muslims. Catalan Jewish financiers had apparently given some help to the conquering army, and it is not surprising that privileges to the Jews rapidly followed the conquest; these privileges were extended to north African Jews as well, such as

[3] F. (later known as Y.) Baer, *Die Juden im Christlichen Spanien. Erster Teil: Urkunden und Regesten*, 1. *Aragonien und Navarra* (Berlin, 1929; repr. with additional material by H. Beinart, Farnborough, 1970).
[4] J. Régné, *History of the Jews in Aragon. Regesta and Documents*, ed. Y. T. Assis from the original publication in separate parts of the *Revue des Etudes juives* (Hispania Judaica, 1, Jerusalem, 1986).
[5] A. Pons, *Los Judíos de Mallorca durante los siglos XIII y XIV*, 2 vols. (Palma de Mallorca, 1957–60); the older work of A. L. Isaacs, *The Jews of Majorca* (London, 1936; Catalan translation as *Els jueus de Mallorca*, Palma de Mallorca, 1986) has a useful register of documents, though the text is very dated. References here are to the page number of the English edition of Isaacs and to the document number shared by the English and the Catalan editions.
[6] Further evidence is to be found in R. Soto Company, 'La aljama judaica de Ciutat en el siglo XIII (época de Jaime I)', *Boletín de la Sociedad arqueológica Lulliana* 36 (1978), 145–84; I am advised by Dr Larry Simon that Soto's transcriptions are at fault; cf. L. Simon, 'Society and religion in the kingdom of Majorca' (unpublished Ph.D. Thesis, University of California, Los Angeles), pp. 205–97.
[7] There is a vast technical literature here; for the context, see F. Fernández-Armesto, *Before Columbus: exploration and colonisation from the Mediterranean to the Atlantic, 1229–1492* (London, 1987).

Salomon ben Ammar of Sijilmasa, the important staging post on the gold routes to Black Africa.[8] In fact, Majorca became something of a haven for foreign Jews, and on one occasion the Jews asked the king to expel some new arrivals who were deemed to be of bad character.[9] Jews in Majorca were certainly closely involved in trade with North Africa, and as at Palermo and elsewhere they played a major part in the slave trade too. Jews might even sell slaves to the king, as a case from 1289 reveals.[10] In July of the same year a Jew petitioned the *baile* of Majorca concerning the seizure of his goods aboard a Christian-operated Majorcan ship *in parte de Tenez*, that is, near Ténès in modern Algeria.[11] Later, in 1326, Jews were to be accused of complicity in the contraband trade to Tlemcen and Mostagem in the same region, at a time when commercial relations with parts of north Africa were officially frozen.[12] Cultural links to the Maghrib appear to have remained strong, while the flight of refugee scholars such as Shimeon ben Zemah Duran to Africa in the late fourteenth century suggests that, under threat of persecution, the African links provided an important lifeline. Many of the leading Jews of Majorca had Arabic surnames; this was not, of course, unusual among Spanish Jews, but it is likely that the Majorcan Jews retained their use of Arabic alongside Catalan and of course Hebrew.

In contrast to the welcome given to the Jews under James I, the Muslims of Majorca were seen as a threat to the new order. The political (as opposed to merely cultural) links of the Majorcan Muslims to the Maghrib raised the possibility that they could form a fifth column on the island, if the ruler of Tunis were to invade. Some Majorcan Muslims were already enslaved in 1229;

---

[8] Pons, II.203, doc. 2; Fita, 'Privilegios', 482–3, no. 110; Isaacs, 225, doc. 2.
[9] Isaacs, 240, doc. 82.
[10] Régné, 354–5, no. 1996; Isaacs, 235, doc. 55.
[11] Baer, 146–7, no. 130; Isaacs, 235, doc. 54. The document does not concern Tunis, as Baer and Isaacs assumed. Majorcan trade with Ténès was already established at this date, as is revealed by a register of licences for ships and sailors leaving Majorca in 1284: David Abulafia, 'Les Llicències per a barques et la commerce de Majorque en 1284', *Les Catalans et la Mer. Mélanges C.-E. Dufourcq*, ed. H. Bresc (Paris, in press); A. Riera, 'La *Llicència per a barques* de 1284. Una font important per a l'estudi del commerç exterior mallorquí del darrer quart del segle XIII', *Faventia*, 2 (1980), 53–73, published also in *Fontes Rerum Balearium*, 3 (1979–80) 121–40; Palma de Mallorca, Arxiu del Regne de Mallorca, RP 1105/1, *Libro de licencias para barcas*.
[12] Fita, 'Privilegios', 187–91, nos. 39–40; Isaacs, 246, docs. 114–15.

nearly all the Minorcan Muslims were enslaved in 1287, but a free Saracen population persisted on Majorca, consisting of artisans, shopkeepers and a few privileged farmers.[13] They had no *aljama* or community organisation that was recognised by the Crown, though they apparently had mosques. Those who were free were free in a hazardous way; they were unattached, unprotected, living almost in a state of vacuum; they paid a poll-tax as individuals, but they had no obvious means to make their grievances felt at court. Their status was thus very different from that of *mudéjares* in Valencia in the same period.[14] Indeed, the denial of *mudéjar* status reached its fullest affirmation in the mass enslavement of the Minorcans.[15]

What distinguished the Jews from the Muslims was the existence of a Jewish *aljama*. The Jews collected their own taxes, which, as elsewhere, were compounded by the whole community; as at Barcelona, they were administered by a board of four elected Jewish secretaries; they maintained their own archives, and marriage contracts and wills were to be valid even when drawn up in Hebrew and Aramaic, as a privilege of 1252 made clear. The dowry contracts of the Jews were in fact to have identical force to notarised Christian acts.[16] In 1278 James II of Majorca reiterated the statement that contracts *in littera hebraica* were to be valid when drawn up before Jewish witnesses; that is, Jewish marriage law was to be binding in the instance of Jewish

---

[13] E. Lourie, 'Free Moslems in the Balearics under Christian rule in the thirteenth century,' *Speculum* 45 (1970), 624–49; repr. in E. Lourie, *Crusade and colonisation. Muslims, Christians and Jews in medieval Aragon* (Aldershot, 1990), essay VI. Other studies of the Majorca Muslims include R. Soto Company, 'La población musulmana de Mallorca bajo el dominio cristiano (1240–76)', *Fontes Rerum Balearium* (Palma de Mallorca, 1978–80), II.65–80, II.549–64, and the same author's study (which I have not seen) 'Sobre mudèixars a Mallorca fins a finals del segle XIII', *Estudis d'història de Mayurqa i d'història de Mallorca dedicats a Guillem Rosselló i Bordoy* (Palma de Mallorca, 1982), pp. 195–221.

[14] Robert I. Burns, 'Muslims in the thirteenth-century realms of Aragon: interaction and reaction', in *Muslims under Latin rule 1100–1300*, ed. James M. Powell (Princeton, NJ, 1990), pp. 57–102.

[15] E. Lourie, 'Anatomy of ambivalence: Muslims under the crown of Aragon in the late thirteenth century,' in Lourie, *Crusade and colonisation*, essay VII, 2–6. This volume is mainly a collection of reprinted articles; the article cited here is published for the first time.

[16] J. L. Villanueva, *Viage literario a las Iglesias de España*, tomos XXI–XXII, (Madrid, 1851–2), XII, *Viage a Mallorca*, XXII, p. 331; summary only in Fita, 'Privilegios', 20, no. 3; Isaacs, 226–7, 229, docs. 7, 21; the reference by Isaacs to contracts in Hebrew is the result of confusion (apparently as far back as 1252) at the use of Hebrew script for Aramaic *ketubot* or marriage contracts, and the text mentions *carta ebraica* and *instrumenta vestra judaica*. Cf. Pons, II.207–8, doc. 8, of 1278, confirming this right.

marriages.[17] Not surprisingly there were Jewish cemeteries, though one was lost in the early fourteenth century when King Sancho, who had grand schemes to build a powerful navy, turned it into a shipyard.[18]

The right to live under Jewish law was an early, and fundamental, concession, matching contemporary practice in areas of the Mediterranean where there existed substantial Jewish or Muslim communities. In 1250 James I confirmed that Jews could settle their own differences among themselves, but insisted that especially grave crimes must be brought to the royal courts; this accords with a wider tendency at this period (for instance, in the Sicily of Frederick II) to insist on the authority of royal courts in such cases as capital crimes.[19] The decree is also reminiscent of the privileges accorded to Italian and Catalan merchants in the Mediterranean, guaranteeing their rights of separate jurisdiction in such places as Acre, Tunis and indeed the City of Majorca itself, where the Genoese had a loggia that was frequented by Italians and by Jews in search of business and of banter about the relative merits of Judaism and Christianity.[20] When Christians brought cases against Jews, there must be Jewish as well as Christian witnesses.[21] This provision was made in 1250 but confirmed after only two years, with particular reference to cases concerning debts to Jews; this suggests that there was some tension between Jews and Christians over the problem.[22] By special royal grace, Muslim slaves were forbidden in 1269 from giving evidence against Jews.[23] Some would have been slaves of the Jews, and the Jews were apparently worried at the danger of vexatious attacks from people who were looking for a chance to cast off their

[17] Fita, 'Privilegios', 27–8, no. 11; Isaacs, 229, doc. 21.

[18] Villanueva, XXII, 330–1; Fita, 'Privilegios', 20, no. 3 (summary); Isaacs, 226–7, doc. 7; Fernández-Armesto, 26.

[19] Villanueva, XXII, 328–30 (not 301 as Isaacs indicates); Isaacs, 226, doc. 5; a case of adultery was brought to the attention of the *baile* in 1314: Pons, II.237, doc. 49.

[20] Fernández-Armesto, 22–3, for the rights of the Genoese; the text of the interesting debate between Majorcan Jews and the Genoese Ingheto Gontardo at the loggia of Majorca City in 1286 is being edited by Dr O. Limor for the Monumenta Germaniae Historica.

[21] Villanueva, XXII, 328–30 (not 301, as Isaacs indicates); Isaacs, 226, doc. 5.

[22] Fita, 'Privilegios', 20–1, no. 4; Isaacs, 227, doc. 8. But in 1269 the king confirmed that the provision applied to all types of civil and criminal charges, not specifically debts: Fita, 'Privilegios', 24, no. 8.

[23] Fita, 'Privilegios', 24, no. 8; Isaacs, 227, doc. 12. See also Pons, II.204–6, docs. 4–5.

shackles.[24] In fact, the slave trade was protected by special tax exemptions for Jewish slave dealers.[25]

Another similarity with the privileges obtained by communities of foreign merchants in Mediterranean ports was that weights and measures were controlled by the *aljama*, as a result of a privilege of Alfonso III of Aragon issued soon after the re-occupation of Majorca by the Aragonese in 1285.[26] In effect this meant that the *aljama* could levy its own taxes on merchandise brought in and out of the Jewish quarter and on sales of goods within the quarter. King Alfonso extended this right to include exemption from trade taxes on Jews of Majorca who traded anywhere in the Aragonese realms.[27] It was an opportunity to celebrate the reincorporation of Majorca into the Aragonese realm and the suppression of the all-too independent Catalan kingdom of Majorca, by bonding the inhabitants of the Balearics to the mainland Aragonese territories from which they had been isolated for several years.[28] Alfonso's warm-hearted approach to the Jews of Majorca was no doubt prompted in part by the awareness that they might help him out of growing financial difficulties.[29] In 1286, he tried to squeeze 10,000 solidi from the *aljama* of Majorca, but 100,000 from the entire city of Majorca. The money was needed for supplies of wheat and barley.[30] Yet it was the same king who created the reserved area, the Call, in which the Jews of Majorca City were required to live.

The transfer of the Jews from the shadow of the Almudaina Palace, where most had lived since the conquest, to the south-east of the old city may simply reflect the need for more space; it also in a sense reflects the increase in privileges for the Majorcan Jews, some of which, such as the right to use their own weights and measures, might be said to be conditional on the existence of a

[24] Fita, 'Privilegios', 24, no. 8 appears to Isaacs, 227, doc. 12, to speak of slaves owned communally by the *aljama*; but the wording seems unambiguous: *captivus vel captiva alicujus judei vel judee aljame predicte*. Most likely this means 'male or female slave of any Jew or Jewess of the said *aljama*'.   [25] Isaacs, 226–7, 230, docs. 4, 12, 27.

[26] Régné, no. 1479 (summary) and 438–9, doc. 20 (full text); Isaacs, 230–1, doc. 27.

[27] Régné, 438–9, doc. 20, and Régné, no. 1481; Isaacs, 230–1, docs. 27, 29.

[28] Abulafia, 'Les *Llicències per a barques* et le commerce de Majorque en 1284', indicates that there was very little direct commercial contact between Majorca and Catalonia in early 1284, when Peter of Aragon and James II of Majorca were taking opposite sides in the Vespers conflict.

[29] See Isaacs, 230–7, docs. 24–68, for a handlist of acts of Alfonso concerning the Jews of the City of Majorca.   [30] Régné, nos. 1595, 1611, 1624; Isaacs, 232, docs. 35–7.

coherent territory in which they could be applied. The exercise of justice by Jewish officials was easier to achieve if there were no non-Jewish neighbours with whom to enter into property or other disputes. James I had already forbidden Jews and Christians to live in the same houses or share the same front door, though he permitted Jews to buy houses from Christians in Majorca City.[31] It was common, too, for Italians and other merchant communities in the Mediterranean to be assigned prescribed areas under their jurisdiction, as at Acre; though the requirement actually to reside in their quarter was not necessarily made explicit.

Early in 1286 Alfonso III issued a privilege to the city of Majorca (and not, in fact, to the Jews) indicating that he wished the Jews to foregather on a specially assigned site in the city, within the next five years. He promised that the Jews would be allowed their own kosher butcher's shop.[32] This part of the privilege can be read as an improvement on the position established by James I in 1273, which was that the Jews were to follow their own rituals in slaughtering animals, but were to arrange for the sale of the meat in Christian butcher's shops.[33] In fact, James I's privilege may have been the more generous, since it enabled Jews to dispose directly to Christians of certain parts of the carcass which Jewish law did not permit to be eaten, or of carcasses that were found to contain certain lesions that prohibited their consumption by Jews.[34] Thus the appearance of a special kosher meat shop was a further stage in the disentanglement of Jews and Christians in Majorca City.

What is visible, then, is a steady process of dissociation of the Jews from the Christian community in Majorca City. Thus the king issued orders in 1288 that Jews should not be obliged by the city administration to contribute to taxes and other royal or municipal levies; the Jewish *aljama* would always be assessed separately. It was the Majorcan Jews who brought this to the king's attention, for fear that they would find themselves liable to

---

[31] Régné, no. 562; Isaacs, 229, doc. 18.   [32] Régné, no. 1483; Isaacs, 231, doc. 31.
[33] Régné, no. 561–2; Fita, 'Privilegios', 26–7, no. 10; Isaacs, 228–9, doc. 17–18.
[34] In Spain, Jewish butcher's shops were generally separate, but this was less often the case in Germany. Some differences between the legal rulings of Sephardi (Spanish) and Ashkenazi (German) rabbis on the fitness for consumption of slaughtered animals may be attributable to this difference; once again, the Sephardim were less strict here than the generally rigorous Ashkenazim: H. J. Zimmels, *Ashkenazim and Sephardim* (London, 1958), pp. 200–1.

double taxation.[35] In 1289 Alfonso ordered the Jews of Majorca to pay taxes to the royal treasurer, Dalmau Suyner.[36] The crown was seeking to exploit Jewish resources, in the awareness that the Jews were themselves a royal possession. Competition from (say) the city government in Majorca in taxation of the Jews was not tolerable.

The aim of transferring the Jews to a defined zone was not forgotten. In late 1290, there were consultations between the king's representative in Majorca, the *baile* Pere de Libian, and prominent Jews.[37] Both the city administration and the Jews of Majorca sent agents to Barcelona to petition the king about the proposed transfer, but the king was too busy to give much thought to the affair.[38] In early December the king confirmed the decision of his *baile* that the Temple and Calatrava areas of the city, in the south-east of the town, were to be enclosed as a Jewish quarter. It is noticeable that Pere de Libian is said to have consulted the consuls and leading men of the city about the choice of a site, which was made *concilio et voluntate non solum dictorum consulum et proborum hominum, immo tocius universitatis Maiorice.*[39]

The king did, nevertheless, show understanding of the special needs of the Majorcan Jews. He stated that the community could build a synagogue, at a time when church policy greatly discouraged new synagogues; the point was, quite simply, that they needed one: *eam habere debent.*[40] A bake-house was also permitted the Jews; this was a right often granted to Italian merchants in their trading colonies, but it had special significance for the Jews, above all at Passover. The rationale cited by the king was not Jewish ritual requirements but the lack of need for them to send for bread outside their quarter. Alfonso may have seen this as another way to reduce undesirable association between Jews and non-Jews in the city. However, he still insisted that the bread tax (*panegia*) should be levied as elsewhere in the city.[41] Later, in 1294, James II of Aragon gave special permission to Juceff ben Salamon Coffe to build a bakery in the Jewish quarter, against a

[35] Régné, no. 1915; Isaacs, 234–5, doc. 52; cf. the earlier privilege of 1254: Pons, ii.204, doc. 3.
[36] Régné, no. 2044; Isaacs, 235, doc. 56.   [37] Régné, nos. 2252; Isaacs, 236, doc. 61.
[38] Régné, nos. 2254; Isaacs, 236, doc. 62.
[39] Régné, nos. 2267–8 (summaries) and 440–1, doc. 22 (full text of no. 2267); Isaacs, 236–7, docs. 63–4.   [40] Régné, no. 2267; Isaacs, 237, doc. 63.
[41] Régné, 441, doc. 22; cf. Régné, no. 2271 and Isaacs, 237, doc. 67.

weighty annual rent of ten gold morabetini; this was to be the sole bakery in the area.[42]

The whole quarter was to be enclosed by a wall, with gates and doors. The intention was to create what Alfonso called a *callem unicum*. This term was translated by Régné to mean 'une rue unique';[43] but the charter of 1290 is clearly speaking of something more substantial, incorporating a substantial network of streets either side of the modern Calle de Montesion; in Barcelona too the term evidently means more than one street.[44] As a matter of fact, the term *rua* or *ruga* was used in merchant settlements such as Acre and Messina to mean not just a street but a whole quarter. There are several possible explanations of the origin of the term Call, notably the reading of Call as *Calle*, 'Street'. But *Calle* is not a Catalan term; it arrived in the Catalan-speaking lands from Castile after the medieval period, and is unlikely to have given rise to the usage 'Call'. Even so, a particular *Calle* in modern Palma deserves attention in this context. The Calle de la Platería in Palma de Mallorca was in modern times the street par excellence of the gold and silversmiths of Jewish descent, the so-called *Xuetas* or *Chuetas*; it lies on the north side of the church of Santa Eulalia, where a mass conversion of Jews took place in 1435. The Platería is divided from the area of the original Call by the church and its Plaza, from which access can be gained to the western end of the old Call, and thence to a modern street called 'Call'; but the Platería was never part of the Jewish settlement.[45] The *Chuetas* were talked of until recent times as 'those of the Street', but what was intended by this term was not the Call but the Calle de la Platería. Almost certainly, the term 'those of the Street' has no connection with the term 'Call'. 'Call' is most likely derived from the Hebrew *qahal*, 'community', and thus means not a single street but the area in which the Jewish community of Majorca City, or, *pari passu*, Barcelona, lived. What is interesting

[42] Isaacs, 238, doc. 72.
[43] Régné, no. 2268; cf. Isaacs, 237, doc. 67, with 'single street', where Régné, no. 2271, has 'call unique'.
[44] E. Lourie, 'A plot which failed? The case of the corpse found in the Jewish Call of Barcelona (1301)', *Mediterranean Historical Review* I (1986), 209, repr. in Lourie, *Crusade and Colonisation*, essay X.
[45] However, the parish of Santa Eulalia technically included part of the Call: Pons, II.214, doc. 16.

is that the use of *callis* seems to be confined to the physical area of the Jewish quarter; the word used for community in the sense of an organised body of people was still *aljama*. The *aljama* was the commune or *universitas* of the Jews of Majorca; the Call was their place of habitation.

King Alfonso wished all Jews to gather there: *quod omnes Judei Majorice habitarent simul in aliqua partita dicta civitatis, ubi facerent callem vestram.*[46] For the privilege of being grouped together, the Jews of Majorca were to pay 12,000 solidi, and those who refused to pay were to be coerced.[47] While the Almudaina district had merely been the focus of Jewish settlement, the Call was to be the home of all the Jews of Ciutat de Mallorca;[48] James II of Majorca was irritated that as late as May 1303 there were still Jews living outside the Call, and issued orders to his lieutenant in Majorca that *non permitatis nec sustineatis, quod aliqui judei stent extra dictum callem, maneant nec morentur.*[49] Pleas of poverty on the part of Jews who could not afford to move to the Call were ignored, but Jews not yet living in the Call were permitted to maintain workshops and to put goods on sale outside the Call.[50] Eventually, in 1320, the bishop complained against this and it seems the permission was revoked.[51] Later, the Jews of the small town of Inca were to experience the same process of separation from the surrounding Christians, as part of a slow but steady tendency to force Jews to live apart.[52]

Having arrived in the Call, the Jews not surprisingly decided that it would be an even worse imposition were they to be forced to move yet again. Soon after the return of James II of Majorca to the Balearics, the restored king promised the Jews that they could remain in perpetuity in the Call. The Jews had already begun to build houses in the area, and they seem to have been worried that space for further building would soon run out. They were therefore to be permitted to encroach on adjoining land, close to the Templar buildings in the far corner of the city: *in locis dicto callo contiguis, et versus dictam domum Templi.*[53] The Jews had begun to build a synagogue, and this had been done with the approval of

[46] Régné, 440, doc. 22.   [47] Régné, nos. 2269–70; Isaacs, 237, docs. 65–6.
[48] Isaacs, 231, doc. 31; Régné, no. 1483; cf. Isaacs, 236–7, no. 63 and Régné, no. 2267.
[49] Pons, II.215, doc. 17.   [50] Pons, II.216–17, doc. 19.   [51] Pons, II.248, doc. 60.
[52] Isaacs, 252, doc. 147; Pons, I.33–42.
[53] Villanueva, XXII, 332–3; Fita, 'Privilegios', 31, no. 14 (summary); Isaacs, 240, no. 78.

the bishop of Majorca; this too could be finished.[54] Worries at a
possible move persisted, and King Sancho (1311–24) again
confirmed that the Call would not be disbanded, either by
expelling the Jews *à la française* or by requiring the Jews to transfer
elsewhere within the city. In the wake of Philip the Fair's
expulsion of the Jews in 1306, the Majorcan Jews, and still more
their brethren in Roussillon, subjects of the Majorcan monarchy,
valde erant timidi et stupefacti.[55] In fact, the Jews of Montpellier,
most of which was held by the king of Majorca from the king of
France, were forced to leave in 1306, and many from there and
elsewhere came as refugees to Majorcan Roussillon, so the realm
of Majorca was not untouched by the French persecutions.

Yet the Call both protected and restricted the Jews. Christian
women were to be chaperoned if they entered the area; but such
rules were perhaps as pleasing to the rabbis as to the churchmen,
who would share a fear that immoral associations might be
formed.[56] In 1296 James II of Aragon decreed that the Lieutenant
of the king in Majorca would have to give special permission
before preachers could enter the Call. Even those who were
allowed to preach could only be accompanied by ten people;
there were to be no large crowds baying at the Jews and
demanding their conversion.[57] When James II of Majorca reissued
these provisions, he also put to an end the practice whereby priests
entered the Call on Easter Saturday and sprinkled Jewish houses
with holy water, in return for which they expected gifts of eggs.
As the king pointed out, this meant nothing to the Jews.[58] The
Jews were not to be forced to go out of the Call to hear sermons.
There were even important limitations on conversions: minors
were not to be baptised, and teenagers were given several days to
think over what they were planning to do before going to the
font.[59]

[54] Pons, II.213–14, doc. 15; Villanueva, XXII, 332; Isaacs, 240, doc. 78, has 'synagogues', but the privilege appears only to refer to a single 'sinagoga in dicto callo'.
[55] Villanueva, XXII, 333–4; Fita, 'Privilegios', 123, no. 17 (summary); Isaacs, 242, doc. 90, (of 1311) for the fears arising from the French expulsion; Fita, 'Privilegios', 131–2, no. 23; Isaacs, 243, doc. 96, for the promise to let the Jews stay put (1318).
[56] Cf. the prohibition in Barcelona in 1319: Lourie, 'A plot which failed?' 209.
[57] Isaacs, 239, doc. 75.
[58] F. Fita, 'Los Judíos mallorquines y el Concilio de Viena,' *Boletín de la Real Academia de la Historia* 36 (1900), 241–2, no. 3; Pons, II.227, doc. 25; Isaacs, 241, doc. 87.
[59] Isaacs, 241, docs. 85–6.

From privilege to persecution

Guarantees for the Jews were dependent on royal goodwill, of course. The relationship between Jews and Christians declined sharply early in the fourteenth century. The Jews of Roussillon and Majorca may have escaped from the fate of the French Jews, but it was clear that anti-Jewish factions were emerging and that they were beginning to influence the Majorcan monarchy. In 1309 a priest named Galceron began to spread rumours that the Jews had put to death a Christian child, and these rumours were firmly suppressed by the crown and indeed the bishop, who was requested to deal toughly with Galceron.[60] He was to be punished in such a way that anyone who thought of repeating such accusations would be struck with terror.[61] More problematic was the case a couple of years later of two German Christians who came to the island and converted to Judaism. In 1315, King Sancho turned on the Jews in fury, fining them £95,000 and confiscating all Jewish property, including the synagogue.[62] Even the Torah bells and crowns, made of silver, were taken into custody.[63] The *aljama* continued to be managed by Jewish officials, or secretaries, but Sancho deprived the Call of all 'privileges, liberties and immunities' granted by himself or former kings.[64] He did permit a replacement synagogue to be built, but it is clear that the Jews had virtually no resources with which to do this, and nothing seems to have been done.[65] The main synagogue was turned into the Church of Santa Fe, but it remained difficult of access, isolated within the Call. Once Sancho had secured the major part of the fine he was claiming from the Jews, he could look more kindly on their grievances. In 1323 he decided to reward the Jews for the help they had given the royal treasury (£2,000) and for their contribution to the cathedral building fund (£300) by transferring the chapel of Santa Fe to the garden of En

[60] Isaacs, 241, doc. 87.
[61] Fita, 'Los Judíos mallorquines y el Concilio de Viena,' 240–1, no. 2; Isaacs, 241, doc. 87; cf. Lourie, 'A plot which failed?' 187–220, and especially 202–3, where she observes that the ritual murder charge had now arrived in the Mediterranean. Its origins lay in Norwich in 1144; neither the closely argued denunciation by Frederick II nor papal condemnation under Innocent IV checked its progress. [62] Pons, II.32–41.
[63] Pons, II.252, doc. 64, recording their return by the Regent Philip in 1326. The *rimonim* (Torah bells) in the Cathedral Treasury are apparently of fifteenth-century Sicilian workmanship and probably never belonged to the Majorcan community; they were made into staffs for the bishop. For illustrations, see Pons, I. plates 3–5.
[64] Fita, 'Privilegios', 132–3, no. 24; Isaacs, 243, doc. 97.
[65] Fita, 'Los Judíos mallorquines y el Concilio de Viena', 249, no. 6; Isaacs, 242–3, doc. 93.

Cassa close to the Temple Gate, on the outer edge of the Call. The king claimed the support of the bishop of Majorca in making this move. Sancho also conceded the Jews the right to open a new gate into the Call at the bottom of the road leading past the disused synagogue and chapel. The old synagogue was not to be restored to Christian use.[66] There was, not surprisingly, a backlash. The bishop apparently assented to the move of Santa Fe, but assumed that the chapel within the Call would still remain Christian property. He was worried that it was about to be turned back into a synagogue, and opposed any transfer of disused churches to Jewish or Muslim hands. No doubt the bishop had received complaints from other churchmen in Majorca City that the king was in breach of canon law.[67]

The Jewish community of Majorca City thus experienced great practical difficulties under King Sancho. There was no central synagogue. At least one of the secretaries of the community was nominated by the crown from the Jewish community of the city.[68] Technically, since part of the massive £95,000 fine was still outstanding, the privileges of the *aljama* were still in a state of abeyance. The climate improved markedly after Sancho's death in 1325. The Regent Philip in 1328 acknowledged that the fine had now been paid and reconstituted the *aljama*, against an annual tribute of £165.[69] The *aljama* secretaries were to be elected by the Jews as in the days of Sancho's predecessors, without intervention by the king or any royal officials.[70]

In 1331 James III (1324–43) finally permitted the Jews to re-establish a synagogue; moreover, the building used was not to be decorated in the sumptuous fashion of the previous Great Synagogue, which had been *curiosam et valde formosam*.[71] James

[66] Pons, II.249–50, doc. 61; Villanueva, XXI, 300–2; Fita, 'Privilegios', 139–42, no. 31 errors in Villanueva); Isaacs, 244–5, doc. 105.

[67] Fita, 'Los Judíos mallorquines y el Concilio de Viena,' 257–8, no. 7; Villanueva, XXI, 302–3; Isaacs, 245, doc. 107.

[68] Fita, 'Privilegios', 197, no. 45; Isaacs, 248, doc. 124. Isaacs, 60, wrongly implies that the king appointed Christian secretaries, but the document says explicitly *judeus secretarius*. In the late fourteenth century, though, Christians were being appointed to the headship of Muslim *aljamas* in the Aragonese mainland territories.

[69] Isaacs, 247, doc. 122; cf. Fita, 'Privilegios', 191–4, no. 41 and Isaacs, 246, doc. 117.

[70] Fita, 'Privilegios', 197–8, no. 45; Isaacs, 248, doc. 124.

[71] Pons, II.271–2, doc. 88; Isaacs, 248–9, doc. 127. One of the candelabra hanging from the ceiling of Palma Cathedral is said to have been brought there from the Great Synagogue. Some idea of how sumptuous a new fourteenth-century Spanish synagogue could be can be obtained

was careful to pay lip service to the requirements of canon law, which had already been cited to deny the Jews the return of Santa Fe. The law as he understood it prohibited the erection of new synagogues in new places, but not by any means the rebuilding of synagogues where they had earlier existed. The new synagogue was not to be thought of as a new building, in fact, so much as the *reparatio et refectio* of what had been in the Call in former times (though he was mostly certainly not offering them back Santa Fe). In fact, it was not to be a synagogue at all, but a 'school' or 'house of prayer'; this was a code word for a synagogue, but understandably the king preferred to avoid using the word that would bring ecclesiastical censure upon him. From the point of view of the Jews this all made little enough difference: synagogues functioned as houses of prayer and of study, as well as assembly halls.[72] He thus advanced a whole range of arguments, some of which almost contradicted one another, in order to justify his policy. At one moment he talked of the building as a synagogue, at the next it was a *domum aliquam decentem ad orandum juxta ritus et consuetudines eorum*. Maybe too he was influenced by the aid he received from able Jewish cartographers; a ruler of impossibly ambitious schemes, James contemplated the conquest of the Canary Islands, and Jewish maps were an important key to the Atlantic. The contribution of the Jews to Majorca's economy was recognised in a privilege of 1329 when King James III pointed out that the Jews of Majorca were primarily engaged in commerce: *judei dicte aljame mercantiliter vivant pro majore parte*.[73]

The fall of the kingdom of Majorca to Peter IV of Aragon in 1343 did not result in a significant change of status for the Jews of the Call. The monarchy continued to give vocal support to the *aljama*, for example against those found guilty of misconduct.[74] Protection was given to African Jews who wished to settle in Majorca.[75] The right of the Jews to operate their own weights and measures was confirmed.[76] A Majorcan Jew was compensated by

from the so-called Transíto Synagogue in Toledo, built in *mudéjar* style for Don Samuel Abulafia, Treasurer of King Pedro the Cruel of Castile, in around 1360.

[72] Hence the use of the term *Scuola* for synagogues in sixteenth-century Venice and Rome, not to mention the continuing use of the term *Schul(e)* among Ashkenazi Jews.

[73] Fita, 'Privilegios', 199, no. 46; Isaacs, 248, doc. 126.

[74] Fita, 'Privilegios', 281–2, no. 61; Isaacs, 252, doc. 149.   [75] Isaacs, 255, doc. 166.

[76] Fita, 'Privilegios', 377–9, no. 81; Isaacs, 257, doc. 179.

the king when a cargo of grain was appropriated for the army in Sardinia.[77] Following complaints from the *aljama*, even the bishop of Majorca concurred with the requirement that Jews had been rushed to the baptismal font faster than canon law permitted.[78] The Jews of Majorca City were commended by the crown for helping efforts to alleviate famine, and the city government was praised for protecting the Jews from angry mobs that were threatening their safety: *molts christians de aqueixa ciutat han comensat e quaix continuen vituperar envilogar e, so que es pijor, avolotar los juheus de la dita ciutat.*[79] It was the Christian population who made scapegoats of the Jews now, in 1374, and then on a much more severe scale in 1391, when a violent wave of anti-Jewish hatred swept through Spain and coincided with social unrest in the Majorcan countryside, and with economic convulsions throughout the lands of the Crown of Aragon.

The slaughter and forced conversions of 1391 and the mass conversion of 1435 stand in direct contrast to the benign outlook of Peter IV of Aragon. Nor, indeed, were the *conversos* of Majorca allowed to forget their origins. They were a caste apart, pursuing in many cases the sort of artisan crafts in gold and silver in which the Jews of medieval Majorca had also been involved; until the twentieth century even wealthy *Chuetas* could only escape from discrimination by travelling to mainland Spain, where their status in Majorca was held of no account. Many were devout Catholics, and the churches of Santa Eulalia and of Montesion became their special places of prayer: the one the place of their ancestors' conversion, the other the site of the Great Synagogue which had been seized from the Jews by King Sancho. They did not retain their religion, but their sense of identity was forced on them, and they maintained a territory which was contiguous with that of the medieval Call.[80]

---

[77] Baer, 435–6, no. 301; Isaacs, 258, doc. 185.

[78] Villanueva, XXII, 253; Isaacs, 259, doc. 190.

[79] Fita, 'Privilegios', 393–4; Isaacs, 260, doc. 195.

[80] There is a large literature on the Chuetas, notably K. Moore, *Those of the street. The Catholic Jews of Mallorca* (Notre Dame, Indiana, 1976); Angela S. Selke, *The Conversos of Majorca. Life and death in a crypto-Jewish community in seventeenth-century Spain* (Hispania Judaica, V, Jerusalem, 1986); B. Porcel, *Los Chuetas mallorquines. Quince siglos de racismo* (6th ed., Palma de Mallorca, 1986).

Religious communities in the urban space

The church of Magdeburg: its trade and its town in the tenth and early eleventh centuries

HENRY MAYR-HARTING

Around 1962, when I had the good fortune to be a member of the department at Liverpool of which Christopher Brooke was Professor, he lent me his copy of Albert Brackmann's book on Magdeburg (1937). This book, though distinctly chauvinistic in tone and also an occasional piece written to mark the millennium of the foundation of the monastery of St Maurice at Magdeburg, was of genuine scholarly importance; and it did much to it lay the foundations of modern knowledge about early Magdeburg. What better return can I make for all the good that has been done to me (*Quid retribuam domino pro omnibus quae retribuit mihi*), than to contribute something on the subject to this *Festschrift*? The contribution is in the nature of the case a modest one, for much of excellent quality has been written on Magdeburg.[1] No subject,

[1] Albert Brackmann, *Magdeburg als Hauptstadt des deutschen Ostens im früheren Mittelalter* (Leipzig, 1937); Robert Holtzmann, 'Otto der Große und Magdeburg', in his *Magdeburg in der Politik der deutschen Kaiser* (Magdeburg, 1936), pp. 47–80; Fritz Rörig, *Magdeburgs Entstehung und die ältere Handelsgeschichte*, Deutsche Akademie der Wissenschaften zu Berlin, Vorträge und Schriften 49 (Berlin, 1952); Berent Schwineköper, 'Die Anfänge Magdeburgs', *Studien zu den Anfängen des Europäischen Städtewesens*, Vorträge und Forschungen 4 (Reichenau Vorträge) (Lindau and Constance, 1958), 389–450; Walter Schlesinger, 'Zur Geschichte der Magdeburger Königspfalz', *Blätter für deutsche Landesgeschichte* 104 (1968), 1–31; Dietrich Claude, *Geschichte des Erzbistums Magdeburg bis in das 12 Jahrhundert*, part II (Cologne and Vienna, 1972), part II (1975); Berent Schwineköper, *Königtum und Städte bis zum Ende des Investiturstreits* (Sigmaringen, 1977); Karl Leyser, *Rule and conflict in an early Medieval society: Ottonian Saxony* (London, 1979). Also to be noted: Siegmund Wolf, 'Die räumliche Entwicklung des Altstadt Magdeburg', *Jahrbuch für die Geschichte Mittel- und Ostdeutschlands* 3 (1954), 33–63; Walter Schlesinger, 'Städtische Frühformen zwischen Rhein und Elbe', *Studien zu den Anfängen*, 297–362; Herbert Jankuhn, 'Die frühmittelalterlichen Seehandelsplätze in Nord-und Ostseeraum', ibid., 451–98; Ernst Nickel, 'Magdeburg in karolingisch-ottonischer Zeit', *Vor- und Frühformen der Europäischen Stadt im Mittelalter*, I, ed. H. Jankuhn et al., *Abhandlungen der Akademie der Wissenschaften in Göttingen*, 3rd ser. 83 (1973), 294–331; Gerd Althoff, 'Das Bett des Königs in Magdeburg', *Festschrift für Berent Schwineköper*, ed. H. Maurer & H. Patze (Sigmaringen, 1982), pp. 141–53.

however, is unsusceptible to being looked at from a slightly new angle, or to being treated with a few mildly different emphases from those previously laid. Besides which, in the present political context it behoves us in Britain to take an interest in what has for the past four decades been Eastern Germany, and to see it as part of a greater historical whole.

Magdeburg is first mentioned in Charlemagne's Capitulary of Thionville (805) as one of the customs outposts of his empire and thus was already an important trading place.[2] It was probably a royal centre, with a *curtis* already in Carolingian times, for there was then no other *burg* in the region of Northern Thuringia, the *Nordthüringau*, and from its name (ek-magadi), which apparently means *burg* (or fortified place) at the tree of the elves, it was presumably a pagan cultic centre and as such a place of resort.[3] It came into its own, however, under the tenth-century Saxon rulers of the East Frankish kingdom, as the linchpin of their missionary strategy amongst the pagan Slavs to the east of the River Elbe, and further south between the Saale and the Elbe. The Elbe in the tenth century was to the Saxon rulers what the Rhine had been in the eighth century to the Carolingians, effectively both their eastern border and an artery of communications between some of their most important churches, palaces, and trading ports. As neither river was by any means impassable to enemies, respectively the Slavs and the Saxons, control of these river basins themselves meant being in control of the eastern side of them. No such control was possible in that age unless these peoples were culturally tamed, which meant converting them to Christianity. That does not mean that missionary effort had no religious motive behind it, only that such effort was bound to be a mixture of religious, military and economic drive.

It is practically certain that the religious foundations of both Quedlinburg and Magdeburg were planned by Henry I, though both were executed only by his son, Otto I, at the beginning of his reign: two foundations both in *East* Saxony, both next to already existing royal palaces, both apparently with an eye to the missionising of the Elbe region; Magdeburg on the west bank of

[2] Trans. in P. D. King, *Charlemagne: translated sources* (Kendal, 1987), c. 23, p. 248.
[3] Schwineköper, 'Die Anfänge Magdeburgs', 395, and 395, n. 21.

the Elbe itself, and Quedlinburg (as befitted a nunnery with
inmates from the ruling family) rather more removed from the
immediate theatre of action and excitement, not to speak of its
being on an impressive and defensive crag with wonderful views
towards the Harz Mountains. The rationale of these foundations
is obvious, as Claude has pointed out. After Henry I's defeat of the
Danes in 934, Bremen constituted an active centre of missionising
in that direction, but there were no similar centres to capitalise on
his victories against the Slavs; the bishopric of Halberstadt in
Saxony had shown few signs of interest, while in Bavaria St
Emmeram of Regensburg was not under Henry's control.[4]

It was quite common in the early Middle Ages for monasteries
such as Fulda, Corvey and Regensburg to serve as missionary
centres, and when the monastery of St Maurice, Magdeburg, was
founded in 937, there was clearly no intention that it should be
elevated to an archbishopric, as it became in 968.[5] If there had
been, the bishoprics of Havelberg and Brandenburg, both east of
the Elbe, would not have been founded in 946 and 948, to the
possible future prejudice of the metropolitan jurisdiction over
them (although it was not prejudiced in practice).[6] The first
evidence of Otto's plan for an archbishopric of Magdeburg comes
in October 955 with a celebrated letter of Archbishop William of
Mainz to Pope Agapetus II objecting to the plan as prejudicial to
his primatial and metropolitan position within the East Frankish
church, and the plan must have arisen as an exaltation of Otto's
missionary strategy after his victories over the Slavs to the east of
the Elbe in 954–5 and his defeat of the Hungarians at the Lechfeld
in 955.[7] Thereafter the intended suffragan bishoprics (Merseburg,
Meissen and Zeitz) were held up until the establishment of the
metropolitan see. The delay of thirteen years between intention
and its realisation was occasioned by the opposition of Archbishop
William of Mainz and Bishop Bernhard of Halberstadt, the one
because his metropolitan authority stood to be cut off to the East,

[4] Brackmann, pp. 2–4, 7–8; Claude, I, 20–2.   [5] Claude, I, 35; Holtzmann, p. 53.
[6] DOI 76, 105; Holtzmann, pp. 60–1.
[7] Text of letter, Jaffé, *Bibl. Rer. Germ, Epistolae Moguntinae* v, 471–72: *tunc quod monachi Magadaeburgensis coenobii eodem privilegio* (as had been granted to Mainz) *a vobis vestrisque antecessoribus sunt adminiculati ; tum quod minorationem nostrae sedis translationemque Halberestetensis aecclesiae me vivo non consentiam.* Thus the transference of the bishopric of Halberstadt to the metropolitan jurisdiction of Magdeburg was at first envisaged. See also Claude, I, 63–85.

the other because he stood to lose part of his diocese. It is singular that both these prelates died within a few weeks of each other in early 968,[8] and the facts about Otto's interventions in the elections of both their successors to secure persons who would agree to his Magdeburg plan are well attested in the sources.[9]

On the face of it, therefore, it might appear that Otto I brought about the archbishopric of Magdeburg by his control of the East Frankish (or German) church, rather than by his Roman imperial policy and the concomitant close association with the pope (who alone could ratify a new metropolitan see), as many historians have seen it. But in Otto I's *mind* there was undoubtedly a connection between his Magdeburg plan and his imperial coronation at Rome by Pope John XII on 2 February 962. For on 12 February 962 this pope issued a bull, with a significant *arenga* connecting Otto's imperial coronation to his conquest of barbarian peoples, setting up the archbishopric of Magdeburg.[10] It does not affect the argument that this bull remained a dead letter for more than six years. There are two other pointers to the connection between the Magdeburg plan and the imperial coronation in Otto's mind at this period. One is his exceptional military push to the East of 963, the year following the coronation, involving both his great marcher lords of the Slav frontier, Gero and Hermann Billung, whose commands, going back to the beginning of his reign, formed the vital political context to the missionary organisation of Magdeburg, as Brackmann pointed out.[11] Gero brought Duke Miesko of the Poles under Saxon dominion, Hermann Billung two important Slav princes, Selibur

---

[8] Claude, I, 30–1, implies an element of pique on Widukind of Corvey's part in not mentioning the church of Magdeburg and its place in Saxon history, because Otto had used monks from far-away St Maximin, Trier, of the Gorze Reform to start the monastery of St Maurice, Magdeburg, whereas he could have drawn on respected monasteries nearer home such as Corvey. But Widukind was writing very much in a profane rather than an ecclesiastical genre. Moreover, remarkably, the only episcopal deaths which he mentions are the two germane to the Magdeburg scheme, those of William of Mainz and Bernhard of Halberstadt early in 968, *Widukindi Monachi Corbeiensis Rerum Gestarum Saxonicarum*, ed. H. E. Lohmann and P. Hirsch, MGH Scriptores rerum Germanicarum in usum scholarium. (Hanover, 1935), III, 74, pp. 150–1.

[9] Hatto of Mainz: *Annales Hildesheimenses*, ed. G. Waitz, MGH Script rer. Germ. in usum schol. (Hanover, 1878), p. 23; Hildeward of Halberstadt: Thietmar (as in n. 12 below), II, 20, pp. 60–2.

[10] *Urkundenbuch des Erzstifts Magdeburg*, ed. F. Israel and W. Möllenberg (Magdeburg, 1937), no. 28, pp. 41–3.

[11] Brackmann, p. 8.

was one very typical of Henry's church policy altogether, to switch the inheritance of the estate from Bishop Wigbert personally to the perpetual corporation of the church of Merseburg. Thus were the endowments of the episcopal churches in the Empire built up during Henry II's reign.[30] For our present purposes, however, two points should be noted: it looks from the story as if this forest-clearing estate, *Godefridesrod*, had been in existence for at least a few decades by 1006, and it is an extraordinary second example of where mining can actually be associated with a forest-clearing name.

Not that the agrarian possibilities of forest-clearing were unimportant. By the same charter of 965 which granted to Magdeburg the iron-workings, it also received the right of pannage, i.e. the right to fatten pigs under oak or beech trees, 'in that wilderness' (*in ipso heremo*), meaning *Gramaningorod*.[31] One assumes that a royal chaplain such as might have drafted this diploma, sitting in bustling Magdeburg (where it was issued), with its learned monks, its Jews, and its urbane merchants, would shudder as he thought of the 'outback' of some perhaps recent forest-clearing, even if not many miles away, and would thus refer to it as 'the wilds'. Whether the monks' interest in bacon extended to its commercial possibilities or was merely for the consumption of themselves and their dependants, we cannot tell, but this is not the only mention of pigs in their early archive;[32] and the more *edge* of wood or forest, such as is gained by forest-clearing, the more scope obviously for fattening pigs under trees. Another activity in the Harz region, which could well have been connected with forest-clearing, was horse-breeding. There is no evidence that Magdeburg was directly involved in this, but amongst the estates granted to Otto's mother, Mathilda, by Henry I as provision for her widowhood (i.e. Quedlinburg, Pöhlde, Nordhausen, Grone and Duderstadt) were stud farms (*equariciae*).[33]

---

[30] See Henry Mayr-Harting, *Ottonian book illumination; an historical study*, Part I (London, 1991), p. 197, for such relations between Henry II and episcopal churches, using Fleckenstein (as in n. 84 below), p. 218.   [31] DOI 214 ...*seu ipso heremo porcos saginandi concessimus.*

[32] E.g. DOI 14 ...*et liceat ut in eis et ligna et herbe in usus sint et porci saginentur*, a phrase which seems to refer more to the numerous places granted to the west of the Elbe than to the three Slav places whose tithe is granted (Claude, I, 34), and whose names immediately precede the phrase.

[33] DHI 20 (929); Leyser, 'Henry I', pp. 35–6.

Forest-clearing requires the availability of cheap labour, so much so that in twelfth- and thirteenth-century England assarting has been taken as one of the primary indices of a rising population. The management of landed estates also of course requires a plentiful supply of labour. In the earliest grants of lands to Magdeburg, numerous families of peasants, or *coloni*, or Slavs/slaves are mentioned: for instance, in *Grimhereslebu* fifteen *familias Sclavorum*, in Frohse twenty-six, in *Pretulitse* eight, in *Triempsitse* twenty, in *Vuiterihhesdorp* twenty-three, *Pizzenitse* seven, *Fridemaresleba* fifty-six, the last being Fermesleben, now a suburb of Magdeburg city, all these in the *Nordthuringau*. The fact that Slavs are distinguished from other kinds of dependent labourers in these texts, *liti* and *coloni*, suggests that the word is being used in an ethnic sense.[34] Whether these Slavs had been purchased in the slave markets of Magdeburg and other entrepôts of the Elbe and its tributaries – there is evidence of slave traffic also in tenth-century Prague – or whether they had been settled as dependent farmers (some of them perhaps long since), quite separately from dealings in these markets, we have no means of knowing, but it seems clear that Slavs formed a major part of the labour force necessary to develop Magdeburg's region to the west of the Elbe in the tenth century. The Saxons also knew the kinds of arrangements for fortress labour embodied in the Anglo-Saxon *trinoda necessitas*, for the church could command the labour of the inhabitants in the surrounding parts to build the walls of the town itself, the *opus construende urbis*, which presumably refers to the walls around the area of the cathedral and royal palace, since excavations have not brought to light any walls of our period round the *Alte Markt* and the merchant settlement, to the north of this area.[35]

Slaves of Slav origin, whether captured by the Saxons in their

---

[34] DOI 14; DOI 21. See also DOI 16. Claude, I, 50–1, mentions the phenomenon of these Slav settlements only in passing. For the identification of Fermersleben, see Schlesinger, 'Zur Geschichte', p. 16; and for the ethnic sense of the word *Sclavi* in this context, Charles Verlinden, *L'Esclavage dans l'Europe Médiévale*, I (Bruges, 1955), p. 219.

[35] DOI 300 (965), and see Schwineköper, 'Die Anfänge Magdeburgs', pp. 440–2. Work on the *burgs* must have been important to the east of the Elbe, where Slav tithes were early collected through the organisation of *burgs* and their attached administrative areas, the *burgwards*; e.g. the tithes from the region between the Elbe and the Oder, excepted in 948 from the endowment of the bishopric of Brandenburg in order to go to the church of Magdeburg, which were attached to certain named *burgs*, or *civitates*. See also Claude, I, 34.

wars or the fruits of warfare amongst the Slav tribes themselves, were undoubtedly a major commodity in Magdeburg commerce, particularly since Jewish merchants are specifically mentioned in the diplomas and in Thietmar of Merseburg to be part of its urban community.[36] In the ninth and tenth centuries Jews were large-scale slave traders, being well qualified culturally to act as intermediaries between the Christian and Muslim civilisations, and ultimately what made the slave trade lucrative in the northern world of the tenth century was the inexhaustible demand for slaves in the Muslim world.[37] The trading journeys which realised so great a profit were indeed long, but then one of the economic advantages of a slave trade is that the commodity transports itself, whether on foot or with oars.

By what routes were slaves exported? Already in the early ninth century Eigil's Life of St Sturm gives us a reference to the overland route from Mainz to Erfurt, the latter in Thuringia and connected to Magdeburg as another of Charlemagne's customs posts of 805. This route crossed the River Fulda, and Eigil describes it as that which the merchants use.[38] It ties in neatly with the reference to another overland route between the Rhine and the Elbe, in a grant of Louis III to the nunnery of Gandersheim confirmed by Otto I in 956, granting it a toll on all merchants crossing from the Rhine to the Elbe and the Saale, by implication a more northerly route than that through Erfurt, a Cologne–Magdeburg rather than a Mainz–Magdeburg route.[39] One likely destination of the traders, where their wares would change hands, would be Verdun, thence to be shipped up the Meuse and down the Saône and the Rhone to Muslim Spain. The merchants of Verdun, among whom Jews appear to have figured large, made an *immensum lucrum* – the words are those of Liudprand of Cremona – from the slave trade in the tenth century.[40] Although

---

[36] E.g. DOI 300 (965); Thietmar, VI, 73, p. 363.

[37] Verlinden, pp. 211–25; see also Alexander Murray, *Reason and society in the Middle Ages* (Oxford, 1978), pp. 40–50.

[38] *Eigilis Vita Sancti Sturmi*, MGH SS II, c. 7, p. 369, trans. C. H. Talbot, *The Anglo-Saxon missionaries in Germany* (London, 1954), p. 186. Also Walter Schlesinger, 'Städtische Frühformen zwischen Rhein und Elbe', pp. 313–14, for Erfurt.

[39] DOI 180, p. 263, lines 24–6. The routes are discussed by Rörig, pp. 16–17, 21.

[40] *Liudprandi Episcopi Cremonensis Opera*, ed. J. Becker, MGH in usum schol. (Hanover, 1915), *Antapodosis* VI, 6, pp. 155–6. Other references to Verdun merchants in the ninth and tenth centuries are given and discussed by Verlinden, pp. 217, 222–3, and in Maurice Lombard,

itself on the Meuse, Verdun could easily be reached from the Rhine by a journey up the Moselle. An eleventh-century tariff of tolls at Coblenz, where the Moselle joins the Rhine, explicitly refers to the slave trade; 'Jews', it says, 'owe four pence for every slave purchased.'[41] We should not overlook, however, the importance of the routes by water down the Elbe (which flows into the North Sea not into the Baltic, a fact of which English people often need reminding, Germans of course never), round the Frisian coast of the North Sea, and into the mouths of the Rhine, or of the Meuse to the south of the Rhine delta. There is good evidence that shipping flourished on the Elbe in the tenth century and earlier;[42] we know that Magdeburg merchants visited such places as Deventer, Tiel, and Bardowick;[43] the monastery/archbishopric itself was given by Otto I important lands and interests, including salt marshes, in and around Deventer.[44] Schwineköper has suggested that although our first evidence of the salted herring trade between Frisia and Magdeburg is no earlier than the beginning of the twelfth century, it could well in fact go back to the tenth; and he has also pointed to the finds of Lotharingian, Rhineland, and even Deventer coins on the Elbe amongst those from the time of Otto III and the early eleventh century, to show that Deventer trade went east as well as south on the Rhine at this period.[45]

What had the slave trade to do with the church of Magdeburg? Everything. Otto I handed over many royal rights and powers in Magdeburg to the church, as Henry II would later do to the cathedral of Bamberg there; he retained the royal palace for his frequent stays, a property later handed over by Otto II to the

---

'La Route de la Meuse et les relations lointaines des pays Mosans entre le vIIIe et le xIe siècle', in *L'Art Mosan*, pp. 16–17. [41] Cited by Verlinden, p. 222.

[42] E.g. Schwineköper, 'Die Anfänge Magdeburgs', 401, 431. According to the Moissac Chronicle (MGH Scriptores II, 258) Charlemagne transported soldiers in ships along the Elbe to Magdeburg; and when Canaparius in his *Vita Adalberti* calls Magdeburg *semiruta domus et malefida statio nautis*, this tendentious statement against Archbishop Gisilher of Magdeburg (early eleventh century) must imply that the writer thought it earlier a secure port for ships. The acquisition of Retha at the confluence of the Fulda and the Weser (DOI, 388 of 970) might suggest an interest by Magdeburg in shipping on that river system also.

[43] Esp. DOII 112 (975), 140 (976).

[44] In DOI 159 (952) Otto I grants all the possessions within the *urbs* of Deventer and in the surrounding region, which he received from his aunt Uta, to the monastery of Magdeburg. *Terra salaritia* is mentioned in a further grant of 960 (DOI 216).

[45] Schwineköper, 'Die Anfänge Magdeburgs', 422–5.

archbishopric, whereafter he and his successors depended upon a right of *hospitalitas* from the church.[46] The church had full control of the market and of the mint, and from the start all tolls on Magdeburg trade, while its *advocatus* had full powers of jurisdiction over the merchants, including the Jewish merchants.[47] One early archbishop at least plainly dealt beneficently with the Jews, for Thietmar of Merseburg tells us that when Archbishop Tagino (1004–12) died, the whole Jewish community mourned his passing.[48] Nor was jurisdiction over the merchants confined to the town of Magdeburg itself, for it extended to their persons almost wherever they were, as we can see from the diplomas which make exceptions to this rule in the case of certain places, namely jurisdiction over Magdeburg merchants at Mainz, Cologne, Tiel and Bardowick.[49] Thietmar seems to recognise a community of merchants at Magdeburg, surely one of the earliest instances of such a phenomenon in German history, articulated as a result of dealings with the archbishops of Magdeburg.[50] At every turn, therefore, there must have been involvement of the church in Magdeburg trade, and profit from it.

Talk of the market and the mint of Magdeburg gains colour from the evidence that large quantities of silver were coming into the Elbe region as a result of Slav tribute, and it should be emphasised that German expansion across the Elbe in the tenth century was not a movement of agrarian colonisation, as in the twelfth, but of military lordship and exaction of tithe and tribute. In 965 Otto I granted to Magdeburg a tenth, or tithe, of all silver due to be paid to his fisc (*ad publicum nostrae maiestatis fiscum*) from the tribute of five Slav tribes, the *Ucrani*, *Riezani*, *Riedere*, *Tolensane*, and *Zerezepani*;[51] and one must assume that a certain proportion of the other nine-tenths went into circulation in the

---

[46] Holtzmann, p. 50; Schlesinger, 'Zur Geschichte der Magdeburger Königspfalz', 16–17; Althoff. For the grant of Otto II in 981, DOII 258 and Wolf, 39–40.

[47] For the market, see esp. DOI 301 (965); the mint, DOI 46 (941); tolls on Magdeburg trade, DOI 15 (937); jurisdiction over merchants DOI 300 (965).

[48] Thietmar, VI, 73, p. 363.   [49] Esp. DOII 112 (975).

[50] It is implicit in his reference to the *ecclesia mercatorum*, see below, and also in DOII 112. Schwineköper, 'Die Anfänge Magdeburgs', 447–8, suggests that the *jus mercatorium* of Quedlinburg, DOIII 155 (994) could have been the model for Magdeburg.

[51] DOI 295. These tribes later formed the confederation of the Liuitizi who rose against Ottonian rule to the east of the Elbe in 983, see Friedrich Lotter, 'The crusading idea and the conquest of the region east of the Elbe', in *Medieval frontier societies*, ed. Robert Bartlett and Angus MacKay (Oxford, 1989), p. 271.

Magdeburg region. Later on, in 971, a tithe of the silver from other Slav regions was also granted to Bishop Folcold of Meissen, one of the suffragans of the archbishopric of Magdeburg deep in Slav territory on the upper Elbe.[52] Even in this matter, however, where Saxon advance to the east of the Elbe at first sight appears the vital condition for this new source of wealth, we should not overlook the western dimension. For Alexander Murray has argued cogently that one of the principal effects of this influx of silver into the west from more eastern sources, both in Saxony and Bohemia, was to stimulate home production, in the Harz Mountains and at Kutna Hora. If that is right, it means that the Saxons' loss of position to the east of the Elbe with the Slav risings of 983 need not be viewed as an unqualified disaster for them, since they could recoup their losses.[53] All the same the advantage to the west of having eastern manpower and wealth available for its development in the tenth century, with Magdeburg church and town at the centre of the whole exchange, is of great historical importance. It explains the geography of why Saxony, so at first sight unpromisingly situated to dominate the East Frankish kingdom with its active Roman and Italian imperial policy, should in fact have done so.

Fritz Rörig in his monograph on the rise of Magdeburg trade, published in 1952, deserves great credit for highlighting the slave trade, since this preceded the publication of Charles Verlinden's *magnum opus* on early medieval slavery, which removed everyone's excuse for not being aware of the subject. None the less, important as this trade was, he arguably emphasised it too much at the expense of other commodities.[54] One of these was honey. In 965 Otto I granted to the church of St Maurice the tithe of honey from whole Slav regions, especially those with rich honey-producing heathlands between the Saale and the Elbe and around the River Mulde to the south of Magdeburg, excepting only the tithe of seven named places which he had already granted to the

[52] DOI 406. Of outstanding interest for Magdeburg and Meissen as exactors of tribute and tithes is Karl Leyser, 'Ottonian government', pp. 87–90, and p. 91 for minting of silver coinage in tenth century Saxony.

[53] A. Murray, *Reason and society*, pp. 50–3; Leyser, 'Ottonian government', pp. 90–1.

[54] But he mentions other commodities at pp. 17–18, and refers at p. 27 to furs, skins, honey and wax, as coming from the east of the Elbe, partly in exchange for cash-payments, partly for other wares, by Rhine merchants.

church of Brandenburg.[55] The idea of honey might bring a smile
to our lips, since the best honey in our society is sold in small
quantities at shops liable to be patronised by cranks; but it was big
business in the tenth century, partly because then it was virtually
the only sweetener, and partly because it was the basis of mead,
the great aristocratic drink everywhere in the Germanic world,
and almost a precondition for bringing warriors into a fit state to
begin lucrative feuds. Again we have to remember that, in dealing
with these obviously valuable grants of tithes, there is the other
nine-tenths of the product to be accounted for, much of it
presumably in the markets.

Moreover, where there is honey there is beeswax, another
highly important commodity. When in 965 Otto I made his grant
of the tithe of Slav silver which we have already mentioned, he
specified that the whole of it should go on the provision of
lighting for the church and the purchase of incense.[56] Perhaps this
suggests that the quantities of silver involved were not so vast as
one might imagine, but, leaving aside for the present the
inscrutable problem of incense, one should not underrate the
lighting bill of Magdeburg, and incidentally that goes also for the
numerous suffragan and dependent churches brought into being
by the realisation of the plan for a Magdeburg archbishopric in
968. It is true that tallow candles would have been much cheaper
than those made of beeswax. An important tenth-century church,
however, in the age of silver candlesticks and candelabra *par
excellence*,[57] would no more have dreamt of suffering the loss of
face involved in using inferior candles for its elaborate liturgy,
much of it taking place in hours of darkness, than a modern
university college would present itself to the world on its street
front with a row of nissen huts. From Otto's grant, therefore, one

---

[55] DOI 303. The grant of 971 to Bishop Folcold of Meissen (DOI 406) also included tithes of honey.
[56] DOI 295 ...*decimam tocius census illius deo sanctoque Mauricio ad concinnanda luminaria Magadeburg sive thimiama emendum offerimus et donamus.*
[57] Because of the intrinsic value of their material, not many silver candlesticks have survived from this period to set beside those of Bishop Bernward still at Hildesheim. But from treasure-lists of *c.* 900–1050 there is no doubting the phenomenon; see Bernhard Bischoff, *Mittelalterliche Schatzverzeichnisse* (Munich, 1967), nos. 39, 40, 43, 50, 55, 62, 74, 76, 77, 93, 103, 125. It is not always stated of what material the candlesticks/candelabra are, and it is likely that in most lists only those for the altar, rather than for general use in the church, are referred to. It is interesting, however, that those lists where large numbers of silver candlesticks are mentioned are at or near the great centres of metal-working on the Meuse, i.e. 21 at Liège Cathedral (no. 43), 13 at Prüm (no. 74), and 6 at St Vincent Metz (no. 55).

may suppose that the ecclesiastical requirement of beeswax must have resulted in quite an injection of silver into the Elbe markets, particularly that of Magdeburg.

Other commodities also come into view as having possible importance in the make-up of Magdeburg trade. Claude has pointed out that land grants from Otto I in the *pagus* of the *Neletici* in 961 brought the monastery into the region of Halle and Giebichenstein with its salt-works (*Giuiconsten cum salsugine eius*), five years after it had already acquired salt marshes from Otto I in Frisia around Deventer.[58] That clothes were produced on some scale in the Elbe region is suggested by Otto I's grant to Quedlinburg in 937 of the tithes of clothes called *lodo* (*decimum vestimentum quod lodo dicitur*, perhaps the origins of the celebrated *Lodenmantel!*) from *Chirihberg* and *Dornburg*; while excavations in Magdeburg itself have turned up evidence of spinning and textile work near the royal palace.[59] In Slav and west-Elbe regions acquired already in 937 the monastery of St Maurice was granted, amongst other things, the use of wood, which not only again argues at least an indirect control of labour, but also points to a likely interest of the monastery in ship-building.[60]

The most problematical issue about the trade of early Magdeburg is what part luxury goods played in it and where they came from. In a famous passage, the chronicler Widukind of Corvey describes the exotic gifts which Otto I received from the legates of Greeks, Romans and Saracens, after his military triumphs of 954 and 955 against the Slavs and Hungarians had made him famous all over the world:

with numerous victories the emperor became glorious and famous, and earned the fear and favour of many kings and peoples. Thus he received many legates, of the Romans, the Greeks and the Saracens, and through them gifts of various kinds; gold, silver and bronze vessels, worked with a wonderful variety of ornamentation; glass vessels and ivory also; rugs of all sorts and sizes (*omni genere modificata stramenta*); balsam and pigments of every kind; animals never before seen by the Saxons, lions and camels, monkeys and ostriches.[61]

The whole of Saxon aristocratic society, secular and ecclesiastical, must have had its appetite whetted for more by these astonishing imports, which so signalised the honour and prestige of its ruler.

---

[58] DOI 232; Claude, I, 48.   [59] DOI 18; Schwineköper, *Königtum und Städte*, p. 62.
[60] DOI 14, quoted in n. 32 above; Claude, I, 34 and 34, n. 115.
[61] Widukind, III, 56, p. 135.

The Saxon rulers themselves assuredly wished to continue to gratify what must in the 950s have been a relatively newly awakened interest, judging by later animadversions made on the material austerity in which Otto I lived compared with Otto II.[62] That they adjudged Magdeburg to be a place from which they could gratify the interest is implied by the account of the handsome presents which both Archbishop Tagino and Archbishop Gero made to Henry II and his courtiers on his visits there.[63]

It has generally been assumed that the Saracens mentioned by Widukind were Spanish Muslims, and that indeed the Jews mentioned as residing in Magdeburg in 965 were Spanish Jews. But although many of the oriental luxury items coming into the North could have come from Spain, given the facts that Otto I had already established contact with the Caliphate of Còrdoba in 953 through the mission of John of Gorze and (significantly) a Verdun merchant,[64] and that the Islamic crescent from east to west was one great free-trade area, nevertheless we ought also to think of another possibility. Ibn Yaqub, himself a Spanish Jew, writing in the tenth century about Prague, which he visited, calls it a great centre of commerce, to which Russian and Slav merchants came from Cracow, and Jewish and Muslim merchants from Turkish lands, who brought various objects and pieces of gold, and took off slaves, furs and lead.[65] There is every reason to think that what was true of Prague, lying on the River Vltava, a tributary of the Elbe, is likely also to have been true of Magdeburg. The fact that in 960 Princess Olga of Kiev, which lies 800 miles to the east of Magdeburg and was connected to the great Muslim

---

[62] See Hartmut Hoffmann, *Buchkunst und Königtum im ottonischen und frühsalischen Reich* (Stuttgart, 1986), pp. 9–10. See also Thietmar, II, 44, p. 92, on Otto I: *Non est ciborum seu aliarum rerum superflua varietas, sed in cunctis delectabat aurea mediocritas* (Horace, Odes II, 10).

[63] Thietmar, V, 43, p. 270; VI, 81, p. 372.

[64] Karl Leyser has written with great interest on this mission, 'Ottonian Government', p. 94, and in his 'Ends and means in Liudprand of Cremona', *Byzantium and the West c. 850–c. 1200*, ed. J. D. Howard-Johnston (Amsterdam, 1988), pp. 119–43.

[65] Quoted by Lombard 'Route de la Meuse', p. 23. For actual economic connections between Prague and Magdeburg/Saxony, see DOIII 71 of 991, granting Magdeburg a third of the royal tribute from Bohemia, and see also on this subject in general, Karl Leyser, 'Ottonian Government', p. 90, and Hartmut Hoffmann, 'Böhmen und das deutsche Reich im hohen Mittelalter', *Jahrbuch für die Geschichte Mittel- und Ostdeutschlands* 18 (1969), 1–62. Otto I spoke with ibn Yaqub about eastern lands at Magdeburg in 965: R. Holtzmann, *Geschichte d. sächsischen Kaiserzeit* (Munich, 1955), p. 229.

trade routes of the east, requested Otto I to send her a bishop to convert her people to Christianity, suggests that Otto had still earlier connections than this with Kiev. And the fact that the person whom Otto sent on this abortive mission, Adalbert, a Saxon aristocrat and monk of St Maximin of Trier, was the very person who became first archbishop of Magdeburg in 968, suggests that Otto saw the archbishopric as an opportunity to put out more feelers far to the east (as Brackmann long ago argued).[66] As to the matter of incense, which was traded between Yemen and Baghdad in the ninth century, it may not have been the most sought-after of eastern luxury goods, but it was a consideration, as the diploma of Otto I which we have mentioned shows. For not only was this the age of the fine silver candlestick; it also witnessed the burgeoning of the liturgical thurible, often of silver or even gilded.[67]

From the moment the monastery of St Maurice was founded, therefore, the economic fortunes of church and town were inextricably woven together in Magdeburg. While Magdeburg could not have achieved its greatness in the tenth century without Saxon eastward expansion, it perhaps needs more emphasis than it has received that the foundations of its material prosperity, certainly that of the church, lay in the developing region to the west of the Elbe. As a place Magdeburg was perfectly positioned to be a centre of commerce between the complementary economic situations to the west and east of the Elbe; the west with its agriculture, its minerals, and its trade routes across Germany to Lotharingia and Burgundy and by water to Frisia; the east with its supply of labour, its silver filtering through from the trade between Scandinavia and the silver-producing regions of the Muslim-controlled silk routes (now in South Russia or northern

[66] Albert Brackmann, 'Die Ostpolitik Ottos des Grossen', *Historische Zeitschrift* 134 (1926), 242–56, esp. 246–7. Whether Thietmar's awareness of Kiev, a city, he says, with more than forty churches, eight markets and an innumerable population, can be read back fifty years earlier to around 968 is not at all certain, and it is of course doubtful that Kiev had developed anything like as much by then; Thietmar VIII, 32, p. 530. Albeit Kiev and the Rus are not mentioned, one may note the importance of eastern legates, including Greeks, Hungarians, Bulgarians and Slavs, at the Easter *Hoftag* of Quedlinburg in 973, Thietmar II, 31, p. 76.

[67] Bischoff, *Mittelalterliche Schatzverzeichnisse* (as in n. 57), nos. 2, 3 (silver), 11 (silver) 39 (gold), 43 (two silver), 50, 55 (gold), 67, 68, 74 (two gold, one silver), 76, 77 (five, one of gold), 93 (silver), 103 (four, one gilded, and a bone incense bowl, Weltenburg *c.* 1000), 124 (silver), 125. The material is not always stated.

Iran),[68] and, riding in on these Slav connections, distant oriental luxury goods. It was the west side of the Elbe, rather than the east, whose development benefited from the exchange; or which exploited the Slavs to add momentum to an economic development already having its own impetus. Thus when the Slav risings of 983 came and the Saxon military position to the east of the central Elbe collapsed, the church of Magdeburg could fall back on the bedrock of its western prosperity. However, scant as is the evidence for the effect on Magdeburg of these risings, if their damage was limited, they must have checked the seemingly limitless possibilities of economic expansion which existed previously, and they probably had an adverse effect on Magdeburg shipping to the north at least temporarily. In the view of Schwineköper, other more safely situated places such as Brunswick, Halle and Quedlinburg, began at the turn of the tenth and eleventh centuries to rival Magdeburg in its rôle of leading trade centre.[69] And though the slave trade continued throughout the eleventh century, it could be that it lost some momentum with the development of political units or tribal confederations in the Slav world.[70]

Finally, what effect had the ostensible raison d'être of the church of Magdeburg, its mission to spread the Christian faith, on its own town? Did mission and pastoral concern begin at home? After all, the Slavs were not the only people who needed missionising; Thietmar of Merseburg had no illusions about residual paganism in the countryside of East Saxony.[71] Notwithstanding the great material build-up of the church, naturally the aspect which has left the most systematic evidence in the sources, there are indications of bishops and priests who took seriously their duties of preaching in general. One of them was the first archbishop, Adalbert (968–81). He was a grandee in Saxon society, intervening on at least one occasion with partisan spirit in the feuds of its secular aristocracy; but we catch a glimpse of him at the time of his death, when Bishop Gisiler of Merseburg was with Otto II in Italy, looking after the diocese of Merseburg,

---

[68] For these routes, see P. H. Sawyer, *The age of the Vikings* (London, 1971), esp. chapters 5 and 8; and for finds of Islamic coins of the ninth to tenth in the Slav region to the east of Magdeburg, Röig, p. 27. [69] Schwineköper, *Königtum und Städte*, pp. 64–66.
[70] E.g. Lotter, 'Crusading idea', and for the eleventh century, Verlinden, pp. 221–3.
[71] See Claude, II, 450–51.

travelling throughout it to teach and administer the sacrament of confirmation. After he had died, his body was brought by ship down the Saale to Magdeburg where it was received with tears by the canons and especially by the monks.[72] When the archbishopric was established in 968 it was not thought possible for the monks to form the cathedral chapter in the English way (e.g. at Canterbury, Winchester and Worcester), as Patrick Wormald has pointed out; secular canons were installed in the cathedral church, the heir to most of the monastery's endowments, while the monks were moved to a neighbouring hill, and became the monastery of St John the Baptist, *Berge*[73]. But Adalbert, the former monk of St Maximin, remained interested in their purity of life, and often came to their church in the dead of night, says Thietmar, 'to watch unexpectedly how the brethren came to matins and who remained in the dormitory'.[74]

Another committed preacher was the priest Boso who had been educated at the monastery of St Emmeram, Regensburg. He surfaces, after long and mainly hidden labours, in the document of Otto I setting up the archbishopric of Magdeburg in 968: 'and because the venerable man Boso has now sweated much to convert the Slav people to God, he is to have the choice (of being suffragan bishop) of either Merseburg or Zeitz'. According to Thietmar, he tried to teach the Slavs in their own language, and asked them to sing *Kyrie Eleison*, explaining to them the usefulness of this; but they turned *Kyrie Eleison* into the German pejorative *ukrivolsa*, and misunderstood much else he said to them, saying, 'so hath Boso spoken'.[75]

It would be a presumption on the part of one whose only visit to Magdeburg occurred as long ago as 1962 to pose as an expert on the ill-evidenced early parochial history of the town. I stick to what appear to be the agreed facts. A parish church dedicated to St Stephen was founded at Magdeburg in the ninth century; it is presumed to be the *ecclesia plebeia* referred to in a diploma of 941, and 'the church of the merchants' referred to by Thietmar in

[72] Thietmar, III, 11, pp. 108–10. For the trial by battle between Count Gero of North Thuringia (not the famous earlier margrave) and Waldo, ibid., III, 9, pp. 106–8. Thietmar says that this fight pleased nobody except Archbishop Adalbert and Margrave Dietrich.
[73] Patrick Wormald, 'Aethelwold and his continental counterparts: contact, comparison and contrast', in *Bishop Aethelwold: his career and influence*, ed. Barbara Yorke (Woodbridge, 1988), p. 38.
[74] Thietmar, III, 11, p. 110.   [75] Thietmar, II, 36–37, pp. 84–86; DOI 366.

connection with visions and voices heard by its custodians one night during his own time at Magdeburg.[76] Another church with parish rights, *extra urbem*, founded in the time of Otto I and built of red wood, is mentioned by Thietmar to have been destroyed by a storm in 1013.[77] Thietmar, with his first-hand knowledge of early Magdeburg from his long education there, provides the fundamental testimony for the whole story, though the archaeological excavations can help us at certain points. For instance archeology suggests that the Market Church of St John, to the north of the cathedral/palace area (the *Domburg*), first mentioned in 1152, was not 'the church of the merchants' or its successor, since there are no signs there of a church earlier than the twelfth century.[78] Thietmar again, in praising the missionary zeal of his predecessor, Bishop Wigbert of Merseburg (1004–9), tells us that he consecrated the third and fourth churches in Magdeburg. Schlesinger has convincingly argued that this must mean parish churches (we cannot now name them), for there were by that time far more than two churches of any description in Magdeburg.[79] Besides the two parish churches already mentioned, we know of the cathedral, the monastery of St John the Baptist, the nunnery of St Lawrence, the round church mentioned by Thietmar (which Schlesinger argues to have been the palace chapel before 937),[80] the church attested in 966 which Margrave Gero had built in honour of St Cyriacus (as with his foundation of Gernrode) on his property in Magdeburg. Perhaps other nobles also had *curtes* with their own chapels in the town.[81]

Two houses of canons, i.e. having pastoral functions, were founded in the early eleventh century. Archbishop Gero fulfilled the intention of his predecessor Walthard, to make the round church into a house of canons, the church of St Sebastian; it later declined and was taken over by the Premonstratensian reformer,

---

[76] DO I 37; Thietmar, I, 12, pp. 16–18 (Thietmar's stay in Magdeburg was 987–1002, at p. 17, n. 6). See also Brackmann, *en passant*, p. 9, and Claude, I, 7–11.

[77] Thietmar, VI, 90, p. 382. See Claude, II, 447; Schlesinger, 'Zur Geschichte der Magdeburger Königspfalz', 10.

[78] Schlesinger, 'Zur Geschichte der Magdeburger Königspfalz', 12, and 12, n. 79; Nickel, 313. For how little help archeology can be in the early parochial history of Magdeburg, see Nickel, 'Magdeburg in karolingisch-ottorischer Zeit', 303, 319–20.

[79] Thietmar, VI, 37, p. 321 ... *preter hanc* (*ecclesiam* i.e. among the pagan Slavs at *Scutibure*), *terciam et quartam in Magadaburg multasque alias ipse dedicavit.* See Schlesinger, 12, Claude, II, 448.

[80] Thietmar, VI, 77, p. 366; Schlesinger, 12–13.

[81] Cited from the *Urkundenbuch* of Halberstadt by Claude, II, 450, n. 61.

St Norbert, in 1129, so that it is impossible to know how effective
and well endowed it was at first. Archbishop Hunfried (1023–51)
founded another house of canons, that of St Nicholas, but no
foundation charter for it survives.[82] Much earlier, in 941, Otto I
endowed a 'hospital' at Rohrsheim near Magdeburg on the road
to Halberstadt to enable the monastery of St Maurice to offer
hospitality to the poor.[83]

Whether all this amounts to adequate pastoral provision for the
town itself is impossible to judge, particularly as there is no
evidence of *how* the parish churches were served in this period.
But two features of the story must, I believe, particularly strike
one. The first is, after Otto I's time, the degree of pastoral interest
shown by prelates of Henry II's (1002–24) appointment.[84] The
second is the amount of pastoral consolidation attempted in the
town in the early eleventh century. Either this was still a period of
expansion in Magdeburg's economic and demographic history
after all; or the church took new initiatives to set its own house in
order pastorally at just the moment when the Gnesen policy
(1000) and an independent Polish church had cut off its prospect
of a really far-reaching field of missionary activity to the East:[85] or
both.

[82] Claude, II, 354, 374, 436.
[83] DOI 41 ... *in hospitales recipiendorum usus pauperum iure perenni in proprium donavimus*; Claude, II, 354–55.
[84] For Henry II's appointments to bishoprics, see H. L. Mikoletzky, *Kaiser Heinrich II. und die Kirche* (Vienna, 1946), pp. 30–41, and Josef Fleckenstein, *Die Hofkapelle der deutschen Könige*, II, *Die Hofkapelle im Rahmen der Ottonisch-Salischen Reichskirche* (Stuttgart, 1966), 208–23. It is the political and economic reasons for these appointments with which both are, for their purposes quite rightly, concerned.
[85] On this see especially Helmut Beumann, *Die Ottonen* (Stuttgart, 1987), pp. 149–56.

The abbot and townsmen of Cluny in the twelfth century

GILES CONSTABLE

The villa of Cluny was described in two documents of 825 as an estate with a church, various types of buildings and fields, vineyards, orchards, woods, waters and water-courses, exits and entries, resident dependants and their families, and 'all things and from all things whatsoever belonging to this villa'.[1] There is no indication of the amount of land, but it was located in an area of small- to medium-sized domains ranging from three to five hundred hectares.[2] In 893 it was given to Duke William of Aquitaine by his sister Ava, to be held after her death,

with all its appurtenances, both in churches and chapels, dependants of both sexes except for twenty dependants, dwellings, fields, orchards, cultivated and

---

The definitions of most technical terms are taken from Niermeyer's *Mediae Latinitatis lexicon minus*. For the dates of the abbots of Cluny in the second half of the twelfth century, see my article on 'The abbots and anti-abbot of Cluny during the papal schism of 1159', *Revue bénédictine* 94 (1984), 370–400 (esp. 371–6). The Latin form of Cluny, which is used as both a noun and an adjective, is normally translated 'of Cluny'. On the terms *villa* and *burgus* (*burgensis*), see nn. 6 and 10 below.

[1] *Cartulaire de Saint-Vincent de Mâcon*, ed. M.-C. Ragut (Mâcon, 1864), with a preface (pp. i–ccxxx) by Th. Chavot (hereafter: *Mâcon*; cited by number followed by page in parentheses), 55 (p. 42), and *Bibliotheca Cluniacensis*, ed. Martin Marrier and André Duchesne (Paris, 1614) (hereafter: *BC*), Notae, col. 13B. See *Recueil des chartes de l'abbaye de Cluny*, ed. Auguste Bernard and Alexandre Bruel (Collection de documents inédits sur l'histoire de France; Paris, 1876–1903) (hereafter: *C*; cited by number followed by volume and page in parentheses), 4–5 (I, 8) for textual emendations and references to other editions. The terms *exitus* and *regressus* (*introitus et exitus* are used in *C* 1516 [II, 566]) probably refer to ways in and out (i.e. access to a property), but Th. Chavot argued that they were revenues in *Mâcon*, pl. lxxv, and 'Des franchises et coutumes de la ville de Cluny au xiie: siècle', *Album de Saône-et-Loire* 2 (1842–43), 68, n. 1. A copy of this valuable article (of which I have not seen the original) was kindly sent me by Madame Germaine Chachuat, author of 'Des rapports entre l'abbaye et les habitants de Cluny aux xie, xiie et xiiie siècles', *Annales de l'Académie de Mâcon*, 3rd ser., 44 (1958–9), 19–26.

[2] Maurice Chaume, 'Les anciens domaines gallo-romains de la région bourguignonne', *Mémoires de la Commission des antiquités du département de la Côte-d'Or* 20 (1934), 305–7.

uncultivated fields, vineyards, meadows, mills, waters and water-courses, exits and entries.[3]

In the foundation charter of the abbey of Cluny, dated 910, William gave the property to the apostles Peter and Paul

with the demesne land and dwellings, and the chapel which is in honour of the blessed mother of God Mary and of St Peter, prince of the apostles, with all the things belonging to it, that is villas, chapels, dependants of both sexes, vineyards, fields, meadows, woods, waters and water-courses, mills, exits and entries, cultivated and uncultivated land, in their entirety.[4]

Since these lists are formulaic – the terminology of the foundation charter was used almost verbatim in a document of 1083[5] – it is hard to say whether the differences between them are significant. The reference in the charters of 893 and 910 to chapels and mills in the plural suggest some growth, and by 910 there were villas within the villa.[6] The domain was still basically agricultural, however, and there was no indication of the urban development that followed the foundation of the monastery.[7]

Cluny was called a *vicus* in some early charters,[8] but the earliest known reference to a town there was in the decree of the council of Anse in 994, which extended its protection to the churches belonging to Cluny and to 'the *burgum* of the same holy place'.

---

[3] C 53 (I, 61–2).   [4] C 112 (I, 125).   [5] C 3599 (IV, 756).

[6] According to Chavot, *Mâcon*, pp. cci–ccii, the *villa* in the Mâconnais 'n'était pas, en effet, une simple agglomération d'habitations, elle avait aussi sa circonscription territoriale'. In the tenth century it was apparently used interchangeably with *vicus*. The old *villa Cluniacensis* was later divided into deaneries, which were also territorial units, of which Cluny was one, with its own dean: C 3726, 4132, and 4143 (V, 77, 476, and 495–6). References to the villa of Cluny in the eleventh century, as in C 3221, 3406, and 3806 (IV, 353 and 512; V, 154), probably do not refer to the town, as some scholars have said. Urban II in 1095 (see n. 25 below) still distinguished the villa and the *burgus* of Cluny. The term villa later developed into the French *village* and *ville*, and by the second half of the twelfth century the town of Cluny was regularly called 'villa'. In a charter of Louis VII in 1166 (cited n. 61 below) villa was used for the town of St Gengoux and *vicus* for the New Town. See Gerhard Köbler, '*Civitas* und *vicus, burg, stat, dorf* und *wik*', *Vor- und Frühformen der europäischen Stadt im Mittelalter*, ed. Herbert Jankuhn, Walter Schlesinger, and Heiko Steuer, 2nd ed. (Abhandlungen der Akademie der Wissenschaften in Göttingen, Phil.-hist. Kl., 3 F, 83–4; Göttingen, 1975), I, 73–4.

[7] On the development of towns around monasteries, see Jacques Flach, *Les Origines de l'ancienne France, X^e et XIe siècles*, II. *Les origines communales. La féodalité et la chevalerie* (Paris, 1893), pp. 311–27 (325 on Cluny); Emile Lesne, *Histoire de la propriété ecclésiastique en France*, VI. *Les Eglises et les monastères, centres d'accueil, d'exploitation et de peuplement* (Mémoires et travaux publiés par des professeurs des facultés catholiques de Lille, 53; Lille, 1943), pp. 389–400 (393 on Cluny); and Ursula Lewald, 'Burg, Kloster, Stift', in *Die Burgen im deutschen Sprachraum*, ed. Hans Patze (Vorträge und Forschungen, 19; Sigmaringen, 1976), I, 155–80.

[8] C 265 and 280 (I, 258 and 276).

The council decreed that no castle (*castrum*) or fortification should be built 'below or next to the same place' and that no one in the vicinity 'should commit robbery in the same *castrum* or in the *burgum* of the same place',[9] which implies that Cluny was fortified and that the *burgus* was in some way dependent on the *castrum*. This is in accord with the view held by many scholars that the decisive feature of a *burgus* was fortification rather than a mercantile settlement.[10] The three factors which promoted the growth of a town around the abbey of Cluny, according to Duby, were political, as a place of security and peace, religious, as a centre of pilgrimage and burial, and economic, owing to its wealth and number of servants. 'By 1049 the town was topographically complete; the monastery was no longer isolated: it was enclosed by buildings on the south and west.'[11] Many references to its physical, economic, and institutional growth are found in charters and other sources of the late eleventh and early twelfth centuries. In about 1094 Humbert, the provost of Cluny (*prepositus Cluniacensis*), was accused by Prior Joceran, among other offences, of usurping some 'land of the town (*terra burgi*), which was of the law of St Peter, on which he built his house'.[12] Two documents of about 1100 concern houses at Cluny, one belonging to a pilgrim to Jerusalem and the other to an archpriest.[13] A few surviving houses in Cluny date from the middle of the twelfth

---

[9] C 2255 (III, 386–7).

[10] André Déléage, *La Vie rurale en Bourgogne jusqu'au début du onzième siècle* (Mâcon, 1941), p. 570 (of text volume), and, more generally, Lesne, *Eglises*, pp. 440–3, and Köbler, 'Civitas', p. 75, who said that a wall was the distinguishing feature of a *civitas* and burg. According to Chavot, *Mâcon*, p. ccii, the appellation *burgus* given to Ouilly in a charter of Hugh of Cluny indicated not a wall but its location next to a castle. For reasons of clarity and consistency, I shall translate *burgus* as town and *burgenses* as townsmen, indicating when they are called *cives*, *parrochiani*, *manentes*, *morantes*, and *habitatores* (see n. 68 below).

[11] Georges Duby, 'La ville de Cluny au temps de saint Odilon,' in *A Cluny. Congrès scientifique…en l'honneur des saints Abbés Odon et Odilon. 9–11 juillet 1949* (Dijon, 1950), pp. 260–2 (quote on p. 260). See also his *La société aux XIe et XIIe siècles dans la région mâconnaise* (Bibliothèque générale de l'Ecole pratique des hautes études, vi^e section; Paris, 1953 and 1971), pp. 267–8 (references here are to the 1971 edition, which is the same as that of 1953 but with different pagination), where he said that 'En 1115…la ville est faite.'

[12] C 3685 (V, 39–40). The 'law of St Peter' presumably referred to the *banlieu* established in 1080 (see p. 156 below). Humbert was allowed to keep for his lifetime what he had before the complaint was brought 'except for the condamine of St Odilo and the gifts and sales of pieces of land in the town of Cluny (*de plastris burgi Cluniacensis*)'. I have found no further references to Humbert's position as provost of Cluny.

[13] C 3755 (V, 108) and *Mâcon* 585 (p. 352). See Duby, *Société*, pp. 267, 271, and 393. The pilgrim Bernard *Veredunus* also had an estate (*honor*) at Varanges.

century. They are among the best examples of medieval domestic architecture in France and show the prosperity of some of the townsmen at that time.[14]

Pope Gregory VII in 1075 confirmed the immunity of the monastery of Cluny 'with the adjacent (*circumjacentibus*) chapels, that is of St Mary, St Maiolus, and St Odilo', and Urban II in 1095 granted the same liberty and immunity as Gregory VII had confirmed 'for the other chapels of this same town (*burgus*)' to the chapel of St Odo 'outside the town (*burgum*)'.[15] The church of St Mary in Gregory's bull was probably that dedicated by the bishop of Chalon in 1064 and not the original chapel in honour of Mary or the church of St Mary within the monastic enclosure.[16] The church of St Maiolus was the scene in 1063 of the efforts of the bishop of Mâcon to exercise his authority over Cluny by preaching and holding a synod.[17] The church of St Odilo was not a parish church. It was located outside the town, according to Chavot, and within the parish of St Mary.[18] The third parish church of Cluny was Hugh's chapel of St Odo,[19] which was replaced in about 1160, according to the Chronicle of Cluny, by the church of St Marcellus.[20] There is a reference in a charter of 1144 to an otherwise unknown church of St Gervais *in loco Cluniaco*, which may refer to the region rather than the town.[21]

[14] See Plate I, which is taken from Prosper Lorain, *Essai historique sur l'abbaye de Cluny* (Dijon, 1839). These houses survived the fires referred to in the Chronicle of Cluny under the years 1159, 1208, and 1233 (*BC*, coll. 1660B, 1664B, and 1665B). On the houses in monastic towns, see Lesne, *Églises*, pp. 416–23.

[15] *Bullarium sacri ordinis Cluniacensis* [ed. Pierre Symon] (Lyons, 1680) (hereafter: *Bull.*, pp. 18B and 23B (also *BC*, col. 516C); Philipp Jaffé, *Regesta pontificum romanorum*, ed. Samuel Löwenfeld, Ferdinand Kaltenbrunner, and Paul Ewald (Leipzig, 1885–8) (hereafter: JL; cited by number), 4974 (dated 1075) and 5551; *C* 3498 (dated 1076) and 3689 (IV, 612, and V, 41).

[16] *Gallia christiana*, IV, 885A. See Jean Virey, *Les églises romanes de l'ancien diocèse de Mâcon. Cluny et sa région* (Mâcon, 1935), p. 259. On the other churches dedicated to Mary see the charter of 910 cited above and Kenneth John Conant, *Cluny. Les églises et la maison du chef d'ordre* (The Mediaeval Academy of America, Publication 77; Mâcon, 1968), p. 65. The church of St Mary off the cloister was probably built by Hugh in 1084/5.

[17] *BC*, col. 509D; *Bull.*, p. 209A; *C* 3395 (IV, 499). This effort was firmly resisted by Hugh: see J.-Henri Pignot, *Histoire de l'ordre de Cluny depuis la fondation de l'abbaye jusqu'à la mort de Pierre-le-Vénérable* (Autun-Paris, 1868), II, 58, and Virey, *Eglises*, pp. 259–60.

[18] Th. Chavot, *Le Mâconnais. Géographie historique* (Paris–Mâcon, 1884), pp. 112–13; Virey, *Eglises*, p. 259.

[19] Calixtus II in 1120 confirmed the right of the priests of the parishes of St Mary and St Odo to receive and reject penitents and to make marriage contracts (*nuptiales chartas*): *BC*, col. 575BC; *Bull.*, p. 39B; JL 6821; *C* 3945 (V, 299).

[20] *BC*, col. 1660C. See Virey, *Eglises*, pp. 256–8. The church is still standing and is the most notable medieval monument of Cluny after the remains of the abbey and the Romanesque houses.

[21] *C* 4083 (V, 436–8). See the note of the editors on p. 437, n. 3.

Plate 1. Cluny, after a lithograph by E. Sagot

From the mid–twelfth century the three parish churches of Cluny were St Mary, St Maiolus, and St Marcellus.[22]

The papacy had long taken an interest in Cluny and helped to establish the special status of the abbey and surrounding *banlieu*, within which the abbot exercised authority.[23] In 1080 Cardinal-Bishop Peter of Albano, acting on behalf of Gregory VII, defined fixed boundaries (which corresponded almost exactly to the town as it existed in the nineteenth century) within which no act of violence could be committed, forbade anyone to attack or disturb Cluny, its inhabitants, 'or those fleeing within the established boundaries', abolished all bad customs, and warned 'the soldiers (*milites*) living in the villa of Cluny' to behave themselves especially 'because the closer they live the more they should avoid injuring the servants of God'.[24] Urban II on his visit to Cluny in 1095, when he dedicated the great church, redefined the region within which no act of violence should be done. 'The certain limits of immunity and security' specifically included the villa and town as well as the monastery, and the ban therefore protected both the townsmen and the monks of Cluny.[25] Lucius II in 1144 extended the boundaries of the *banlieu* yet again and decreed that only the pope or the abbot of Cluny could require the priests or parishioners of Cluny to attend a synod or meeting.[26]

The common interests of the monks and townsmen are illustrated by the privileges freeing them from the payment of tolls, which were intended to benefit the monks but which also protected pilgrims, travellers, and merchants as Cluny's im-

[22] Chavot, 'Franchises', p. 86, n. 89; Virey, *Eglises*, p. 263.
[23] Chavot, in *Mâcon*, pp. cxc–cxciv, translated the relevant passages in the papal bulls, and identified the places defining the *banlieu*. See, generally, the unfinished chapter in Lesne, *Eglises*, on 'Territoire, *procinctus*, banlieue'.
[24] *BC*, col. 512BD; *Bull.*, p. 210; *C* 3549 (IV, 677). Here and below I have translated *milites* as 'soldiers' or 'fighting men' unless it clearly means 'knights', as in Peter the Venerable's Letter 191 cited n. 52 below.
[25] *BC*, col. 518–20; *Bull.*, p. 25AB; JL, I, 681; *C* 3689 (V, 41). 'We therefore establish the boundaries of the sacred ban for the monastery of Cluny and likewise for the villa and town and we assign these limits in full certainty, ordering in the name of the lord God Almighty and by the authority of the apostles Peter and Paul [and] admonishing all of you and every man who reads or hears this not to infringe this ban knowingly and each and all to keep its law.' Louis VI in 1119 confirmed the authority of the abbot and forbade any except royal castles and fortifications but made no specific reference to the town: *C* 3943 (V, 295–8). See Achille Luchaire, *Louis VI le Gros* (Paris, 1890), p. 130, no. 276.
[26] *BC.* col. 1383C–4A; *Bull.*, pp. 52B–3A; JL 8621; *C* 4085 (V, 439). See Chachuat, 'Rapports', p. 22.

portance as a religious and commercial centre grew.[27] In a joint
privilege for the Bishop of Langres and the monks of Cluny issued
in about 1070, Landric *Grossus* of Uxelles agreed not to demand
'the exaction which they commonly call *pedituram*' from those,
free or servile, who travelled across his lands 'for the sake either of
trade or of prayer'.[28] Pascal II in 1107 forbade any tolls or new
exactions to be levied on the main roads leading to and from
Cluny and protected the persons and possessions of travellers.[29]
Grants to Cluny of freedom from tolls were made in 1130 by
King Louis VI, in 1140 by Hugh of Berzé, and in about 1150 by
Raymond of Toulouse, who freed from all kinds of tolls 'the
agents (*nuncios*) who do anything for the food and clothing of the
holy convent of Cluny or for their other work'.[30] Some of these
nuncii may have been monks but many of them were certainly
servants and other laymen engaged in supplying the needs of the
abbey.

The inhabitants of Cluny in the eleventh century were mostly,
if not all, dependants of the abbey. 'Cluny attracted men',
according to Duby, 'while nearby hamlets, like Mailly, were
emptied, and Ruffey and Merzé lost their former importance.'[31]
The earliest known use of the term *burgenses* was in a charter of
996/1031 which defined a holding of land at Mailly as bounded
by *terra francorum qui Buggencii [Burgentii] vocantur*. Déléage (who
was followed by Duby) proposed that these 'free men who are
called townsmen' lived in Cluny but stressed that many freemen
at that time were agricultural workers and that there was still no
urban community.[32] There is no proof that these townsmen were

[27] On the routes through Cluny, which was located at an important crossroads, see Déléage, *Vie rurale*, pp. 172–3, and Duby, *Société*, pp. 265–6. On tolls (*pedagie, péages*), see Chavot, 'Franchises', pp. 70–1; Duby, *Société*, pp. 260, 266, 312, etc.; and Jean Richard, *Les Ducs de Bourgogne et la formation du duché du XIᵉ au XIVᵉ siècle* (Paris, 1954), p. 353.
[28] *C* 3440 (IV, 550). On Landric and the lords of Uxelles, who became the lords of Brancion in the twelfth century and played an important rôle in the history of Cluny, see Constance Bouchard, *Sword, Miter, and Cloister: Nobility and the Church in Burgundy, 980–1198* (Ithaca–London, 1987), pp. 303–4 (and 295–307 generally).
[29] *Bull.*, p. 34AB; JL 6113; *C* 3851 (V, 203).
[30] *BC*, col. 1392 (see Luchaire, *Louis VI*, p. 213, no. 456); *C* 3908 (V, 258 and 846 on date); and *C* 4069 (V, 420). See also *C* 4275 (V, 638); *BC*, col. 1442 (*C* 4276 [V, 638]); *C* 4346 (V, 711); and *C* 4351 (V, 713). The terms *nuncii* and *missi* in these and other twelfth-century Cluniac charters clearly mean 'agents' or 'couriers' rather than 'messengers' or 'representatives'.
[31] Duby, 'Ville', p. 261.
[32] *C* 2331 (III, 449). See Déléage, *Vie rurale*, p. 570; Duby, 'Ville', pp. 261, n. 1, and 263, n. 1, and *Société*, p. 46.

in fact from Cluny, and according to Chavot and Chachuat there were no clear references to *burgenses* before the time of Hugh, who was the first abbot to confirm the customs of the townsmen of Cluny.[33] This charter is known only from later references. Chavot argued that it postdated Peter of Albano's privilege of 1080, which would have mentioned a commune had it existed,[34] but there were many other types of urban privileges which Hugh could have granted. He is known to have taken an interest in the question of personal freedom. In 1103/4 three Cluniac deans, acting on his instructions, secured the freedom of some serfs in a village belonging to Cluny. The names of the *rustici* 'who were freed from the yoke of servitude by the service of St Peter' were listed in the resulting charter.[35]

The first unequivocal reference to the *burgenses* of Cluny as a group was in a charter of 1108 listing three groups of witnesses *de monachis*, *de militibus*, and *de burgensibus vel servientibus*.[36] The population of the town was varied, though probably still not large,[37] and included not only the groups mentioned here but also clerics, such as the parish priests and the archpriest whose house has been mentioned. Peter the Venerable in his *Dispositio rei familiaris Cluniacensis*, which dates from 1147/8, referred to 'some noble little clerics (*clericellos nobiles*) who were educated in the town of Cluny'. He also mentioned 'a crowd of guests' at the

---

[33] Chavot, 'Franchises', p. 68, who added after saying that no *burgensis* appeared in the charters of the abbots before Hugh that 'Les chartes même de son temps ne nous ont laissé aucune trace de ce fait'; Chachuat, 'Rapports', p. 20. See also Joseph Garnier and Ernest Champeaux, *Chartes de communes et d'affranchissements en Bourgogne. Introduction* (Dijon, 1918), p. 65. For the references to Hugh in the confirmations of Abbots Stephen and Hugh IV, see pp. 165 and 168 below.   [34] Chavot, 'Franchises', p. 69.

[35] C 3822 (v, 178–9). See Chachuat, 'Rapports', pp. 20–1. The case was brought by three Cluniac deans in the court of Brancion and Sennecy.

[36] C 3874 (v, 229). The editors (see v, 549, n. 1) cited this as the first use of the term *bourgeois* for the townsmen of Cluny. Johannes Fechter, *Cluny, Adel und Volk. Studien über das Verhältnis des Klosters zu den Ständen (910–1156)* (Diss. Tübingen, 1966), p. 13, dated the earliest reference to a *burgensis* in 1136, citing C 4056 (see n. 39 below). The meaning of *servientes* and force of *vel* in *de burgensibus vel servientibus* is unclear (cf. n. 64 below). *Serviens* had a wide range of meanings. Here it probably means the servants or *famuli* of the abbey. It is also uncertain whether the *milites* lived in the town of Cluny or in the surroundings, like the *milites* in the privilege of Peter of Albano cited n. 24 above. The *miles de Cluniaco* in C 3299 (IV, 395) may have been from the villa. Bernard *Veredunus*, who had an *honor* in Varanges as well as a house in Cluny (n. 13 above), was a man of some standing but was not called a *miles*. Cf. Duby, 'Ville', p. 262, n. 1, and *Société*, p. 271, n. 36.

[37] See Chavot, 'Franchises', p. 70; Garnier and Champeaux, *Chartes*, p. 65; and Duby, *Société*, pp. 271, 274, n. 47, and 347, n. 2, and 308–9, where he estimated the population of Cluny in the twelfth century at about 555 adult men.

monastery and 'an infinite number of poor men', who presumably lived in the town.[38] Some townsmen were rich, however. 'A certain townsman of Cluny, named Girbertus' became a monk in about 1136 'because he overflowed with goods in this world' and desired some in the next.[39] There were also many ranks and types of dependants, including the monastic servants or *famuli*, who sometimes brought food stolen from the infirmary to their wives and children in the town.[40] Henry of Winchester's *Constitutio expensae Cluniaci*, drawn up in the middle of the twelfth century, shows that there were various types of tenures within the villa of Cluny, and perhaps also in the town, where some tenants held for rents in cash and others in kind.[41] It is hard to say whether or not they were all free,[42] and the main link between them was their common residence in the town of Cluny. The concept of the *burgenses* as a social category was by now well established in Burgundy and the Auvergne. Peter the Venerable in two letters written to the pope about 1150 listed 'the lords of castles, soldiers of lesser degree, townsmen, country folk, and all types of laymen' in Auvergne and the clerics, monks, townsmen, and 'those who are the usual prey of plunderers and food of wolves, the countrymen (*rustici*), peasants (*agricolae*), poor men, widows, orphans, and all types of commoners' in Burgundy.[43]

The townsmen of Cluny first appeared on the larger scene of history as supporters of Abbot Pontius in his attempt to re-establish himself at Cluny, probably in 1126, four years after Peter

[38] *C* 4132 (v, 475 and 479). See Lesne, *Eglises*, p. 415. On this document and the problems created for the abbey by the progressive replacement of a domainal by a money economy, see Georges Duby, 'Economie domaniale et économie monétaire. Le budget de l'abbaye de Cluny entre 1080 et 1155', *Annales* 6 (1952), 155–71. [39] *C* 4056 (v, 409).

[40] Peter the Venerable, *Stat.* 24, ed. Giles Constable, in *Corpus consuetudinum monasticarum*, VI (Siegburg, 1975), 61. On the *famuli* living in the town of Cluny see Duby, *Société*, pp. 274, n. 47, and 347, n. 2.

[41] *C* 4143 (v, 495–6). See Chavot, 'Franchises', pp. 69–70, and *Mâcon*, p. ciii; Chachuat, 'Rapports', p. 25; and, more generally, Georges Duby, 'Un inventaire des profits de la seigneurie clunisienne à la mort de Pierre le Vénérable', in *Petrus Venerabilis, 1156–1956. Studies and Texts Commemorating the Eighth Centenary of his Death*, ed. Giles Constable and James Kritzeck (Studia Anselmiana, 40; Rome, 1956), pp. 128–40.

[42] The serfs mentioned by Duby, 'Ville', p. 263, n. 1, may have lived in the villa rather than the town of Cluny. The free men and serfs given to Cluny by Bernard *Grossus* of Uxelles in 1117 were 'inside and outside the town of Cluny': *C* 3929 (v, 282–3). Chavot, 'Franchises', p. 69, suggested that the free men and women lived in the town and the serfs in the environs.

[43] Peter the Venerable, *The letters of Peter the Venerable*, ed. Giles Constable (Harvard Historical Studies, 78; Cambridge, Mass., 1967), I, pp. 406 and 410.

the Venerable was elected abbot. Before his return, according to the *Chronologia abbatum*, Pontius made sure 'of the agreement concerning himself both of the monks and of the townsmen of Cluny', and Ordericus Vitalis wrote that

The soldiers and people of the region (*milites...et comprovinciales*), both countrymen and townsmen, rejoiced at the coming [of Pontius], whom they greatly loved for his friendliness and hospitality (*affabilitate...et dapsilitate*). These men broke into the monastery when the schism among the monks became known, and they introduced Pontius and his men with violence, though he himself did not want this.[44]

Pope Honorius II condemned the townsmen in his bulls of 24 April and 20 October 1126, where he required them to give back what they had taken from the abbey and to make reparation for any other damage.[45] The reasons for their support of Pontius are unclear aside from his open-handedness and Peter's policies of economy and of excluding laymen from the abbey, which may have hurt the interests of the townsmen.

There was also trouble with the townsmen of La-Charité-sur-Loire, who in 1130 swore to the count and bishop of Nevers and other dignitaries that

Henceforth they would not attack, strike, or kill the lord Peter abbot of Cluny or his successors or the monks of Cluny, both present and future, and that they would neither take their property by violence nor harm these abbots, monks, servants, or their associates or agents or any of their property.

They swore furthermore to persevere faithfully in this fealty and not to rebel against the abbot and monks of Cluny or their men.[46]

---

[44] *BC*, col. 1623A, and Ordericus Vitalis, *Historia ecclesiastica*, XII, 30, ed. M. Chibnall (Oxford Medieval Texts; Oxford, 1969–80), VI, 312. Peter the Venerable in his account of the affair in *De miraculis*, II, 12, ed. Denise Bouthillier (Corpus Christianorum: Continuatio mediaevalis, 83; Turnhout, 1988), pp. 119–20, mentioned *milites*, 'the arms of common men', and women who entered the abbey but not specifically townsmen. Among many works on this affair, see with reference to the rôle of the townsmen, Adriaan Bredero, 'Cluny et Cîteaux au XIIème siècle. Les origines de la controverse', *Studi medievali*, 3 s., 12 (1971), 158 and n. 95, reprinted in his *Cluny et Cîteaux au douzième siècle* (Amsterdam–Maarssen, 1985), p. 41 and n. 93; Piero Zerbi, 'Intorno allo scisma di Ponzio, abate di Cluny (1122–26)' in his *Tra Milano e Cluny* (Italia sacra, 28; Rome, 1978), pp. 332–3; Nadine Fresco, *L'"affaire" Pons de Melgueil, 1122–1126* (Diss. Paris I, 1973), I, 147 (n. 82) and 150, who argued that the townsmen were Pontius's principal supporters; and H. E. J. Cowdrey, 'Two Studies in Cluniac History 1049–1126', *Studi Gregoriani* 11 (1978), 238–40.

[45] *PL*, 166.1260AC and 1267D–8A (*Bull.*, p. 44A); JL 7261 and 7268; *C* 3991 and 3994 (V, 344 and 346).

[46] *C* 4009 (V, 365). See Pignot, *Cluny*, III, 257–8. The charter is inscribed on the back 'That the townsmen of La Charité swore in perpetuity not to oppose the abbot of Cluny.'

A few years later the prior of La Charité wrote to Peter the Venerable thanking him for some gifts and saying that 'Your paternity should know that both we and our townsmen derive great comfort from these and great certainty of your holy love.'[47]

In January 1145 Peter took the important step of requiring all the townsmen of Cluny and men in the deaneries who were over the age of fifteen to swear (1) to be faithful to the abbot and church, (2) not to assist any declared enemy of the church, and (3) to go out armed if summoned by an agent of the abbot, unless they were physically infirm, were chosen to guard the town by the abbot and 'the better townsmen (*meliores burgenses*)', or sent suitable substitutes. Anyone who was killed on an expedition 'in defence of the church' would be brought to Cluny, received by the community, buried without charge, absolved of his sins, and made a participant in the liturgical benefits of the church. Anyone who was liable to give compensation for killing or harming an enemy of the church should make no payment and would be included in the peace made by the church with his adversary. He would be supported and protected at home by his dean and, if necessary, at Cluny by the dean and chamberlain of Cluny until he could safely return home. Depending on by whom, to whom, and where (inside or outside the apostolic ban) the deed was done, payment would be made by the church, the townsmen, or those from outside.

Since all this was established for the good of peace and common utility, the lord abbot granted the townsmen that for a fixed time after these agreements (*ex his paccionibus prefixo tempore transacto*) no custom could be exacted from them or imposed upon them or in any way reimposed to the harm of themselves or their heirs.[48]

So far as is known, there was no statement at this time of the respective rights and obligations of the abbot and townsmen aside from the lost grant of Abbot Hugh, but the imposition of the oath

[47] Peter the Venerable, *Ep.* 41, ed. Constable, I, 136.
[48] This charter is printed (numbered 4098 bis) in the additions to the errata to volume V in C VI, 958–60. It was described as unedited by Paul Séjourné in the *Dictionnaire de théologie catholique*, XII.2, col. 2067, and republished by Jean Leclercq, *Pierre le Vénérable* (Figures monastiques; Abbaye S. Wandrille, 1946), pp. 371–4. See Jean Richard, 'La Publication des chartes de Cluny', in *A Cluny* (n. 11 above), p. 159; Duby, *Société*, p. 313; Fechter, *Cluny*, p. 101; and Chachuat, 'Rapports', pp. 25–6.

of fidelity and military service shows that the abbot had power over all the men in both the town and the deaneries.[49] He also benefited from various customary payments. Peter the Venerable in his *Dispositio*, drawn up in 1147/8, said that the chamberlain received a hundred pounds and five hundred Cluniac *solidi* 'in the town of Cluny'.[50] Soon afterwards Henry of Winchester gave a more detailed account of the revenues from the deanery of Cluny, including four pounds and ten *solidi* 'from the gardens next to the water', sixty *solidi* from the holdings of borderers, ten pounds of census at the feast of St John, thirty *solidi* from markets (*feriis*), six pounds from the monopoly of wine, six pounds from the census of houses and from fees or fines (*bannis*), three shillings from the sale of salt, and forty pounds from legal pleas and approvals.[51] These payments may not all have come from the town, but they give an idea of the extent of the abbot's rights and revenues.

The most striking feature of the oath of 1145 was the obligation of military service it imposed on the townsmen and men of the deaneries. Peter clearly wanted to strengthen the position of Cluny in view of the growing disturbances and pressures from its enemies in the middle of the twelfth century. He wrote to the pope after his return from Italy in 1152 that 'I found all of our neighbors, including the *milites* and castellans as well as the counts and dukes of our Burgundy ... urging our men everywhere to take up arms.' He was particularly alarmed by the castle built near Cluny by Hugh *Discalciatus* of La Bussière, who eventually agreed, in return for two hundred and twenty pounds, to destroy the castle, give the site to Cluny, and build no further fortifications between Cluny and La Bussière.[52] In 1153 or 1154 a council

---

[49] See Duby, *Société*, p. 273 and n. 43, on this and other rights of the abbot.

[50] *C* 4132 (v, 480). He also said (p. 478) that Abbot Hugh had transferred 'certain ovens in the villa of Cluny and their revenues' from the chamberlain to the almoner to support commemorative distributions to the poor. See, on the *Dispositio*, n. 38 above, and on the money of Cluny, Chavot, 'Franchises', pp. 78–82, and *Mâcon*, pp. cxxxvi–cxl, and Duby, *Société*, pp. 281 and 362.

[51] *C* 4143 (v, 495–6). The other revenues were from places outside Cluny, agricultural produce, and a mill. The total was 90 pounds plus 47 measures of grain as compared to 125 pounds in Peter's *Dispositio*: see the chart in Duby, 'Inventaire', between pp. 134–5, and *Société*, p. 273, n. 43.

[52] Peter the Venerable, *Ep.* 191, ed. Constable, I, 442–3. In the commentary (II, 225–6) I missed the description of the terms and circumstances of this agreement (in terms similar to Peter's) in a charter of 1173 (*C* 4244, cited n. 65 below). According to Peter (but not the charter), Hugh 'promised that he would make (*sese facturum*) a document containing this [agreement] by the

(known only from an entry in the later Chronicle of Cluny) met at Mâcon in order to restore 'the peace of the church of Cluny' and decreed that its monks, laymen, and property should remain in full and secure peace within the region bounded by the Saône, Loire, and Rhone rivers, Autun, and a castle (perhaps Chagny or Château-Chalon) beyond Chalon, and that travellers to and from Cluny 'should remain and be kept secure and peaceful with regard to themselves and their property'.

At the same time... the inhabitants of the town (*civitas*) of Cluny promised to go out armed with the aforesaid nobles and lords as often as they were required to do so, etc., and the prelates promised on their part that they would likewise go out against such men, etc.[53]

A decade later, in 1163, Pope Alexander III urged the counts of Forez and Mâcon and some of the lords who had attended the council at Mâcon to preserve 'the sworn peace of the church of Cluny'.[54]

These troubles may have been the result of purely local disturbances and the lack of any central power in Burgundy,[55] but they have been associated by some scholars with the growing ambitions of Frederick Barbarossa on the other side of the Saône.[56] Abbot Stephen of Cluny wrote at least seven letters to

authority and witness of the archbishop of Lyons and his co-bishops, count William, and other nobles of the region'. On the significance of the use of the future here see n. 53 below.

[53] *BC*, coll. 592D–3B and 1650C–1B; *Mâcon*, pp. cclviii–lix (the fourth council of Mâcon). See Chavot, 'Franchises', p. 72; Duby, *Société*, p. 312; and the commentary on Peter's letter 191 cited n. 52 above. This council was called at the request of Peter and his friends, presided over by the Cardinal-Legate Odo, and attended by the archbishop of Lyons (Peter's brother Heraclius), the bishops of Autun, Mâcon, and Chalon, the counts of Burgundy and Chalon, the lords of Beaujeu, Berzé, Brancion, and La Bussière, and other notables. If the account in the Chronicle is to be trusted, the townsmen of Cluny repeated their oath of 1145, and Hugh *Discalciatus* may have presented the document to which Peter referred in his *Ep.* 191 (n. 52 above).   [54] *Bull.*, pp. 74–5; JL 10908; *C* 4214 (v, 561).

[55] This was the view of Peter the Venerable in the letters cited nn. 43 and 52 above. The rising tide of disorder is reflected in the statutes of the Cistercian general chapter, which decreed in 1157 that 'No abbot should give anything or assist fighters in time of war', to which the Charleville MS added 'That we should not lend or give anything, either grain or horses, to those who make war among themselves': *Statuta capitulorum generalium ordinis Cisterciensis*, ed. J.-M. Canivez (Bibliothèque de la Revue d'histoire ecclésiastique, 9–14; Louvain, 1933–41), I, 58 (1154.19) and 62 (1157.23), cited and dated together by Chrysogonus Waddell in his forthcoming article 'Towards a new provisional edition of the statutes of the Cistercian chapter general *c.* 1119–1189'.

[56] Ernest Petit, *Histoire des ducs de Bourgogne de la race capétienne* (Dijon, 1885–Paris, 1905), II, pp. 163–4; J.-Louis Bazin, *Les comtes héréditaires de Chalon-sur-Saône* (Mémoires de la Société d'histoire et d'archéologie de Chalon-sur-Saône, 2 s., 4.1; Chalon-sur-Saône, 1911), pp. 72–5;

Louis VII describing the problems, in one of which he referred to the attacks of the Germans 'whom they call Brabançons' and urged the king to intervene to protect his own interests and those of his subjects.[57] Matters came to a head in the spring of 1166, when Count William of Chalon occupied the Cluniac castle of Lourdon. 'The older men together with the younger men went out from the town (vicus) of Cluny', wrote Hugh of Poitiers, but they were attacked and almost all killed by the count's men,[58] who 'atrociously massacred more than five hundred of the townsmen of Cluny like sheep', according to the History of Louis VII, which gave a lurid account of the affair, saying that the count, inspired by the Devil, gathered an army of Brabançons in order to attack and despoil the monks of Cluny.[59] Louis VII's consequent campaign against the count, who was duly punished, marked an important step in the expansion of royal authority in Burgundy,[60] as did his association with Cluny in the ownership of St Gengoux, henceforth known as 'le Royal' (and, later, 'le National'). In the charter of pariage, which Luchaire dated between 24 April and 11 July 1166 (that is, after the count's attack but probably before the royal campaign), Louis said that the abbey of Cluny until recently had flourished and given help to others but now was forced to seek help for itself 'by the wars

Ch. Perrat, L'Autel d'Avenas. La légende de Ganelon et les expéditions de Louis VII en Bourgogne (1166–1172) (Lyon, 1932), pp. 48–9; and Heinrich Büttner, 'Friedrich Barbarossa und Burgund', in Probleme des 12. Jahrhunderts (Vorträge und Forschungen, 12; Konstanz-Stuttgart, 1968), pp. 103–4. On Frederick's support of the expelled Abbot Hugh III of Cluny, see Constable, 'Abbots', pp. 392–4.

[57] Historiae Francorum scriptores, ed. André Duchesne (Paris, 1636–49), IV, 665, no. 279, and other letters referred to in Constable, 'Abbots', p. 397, n. 111. This letter can be dated 1166 from its reference to the excommunicated imperial candidate for the archbishopric of Lyons: Jean Beyssac, Les Chanoines de l'église de Lyon (Lyon, 1914), p. 32, and Büttner, 'Friedrich', p. 104. This is the first known reference to Brabançons, according to Herbert Grundmann, 'Rotten und Brabanzonen. Söldner-Heere im 12. Jahrhundert', Deutsches Archiv 5 (1942), 445.

[58] Hugh of Poitiers, Chron., IV, ed. R. B. C. Huygens, Monumenta Vizeliacensia (Corpus Christianorum: Continuatio mediaevalis, 42; Turnhout, 1976), p. 589. The term egressi sunt resembles the oath ut omnes exeant in 1145.

[59] De glorioso rege Ludovico, Ludovici filio, c. 23, in Vie de Louis le Gros par Suger, ed. Auguste Molinier (Collection de textes pour servir à l'étude et à l'enseignement de l'histoire, 4; Paris, 1887), pp. 172–3. Grundmann, 'Rotten', pp. 446–7, suggested that the Brabançon mercenaries used by the count were on their way to Italy, which they entered in the fall of 1146. Duby, Société, p. 408, n. 31, questioned the number of men killed.

[60] See, in addition to the works of Petit, Bazin, and Perrat cited n. 56 above, Duby, Société, pp. 314 and 407–8; Richard, Ducs de Bourgogne, pp. 184–5; and Marcel Pacaut, Louis VII et son royaume (Bibliothèque générale de l'Ecole pratique des hautes études, VIᵉ section; Paris, 1964), p. 89.

which are spreading everywhere and the evil raging on every side'.[61] A memorial to the massacre of the townsmen of Cluny is found in the necrology of St-Martin-des-Champs under July 14:

P[eter] died and many others who were killed by the Brabançons for the protection of liberty and out of fidelity to the church of Cluny. Let the office be celebrated with hoods in the choir.[62]

The monks as well as the townsmen thus fulfilled their obligations under the oath of 1145, and the memory of those who died for Cluny was solemnly preserved at Paris as well, presumably, as at Cluny and other Cluniac houses. It must have helped to seal the alliance between the monastery and the town and to usher in the period which saw two confirmations of the rights and customs of the townsmen.

The first was issued by Abbot Stephen, who was abbot from 1162/3 until 1173.[63]

Desiring to know and preserve the good customs of this place and the practices rightly established by St Hugh and other blessed abbots of the same town

[61] *C* 4223 (v, 571–3). The charter said that Abbot Stephen and the monastery associated (*consociaverunt*) the king 'in the town (*villa*) called St Gengoux and in all the possessions belonging to the authority (*potestatem*) of that town, and especially in the settlement called the New Town (*nominatim vico qui dicitur Burgum Novum*)'. See Achille Luchaire, *Etudes sur les actes de Louis VII* (Paris, 1885), p. 267, no. 527, and, on the pariage of St-Gengoux, Petit, *Ducs de Bourgogne*, II, 169; Achille Luchaire, *Histoire des institutions monarchiques de la France sous les premiers capétiens (987–1180)*, 2nd ed. (Paris, 1891), II, 196–7 and 201; Léon Gallet, *Les Traités de pariage dans la France féodale* (Paris, 1935), pp. 21 (misdated 1266), 29, and 131; Duby, *Société*, pp. 412 and 415; and Richard, *Ducs de Bourgogne*, p. 184. These authors do not discuss the provisions concerning the *burgus Clun.* (p. 572), which apparently refer not to the town of Cluny but to the town of St Gengoux (as distinct from the New Town), where Cluny continued to exercise special rights. The date of this charter suggests that Petit was right in calling it the price of Louis's intervention. He was well aware of the situation, and in November 1166 issued a privilege for the Cluniac priory of Ambierle 'because with wars spreading everywhere in our homeland, evil men try to oppress the churches and take their goods': *C* 4224 (v, 574). See Luchaire, *Louis VII*, p. 267, no. 529.
[62] *Obituaires de la province de Sens*, I. *Diocèses de Sens et de Paris*, ed. Auguste Molinier and Auguste Longnon (Paris, 1902), p. 447, and *Synopse der cluniacensischen Necrologien*, ed. Joachim Wollasch with Wolf-Dieter Heim, Joachim Mehne, Franz Neiske, and Dietrich Poeck (Münstersche Mittelalter-Schriften, 39.1–2), II, 391. See Auguste Molinier, *Les Obituaires français au moyen âge* (Paris, 1890), p. 41, n. 7 (on p. 42).
[63] There are three editions of this document: (1) Chavot, 'Franchises', pp. 72–5 (with a French translation and commentary on pp. 75–8); (2) A. L'Huillier, *Vie de saint Hugues, abbé de Cluny, 1024–1109* (Solesmes, 1888), pp. 635–7 (from Chavot); and (3) *C* 4205 (v, 548–51), which is used here. Before knowing the text was published, I transcribed it from the two manuscripts (Paris, Bibl. nat., N.a.l. 2265, nos. 10 and 11; see the descriptions by Chavot and by Bruel), and it has been checked again by Professor Alan Bernstein of the University of Arizona. The only significant emendations (none of which affect the sense) are p. 548, line 1] add *nostri after* Domini; p. 550, lines 4, 5, 9] *solidos for solidorum*; and p. 551, line 14] *annone for avene*.

(*ville*), he [Stephen] ordered the older men of this place to come together, to examine by discussing among themselves the state of the town (*ville*) and the practices established and preserved by the previous holy abbots, to bring them to memory, and to gather them in writing for the aforesaid venerable Abbot Stephen.

The eighteen customs fell into five categories, concerned respectively with personal status (1–3), public order (4–10 and 18), marriages (11), inheritance (12–14), and banalities (15–17). The first three established that the church (meaning the abbey of Cluny, as in the oath of 1145) (1) would treat as a citizen (*civis*) anyone who lived in Cluny for a year and a day, (2) would defend an inhabitant or parishioner who was accused of servile status, and (3) would let the accused, if convicted, leave the town with his property and not deliver him to the accuser. From this it appears that all townsmen were considered free and that *burgensis* was equated with *civis*, *habitator*, and *parrochianus*.[64]

The second group, dealing with public order, began with (4) that no harm should be done to the person or property of an inhabitant or parishioner against whom a complaint had been made to the magistrate (*potestas*) if he was ready to do justice or provide suitable security. (5) A dispute between townsmen could be settled by themselves without lodging a complaint with the magistrate (*potestas*), unless it was a case of *fractum ville*, which involved a blow, theft, or adultery and must be brought before the magistrate (*magistratum*). Articles (6) and (7) established the fines for a blow with bloodshed at sixty *solidi* and for a blow without bloodshed or for calling someone a thief, serf, rotter (*putidus*), perjurer, leper, or traitor, if a complaint was made to the magistrate, at six *solidi*, to be divided between the lord and the injured party. (8) The person and property of a convicted thief were at the discretion (*in placito et miseratione*) of the lord. (9) A man and woman guilty of adultery must run together naked through the town. (10) The fine for subsequently reproaching them with the crime or the penalty, if a complaint was made, was six *solidi*, to be divided between the lord and the accused. To this group should be added the final article (18) permitting a respectable man or woman who was abused in word or deed by

---

[64] In article 4 the text reads *burgenses uel ... habitantes*, but the force of the *uel* (cf. n. 36 above) is uncertain.

a *glutus* (pander?) or whore to take immediate revenge and forbidding the magistrate to intervene. The *dominus* in these articles was probably the abbot of the *ecclesia* of Cluny. The *potestas* or *magistratus* who was directly responsible for maintaining law and order presumably acted for the abbot.

Article 11 regulated the compensation given to chaplains at weddings. The three following articles dealt with inheritances and established that (12) a legal will must be observed. The goods of an intestate went either (13) to his nearest relation, who was responsible for his burial and benefactions for his soul, or (14) to the church, if he had no heir or wife. The remaining three articles define the payments, in cash or kind, for using the oven to bake bread for (15) sale or (16) personal use and (17) for grinding grain at the mill. It is known from the *Dispositio* of Peter the Venerable and the *Constitutio* of Henry of Winchester that the abbey derived revenues from ovens and mills, which were clearly seigneurial monopolies at Cluny. The two bakers – the *major* and his *socius* – were probably both appointed by the abbey, but Chavot proposed that one was responsible to the monastery and the other to the town.

The townsmen and abbots continued to cooperate under Abbot Stephen's successors. The charter renewing the peace between Cluny and Hugh of La Bussière in 1173 was witnessed by nine townsmen, including John 'the *famulus* of the prior of Cluny'. After reviewing the controversy between Hugh and Peter the Venerable, and its settlement, the charter said that another dispute developed under Abbot Ralph 'because some things were less explicit (*minus expressa*) in the previous agreements'. Hugh agreed to allow the monks to fortify Massilly and withdrew his complaints against Cluny in return for three hundred *solidi* for himself and a hundred for his counsel. 'The monks could make a complaint when they wished concerning the toll which he established in our land.' Hugh furthermore accepted only those customs of Saint-Point and *Mons Franciae* 'which he would follow for justice or ancient usage according to the testimony of the senior men'.[65] This left several loopholes, and in 1180 a further dispute between Cluny and Hugh's son Guy of La

---

[65] C 4244 (v, 598–9). See n. 52 above. I cannot find *Mons Franciae* among the place-names in *Mâcon*; Déléage, *Vie rurale* (appendices); or Duby, *Société*.

Bussière was settled on the basis of evidence going back to the time of Guy's grandfather Guigo. The charter recording the agreement was made in the chapter of Cluny and witnessed, among others, by seventeen townsmen.[66] This was under Abbot Theobald, who, according to the Chronicle of Cluny, acquired the tithes of Cluny and began the town wall, and during whose abbacy a townsman named Stephen, who may be one of the several Stephens who witnessed the charters of 1173 and 1180, made many gifts to Cluny and later became a monk there.[67]

The second surviving confirmation of the customs of Cluny was issued in 1188 by Abbot Hugh IV.[68]

Wishing to promote in all ways the peace and advantage of the townsmen of Cluny and of all residents there, I have with the counsel of our senior [monks] granted to these townsmen and their successors that they may henceforth freely and peacefully use the good practices and customs which their ancestors obtained from our predecessors in any just way. We freely grant them whatever promotes peace in order that they and their successors, from being submissive, may become yet more submissive to us and the church of Cluny.

In the conclusion he again granted whatever his predecessors Hugh and Stephen had granted to the townsmen 'for the peace and improvement of the town (*ville*)'. There were five new or additional customs. (1) No claim could be brought for any property peacefully held by a resident of Cluny for thirty-one years.[69] (2) A buyer of stolen or plundered property who failed to give it up and swear that he bought it unknowingly in the open market (*in communi foro*) was guilty of buying stolen property. (3) The agent (*serviens*) of the lords could take a pledge from someone who could not pay the annual census and sell it after seven days. Someone who withdrew a pledge had to pay seven *solidi* for withdrawal. If someone could not give a pledge, the lord might turn to his property and keep it in his power until

---

[66] C 4280 (v, 648–50). The copy in D518 lists eight more townsmen.   [67] BC, col. 1662DE.

[68] This document is edited in Chavot, 'Franchises', pp. 82–4 (with a French translation and commentary on pp. 84–7) and C 4329 (v, 690–2), both of which accurately transcribe MS. Paris, Bibl. nat., N.a.l. 2265, no. 14. The heading describes it as 'The charter in which Hugh IV, abbot of Cluny, granted many new customs to the town of Cluny and confirmed the ancient customs granted by Abbots Hugh I and Stephen I'. *Burgenses* were apparently distinguished from *manentes* (*morantes*) in the preface and in articles 1, 4, and 5, but it is unclear whether there were two distinct groups.

[69] Thirty-one year prescription is found in a charter of 1097: C 3726 (v, 76). See Chavot, 'Franchises', p. 84.

satisfaction was given.[70] (4) Residents of Cluny should not use lawyers (*legistas*) in disputes between themselves, which should be settled by the court (*judiciali ordine*) in accordance with the practices of the town. (5) A resident of Cluny might use the legal advocate (*legistam advocatum*) of the town of Cluny in a dispute with an outsider who used lawyers (*legis peritos*).

This charter throws light not only on the relations between the abbot and townsmen of Cluny but also on the development of urban institutions and judicial procedures. The *potestas* and *magistratus* of Stephen's charter were apparently incorporated into the *judicialis ordo*, and the town seems to have had its own legal adviser. The prohibition to use lawyers in internal disputes may reflect a growing number of cases not covered by local custom, in which lawyers were needed. The most interesting and puzzling article is number 3, which suggests that there were several lords (unless this means the abbots or monks) and that they were entitled, through their agent, not only to collect an annual census but also to take and sell pledges and ultimately to seize a debtor's property. If this refers, as seems probable, to the abbot of Cluny, he still exercised a high degree of control over the town and its residents.

It may have been problems of this sort that led to the formation of the commune, which was the subject in 1206 of a charter of Abbot Hugh V, who

for the good of peace and love remitted and pardoned our townsmen of Cluny all the complaints which we have hitherto had against them on account both of the expenses incurred on the occasion of the war of Berzé and the commune (*communie*) and of all the other past injuries and troubles brought on us by or through them.

The townsmen in return renounced the obligation and sacrament of the commune (*obligatio et communie sacramentum*). Peace was thus made again between the abbot and the townsmen, the charter continued, saving the right (*ius*), power (*dominium*), and jurisdiction (*justicie potestas*) of the abbot and the good practices and

[70] The text reads *dominus ad possessionem se vertet, et in dominium suum illam reducet donec reus ei satisfecerit*, which Chavot ('Franchises', p. 83) translated 'le seigneur s'en prendra à sa possession, la remettra en son domaine et la gardera jusqu'à ce que le débiteur se soit acquitté'; it is uncertain just what the lord took and kept, but it was presumably immovable property which could not be pledged.

ancient customs of the abbot and the town (*ville*), both written and unwritten, 'as they were reasonably observed between us and them before the time of the commune'.[71] It is not known exactly when or why the commune was created, but it must have been between 1188 and 1206 and may have been associated with the demands put upon the townsmen in connection with 'the war of Berzé' and other difficulties with local lords.[72]

The late twelfth and early thirteenth centuries were marked in particular by quarrels with the house of Brancion. The lady of Brancion – the widow of Joceran IV and mother of Henry I, who died respectively in about 1175 and 1206 – was a sister of the count of Chalon who attacked Cluny in 1166 (and was consequently dispossessed by Louis VII), and she was probably not well-disposed towards the abbey. According to a charter of 1203/14 'a discord developed between, on one side, the church of Cluny and the townsmen of this town (*ville*), and on the other, the lady of Brancion and her sons and men and supporters', who inflicted 'many and immense injuries' on the townsmen, who in return 'descended with an armed and powerful hand on the castles of Brancion and Nanton and the town of Chassigneules and perpetrated many evils on these and adjacent places'. In the ensuing settlement, which was arranged by the bishop and countess of Chalon, each side swore peace towards the other.

The church of Cluny, on behalf of itself and its men, made peace over these matters with the aforesaid lady and her men and two townsmen from the common counsel of the church and the town swore that this peace would be firmly observed by all its men.[73]

This document shows that the abbey and townsmen worked together when they were under pressure and in particular that two townsmen were empowered to act on behalf of the church and town. It also shows the growing self-confidence of the townsmen. They were no longer the reluctant recruits who were required to swear fealty by Peter the Venerable, or the unwary and inexperienced troops massacred by the count of Chalon.

[71] C 4425 (v, 797).

[72] See Duby, *Société*, pp. 314 and 330, and Richard, *Ducs de Bourgogne*, p. 234. Previous relations with the house of Berzé were relatively good, and Hugh of Berzé acted as mediator in the disputes with Hugh of La Bussière in 1152 and 1173.

[73] C 4410 (v, 785–7). See Richard, *Ducs de Bourgogne*, p. 234, and Bouchard, *Sword*, pp. 301, 305–6, and 308. Subsequent disputes with Joceran V were settled in 1214; C 4482 (VI, 35–8).

Now, when they were attacked, they struck back 'with an armed and powerful hand'. Some of this assertiveness and confidence may have inspired the formation of a commune, by which the townsmen bound themselves, presumably by an oath of mutual support, against the claims of the abbot.[74] Faced with such organised opposition, Hugh made peace with the townsmen, who renounced the commune and let the abbot keep his right, power, and jurisdiction, on condition that both sides kept their good practices and ancient customs. During the century since the townsmen first appeared as a recognisable group, therefore, they became a force to be reckoned with by both the abbey and the local aristocracy and established themselves less as dependants than as partners of the abbot, to whom they were bound by common political, economic, and military interests. The alliance was uneasy, however, and many tensions remained, since the townsmen showed themselves to be at the same time among the most loyal supporters and most determined opponents of the abbot.

[74] On the hostility of the church to the communal movement, especially in the north of France but also closer at hand, as at Vézelay, see Achille Luchaire, *Les Communes françaises à l'époque des capétiens directs*, ed. Louis Halphen (Paris, 1911), pp. 235–50.

The cathedral as parish church: the case of southern England

MICHAEL FRANKLIN

Much has been written about the relationship between bishops and their cathedral churches in the late medieval period. Many bishops became positively unwelcome in the precincts of their own cathedrals because of the clash between their own jurisdictions and that of their chapters. Deans, to varying degrees, became their own masters within the chapter precincts, particularly in spiritual matters, where it was rarely doubted that they had the responsibility of the cure of souls within the cathedral enclosure. Deans could be said to be, in some senses, rectors of cathedrals. But who could be said to be a cathedral's parishioners? The cathedral clergy obviously, that is the chapter itself and the variety of other clerks, incorporated to varying degrees, which abounded in the medieval cathedral; the vicars, the choristers and the like. It is well known that the laity attended cathedrals in large numbers, even when the cathedral concerned was notionally monastic, and therefore, supposedly, in some sense at least, closed to the world. But were such visitors truly parishioners, except in so far as the terms *parochia* and *diocesis* had once been virtually synonymous, with the consequence that all Christians in a diocese had in some sense a claim to be so described?

One of the most important facets of Christopher Brooke's work is that concerned with the study of parochial origins. In his work on medieval London particularly he drew attention to the importance of the worshipping community in the formation of urban parishes. This paper aims to survey what evidence there is for actual local worshipping communities using English cathedrals of the southern province for the essentially parochial functions of baptism and burial. This aspect of cathedral history has been little studied, but it is one which is of considerable importance. For those cathedrals which have always been of such a status, for example Canterbury or St Paul's, this survey may tell us something about the extent of the pastoral responsibilities expected of these early institutions. For those which had greatness thrust upon them, as it were, it may provide some indication of why bishops chose to set up their sees there.

Reflecting perhaps the amount of effort that has been put into the study of the history of medieval Winchester, perhaps the most is known about the parochial standing of the cathedral in Winchester.[1] Throughout the medieval period the cathedral there seems to have been dominant as mother church in some ways over all the parish churches of the city and the suburbs. This is not to say that the clergy of the churches of Winchester were not true parish priests, in the sense of having the cure of souls, for the evidence, such as it is, argues that they did indeed have this right. However, the full range of parochial rights, and particularly those of baptism and burial, seem to have been denied to the Winchester churches until right to the end of the Middle Ages. To the episcopal administration all the churches of the city remained technically *capelle*, as can be seen from a list apparently compiled *c.* 1270,[2] though in the secular sources invariably the term *ecclesia* was used, clearly demonstrating the real function of these churches as their parishioners saw them.[3] A document of 1331 summarises the cathedral's extensive claim to burial rights,[4] which amounted practically to a ban on intra-mural burial except in the great cemetery on the north and west sides of the cathedral. It is interesting that in Winchester it can be shown that this claim definitely did not grow out of the establishment of the see in 662, for there were at least two small burial-grounds within the walls of Winchester, active into the eighth century, which were well away from the Old Minster.[5] However, once the claim was

[1] This section, of necessity, relies heavily on D. Keene, *Survey of Medieval Winchester*, Winchester Studies 2 (Oxford, 1985), (hereafter *Winchester Studies 2*) 106ff.
[2] *Registrum Johannis de Pontissara episcopi Wintoniensis a.d. 1282–1304*, ed. C. Deedes, 2 vols., (Canterbury and York Society, 1915–24), pp. 597–9.   [3] *Winchester Studies 2*, 108.
[4] Winchester Cathedral Library MS Records 1 fo. 38 (no. 119); another copy appears in BL Additional MS 29436 fos. 67–71.
[5] *Winchester Studies 2*, 741, 761. The theory that the Old Minster began as a church designed to serve an adjacent royal residence and not as a cathedral at all is discussed in F. Barlow, M. Biddle, O. Von Feilitzen and D. J. Keene, *Winchester in the early Middle Ages*, Winchester

established, it took until the fifteenth century for men of substance
to begin to seek to express their status by avoiding interment in
the common graveyard. The other minster churches in the city
also acquired important rights of exemption which ran contrary
to the Old Minster's monopoly. The rights of the New Minster to
receive citizens for burial at their will were specifically inherited
by its successor institution at Hyde.[6] Most of the inhabitants of the
northern suburb in the medieval period seem to have taken
advantage of this freedom. That the New Minster had this right,
for it seems to have been well established before the move to
Hyde, and there is no reason to suppose that it was then a recent
introduction, would make sense, if indeed the purpose behind the
New Minster was to provide a church for the new *burh* and its
rapidly growing population.[7] It would appear from the evidence
of late-medieval wills that the Nunnaminster also seems to have
had this right, though apparently it never gained a monopolistic
position for any particular area of the city. The darkness which
descends upon the history of the Nunnaminster from after the
period of Æthelwold's reforms until the early twelfth century
makes it impossible to say any more about its rôle in the parochial
development of the city. What would seem to be clear is that the
Old Minster of late Anglo-Saxon Winchester eventually acquired
a pre-eminence in parochial matters, a superiority which was only
challenged by the other major royal minsters of the city and then
only in its monopoly of burial rights.

It is possible that the sack of the city in 1141 caused bishop
Henry of Blois to address the issue of the city's parochial affairs. A
record written in a hand of the fourteenth century in a Hyde

Studies 1 (Oxford 1976), (hereafter *Winchester Studies* 1) 306. The short gap between the
foundation by Cenwalh in 648 and the consecration of Bishop Wini in 661 does not explain the
survival of the burial grounds. They must have been in use while the Old Minster was a
cathedral and thus taken out of use, as a matter of policy, some time later.

[6] In 1110: *Reg. Pontissara*, 441.

[7] 'The character of the church itself and the citizen's right of burial in its cemetery may thus
suggest that a close relationship existed between New Minster and the people of Winchester
from a time early in the monastery's history, and possibly from the moment of its foundation.
Edward's purpose, (and perhaps his father's wish) in establishing a new church in the centre of
the city, so close to the existing cathedral, may therefore have been to provide for the needs of
the new *burh* and its rapidly growing population. While Old Minster remained the bishop's see,
New Minster was to be the *burh* church...': *Winchester Studies 1*, 314. Thus Biddle and Keene
explained the complexities and the cost of the inconvenient location of the spacious New
Minster cheek-by-jowl with the crowded Old Minster. (N.B. Biddle and Keene calculated that
the New Minster nave alone enclosed 790 sq. metres, while Old Minster's overall area was 354
sq. metres.)

abbey manuscript of the eleventh century purports to be a record
of a synod, said to have been convened by Bishop Henry in 1150
(more likely 1143), to consider the problem of the churches
destroyed in 1141 and their parishioners.[8] There are good reasons[9]
for suggesting that this is not a contemporary record but a
distortion of the 1330s or 1340s, when the bishop and St Swithun's
were in dispute with the citizens over the extent of the cathedral
cemetery, for its sole recorded decision seems to have been to
define the extent of the parish of St Lawrence, a church owned
by the abbot of Hyde. None the less the point that Bishop Henry
seems to have been concerned with pastoral care is borne out by
a study of his *acta*,[10] so it is reasonable to assume that some
intervention was made by him. As Keene points out:

The later record may therefore preserve a genuine, if garbled, memory of the
bishop's activity in the city's parochial affairs and may indicate that by c. 1150
parochial areas assigned to individual churches both inside and outside the walls
were formally defined.[11]

It is significant too that the bishops came to control a high
proportion of the patronage of the Winchester churches. Of the
fifty-five churches in Winchester still active c. 1300 the patronage
of forty-eight is known. The patronage of thirty-two of these
forty-eight was the bishop's, twenty-nine of these had once been
in the hands of St Swithun's.

The continuing importance of the cathedral as a mother church
can be demonstrated by its enduring dominance of the liturgical
life of the city. The Palm Sunday procession from the centre of the
city to the church of St James high up in the western suburb was
an important part of the religious soul of the city.[12] Although by
the time of our knowledge of it, the royal charter of 1114,[13] which
dealt with the changes to it necessitated by the moving of the New
Minster to Hyde, many of the Carolingian-inspired aspects of the

[8] *Liber Vitae: Register and Martyrology of New Minster and Hyde Abbey*, ed. W. de Gray Birch,
(Hampshire Record Society, 1892), 1–3. The manuscript is BL Stowe MS 944 (Davis no. 1050).
[9] Discussed in *Winchester Studies 2*, 565.
[10] See my forthcoming volume in the series *English Episcopal Acta* and, in addition the remarks in
M. J. Franklin, 'The bishops of Winchester and the monastic revolution', *Anglo-Norman
Studies* 12 (1990), 55–6. [11] *Winchester Studies 2*, 116.
[12] The Easter Guild, probably a body of men living outside the West Gate, had owned land in
1066, according to the Survey of 1110: *Winchester Studies 1*, 50 (Survey 1, no. 105).
[13] *Regesta* II, no. 1070. The text appears in *Monasticon* II, 444–5 and *Reg Pontissara*, pp. 439–41.

procession specified by the *Regularis Concordia* had been modified by Archbishop Lanfranc, the fact that all the principal clergy of the city's churches were still to be involved in it showed how important this procession was. The popular impact of such processions might well have changed as a consequence of the adoption of the Use of Sarum, for rites concentrating on the cathedral and its immediate precincts would have been introduced, replacing several of the ancient forays out into the city.[14] The Rogationtide and Corpus Christi processions may well have come to replace the Palm Sunday and Candlemas ceremonies in terms of popular attractiveness. Nevertheless all these processions survived to emphasise the family relationship between the mother church and those of the surrounding countryside. It is known that in eighth- and ninth-century Metz and St Riquier the association of quite distant churches (five or six kilometres) with the mother church were emphasised by their inclusion in processions.[15] This may have been paralleled in the Winchester of the early Middle Ages.

Relatively little is known of any parochial functions of the cathedral in Canterbury. An *actum* of Archbishop Theobald of 1150 × 8 in favour of Christ Church establishes the existence of a claimed right of burying dead townsmen superior to that of any parish priest in the city:

inhibemus ne quis ullum ex parrochianis suis vel alium quemlibet qui in cimiterio Cant' ecclesie se sepeliri peterierit vel amici sui pro impedire presumat. Clericus eciam, in cuius parrochia defunctus erit, usque ad ecclesiam corpus defuncti commitetur. Quod si noluerit monachi libere defunctum ad ecclesiam obsequiis rite peractis deferant et sepliant...[16]

The *actum* goes on to detail the monks' exclusive right to jurisdiction over crimes committed in the precincts of the cathedral, an entirely separate matter. It is important to recognise that this first right cannot have been an inheritance from Augustine's times, because of the well-known Roman prohibition on intra-murine burial. It is known that until the time of Archbishop Cuthbert (740–60) no burials were permitted at

---

[14] T. Bailey, *The Processions of Sarum and the Western Church* (Toronto, 1971), 105–6.

[15] *Winchester Studies 1*, 270 n. 4 and the reference there cited.

[16] A. Saltman, *Theobald, archbishop of Canterbury*, Univ. of London Hist. Studies 2 (London, 1956), no. 50.

Christ Church; according to Eadmer he built the church of St John, abutting the east end of Augustine's church, for three purposes, baptisms, judicial functions (presumably the ordeal and the like) and to provide a burial site for the archbishops.[17] As an architectural commentator Eadmer has his limitations,[18] but what little independent evidence there is has shown him to be reasonably accurate. In particular his description of the pre-Conquest cathedral as a bi-polar church is independently confirmed by a surviving pre-Conquest pontifical:[19] hence his reference to the laity standing in the body of the nave of the church of Christ Church to receive mass on Sundays and major festivals from the altar of St Mary at the West end is most important for our purposes because it shows that townsmen used at least part of the cathedral in immediately pre-Conquest times.[20] It is possible that the laity of Canterbury at this time also had the right to be buried in the precincts of St Augustine's; the objection that the monks of that house made in the time of Lanfranc to the diminution of their right of *generalis sepultura* is only explicable in these terms.[21]

At nearby Rochester more concrete data are available owing to the survival of a series of documents, culminating in an indenture of 1327 between the priory and prominent parishioners on behalf

[17] 'Is [sc. Archbishop Cuthbert] inter alia bona fecit ... ecclesiam in orientali parte maioris ecclesie eidem pene contiguam; eamque in honorem beati Johannis baptiste solemniter dedicavit. Hanc ecclesiam eo respectu fabricavit ut baptisteria et examinationes iudicium pro diversis causis constituorum que ad correctionem scleratorum in ecclesia Dei fieri solent inibi celebrentur et archiepiscoporum corpora in ea sepelirentur: sublata de civitatem in ecclesia beatorum apostulorum Petri et Pauli ubi posita sunt corpora omnium antecessorum suorum ...': Eadmer, *Vita sancti Bregowini*, in H. Wharton, *Anglia Sacra*, 2 vols. (London, 1691) II, 186, also in H. M. Taylor, 'The Anglo-Saxon cathedral at Canterbury', *Archaeological Journal* 126 (1969), 126 and ed. B. W. Scolz, *Traditio* 22 (1966), 139–40.

[18] In particular it must be remembered that he can have been at most seven years old when the building he was describing was utterly destroyed by fire and that he was writing some fifty years later with a particular axe to grind: N. Brooks, *The early history of the church of Canterbury* (Leicester, 1984), p. 39. The existence of St John's *c.* 800 is confirmed by a charter of King Coenwulf of Mercia (798–821): Sawyer no. 1618.

[19] Cambridge, Corpus Christi College MS 44 fos. 273–274, cited Brooks, *Early history*, p. 337 n. 5.   [20] Brooks, *Early history*, p. 45.

[21] Brooks, *Early history*, pp. 36f. 'Ad haec primorum patrum decreto hoc institutum est, ut omnes tam archiepiscopi quam monachi, cives etiam et suburbani post obitum nobiscum [sc. St Augustine's] sepelirentur. Erat enim tunc temporis ecclesia nostra unicum et singulare civitatis Cantuariensis cimiterium. Haec erat, reverende pater, ex institutione beati Augustini et successorum ipsius unitas et concordia, quam istis temporibus nobis subtractam esse dolemus acriter et ingemiscimus ...': *Gervasii Cantuariensis opera historica*, ed. W. Stubbs, 2 vols., RS (London, 1878–80), I, 81.

of the city.[22] This document is interesting for a number of reasons. First, it confirms the existence of a distinct worshipping community attached to the cathedral. The community was known as 'parishioners of the altar of St Nicholas in the nave'. Second, it shows that the nave of Rochester cathedral was used for parochial purposes as late as the fourteenth century. The indenture makes it clear that this was not the first time there had been a difference of opinion between the parishioners and the monks. The *ultima composicionis*, referred to in 1327, which determined the nature of the services available from the altar of St Nicholas was probably made in 1312. In that year, following an attempt by the monks to move the parochial altar,[23] it was agreed that, henceforth, mass would be said every Sunday and on All Saints' Day, St Nicholas' Day, Christmas Day and Purification.[24] However, tensions between the regular community and the townsmen seem to have been inevitable. Access by the latter seems always to have been the flashpoint. Archbishop Peckham, on metropolitical visitation in 1283, picked up the point. He wrote as follows:

Preterea est aliud inconveniens quod non potest aliqualiter tolerari quia videlicet populus civitatis parochialem non habet ecclesiam nisi ipsam basilicam cathedralem que clausis prioratus januis nocturno taliter continue observatur tempore quod nec ad ipsam ecclesiam patet accessus confugis nec aegrotantibus viaticum nec cetera ecclesiastica sacramenta nec de die umquam dicitur cum nota populo matutinum, nec horas etiam canonice in eadem ut nobis fideliter est relatum. Unum ergo istorum oportet fieri necessario vel quod infra septa monasterii fiat ecclesia parochialis, que dudum fuerat inchoata et fuit consequenter perniciose destructa, vel quod paretur omni tempore accessus ad maiorem ecclesiam pro rationibus supradictis et quod in eadem dicatur populo matutinuum, cum ceteris horis canonicis cum missa et solempnitate debita omni die. Cogatis etiam sacristam conplere ecclesiam maiorem continuato processu, iuxta quod sufficiunt ecclesiae facultates.[25]

The archbishop's reference to a long-since abandoned project for a separate parish church is interesting. We are left to speculate whether some ruin of one of the Saxon predecessors of Gundulf's Norman cathedral was being mis-interpreted by the archbishop as

[22] Appendix no. 1.
[23] 'occasione amocionis dicti altaris parochialis sancti Nicholai per dictos religiosos contra voluntatem parochianorum altaris supradicti in alio loco dicte ecclesie situati': *Registrum Roffense*, ed. J. Thorpe (London, 1769), p. 545.   [24] Ibid.
[25] *Registra Epistolae Johannis Peckham archiepiscopi Cantuariensis*, ed. C. Trice Martin, 3 vols., RS, (London, 1882–5), I, 624–5.

part of an attempt to build a separate parish church.[26] If the foundations to the west of the cathedral are indeed those of Ethelbert's church of St Andrew, the ruins allegedly found by St John Hope in the angle between the nave and the south transept, which might possibly be said to be 'infra septa monasterii', might well be those of an original, and early, church of St Nicholas.[27] That archaeology points to the possibility of there being two churches replaced by Gundulf is significant because of the terms of the 1327 indenture. To deal with the entirely proper needs of the townsmen to have access to the host for the sick they were still to have access to the cathedral at night, but once the changes mentioned in the indenture had been finally implemented this was no longer to be the case, except on three specific occasions, Christmas, All Saints and the feast of St Nicholas. The preservation of this right of access on the feast of St Nicholas, rather than on the feast of St Andrew is interesting, for it suggests that considerable importance was attached to it. Since we know that Ethelbert's church in Rochester given to Bishop Justus, the first bishop of Rochester, was dedicated to St Andrew from Bede,[28] and that this has always been the dedication of the cathedral, this suggests that the focus of parochial devotion was never Ethelbert's church and never to St Andrew. It would be interesting if it could be shown Bishop Gundulf, who introduced regulars into the cathedral,[29] was in fact responsible for the difficulties perceived by his successors, by abolishing an ancient arrangement whereby the community of St Andrew served its church while the townsmen worshipped in their nearby church of St Nicholas. Of course to a Norman prelate like Gundulf, this difficulty simply would not exist, for the sheer size of Norman naves of English cathedrals and monasteries cannot be explained other than by the inference that the laity were expected to make use of them.

[26] On Saxon Rochester see H. M. and J. Taylor, *Anglo-Saxon architecture*, 3 vols., (Cambridge, 1965–78), II, pp. 518–19.
[27] I am informed by Mr Tatton-Brown, at present consultant archaeologist to the Dean and Chapter of Rochester, that there is little of substance in St John Hope's claims. Moreover, it must be remembered that at Rochester, because of the constricted site, the cloister has never been in the conventional location, that is to the south-west of the crossing, but to the south-east.
[28] *Bede's Ecclesiastical History of the English people*, ed. B. Colgrave and R. A. B. Mynors, (Oxford Medieval Texts, 1969), II.3. The charter of foundation is Sawyer no. 1.
[29] He replaced the five secular canons with originally twenty-two Benedictine monks – D. Knowles and R. N. Hadcock, *Medieval religious houses: England and Wales*, 2nd edn., (London, 1971), p. 74.

On the point of disputed access the indenture of 1327 is also explicit: the question at issue was the custody of the key to the nave. To obviate the townsmen having access to the church the monks were prepared to build a chapel in the corner of the nave abutting the north door – *unum oratorium in angulo dicte navis ecclesie iuxta hostium boriale*. This was doubtless a cheaper solution than the building of an entirely separate church. A further, and purely conceptual, point of interest, can be made here – the 'nave', which modern architectural historians would apply as a term to the compartment bounded on its north and south side by the aisles, here clearly refers to the whole space west of the crossing, or otherwise the chapel cannot possibly be built in the corner of the nave abutting the north door.[30] Such compromises never really worked; even in 1312 it had been recognised that the building of a separate church for parochial devotions was the only really viable solution.[31] In Rochester, however, the building of the present St Nicholas' church did not finally take place until the end of the first quarter of the fifteenth century. On 18 December 1423 the parishioners finally renounced their rights in the cathedral church and took up occupation in what was clearly considered as the new town parish church.[32] The terms of the agreement, which took some five years to achieve and which required the involvement of both the Bishop of Rochester and the Archbishop of Canterbury, are interesting. The Bishop's original plan, enunciated in a charter of May 1418, was that once the church was built all costs should henceforth fall on the parishioners, the monks only receiving an annual pension of forty shillings.[33] But there were clearly many matters of dispute: it was agreed, following the archbishop's intervention, that the new church was to contain a font, that it was to have a bell tower at the western end on its North side, that it was to have its own cemetery in *Grenechirchehaw*, that is in the space between the cathedral and the

---

[30] The present north door on this aisle is clearly of a later date. Owing to considerable refacing in the eighteenth and nineteenth century the present fabric has little to tell us.

[31] The agreement was to run pending the building of a new church – 'prior et capitulum extra suam cathedralem ecclesiam prefatam ad opus dictorum parochianorum construi fecerunt ecclesiam competentem', *Registrum Roffense*, p. 545.

[32] 'ad usum parochianorum civitatis Roff' et suburbiorum predictorum': *Registrum Roffense*, p. 568.

[33] Bishop Young sanctioned 'pro ecclesia fienda in cimiterio dicte ecclesie nostre in parte borealis fabricandi': ibid., pp. 560–1.

new church, but that each use of the same was to incur a fee of fourpence to the cathedral.[34] Here are all the points at issue laid out for us, who was to baptise and who was to bury on the parishioners' behalf? While the monks were prepared by the fifteenth century to forgo the privilege of baptism, probably the most ancient of the symbolic rights of a mother church, as the glory of the ancient baptistery in Florence always reminds us, the fees associated with the burial of the dead was something they were not quite ready to concede.

Hereford, also one of those cathedrals whose position as a bishop's seat was never in doubt, seems also to have had a burial monopoly. The history of this claim can be traced in a series of incidents from the twelfth to the fifteenth centuries. In *c.* 1108 Bishop Rheinhelm was prepared to go as far as to travel into the next diocese, to Gloucester, and dig up the body of one of his parishioners, Ralph fitz Ansketill, who had been buried by the Abbot of Gloucester in his abbey church contrary to the rights of his cathedral.[35] In 1203 × 18 a dispute between Llanthony and the Chapter of Hereford lead to a succint definition of the privilege – *nullum parochianorum Herefordensis ecclesie, nisi impetrata licencia a decano et capitulo Herefordie, ad sepulturam admittent...*[36] What is interesting is the size of the geographical area over which this privilege remained enforceable. In 1288 Bishop Swinfield ruled that the parishioners of Hampton Bishop, a village located some five km to the South East of Hereford, who died with goods worth more than six shillings had to be buried in the cathedral, and not in their parish church.[37] In 1318 Bishop Orleton declined to consecrate a cemetery in Allensmore on the grounds that *sepultura omnium et singulorum parochianorum ecclesie de More Alani predicte pertinet ad ecclesiam cathedralem ut matricem ecclesiam...*[38] In 1385 the Chapter successfully sued for its due pension from the rector of Credenhull, whose church lay some eight km to the North West of Hereford, *pretextu quorundam jurium spiritualium*

[34] Ibid., pp. 563–4.
[35] *CS*, 703; M. Brett, *The English church under Henry I* (Oxford, 1978), p. 98.
[36] *Charters and records of Hereford Cathedral*, ed. W. W. Capes (Cantilupe Society, 1908), p. 44.
[37] *Registrum Ricardi de Swinfield episcopi Herefordensis a.d. 1283–1317*, ed. W. W. Capes (Canterbury and York Society, 1909), p. 213.
[38] *Registrum Ade de Orleton episcopi Herefordensis a.d. 1317–22*, ed. A. T. Bannister (Canterbury and York Society, 1908), p. 67.

ecclesie cathedrali Herefordensi de ecclesia de Credenhulle debite ab antquo,[39] showing that in some cases the monopoly could be sold off, either permanently, or possibly in an individual situation. As an example of the latter practice we may cite the licence given in 1404 to bury a single parishioner of Moreton in his own parish: *non obstante quod omnes parochiani utriusque sexus de Moretone predicta suas haberent et habere deberent sepulturas in cimiterio ecclesie cathedralis Herefordensis...*[40] Moreton is six km North of the cathedral city. So vast a claim was bound to come under attack, once the developing canon law began to give some support, for the wealthy at least, to the principle of individual freedom to choose the place of burial.[41]

Any analysis of the cathedral of Lichfield in this regard must be coloured by the saga of the migration of the bishop's chair in that particular diocese. Undeniably the cathedral is ancient, since it was in existence certainly by 700,[42] but a certain amount of darkness extends over its internal history because of the movement of the see first to Chester in 1075, and thereafter to Coventry. There is no obvious evidence of continuity between the Saxon head-minster, which we might expect to have had some parochial function, and its medieval successor. Virtually nothing is known of Saxon Lichfield, except that Bishop Æthelweald is supposed to have established canons there, presumably following the rule of Chodregang, in 822.[43] Closer analysis of certain fragments of late evidence, however, permits some speculation. According to one Lichfield source, Bishop Roger de Clinton (1129–48) was responsible for re-organising the constitution of the Norman cathedral begun by his predecessor, Bishop Robert de Lymesy (*ob.* 1117).

Hic primo constituit collegium canonicorum apud Lichefeldiam, nam antea erat ibi nisi quinque sacerdotes deservientes quinque capellis singuli singulis.[44]

The entry in Domesday Book which mentions five canons holding three ploughs[45] would seem to confirm the existence of these particular priests. A tradition recorded from the thirteenth

---

[39] *Charters of Hereford*, p. 246. [40] Ibid., p. 258.
[41] 'Ubi autem quisque tumulandus sit, legibus expressum non est, et ideo in voluntate tumulandi consistit, unde B. Gregorius ait, "Ultima voluntas defuncti modis omnibus conservetur"': *Decretum*, c. 13 q. 2 c.3–4. [42] Knowles and Hadcock, *Houses*, p. 419.
[43] Wharton, *Anglia Sacra*, I, pp. 423ff. [44] *Monasticon* VI, 1243, vi.
[45] *Domesday Book* I, 247a.

century onwards mentions five particular prebends with a special duty of serving at the high altar of the cathedral.[46] These prebends are named in the sixteenth century as those of Freeford, Stotfeld, Longdon, Hansacre and Weeford.[47] It has been pointed out that all these places are in or near Lichfield itself. That these five prebends had some special dignity in the medieval cathedral, coupled with their location and the fact that the number of them is significantly five, permits the hypothesis that these might have been the original 'prebends' of Lichfield, that is the *parochia* served by Æthelweald's canons.

Discussion of parochial aspects of the history of St Paul's is also, inevitably, prejudiced by the fact that the medieval cathedral perished in the fire of 1666. Nevertheless Wren's church seems to have inherited a parochial rôle from its predecessor. Until 1878 the parishioners of St Faith had the use of the eastern end of the north aisle of the crypt which was shut off by railings from the rest of the church. At that date these were removed, but the memory of the worshipping community was preserved in inscriptions.[48] Before the Fire, it was the main body of the medieval crypt which formed the church of St Faith.[49] However, it appears that this was not a particularly ancient arrangement, dating merely from the period of the 'new work' in the medieval cathedral, that is the work commencing in 1256 which extended the Norman cathedral eastwards.[50] The church of St Faith, the earliest reference to which

---

[46] VCH, *Staffs.*, III, 141. The earliest reference is to the statutes of Bishop Hugh Nonant (1188–98): 'Dignitates autem quinque capellanorum haec est quod nullius preter ebdomadarii licentiam in magno altari celebret episcopo tantum et decano exceptis quorum interest in maioribus duplicibus festis divinum officium exercere' (*Monasticon* VI, 1257).

[47] VCH, *Staffs.*, III, 141. Freeford, Hansacre and Weeford are among the berewicks listed as being dependent on the bishop's manor of Lichfield in 1086: *Domesday Book*, I, 247b.

[48] *Documents illustrating the history of St Paul's cathedral*, ed. W. S. Simpson, Camden Society new series 26 (1880), 193. The inscriptions were, at the west end 'Limen ecclesie antiquae parochialis sancte Fidis virginis et martyris', and, on the south side, 'Limitem meridionalem antique ecclesie parochialis s. Fidis virginis et martyiris, olim cancellis inclusae, difinuerunt tesserae a.d. MDCCCLXXVIII positae.'

[49] C. N. L. Brooke, in *A history of St Paul's cathedral*, ed. W. R. Matthews and W. M. Atkins (London, 1957), p. 97; cf. W. Dugdale, *The history of St Paul's cathedral in London*, with a continuation by H. Ellis (London, 1818), p. 75. Pepys mentions that the vault of the old cathedral crashed down into St Faith's.

[50] 'Building operations were commenced at a distance of about 170 feet east of the Norman choir. The site was occupied by a short alley that ran from Cheapside to Watling Street and by the parish church of St Faith the Virgin that served the dwellers in the cathedral precincts and Paternoster Row. Both alley and church were demolished': G. H. Cook, *Old St Paul's cathedral* (London, 1955), p. 34.

that I have been able to locate is only *c.* 1200,[51] was engulfed by
the extension of the cathedral: its parishioners were naturally
provided with facilities in the new building. However, the fact
that St Faith's was a peculiar of the Dean and Chapter, which was
both patron and ordinary for the parish,[52] may be the only
surviving residual facet of the ancient rôle of St Paul's minster.[53]
Christopher Brooke's own currently expressed view, based on the
dedication, is that St Faith's is unlikely to be earlier than the ninth
century, and probably of the eleventh century.[54] It should also be
remembered that there was another church in immediate
proximity to medieval St Paul's, which might be even earlier. This
was St Gregory's, destroyed in 1631 to make way for a new
church by Inigo Jones.[55] A *porticus* altar, dedicated to Augustine's
mentor, could well have turned into a parish church, as may have
been the case at Canterbury and York.[56]

When discussing Worcester cathedral we have the inestimable
assistance of one of the few documents to survive from a diocesan
synod held by an eleventh-century bishop. The account of Bishop
Wulfstan's synod of 1092 does not now survive as an original, but
it did in the seventeenth century and was printed by Wharton in
his *Anglia Sacra*.[57] There is no reason to doubt its authenticity. The
document says that Bishop Wulfstan held the synod *in monasterio
sancte Marie in criptis*, that is 'in the crypt of St Mary's minster',
because he felt the need to put the affairs of his diocese in order
before his death.[58] Its sole recorded business was the dispute,

---

[51] *Early charters of the cathedral church of St Paul, London*, ed. M. Gibbs, Camden 3rd Series, 58 (1939), no. 115.   [52] Dugdale, *St Paul's*, p. 75.

[53] The fire in 962 which destroyed St Paul's minster (Anglo-Saxon Chronicle, *sub anno*) may well be significant here. There seems to have been no attempt to introduce monks into St Paul's by Dunstan and the Reformers, but we would expect them to be unconcerned in consequence with the rights of St Paul's minster. In Worcester the reverse was true – see below. It is to be hoped that the results of Dr Keene's *Survey of medieval London* will permit considerable modification of this paragraph.

[54] Brooke, 'London', in *Atlas of Historic Towns*, III, ed. M. D. Lobel (London, 1989), p. 35.

[55] Cook, *Old St Paul's*, p. 83.

[56] Ibid., citing W. Levison, *England and the continent in the eighth century* (Oxford, 1946), pp. 264–5.

[57] The best edition of this document is *The cartulary of Worcester cathedral priory (Register I)*, ed. R. R. Darlington, PRS new series 38 (1968 for 1962–3), no. 52. Professor Darlington, as Hearne in his edition of Hemming's cartulary had done before him, prints the document from the thirteenth century cartulary, but collates this with Wharton's text. The original was no. 44 in Dugdale's list – ibid., xii, n. 1.

[58] 'Eo quod ego longemus dierum imbecillitatem mei corporis sentiens et finem vite mee iam instare intelligens cupiebam res ecclesiasticas nostre cure commissas canonice tractare et queque

which had arisen between Ælfnoth, the priest of St Helen's church and Alan, the priest of St Alban's church, concerning the parishes and customs of their churches. A sub-committee of senior clergy declared that there was no case to answer, since the only church with parochial rights in the city was the cathedral itself (*nullam esse parochiam in tota urbe Wigrac' nisi tantum matris ecclesie*). To justify the dependency of St Helen's on the cathedral they then made an interesting appeal to history and the period of the replacement of clerks with monks by Oswald. This was necessary because the then cathedral, newly rebuilt by Wulfstan, was known not to have been the original mother church of the city. The church of St Helen had existed from the time of Æthelred and Archbishop Theodore and the foundations of the see (i.e. *c.* 680) and its dependency on the then cathedral was undoubted. In St Oswald's time (i.e. *c.* 969) the priest of St Helen's was called Wynsige. Modern scholars would probably view him as one of the secular clerks of St Peter's (secular) cathedral, which Oswald was to transform into the entirely monastic establishment of (new) St Mary's.[59] Wynsige responded to the appeal to change his vocation, and in fact three years later became prior of St Oswald's new community, but he brought with him to the monastery, symbolically, the keys of his church, that is he brought it with him. Oswald's monastery then received an important grant which confirmed its assimilation of all the dependencies of the old cathedral, the prior was to be *summus decanus episcopi* and as such the superior of all the city clergy.[60] It was an interesting assertion for the prior to claim to be, on the one hand, the legitimate successor of Wynsige, the priest of St Helen's who became Prior, and, on the other, the recipient of a grant by Edgar, St Dunstan and St Oswald of being *summus decanus episcopi*. The status of St Helen's as an important mother church in the city is confirmed by other documents, above all the notification by Fritheric, one of Bishop Wulfstan's chaplains, issued *c.* 1100, which lists the appurtenances of the church. These number some eleven chapels together with tithes from a large area.[61] There are problems with some aspects of the view of history propounded in the account of

emendanda forent, illorum sapienti consilio corrigere et emendare': *Cartulary of Worcester*, no. 52.   [59] Knowles and Hadcock, *Houses*, p. 81.   [60] Appendix no. 2.   [61] *Cartulary of Worcester*, no. 53.

the synod of 1092. The old church of St Peter, whatever its precise location,[62] seems definitely to have remained until as late as the middle of the eleventh century.[63] In 991 it still contained the bishop's throne,[64] and hence may not have been as dead a minster as the monks of St Mary's would have liked to think.

It would seem logical to consider those churches which have always had the status of cathedrals as a separate category from those where this was not always the case. In the eleventh century, following the Conquest, several sees were moved. When moving his see into a large town it would be natural for a bishop to choose for the new location of his see an already reasonably wealthy institution, such as a pre-existing minster church with parochial responsibilities. Chichester would appear to be a prime example of this practice. Before the Conquest, according to William of Malmesbury, Chichester was the site of an ancient minster, housing a community of nuns. Chichester was *ubi antiquitus et sancti Petri monasterium et congregatio fuerat sanctimonialium*.[65] In 1075 the canons of Bishop Stigand's cathedral at Selsey moved into their new home at Chichester; the nuns of St Peter's minster henceforth disappear from the historical record.[66] This reference by William of Malmesbury need not be dismissed as fanciful; it has been pointed out that communities of nuns could be extremely conveniently located in secular minsters where the prebendaries would be available to assist the nuns with the management of secular affairs and to serve their churches.[67] This may well have been much more common in Anglo-Saxon England than has hitherto been realised. Shaftesbury, Wilton, Wherwell, Romsey

---

[62] It seems reasonably certain that Oswald built St Mary's in the cemetery of St Peter's. Both Hemming and William of Malmesbury, relying presumably on the oral traditions preserved in the monastery, thought thus: C. C. Dyer, 'The Saxon cathedrals of Worcester', in *The origins of Worcester*, ed. P. Barker, *Transactions of the Worcestershire archaeological society* 3rd series 2 (1968–9), 34. Given that the present cathedral presumably lies on the site of his tenth-century church, this would suggest that St Peter's lay to the north, provided that its cemetery was, as custom would suggest, on the south side of the church. This is, however, not certain; if it were so the present site of St Helen's church, only some 200 m. away from the cathedral, seems rather too close.

[63] In the 1030s a tomb in the cemetery was demolished to provide building material to enlarge the presbytery of St Peter's: *Hemingi Chartularium ecclesie Wigornensis*, 2 vols., ed. T. Hearne (Oxford, 1721), I, p. 189.   [64] Ibid., I, p. 232.

[65] *Willelmi Malmesbiriensis monachi de gestis pontificum Anglorum libri quinque*, ed. N. E. S. A. Hamilton, RS (London 1870), 205.   [66] VCH, *Sussex*, II, 47.

[67] M. J. Franklin, 'Another Lewes forgery?', *Journal of the Society of Archivists* 9 (1988), 34.

and St Mary's, Winchester may not be anomalous 'royal' nunneries, but merely the houses of a once common, but outmoded type which survived precisely because they had royal patrons. Though the nuns of St Peter's minster vanish from the record, both the dedication of their church and its parochial rôle in the religious life of Chichester survived.[68] An extra stimulus to the preservation of these ancient parochial functions seems to have arisen because these rights became intertwined with the claims of the Deans of Chichester to be exempt from the control of the bishop in their peculiar jurisdiction, which approximated to the city liberties. The other parish churches in the city seem technically to have been regarded as *capelle* dependent on the cathedral, or more correctly the parochial altar of St Peter within it.[69] This parochial rôle for the cathedral seems to have survived into the nineteenth century, when the church of St Peter in Chichester was finally built to take over this function.[70]

At Lincoln the evidence for parochial functions being performed in the Minster is coloured by the varying interpretations of the origins of that church. While it is apparently obvious that in discussing Lincoln we are not talking about an ancient episcopal seat like Canterbury or Hereford, it is important to know whether we are dealing with a case *sui generis*, or one of a new cathedral on a virgin site (like Old Sarum), or of one sited in a pre-existing church of some parochial status. Dr Owen's attractive argument[71] that the primary motive for the location of the new cathedral in

[68] It has been suggested – VCH, *Sussex*, III, 106 – that a representation of a pre-Conquest looking building on a seal of the Dean and Chapter of Chichester of the thirteenth century (pictured VCH, *Sussex*, II, 16) might be meant to be this building. It is dangerous, however, to argue that representations of buildings on seals are anything other than stylised representations; moreover, a representation of the former cathedral at Selsey is just as likely in this case. Cf. Brooks, *Early history*, 48 where the theory that the 'first' seal of Christ Church, Canterbury, in use in the early part of the twelfth century, bears a representation of the pre-Conquest Cathedral is dismissed.

[69] 'The church of St Peter Subdeanery ... seems to have been considered the mother church of all the churches in the city, except perhaps All Saints in-the-Pallant belonging to the archbishop. At the parish altar of St Peter in the nave of the cathedral church, where the parish services were conducted, the visitations of the city churches were held. In the thirteenth century we find the churches of St Olave, St Andrew-in-the-Market and St Andrew-in-the-Pallant described as 'chapels': VCH, *Sussex*, III, 165. For an example of grants to this altar see *Chartulary of the High Church of Chichester*, ed. W. D. Peckham, Sussex Record Society 46 (1946 for 1942–3), nos. 361, 388.

[70] In 1850: VCH, *Sussex*, III.160. In fact fifteenth-century furnishings from the cathedral seem to have been moved to the new church. For a description of the old arrangement see BL Additional MS 5699 fo. 182r.

[71] D. M. Owen, 'The Norman cathedral at Lincoln', *Anglo-Norman Studies* 6 (1983), 192.

the immense diocese of Dorchester was short-term and pragmatic, to wit the need to protect the Conqueror's new kingdom from a Viking repetition of the expedition quashed by Harold at Stamford Bridge, has much to commend it. The question is what institution, if any, did the new cathedral church of St Mary supersede?

Henry of Huntingdon, who had every reason to know the truth of the matter, because he served as a member of Bishop Remigius' *familia*, and who is the nearest to a contemporary source on the point, makes no mention of any precursor to the new Minster.

Mercatis igitur praediis in ipso vertice urbis iuxta castellum turribus fortissimus eminens in loco forti fortem, pulchro pulchram, virgini virginum construxit ecclesiam; que et grata esset Deo servientibus et ut pro tempore oportebat invincibilis hostibus...[72]

It is manifest, none the less, that this passage, with its threefold alliteration, is written primarily for rhetorical effect, not necessarily with historical accuracy in mind. The only account which mentions a pre-existing church on the site of the Lincoln Minster is that of John of Schalby, Bishop Sutton's devoted registrar, who wrote in the early fourteenth century. His account is therefore hardly to be dignified with the status of a contemporary record, though he probably did have access to the *Liber fundationis* which is known to have been in the Chapter library *c.* 1160 at least.[73] Schalby reports that the cathedral was founded by Bishop Remigius on the site of the church of St Mary Magdalen in the Bail of Lincoln. An altar in the cathedral nave with the same dedication served by a priest from the cathedral was provided for the erstwhile parishioners of St Mary Magdalen's, until Bishop Sutton had a new church built for them just outside Exchequer Gate to the west of the Minster.[74] Explaining this story has been the subject of considerable discussion,[75] for the amount of hard

---

[72] *Henrici archidiaconi Huntendunensis historia Anglorum*, ed. T. Arnold, RS (London, 1879), 212.
[73] Owen, 'Norman cathedral', 189.
[74] Appendix no. 3. Schalby's text is also available in translation in *Lincoln Minster Pamphlets* no. 2, ed. J. H. Srawley (1949).
[75] Owen, 'Norman cathedral' substantially revises the standard account where the minster is founded in a pre-existing minster of St Mary; cf. J. W. Hill, *Medieval Lincoln* (Cambridge, 1948), pp. 61–81.

evidence for the existence of a substantial minster church on the site Remigius chose for his new cathedral is in reality very limited. Moreover, St Paul-in-the-Bail on the site of the Roman *forum*, as the archeologists have confirmed recently is a much more likely candidate for the status of mother church of the city. It was here that the eponymous Paulinus consecrated Honorius as Justus' successor as archbishop of Canterbury in 631,[76] and even if by the eighth century, as Bede says, the church was damaged, the church could easily have subsequently been repaired. It is difficult to show that the pre-Conquest stones now in the Cloister, usually mentioned in support of the St Mary's head-minster theory, are definitely pre-Conquest, let alone definitely associated with a structure on the site earlier than Remigius' Minster.[77] The 'Marycorn' due to St Mary of Lincoln might be conclusive evidence of an ancient episcopal minster, if it could be shown that this render was paid before 1066. Unfortunately the evidence is twelfth-century, a papal privilege of 1163,[78] and complicated by the fact that the claim is extended to the whole of Lincolnshire, not just Lindsey alone, and nobody has ever claimed that Kesteven and Holland were a part of the same diocese in earlier times. 'Marycorn' is more likely as Dr Owen has suggested, to be[79] merely the invention of a revenue-hungry twelfth-century dean, than a folk memory of a more ancient time. There is no evidence either in Domesday Book or the papal privilege of 1061 confirming the Bishop of Dorchester's rights to Lindsey[80] of episcopal involvement in Lincoln. What evidence there is for a St Mary's church in Lincoln in 1066 does not support the inference that it was a major church. In the account of the twelve carucates in the fields of Lincoln in Domesday Book is the single reference of relevance ... *residuum dimidiam carucatam terre habuit et habet sancta Marie de Lincoln in qua nunc est episcopatus* ...[81] Half a carucate is not much of an endowment for a putative minster, even if this reference does suggest the existence of St Mary's, Lincoln *TRE*. I find myself inclined to agree with Dr Owen's suggestion[82] that

[76] Bede, *Historia Ecclesiastica* II.16, 18.   [77] Owen, 'Norman cathedral', 194.
[78] *The Registrum Antiquissimum of the Cathedral church of Lincoln*, ed. C. W. Foster and K. Major, 10 vols., (Lincoln Record Society, 1931–73), no. 255.
[79] Owen, 'Norman cathedral', 195.   [80] *Registrum Antiquissimum*, no. 247.
[81] *Domesday Book, seu liber censualis* ..., ed. A. Farley 2 vols., (Record Commission, 1783). I, 344a.
[82] Owen, 'Norman cathedral', 195.

the precursor of the Minster in Lincoln was, if anything, a small poorly endowed worshipping community church whose memory was perpetuated in the nave altar said by Schalby to have been dedicated to St Mary Magdalen. Against this theory, it must be said, is the fact of the continuing colloquial usage of the term *minster* in Lincoln.[83] Perhaps of more interest, however, is Leland's story that where the Dean's house was in the Close there had been a monastery of nuns (presumably Leland's source, whatever it was, used that oft-mistranslated word *monasterium*; minster is doubtless to be preferred) before the time of Remigius and that fragments yet remained in his time.[84] My own observations on the nuns of Spinney near Melton Mowbray (Leics.)[85] have shown that a nunnery this far north in the eleventh century is not out of the question, as once might have been thought. Hence it is just as likely that Lincoln is to be equated with Chichester in that it seems likely to have been founded in the shell of a former nunnery.

Exeter became a cathedral only as a result of the changes associated with the Conquest. Despite this it would seem that the cathedral was able to maintain a monopoly of the right to burials roughly analogous to those in Winchester. This points to a pre-Conquest institution of some importance. According to Bishop Grandisson in 1354 there was still a single *commune civitatis poliandrum iuxta ecclesiam*.[86] In 1389 the rector of the church of All Hallows, Goldsmithry in Exeter, described as *ecclesia sive capella curata* was involved in a dispute with the Chapter over mortuaries.[87] Much is confused in the history of Exeter's parochial development, however, because of the rôle of that shadowy figure, the Dean of the Christianity of Exeter. In some sense the leader of the city's clergy, none of whose churches was technically any more than *capella curata*, there is some evidence that he was responsible for the distribution of their income. A twelfth-century manuscript informs us that *infra xv dies post Pascha*

---

[83] This is true not only today, which might well be the result of conscious or unconscious archaism in the last century, but also of the sixteenth century. Hill, *Medieval Lincoln*, p. 79, n. 3 draws attention to the sixteenth-century Common Council minutes where 'the minster' is frequently spoken of. [84] *Leland's Itinerary*, ed. L. Toulmin Smith, v, p. 123.
[85] Franklin, 'Lewes', 33 discussing *English Episcopal Acta* I no. 356.
[86] *The Register of John de Grandisson 1327–69*, ed. F. C. Hingeston-Randolph, 3 vols. (London, 1894–9), p. 1125. This section relies heavily on F. Rose-Troup, *The lost chapels of Exeter*, History of Exeter Research Group Monograph no. 1 (Exeter, 1923), and the references cited therein.
[87] Exeter D&C MS 3550 fo. 59d.

solvendi sunt xxid xxix capellis per manus prepositorum Exonie quos dedit rex Willelmus de collecta gepgabuli,[88] that is that the city Provost shall pay money to the city's clergy from the town's revenue, by virtue of a royal grant. That these payments, according to a manuscript of the next century, were made on St Martin's Day and on Okeday,[89] leads me to speculate whether there was some connection between this Dean and an important former minster in the city. Churchscot, a key perquisite of a minster was paid on St Martin's Day.[90] So strong was the right of the ancient church that in the twelfth century the monks of Battle had to fight long and hard, and probably ultimately unsuccessfully, to establish the right of their church in the city to bury benefactors of their house: despite the support of Archbishop Anselm,[91] who managed to extract from Bishop Osbern a concession permitting the monks' bells to be rung,[92] bulls still needed to be extracted from both Paschal II[93] and Eugenius III, the latter commanding Bishop Robert Warelwast to consecrate a cemetery within three months on pain of interdict.[94] It is not clear whether this was ever done.

Ely is a most interesting case since there is no doubt that the cathedral began life as the church of a monastic community. There is considerable evidence that part of the cathedral was used by a parochial community, some as early as the twelfth century. Archiepiscopal commissioners on visitation in 1315 reported on the rights of two parishes in the city of Ely then known as 'the church of St Peter' and 'the church of St Mary'.[95] These seemed to have grown out of groups of worshippers at the nave altar, or altar of the Holy Cross,[96] doubtless from the rood on the

[88] Exeter City Archives Muniment Book 53A fo. 36r: Miss Rose-Troup corrects the last word to *chepgabuli*, the city due; Rose-Troup, *Lost chapels of Exeter*, p. 12.

[89] Historical Manuscripts Commission, *Report on the records of the City of Exeter* (London, 1916), p. 387.　　　　[90] *CS*, 512 (Cnut's letter of 1027).

[91] *Sancti Anselmi Cantuariensis archiepiscopi opera omnia*, ed. F. S. Schmitt, 6 vols. (Edinburgh, 1938–61), IV, pp. 53–4.

[92] *The Exeter book of Old English poetry*, ed. R. W. Chambers, M. Forster and R. Flower (London, 1933), p. 49.　　　　[93] *Sancti Anselmi opera* IV, p. 131.

[94] W. Holtzmann, *Papsturkunden in England*, Abhandlungen der Gesellschaft der Wissenschaften in Göttingen, phil.-hist. klasse, 3 vols. (Berlin and Göttingen, 1930–52), II, no. 54.

[95] BL Additional MS 41612 fos. 33v–36v.

[96] It was described by the visitors of 1315 as *esse constructum contra ius commune infra ecclesiam conventualem monachorum non longe a choro distans eorundem* (ibid., fo. 35v). There is a direct parallel, of immense intrinsic interest, in the much smaller church of Daventry where the parish

pulpitum. The earliest reference to the church of St Mary is in 1109,[97] and it is clear from the surviving sacrists' rolls of the priory that the revenues gained from the offerings made by both these groups were of considerable importance to the monks.[98] Both parishes were served by chaplains appointed by the monastic sacrist,[99] and the former had spawned a daughter chapel at Stuntney probably by the mid-twelfth century.[100] Bishop Eustace (1198–1215) seems to have rebuilt the church of St Mary some time before 1208,[101] presumably thus solving some of the difficulties caused by the parishioners in the monastic church, but the Holy Cross community had to await the mid-fourteenth century before the difficulties caused by their presence were addressed. Work on their new church, a ramshackle lean-to built on to the wall of the north aisle, probably only began in 1341–2, when 3s 8d was spent by the sacrist *pro fundamentis ecclesie parochialis*,[102] and was completed sufficiently to come into use by 1362, or perhaps 1367.[103] This church was then possibly re-dedicated to the Trinity, for it was known by this name at least from as early as 1373.[104] Never satisfactory and only fully

which developed out of the pastoral functions of the collegiate pre-Conquest minster there also took its name from the rood in the nave where they worshipped: cf. *The cartulary of Daventry priory*, ed. M. J. Franklin, Northamptonshire Record Society 35 (1988), xxxvi. We are reminded, yet again, of the many meanings of the word *mynster* or *monasterium*, a point which Christopher Brooke himself made most succinctly – C. N. L. Brooke, 'Rural ecclesiastical institutions in England: the search for their origins', *Settimane di studio del Centro italiano di studi sull'alto medioevo* 28 (Spoleto, 1982), 697. The important churches of eleventh and twelfth-century England, be they 'monastic' in a sense that St Æthelwold would have accepted, let alone St Bernard, could not turn out the laity completely because they often had their origins in institutions of the Conversion age when such contacts were positively encouraged.

[97] CUL MS EDR G/3/28 [Ely 'Liber M'] 143b.

[98] The revenues from offerings made *altare ad crucem* and *de ecclesia beate Marie* are tabulated from the surviving fourteenth-century sacrists' rolls in *Sacrist of Ely Rolls*, ed. Chapman, 2 vols. (Cambridge, 1907), I, 119.

[99] *Sacrists' Rolls* ed. Chapman, I.114; II.121; cf. CUL MS EDR G/3/28 p. 178 an *actum* of Bishop Hugh de Northwold, dated 1232, which is attested by Everard and John, *capellani* of St Cross, and William and Peter, *capellani* of St Mary's. Cf. BL Additional MS 41612 fo. 35r where the sacrist's right to appoint two chaplains for each of the two churches within the city is referred to.

[100] This is by the evidence of the fabric – VCH, *Cambs.*, IV, 85. Documentary evidence of dependence can be found from the late fifteenth century – CUL MS EDR G/1/5 [Bishop Gray's Register] fo. 224v – a list of churches in the diocese where are mentioned *ecclesie sancte Trinitatis et sancte Marie cimiterii Elien cum capellis suis de Stonteney et de Chetesham appropriate officio sacristarie Eliens'*.

[101] CUL MS EDR G/3/28 p. 165b attested by Richard, archdeacon of Ely (*Fasti Monastic Cathedrals*, 50–1).   [102] *Sacrists' Rolls*, II, 121 – Roll IXB for 15 Edward III.

[103] *Sacrists' Rolls*, II.121, cf. 192ff.   [104] VCH, *Cambs.*, IV, 83 n. 15.

completed in 1459–60,[105] the parish abandoned using this structure when the use of the Lady Chapel was obtained in 1565,[106] a situation which was to endure until 1938.

In dealing with the diocese of Bath and Wells in this survey there is a certain amount of difficulty in deciding which of the two 'cathedrals' to deal with. The *Historiola de primordiis episcopatus Somersetensis*, from an early-fourteenth-century manuscript now preserved in Lincoln's Inn, mentions changes at Wells instituted by Bishop Giso (1061–88). He

tunc ecclesiam sedis mee perspiciens esse mediocrem clericos quoque quatuor vel quinque absque claustro et refectorio...claustrum vero et refectorium et dormitorium illis preparari et omnia que ad hec necessaria et impetrantia fore cogiari...[107]

as well as causing the first dean of the cathedral to be elected. Bishop John, Giso's successor, who tried to transfer the see to Bath, destroyed much of Giso's work,[108] but was opposed primarily by John the archdeacon, probably a representative of the old order since he claimed by hereditary right his priestly inheritance.[109] These fragments of probably mainly legendary history add weight to the inferences drawn from Warwick Rodwell's excavations, which show that, when the diocese of Somerset was created in 905, a substantial pre-existing minster complex was used.[110] Although Wells only became a see in 909, there is documentation concerning St Andrew's minster dating from 766.[111]

There is little to be said about the cathedral which served the diocese of Wiltshire. Since both Salisbury and its predecessor at Old Sarum were built on virtually virgin sites there is little to comment on in this context. If the cathedral of Old Sarum grew out of any pre-existing institution the only comparison is with free chapels which grew up in royal castles. Similarly at Norwich there appears to be no evidence of parochial use of the cathedral. This might possibly be expected, for Bishop Losinga's intention

---

[105] Ibid., 83.   [106] Ibid., 60.

[107] *Historiola de primordiis episcopatus Somersetensis* in *Ecclesiastical Documents*, ed. J. Hunter, Camden Society 1840, 16–17; 19. This is an edition of part of Lincoln's Inn MS 185.

[108] Cf. Knowles and Hadcock, *Houses*, p. 442.   [109] *Historiola*, p. 22.

[110] W. Rodwell, *Wells cathedral: excavations and discoveries*, 3rd edn. (Wells, 1980), esp. p. 3.

[111] = 774; Sawyer no. 262.

was to build from scratch a Carolingian-style episcopal monastic complex; he seems to have cared little for pre-existing ecclesiastical rights. None the less it would seem that at least two churches, dedicated to Christ Church and to St Michael, were destroyed in the process of creating his new cathedral,[112] and it is strange that little or no data concerning the provision made for these worshipping communities seem to be available.

It would appear that it was entirely conventional for certain members of the laity to use a cathedral for what later canon law was to define as the essentially parochial functions of baptism and burial, irrespective of whether that cathedral was monastic or not. In many cases this was a function of the origin of individual cathedrals. When a bishop set up his *cathedra* either for the first time in a particular see, or in a new location, he seems to have chosen a well established, and presumably reasonably wealthy institution. This was the case both before and after the Conquest. There was clearly little difference in the decision taken by Bishop Æthelhelm to set up his establishment in Wells in 909 and that by Bishop Leofric to move from Crediton to Exeter in 1050 or Bishop Stigand to move from Selsey to Chichester in 1075. All three chose established minsters of differing types. It seems to have been rare for a cathedral to be built on a virgin site like Old or New Sarum, even when motives were coloured by political or other considerations, as in the case at Lincoln or Norwich. When the more ancient institutions are considered it becomes clear that the history of these rights cannot be traced back much earlier than the eighth or ninth century. At Canterbury it is explicitly recorded that until archbishop Cuthbert built the church of St John no burials were permitted at Christ Church,[113] and the claims of the monks of St Augustine that their church was the original burial place for the whole city,[114] might well have an element of truth. At Winchester, where most is known, it is clear that what history tends to regard as a cathedral monopoly was probably in reality part of Edward the Elder's grand design for his capital city and its three major minster churches. None the less, and significantly, the one instance where there is substantial specific medieval documentary evidence, at Worcester, the picture is confused. It is clear

---

[112] 'Norwich', in *Atlas of Historic Towns 2*, ed. M. D. Lobel (London, 1975), p. 3.
[113] See above, n. 17.   [114] See above, n. 21.

that the clergy of Worcester in 1092 thought that the cathedral *ought* to be the only parish in the city, and that this claim ought to emanate from the very earliest days of the see. Whether their appeal to history was valid, however, is another story. It shows how important burial dues must always have been to cathedral finances, as do the long drawn-out sagas of conflicts between monks and worshipping communities. The example of Ely shows that a major pre-Conquest monastery was expected to have a *parochia*.

APPENDIX

I ROCHESTER CATHEDRAL

Maidstone, West Kent Archives Office, MS DRC/L7 (bi-partite indenture with seal attached: obverse, impression of Priory seal, reverse city seal).

Per istam indenturam cunctis pateat evidentis quod anno millesimo trecentisimo vicesimo septimo decimo octavo kalendis Julii mota contentione inter priorem et conventum ecclesie cathedralis Roffens' ex parte una et parochianos altaris sancti Nicholai in navi dicte ecclesie Roffens' situati ex parte altera super custodia clavis dicte ecclesie navis sit concordatum est intra partes videlicet quod dicte religiosi facient dictis parochianis unum oratorium in angulo dicte navis ecclesie iuxta hostium boriale cum hostio et fenestra ex parte exteriori dicte ecclesie ad respondendum corpus domini pro infirmis in nocturis horis futuris temporibus ministrandi cum libero introitu et exitu ad dictum oratorium. Et quis ante completionem dicti oratorii propter defectum ingressus ecclesie ut pluribus parochianorum visum fuerat pro eventus fortuitos pericula contingere possent ex benignitate dictorum religiosorum concessum est et concordatum quod die et nocte usque ad dicti oratorii complectionem pro infirmis ministrandis liberum in dictam ecclesiam habeant ingressum. Oratorio vero perfecto et clavis hostii dicti oratorii eisdem parochianis tradita. Ingressus dicte ecclesie decetero eis per noctem totaliter denegetur noctibus: nativitate domini, omnium sanctorum et sancti Nicholai dumtaxat exceptis. Observate tamen quod dicti parochiani omnia sacramenta et sacramentalia ac eciam omnia servicia sua in dicta navi ecclesie habeant sicut prius usi sunt et habere solebant a tempore ultime composicionis inter eosdem facte. In cuius rei testimonium parti indenture remanenti penes religiosos predictos sigillum commune civitatis Roffens' est appensum et parti indenture remanenti penes parochianos predictos appensum est sigillum commune religiosorum predictorum. Dat' Roffe' in ecclesia cathedrali predicta xii Kalendis Julii anno domini supradicti.

2 WORCESTER CATHEDRAL

The cartulary of Worcester cathedral priory (Register I), ed. R. R. Darlington, Pipe Roll Society new series 38 (1968 for 1962–3), no. 52.

... Huius pii patris Oswaldi temporibus Winsius sancte Elene presbyter uicarius huius sancte matris ecclesie extitit. Hic idem monitis sancti Oswaldi cum ceteris qui in clericali habitu huic ecclesie ut cumque seruiebant mundo posthabito monastice religionis habitum suscepit, et claues ecclesie sancte Elene quarum ipse sicut vicarius custos extiterat cum terris decimis ceterisque redditibus ad communem usum monachorum reddidit. Winsio proinde monacho facto cum ceteris qui secum sponte elegerunt conuerti, tam supradicta ecclesia quam ceter que nunc usque monachorum sunt ecclesie terre decime sepulture uel quelibet alie consuetudines sue dignitates ecclesiastice que clericorum quasi propria hactenus extiterant in ius monachorum tunc transierunt et in communem usum illorum redacte sunt, assensu Eadgari et beati Dunstani sanctique Oswaldi archiepiscoporum. Anno tercio conuersionis Winsii presbyteri beatus Os- waldus prioratum ei super monachos huius ecclesie concessit, assensu eiusdem regis. Concessit eciam illi omnibusque suis successoribus suis prioribus huius ecclesie decanos esse super omnes ecclesias suas et presbyteros ita uidelicet quod nullus decanus nullus archidiaconus de monachorum ecclesiis seu clericis se intromittat, nisi per priorem ecclesie. Omnes ecclesiasticas consuetudines prior sicut summus decanus episcopi pro suis ecclesiis episcopo persoluat...

3 LINCOLN MINSTER

a) John of Schalby, concerning the pre-history of his cathedral: *Giraldi Cambrensis Opera* VII, ed. J. F. Dimock, Rolls Series, London 1877, 194.

In loco autem in quo ecclesia beate Marie Magdalene in ballio Lincolniensi sita erat, dictus Remigius erexit suam ecclesiam cathedralem. Et in certo loco ipsius ecclesie cathedralis parochiani dicte ecclesie beate Marie Magdalene divina obsequia audierunt ac in fonte cathedralis ecclesie eorum parvuli baptizati fuerunt, et in ipsius cimiterio corpora parochianorum in obitu sepulture tradita extiterunt; per quemdam presbiterum de ecclesia cathedrali qui eis alia sacramenta et sacramentalia ministravit ad hos specialiter deputatus per decanum et capitulum dicte ecclesie cathedralis penes quos proprietas jurisdictionis ordinarie, sede vacante de iure et sede plena ipsius exercitium in ecclesia et ipsius prebendis ac ecclesiis de communa de introducta consuetudine pertinebat. Et iste presbiter per dictos decanum et capitulum et non per episcopum cure huiusmodi deputatus jurisdictionem ordinariam super dictos parochianos ex commissione capituli exerebat tam in correctionibus quam in ... et in eis. Si excessit, vel alias incuriose processit ad capitulum appellatum fuit de consuetudine memorata. Decimis oblationibus et ceteris provenientibus ex dictis parochianis provenientibus sibi pro stipendio assignatis...

b) John of Schalby, concerning the construction of a new church of St Mary Magdalen by Bishop Sutton: ibid., 209.

...ob quietem ministrantium in ecclesia cathedrali frequenter tribatam per confluentiam parochianorum olim ecclesie beate Marie Magdalene qui a fundatione ecclesie cathedralis in occidentali parte eiusdem ecclesie divina audierant et sacramenta et sacramentalia perceperant prout in principio huius tractatus plenius memoratur – quandam capellam in honore beate Marie Magdalene in atrio dicte ecclesie cathedralis, competenti spatio distantem ab ea erigi procuravit...

'Except the Lord keep the city'[1]: towns in the papal states at the turn of the twelfth century

BRENDA BOLTON

With his surprise election on 8 January 1198[2] came Innocent III's first, immediate and practical concern. This was to remove from those lands around Rome the 'intolerable German tyranny' which was still oppressing the people.[3] The area of 'middle Italy' with its mountains and narrow coastal stretches consisted mainly of towns or fortified villages dominated by agriculture. Some of them had existed since Roman or even Etruscan times[4] but it would be a great mistake to think of them in any way as successors to the Roman cities or as forerunners of those great city-states of northern Italy.[5]

The structure of the region, Rome and the towns, both simplified and yet made more difficult Innocent's task.[6] It was

---

[1] Psalm 127 (126), verse 1.

[2] M. Maccarrone, 'Innocenzo III, prima del pontificato', *Archivio della Società Romana di Storia Patria* (hereafter *ASRSP*) 9 (1942), 1–78 especially 64–78; W. Maleczek, *Papst und Kardinalskolleg von 1191 bis 1216: die Kardinäle unter Coelestin III und Innocenz III* (Vienna, 1984), pp. 101–4; M. L. Taylor, 'The election of Innocent III', in *The Church and sovereignty*, ed. D. Wood, *Studies in Church History, Subsidia* 9 (Blackwell, 1991), pp. 97–112.

[3] 'Propter importabilem Alemannorum tyrannidem', *Gesta Innocentii PP III*, (hereafter *Gesta*) *PL* 214–17 (Paris, 1855), 17–228, especially 26–7.

[4] J. Ward-Perkins, 'Etruscan towns, Roman roads and medieval villages: the historical geography of southern Etruria', *The Geographical Journal* 128 (1962), 389–405; T. W. Potter, *The changing landscape of South Etruria* (London, 1979), pp. 138–67.

[5] P. Racine, 'Innocent III et les Communes italiennes', *Religion et culture dans la cité italienne de l'antiquité à nos jours*, Actes du Colloque du Centre Interdisciplinaire de Recherches sur l'Italie, des 8–9–10 novembre 1979, Bulletin du C.I.R.I., 2e serie (Strasbourg, 1981), 73–87. Compare M. Pacaut, 'La Papauté et les villes italiennes (1159–1253)', *I problemi della Civiltà Comunale, Atti del Congresso Storico Internazionale per il viii centenario della prima Lega Lombarda*, (Bergamo, 4–8 settembre 1969), a cura di Cosmo Damiano Fonseca (Bergamo, 1971), pp. 33–46.

[6] P. Toubert, *Les Structures du Latium médiéval. Le Latium méridional et la Sabine du IXe siècle à la fin du XIIe siècle*, 2 vols. Bibliothèque des écoles françaises d'Athènes et de Rome, vol. 221 (Rome, 1973). For two vastly different yet complementary studies of the historiography of the region see K. Walsh, 'Zum *Patrimonium Beati Petri* im Mittelalter', *Römische Historische Mitteilungen* 17 (1975), 193–211 and S. Rubin Blanshei, 'Perugia 1260–1340: conflict and

simplified because of its geographical connection with Rome or made more difficult because these towns were either isolated on their rocky promontories or were way-stations to meet the needs of trade or pilgrims passing through the area. Insignificant many of these towns may have been but their inhabitants were certainly not lacking in awkwardness, especially in relation to the church in Rome.[7] The death of the Emperor Henry VI in 1197 and the consequent attempt by the church under Celestine III to restore control only served to heighten this awkwardness.[8] Innocent, the new shepherd and bishop of the area, wasted no time in setting out on his task. His aim was to recover those lost areas of the patrimony of St Peter and to remedy the unhappy state into which they had sunk.[9]

The towns concerned surrounded the great city of Rome. Those to the north, in present-day Lazio, then proudly belonged to the area of Tuscia Romana,[10] which should not be confused with modern Tuscany, then known as Tuscia Lombarda. Towns to the south, also now in Lazio, were then in Campania and Marittima, stretching as far as the bridge over the River Liri at Ceprano in the shadow of Monte Cassino and with Terracina being one of the most important.[11] In the view of Innocent III, the patrimony covered the area from Radicofani in the north to Ceprano in the south[12] and although the actual borders may have reached further

change in a medieval Italian urban society', *Transactions of the American Philosophical Society* 66 (1976), 1–128, especially 7–11.

[7] For example, L. Lanzi, 'Un lodo d'Innocenzo III ai Narnesi: specialmente per la terra di Stroncone', *Bolletino della Società Umbra di Storia Patria* 1 (1895), 126–35.

[8] M. Maccarrone, *Studi su Innocenzo III*, Italia Sacra 17 (Padua, 1972), 9–22.

[9] 'Status Romanae Ecclesiae pessimus erat', *Gesta*, col. 1. See also C. Lackner, 'Studien zur Verwaltung des Kirchenstaates unter Papst Innocenz III', *Römische Historische Mitteilungen* 29 (1987), 127–214 for an extensive discussion of 'päpstlicher Territorialpolitik' and useful prosopographies.

[10] *Gesta*, cols. 28–30; T. F. X. Noble, *The republic of St Peter: the birth of the papal state 680–825* (Pennsylvania, 1984), p. 37. For a visual and documentary record see J. Raspi-Serra, *La Tuscia Romana: un territorio come esperienza d'arte: evoluzione urbanistico-architettonica* (Rome, 1972).

[11] G. Falco, 'I comuni della Campagna e della Marittima nel Medio Evo', *ASRSP* 42 (1919), 537–605; 'Le origini ed il primo comune (sec. IX–XII)'; ibid., 47 (1924), 116–87. Neither of Falco's articles, although frequently cited by historians, contains much useful information for the period 1198–1216. See also A. Contadore, *De historia terracinensi: libri quinque* (Rome, 1706); A. Bianchini, *Storia di terracina* (Tivoli, 1952).

[12] 'A Radicofani usque Ceperano', *Gesta*, col. 24; Lackner, 'Des Kirchenstaates', p. 129, 117–86. See Noble, *Patrimony* pp. xxv–xxix for a persuasive discussion on the existence of a papal state before the eighth century and a critique of D. Waley, *The papal state in the thirteenth century* (London, 1961) and P. Partner, *The lands of St Peter* (London, 1972).

to the north east by the end of his pontificate, it is the towns of the smaller area which are most interesting in relation to Rome and the church.

One of our main sources will be the *Gesta Innocentii PP III* where the pope's biographer paints a most depressing picture of the grave servitude in which his subjects found themselves:[13] of dangerous assaults and hijackings on the roads; of a vastly depreciated currency; of oaths broken everywhere and the church's power usurped in town and village alike.[14] No one was safe. Had not even Octavian, cardinal bishop of Ostia been hijacked in 1192 at Monte S. Maria by Conrad 'Flybrain' and detained against his will?[15] Did not thugs abound, such as those at Rispampani where Guy and Nicholas, of noble origin, exacted illegal tolls[16] at the bridge where the Via Cassia from Radicofani to Aquapendente crossed the River Rigo?[17]

The *Gesta* goes on to give evidence of Innocent's practical help in regard to the roads of the region. He aimed to keep them open and Guy and Nicholas were, after, a hard fight, forced to swear that they would henceforth leave the roads in peace.[18] Papal peace was imposed for all faithful pilgrims and for travellers, particularly on that dangerous stretch of the Via Cassia between Vetralla and Sutri.[19]

[13] Y. Lefèvre, 'Innocent III et son temps vus de Rome', *Mélanges de l'Ecole Française de Rome* 61 (1949), 242–5; V. Pfaff, 'Die *Gesta* Innocenz' III und das Testament Heinrichs VI', *Zeitschrift der Savigny-Stiftung für Rechtsgeschichte, kanonistische Abteilung* 50 (1964), 78–126, especially 79–90; B. M. Bolton, 'Too important to neglect: the *Gesta Innocentii PP III*', *Church and chronicle in the middle ages: essays presented to John Taylor*, eds. G. A. Loud and I. R. Wood (London, 1991). [14] *Gesta*, cols. 26–9.

[15] Ibid., col. 25; O. Hageneder, W. Maleczek and A. Strnad, *Die Register Innocenz' III. 2. Pontifikatsjahr, 1199/1200* (Rome–Vienna, 1979) (hereafter *Register* II), 166 (175), p. 322; PL 214. 725; Potthast, 826; Maleczek, *Päpst und Kardinalskolleg*, pp. 80–3 and especially p. 82 for the activities of Conrad von Lützelnhart.

[16] *Gesta* xv, col. 29; I. Ciampi, *Cronache e Statuti della città di Viterbo* (Florence, 1872), p. 325; Lackner, 'Des Kirchenstaates', p. 152, n. 77–9. 'Senescallo et rectoribus patrimonii S. Petri in Tuscia super captione Guittonis et Nicolai et super tractatu habito cum eisdem' in A. Theiner, *Vetera Monumenta Slavorum Meridionalium Historiam Illustrantia, 1198–1549* (Rome, 1863), doc. 187, p. 61.

[17] C. R. and M. G. Cheney, 'A draft decretal of Pope Innocent III on a case of identity', *Quellen und Forschungen* 41 (1961), 29–47, especially 31, n. 10; G. Caselli, *La Via Romea* (Florence, 1990), pp. 138–41.

[18] Compare the oath of 1201 taken by the citizens of Viterbo, 'Domnus papa Innocentius (III) fecit (? con) firmatione pacis…de Nicola et Guitto de Strata…firmiter servabo et fideliter adimplebo sicut exprimunt', Ciampi, *Cronache*, p. 325; Caselli, *Via Romea*, pp. 146–7.

[19] *Gesta*, col. xxix 'In super domino papae fidelitatem, secundum morem et consuetudinem aliorum fidelium, juraverunt.' Compare PL 214.359, n. 65 which Migne linked, perhaps erroneously, with this case.

In his general aim of returning the papal states to the sphere of influence of the church, some political measures would be needed to restore the temporal dominion and Innocent was well aware of what had gone before. The provisions of the *Ludovicianum*,[20] the pact of 817 between Louis the Pious (814–43) and Pope Paschal I (817–24) would have been well known at the Curia. It had, after all, been only recently copied into the *Liber Censuum*, or *Book of Taxes*, a compilation of the customs, rents and payments owed to the Roman church, made by Cencio, the papal chamberlain and completed by him in 1192.[21] Although the actual revenues received by the church were not very great, it was important to Innocent that he stated his right to them, even if he then generously waived them on suitable occasions as at Fossanova in 1206.[22] His main concern was to establish this part of central Italy as a unified region with its own special identity and purpose, having strong links with the church.[23] He was keen to establish a successful model which he could then use elsewhere. The region was quite simply to be one 'Italia' and in its creation the towns of the area were to be set apart as particular agents of the pope.[24] In return for their support, they were rewarded with a period of papal residence, an event which enriched them because papal favour brought real profit as the entourage and the inevitable hangers-on attracted traders of all descriptions.[25] Those towns not fortunate to be visited by the pope himself made the best of what they could with lesser visits by cardinal-legates.

The *Gesta* sets down the pope's deeds with considerable bravura. It gives a long list of those areas recovered in the first two years of the pontificate.[26] One by one, they come back into the fold – a medieval version of the 'domino theory' so beloved of today's strategists. The list seems endless: from the March of Ancona in the north east through the Duchy of Spoleto. It then

[20] Noble, *Republic of St Peter*, pp. 148–53.
[21] *Le Liber Censuum de l'Eglise Romaine*, ed. P. Fabre and L. Duchesne, 3 vols. (Paris, 1889–1905), I, pp. 363–5; J. E. Sayers, *Papal government and England during the Pontificate of Honorius III (1216–1227)* (Cambridge, 1984), pp. 1–12.
[22] W. E. Lunt, *Papal revenues in the Middle Ages*, 2 vols. (Columbia, 1934), I, pp. 57–136, especially 69; II, pp. 62–4; 'Chronicon Fossanovae', ed. L. A. Muratori, *Rerum Italicarum Scriptores* 7 (Milan, 1725), 853–97, especially 886.   [23] Maccarrone, *Studi*, p. 16, n. 1.
[24] O. Hageneder and A. Haidacher, eds., *Die Register Innocenz' III*, I. *Pontifikatsjahr 1198–99* (Graz-Vienna-Köln, 1964–68), 401, pp. 599–601; *PL* 214. 377–8; Potthast, 403.
[25] William of Andres, *Chronicon*, MGH SS, 24, ed. G. H. Pertz (Hanover, 1897), pp. 690–773, especially p. 743; Maccarrone, *Studi*, pp. 55–61.   [26] *Gesta*, cols. 24–30.

peters out towards the south where the Germans had been stronger and where it was 1208 before Innocent was able to make any substantial journey to this area.[27] This strong German influence must have been in Innocent's mind in his general approach to Campania and Marittima. He was eager to replace the scarce and short-weight money of Flora used in this region, by so-called 'money of the Senate', *de jure* papal but *de facto* Roman. In so doing, he hoped to increase commerce in the south.[28] The attention he gives to the town of Terracina is another indication of this concern.[29] The situation there had been made even more difficult by the strength of the Frangipani brothers.[30] Anything Innocent could do to demonstrate the benign influence of the papacy would have been useful. It is most likely that he improved the 'triumphal arch' of the duomo of Terracina as he had already done in Città Castellana to indicate to the inhabitants the pride they should have in guarding these significant points of entry to the increasingly important patrimony.[31] All in all, the author of the *Gesta* is more accurate about the 'labour and expense'[32] involved in returning these towns to the pope than he is in his timescale. Recovery was a far longer process than the *Gesta* suggests, beginning in 1198 and still far from total in 1216.[33]

Innocent's approach to reclaiming what he felt belonged by right to the church was a mixture of temporal and spiritual, of 'force and blandishment'[34] and the power of his office together with the gospel message, pastoral care and the promise of salvation. He regarded his temporal activities as an unavoidable diversion.[35] He expressed his deep distaste at the thought that by using methods resorted to by factious local lords, the church might be said to have abandoned its spiritual principles. His letters continually express his awareness of the risk and his papal qualms appear perfectly genuine.[36] Indeed, it is precisely in this area that

[27] Lackner, 'Des Kirchenstaates', pp. 164–82.   [28] *Liber Censuum*, I, pp. 14–5.
[29] Contadore, *De Historia Terracinensi*, p. 174 for the text of the Bull *Satis Vobis*, 28 June, 1204.
[30] James, Deodatus, Manuel, Odo and Peter, Bianchini, *Storia di Terracina*, pp. 143–52; Lackner, 'Des Kirchenstaates', pp. 169–73.   [31] Ibid., pp. 205–8.
[32] 'Quia labor erat magnus et fructus parvus', *Gesta*, col. 30.
[33] Compare *Regestum Innocentii III papae super negotio Romani imperii*, ed. F. Kempf, *Miscellanea Historiae Pontificiae* 12 (Rome, 1947) 56, 150–3, especially 153 for Innocent's claim made at the end of October or early November 1201 that he held Rome. Also Bolton, *The Gesta Innocentii PP III*, pp. 95–7.   [34] Maccarrone, *Studi*, pp. 9–19.
[35] *PL* 214. 751; Maccarrone, *Studi*, p. 12.   [36] *Gesta*, col. 30; Maccarrone, *Studi*, p. 11.

the author of the *Gesta* comes closest to understanding Innocent's innermost feelings when he cites the text from Ecclesiastes, 13.1: 'Whomsoever toucheth pitch shall be defiled.'[37] There is no doubt that whatever method was used, the pope's solicitude for his subjects was paramount.[38]

In his activities around the patrimony, Innocent was well aware of the importance of both the historical and biblical dimensions of papal claims. He read avidly the *Liber Pontificalis*[39] and much admired his great predecessor, Gregory I (590–604) whose pragmatic and practical attitude towards the patrimony had led to a more systematic organisation[40] – even a 'Romanisation'[41] – whilst, at the same time, never losing sight of the pastoral duties involved. Innocent constantly used Bible references in the sermons which he, as a noted preacher, frequently delivered.[42] In the second of his *Sermones Communes* he develops the theme of Psalm 127.[43] 'Except the Lord build the house, they labour in vain that build it. Except the Lord keep the City, the watchman waketh but in vain.' His powerful text was composed for general use on feast days *in communi apostolorum* and also as a circuit-sermon for use on journeys around the patrimony. This is the guide to his approach to the towns and those who dwelt within them. 'The King of Kings, dearest brothers, has different cities in different regions, that is to say, heavenly and earthly, spiritual and corporal.' 'These four cities', he tells us, 'represent the Churches Triumphant and Militant, the whole body of the faithful and Jerusalem, the Wonderful.' The cities are threatened from above and below, from within and without by fallacious demons, 'the little foxes' of heresy, carnal concupiscence and alluring inducements. The rectors of the church are to keep the four watches: *conticinium*, the first part of the night, *intempestum* or dead of night,

---

[37] *Gesta*, col. 30; Maccarrone, *Studi*, p. 11.

[38] 'Propter curam et sollicitudinem apostolica patrimonium', 11 October 1199, *Register* II, 193 (202), pp. 367–8; *PL* 214. 750–1; Potthast 848.

[39] *Le Liber Pontificalis* ed. L. Duchesne, 3 vols. (Paris, 1886–92); *The book of pontiffs* (*Liber Pontificalis*) translated by R. Davis (Liverpool, 1989); S. J. P. Van Dijk and J. Hazelden Walker, *The origins of the modern Roman liturgy* (London, 1960), pp. 126–8.

[40] Sermo XIII, *De Sanctis, In festo D. Gregorii Papae, Hujus Nomine* I, *PL* 217. 513–22; Noble, *Republic of St Peter*, pp. 9–11; J. Richards, *Consul of God: the life and times of Gregory the Great* (London, 1980), pp. 128–39. [41] Ibid., p. 132. [42] *PL* 217. 309–688.

[43] 'De diversis civitatibus Dei, nimirum coelesti, terrestri, spirituali et corporali', *PL* 217. 601–6; Psalm 127 (126) verse 1.

gallicantium or cockcrow and *antelucanum*, just before daybreak.[44] They are the custodians of the cities, the *apostolici viri*, who ought to watch and take care of the flock throughout the night. 'Nothing', says Innocent, 'is to divide the head from the members, to keep fathers from sons, the shepherd from his sheep.' The gravest danger of all is heresy, to be guarded against as securely as men guard their riches.[45] Hence, the rector's rôle, as agent of the pope, is conceived of as highly supportive.

In a series of letters addressed to the cities of the patrimony, Innocent expatiates further on the implications of papal solicitude. The pope's yoke, like that of Christ, would be easy and the burden light.[46] Henceforth, all would walk, not in darkness but in the light and the recovered dominion would be a restored 'Italia', saved from foreign domination and kept in perpetuity for the church.[47] Innocent aimed to transfer to 'Italia' what Leo I and the medieval tradition had attributed to Rome.[48] In future, the towns would satisfy their desire for autonomy, linked together in the privilege of being the seat of the principality of the church as Rome had once been the seat of emperors. The sons of the patrimony would no longer be servants, nor would *minores* be oppressed by *majores*.[49] Some might even have the opportunity to be raised up to the status of *filii speciali*, an honorific title bestowed on prominent citizens and ecclesiastics whose activities the pope wished to recognise.[50] There would be a fair administration of justice and wherever necessary, the observance of a papally inspired truce would encourage *pax et concordia* in disputes amongst the towns of the patrimony.[51] Brotherly love would abound and the political fragmentation inherent in the geographical, historical and other characteristics of the patrimony would melt away before Innocent's unifying vision. Even with

---

[44] *PL* 217. 604.   [45] *PL* 217. 604–5.

[46] 'Jugum meum suave est et onus meum leve' (Matt. 11:30). Compare the parallel letter to the consuls and people of Sutri, *c.* 15 October 1199, *Register* II, 194 (203), pp. 369–71; *PL* 214. 751–2; Potthast, 849. A similar letter was also sent to the consuls and people of Nepi, Spoleto, Narni, Orte, Rieti, Città Castellana, Amelia, Città di Castello, Tuscania, Vetralla, Todi, Assisi, Bagnoreggio, Centocello, Perugia, Foligno, Orvieto and Corneto. Compare Maccarrone, *Studi*, pp. 14–15.   [47] *Gesta*, xxvi; Maccarrone, *Studi*, p. 15.

[48] *Register* I, p. 600; *PL* 214. 377; Potthast, 403.

[49] 'Ne filii fiant servi, neque minores maioribus opprimantur', *Register* I, p. 600; *PL* 214. 377.

[50] *Register* I, I, p. 5; *PL* 214. 2; Potthast, I.

[51] For one such exhortation given on 23 September, 1207, *PL* 215. 1228; Maccarrone, *Studi*, p. 17.

Innocent, ambitious schemes did not always materialise; and by 1213, when he sent out his crusade encyclical *Quia Maior*, the hoped-for unity was still not achieved.[52] Perhaps he was expecting and demanding too much.

To return to his methods, we must first look at the way in which he presented his programme through the institution of rectors in various parts of the patrimony.[53] Regretting his inability to be everywhere at once, but rejoicing that others could act on his behalf, he sent circular letters to the bishops and leading citizens, asking them to receive his rectors.[54] Gregory I seems to have appointed only clerical rectors but Innocent had a mixture of both clerical and lay.[55] In 1203, he created as rector his *cognatus* and thus possibly a relation, one Stephen Romano Carsoli,[56] whom he strategically based at Montefiascone, a former imperial fortress. He praised the purity of the man's faith, his hard work and discretion and stated that he had absolute trust in him.[57] Obviously these were the qualities which the pope hoped for in all his rectors. Another relation, his cousin James the Marshall, was deemed worthy of this position in 1215.[58]

A rector's tour of duty seems to have lasted about a year, perhaps the limit of endurance and effectiveness which could be expected as the pressure of work was considerable.[59] Rectors were responsible for collecting the *fodrum*, the traditional hospitality tax,[60] for keeping the peace, for dealing with appeals from lower courts and arbitration in regard to claims made by one subject against another.[61] Should the rectors be also cardinals, they were

---

[52] L. and J. Riley-Smith, *The Crusades: idea and reality 1095–1274* (London, 1981), pp. 118–24.

[53] On the office of rector and the administration of the patrimony in general, see M. Moresco, *Il Patrimonio di San Pietro* (Turin, 1916); J. Richards, *The popes and the papacy in the early Middle Ages 476–752* (London, 1979), pp. 307–22; Waley, *Papal state*, pp. 52–3.

[54] 'Romanus pontifex pro defectu conditionis humanae per se ipsum omnia expedire non potest, iuvetur subsidiis aliorum', *Register* II, 194 (203), p. 369; *PL* 214. 750; Potthast, 849.

[55] Richards, *Consul of God*, p. 134; Lackner, 'Des Kirchenstaates', pp. 197–205.

[56] *PL* 215. 112; Lackner, 'Des Kirchenstaates', p. 200.

[57] 'Cum ergo de tuae fidei puritate indubitam fiduciam habeamus, et de tuae discretionis industria', *PL* 215. 112.   [58] Prosopography in Lackner, 'Des Kirchenstaates', pp. 200–3.

[59] Waley, *Papal state*, p. 96.

[60] C. R. Brühl, *Fodrum, Gistum, Servitum Regis*, 2 vols. (Köln-Graz, 1968) I, pp. 578–761. For various insights into the imperial *fodrum* see *Chronicon Fossanovae*, ed. L. A. Muratori, *Rerum Italicarum Scriptores* 7 (Milan, 1725), 853–97, especially 886 and 889.

[61] For the oaths taken from rectors, Waley, *Papal state*, p. 97. See also G. Ermini, 'I rettori provinciali dello Stato della Chiesa da Innocenzo III all'Albornoz', *Rivista di Storia del Diritto Italiano* 4 (1931), 5–6.

made responsible for working with bishops in their dioceses.[62] A novel form of *Parliamentum*, consisting of all estates, clerics, nobles and citizens, was summoned by Innocent to meet together for three consecutive days at Viterbo in 1207.[63] On 21 September, he set out the law of the Roman church and received the oaths of the laity.[64] On 22 September, he adjudicated quarrels and complaints between his vassals[65]; whilst on 23 September, the last day, he promulgated statutes to promote peace and justice, including the repression of heresy.[66] At the same time, he formalised the office of rector. Thereafter, most appointments seem to have been laymen close to the pope, who could be trusted to carry out his policy, particularly when new fortifications, manned by Innocent's own castellans, were necessary.[67]

Whilst most rectors were concerned with large areas, the office itself also existed in some of the towns. The *Gesta* refers to the events of 1197 when the citizens of the northern part of the patrimony had appointed their own 'rectors' and joined in the league of Tuscan cities.[68] Whilst this league claimed to serve the Holy See, Innocent seems to have given them little more than a letter of greeting and commendation.[69]

In addition to the rectors, the bishops were most important agents of the pope, immediately subject as they were to him, in his position as archbishop of the region.[70] All these bishops were bound to swear an oath of recognition to the pope, promising obedience and reverence and, in return, receiving his special vigilance and protection.[71] As there were more than twenty episcopal towns throughout the patrimony,[72] Innocent might

---

[62] Compare the letter of March 1198 to all the bishops of the Marches, *Register* I, 38, pp. 56–7; *PL* 214. 31–2; Potthast, 40.   [63] *Gesta*, cols. clxi–clxii; *PL* 215. 1226–8.
[64] Ibid., 1227, 'Cum ex officii nostri'.   [65] 'Cum juratum sit', ibid., 1228.
[66] 'Ad eliminandum', ibid., 1226–7.
[67] Lackner, 'Des Kirchenstaates', pp. 197–205 for prosopographical studies of the rectors. In Tuscia Romana: John Cencio (1199); Gregory Ceccarello, Cardinal–Deacon of S. Giorgio in Velabro (1199–1200); Peter de Vico, Prefect of Rome (1199–1201/2); Stephen Romani Carsoli (1203), *cognatus*; James, the Papal Marshal (1213–16). In Campania-Marittima: Lando de Montelongo, *consobrinus* (1199–1203); Peter de Sasso (1208–12).
[68] *Gesta* cols. xxvi–xxvii; Lackner, 'Des Kirchenstaates', p. 147.
[69] *Register* II, 198 (207), pp. 377–9; *PL* 214. 55–6; Potthast, 870.
[70] C. Eubel, *Hierarchia Catholica Medii Aevi* (Regensburg, 1913), p. 540.
[71] Maccarrone, *Studi*, pp. 302–5, especially n. 1, p. 302.
[72] In the Province of Rome: Tivoli, Segni, Anagni, Alatri, Veroli, Ferentino, Terracina, Grosseto, Bagnoreggio, Montefiascone, Viterbo, Nepi, Sutri, Orte, Città Castellana. In Umbria: Rieti,

have been forgiven for being complacent over this apparent support. He could not afford to be so. The problem of Catharism was a grave difficulty which had, before 1198, infiltrated Viterbo and Orvieto and was there for him to deal with.[73]

The task of each bishop was to defend his flock, maintain its faith by preaching and example, administer the goods of the diocese so that he could hand them on undiminished to his successor and generally to show united allegiance to the pope and the church in Rome. In Orvieto, the inadequacy of the aged bishop Richard (1178–1202) was so apparent in dealing with heretics and his sympathies were so much in doubt that Innocent was forced to keep him in Rome under house arrest for nine months in 1198.[74] The faithful of the city, seeking reconciliation with the pope, appealed for a 'rector' to extirpate the heresy.[75] Peter Parenzo was selected by Innocent and was then promptly murdered in May 1199.[76] The shock of his death provoked a reaction strong enough to eliminate heresy in Orvieto.

Orvieto's neighbour and the former imperial stronghold, Viterbo, proved a far more serious threat.[77] Heresy here was deep-rooted and one of Innocent's letters to the city became a model decretal forming the basis for Canon III of the Fourth Lateran Council.[78] *Vergentis in Senium* of 25 March 1199 and addressed to the clergy and people of Viterbo, established heresy as a treasonable offence.[79] *Si adversos vos* dated 4 June 1205,[80] in the opinion of Luchaire possibly the most virulent letter ever to emerge from Innocent's chancery,[81] revealed that the chief official of Viterbo, the *camerarius* John Tigniosi, and the consuls of the city were not only heretics but also excommunicates.[82] The Bishop

Narni, Terni, Amelia, Castro, Perugia, Città di Castello, Assisi, Foligno, Gubbio, Nocera, Orvieto, Todi and Spoleto.
[73] On Catharism in the region, see V. Natalini, *S. Pietro Parenzo: la leggenda scritta dal Maestro Giovanni, Canonico di Orvieto, Lateranum*, new series 2, (Rome, 1936); Maccarrone, *Studi*, pp. 30–51; Lackner, 'Des Kirchenstaates', pp. 148–54; D. Waley, *Mediaeval Orvieto* (Cambridge, 1952), pp. 12–21. [74] Natalini, *S. Pietro Parenzo*, p. 104; Maccarrone, *Studi*, pp. 28–9.
[75] Maccarrone, pp. 33–5. [76] Natalini, *S. Pietro Parenzo*, pp. 163–4.
[77] I. Ciampi, *Cronache e Statuti della Città di Viterbo* (Florence, 1872); P. Egidio, 'Le croniche di Viterbo', *ASRSP*, 24 (1901), 197–252; N. Kamp, *Istituzioni communali in Viterbo nel Medioevo. I. Consoli, Podestà, Balivi e Capitani nei secoli XII e XIII*, Biblioteca di Studi Viterbesi, 1 (Viterbo, 1963).
[78] *Conciliorum Oecumenicorum decreta*, ed. J. Alberigo et al. (3rd ed. Bologna, 1973), pp. 263–4.
[79] *Register* II, 1, pp. 3–5; *PL* 214. 537–9; Potthast, 643. [80] *PL* 215. 654–7; Potthast, 2532.
[81] A. Luchaire, *Innocent III: Rome et l'Italie* (Paris, 1905), p. 93.
[82] *PL* 215. 652; Potthast, 2532.

seemed to be nowhere. Two weeks later, in a joint letter to the Bishops, Rainier of Viterbo[83] and Matthew of Orvieto,[84] Innocent ordered that 'Brother Viterbo' should immediately go to the rescue of his flock whom he had deserted, whilst 'Brother Orvieto' was ordered 'not to wait at a distance with dry eyes' but must immediately assist, even if it meant laying down his own life.[85] The systematic, firm and energetic actions which followed were to be a model for use elsewhere, but there is evidence that the degree of success in Viterbo itself was very slight.[86] The Statute *Ad Eliminandum*, promulgated at the Viterban Parliament in 1207,[87] dealt harshly with heretics but the matter seems not to have been resolved. In due course, Bishop Rainier seems to have been suspended for incompetence and incapacity.[88]

In spite of heresy not having been eradicated, the bishops of the region began to play a greater part in restoring peace and concord, especially in negotiating the settlement of disputes between the cities. In so doing, they followed the pope's overall duty. The language Innocent uses in this is surprisingly similar to that he used to monarchs.[89] The Roman church is regarded as the pious mother, who is unable to forget the sons she has borne.[90] Yet he believes in firm, direct and hard-hitting intervention where needed. In 1198–9, he freed Aquapendente from domination by Orvieto[91] and protected Vitorchiano from its predatory neighbour Viterbo.[92] He showed himself willing to move firmly against Narni in 1208[93] where he accused the people of having been stained by pitch. He intervened to settle rivalries between Todi, Amelia and Orvieto[94] saying that too many casualties had been caused and that all their attempts at mediation had been in

---

[83] Rainier (1199–?1221): Eubel, p. 532, n. 1.
[84] Matthew of Orvieto (1201–?1221): Eubel, p. 508; Ciampi, *Cronache*, pp. 326, 335.
[85] *Cum lupi rapaces*, PL 215. 673–4; Potthast, 2539.
[86] Ciampi, *Cronache*, p. 326 cites an undated letter from Bishop Rainier about the heresy of Master Robectus who appears to have practised a thorough-going form of Cathar dualism, denying the value of baptism and using such obscenities that Ciampi felt unable to print them.
[87] *Gesta*, cols. clxi–clxii: PL. 214.1226–7.
[88] Eubel, *Hierarchia*, p. 532, n. 1: Ciampi, *Cronache*, pp. 326, 335–6.
[89] Compare B. M. Bolton, 'Philip Augustus and John: two sons in Innocent III's Vineyard?', *The church and sovereignty*, pp. 113–34. [90] PL 214. 400–1; Maccarrone, *Studi*, p. 72, n. 1.
[91] *Gesta*, col. xxvii; Natalini, *S. Pietro Parenzo*, pp. 155–6; Maccarrone, *Studi*, pp. 22–30; Waley, *Papal state*, p. 36. [92] *Gesta*, cols. clxxix–clxxxiii.
[93] PL 215. 1458–9; Lackner, 'Des Kirchenstaates', pp. 158–9; Lanzi, 'Un lodo d'Innocenzo III ai Narnesi', pp. 126–35. [94] Maccarrone, *Studi*, pp. 70–3.

vain. When called upon by both sides to resolve the disputes, the pope insisted on receiving their oaths personally so that a real and lasting peace could be agreed.[95]

In some of these towns there already existed *podestà*, consuls and other urban officials; but the *ius elegendi potestatem*, that is, the right to elect their own, enjoyed by the Lombard League in the North, had not been easily transposed to Tuscia Romana.[96] Some towns had to ask permission or approval from the pope himself or from his rector. In May 1199, the citizens of Città Castellana promised not to elect their rector without papal permission[97] and Innocent agreed to approve their candidate, John, as he had been elected *communiter*, by all the people.[98] Quite the reverse seems to have happened at Velletri in 1201 where John Nicholas was forced to step down.[99] In the same year, Innocent conceded that the people of Aquapendente might receive John of Orvieto[100] but, by 1203, the pope was intervening once more to prevent a Viterban noble from holding office there.[101] In 1206, he acted against the strategic frontier town of Radicofani.[102] 'On this occasion', says Innocent, 'the people have not lightly but seriously offended by electing consuls without his permission.'[103] The blessings of the Holy See which are extended to *nationes* ought to be shown equally to *domestici* and vassals who are the proper concern of papal solicitude. Interestingly, in the same year, the pope had written to the people of Sutri, a great pilgrim centre on the Via Cassia, instructing them at no time to receive strangers into the government of the town.[104] Sutri epitomised the problems faced by pilgrim towns in regard to the influence of strangers from outside its borders. Much of Sutri's prosperity derived precisely

---

[95] 'Receptis ab utraque parte iuramentis aliisque securitatibus...talem inter eos pacem et concordiam...duximus statuendam', Ibid.

[96] G. Ermini, 'La libertà communale', *ASRSP* 49 (1926), 4–7.

[97] Bonus de Fordevolie, elected without papal consent, PL 214. 617–18; Ermini, 'La libertà communale', p. 9; A. Theiner, *Codex Diplomaticus domini temporalis S. Sedis*, 3 vols. (Rome, 1961), I (756–1334), p. 32.

[98] 22 December 1199, *Register* II, 246 (256), p. 470 (where Città Castellana and Città di Castelle appear to be confused); PL 214. 815–16; Potthast, 911; Waley, *Papal state*, p. 70.

[99] 'Quem contra inhibitionem sedis apostolice elegerunt in Rectorem', Theiner, *Vetera Monumenta*, 237, p. 54.   [100] Ibid., 235, p. 54.

[101] 13 January 1203, PL 214. 1147–9; Potthast, 1804; Maccarrone, *Studi*, p. 63.

[102] PL 215. 796–7; Ermini, 'La liberta communale', p. 55.

[103] 'Hac vice non leviter offenderitis', PL 215. 795.

[104] Theiner, *Codex Diplomaticus*, 48, p. 40.

from its position on the principal road to north Italy. Nepi enjoyed a similar position on the Via Amerina and Città Castellana on the Flaminia.[105] The patrimony was, in fact, much more than a papal dominion. It was a permanent area of transit with highways and byways all leading to Rome. The whole area between Sutri in the north and Albano to the south was regarded as a pilgrim zone in which papal protection was necessarily sought and freely given. In return, the pope possessed several rights there. For example, in Sutri, if a pilgrim fell so ill in the town as to need a priest for the last rites, he was warned that he should also have present either the administrative official known as the *gastaldus curie* or two vassals of the Roman church.[106] This was a necessary precaution to enable the pilgrim to dispose of his worldly goods as he wished. If this testamentary deposition was not carried out to the letter, the will of the pilgrim would be judged invalid. Priests were particularly instructed to point out to solitary pilgrims that if they were to die intestate, within the pilgrim zone, the Curia would have the right to claim all their goods. Perhaps some of these goods were used towards Innocent's hospital foundations for pilgrims and strangers in Rome (1204)[107] and Anagni (1208).[108]

The problems which arose in towns such as Orvieto and Viterbo exemplify the importance Innocent gave to the visits he made to different parts of the patrimony throughout the eighteen years of his pontificate.[109] In this time, Innocent made four visits to Viterbo, in 1207,[110] 1209,[111] 1214[112] and 1216,[113] totalling about twelve months in all, although his final visit there was fleeting. The amount of time spent in Viterbo was only matched

---

[105] Waley, *Papal state*, pp. 83–4.

[106] 'Consuetudines et iura, que habet dominus papa in Burgo Sutrino', Theiner, *Codex Diplomaticus*, p. 29. On the gastald see G. Tabacco, *The struggle for power in medieval Italy: structures of political rule*, translated by R. Brown Jensen (Cambridge, 1989), pp. 102–3.

[107] 19 June 1204, *Inter opera pietatis*, PL 215. 376–80.

[108] 26 August 1208. See R. Ambrosi de Magistris, 'Il viaggio d'Innocenzo III nel Lazio e il primo ospedale in Anagni', *Storia e Diritto* 19 (1898), 365–78.

[109] L. Delisle, 'Itinéraire d'Innocent III dressé d'après les actes de ce pontife', *Bibliothèque de l'Ecole des Chartes* 18 (1857), 500–34.   [110] William of Andres, *Chronicon*, p. 737.

[111] From mid-May to mid-September, Delisle, p. 509; Potthast, 3727–3802; Maccarrone, *Studi*, pp. 56–7.   [112] From 23 June–19 September 1214, Potthast, 4932–8.

[113] Maccarrone, *Studi*, pp. 7–8. Compare *Cronaca di Luca di Domenico Manente (1174–1413)* in *Ephemerides Urbevetanas*, in *Rerum Italicarum Scriptores*, 15, ed. L. A. Muratori, 2nd ed., ed. L. Fiumi, 2 vols. (Città di Castello, 1920), pp. 269–414, especially p. 288.

by his time in Anagni, a favourite southern seat and a safe refuge during times of difficulty with the city of Rome.[114]

The whole pattern of Innocent's itineration is of interest. Between July and October 1198, in a massive display of personal authority in towns which had recently returned to the dominion of the Church, he progressed to Rieti, Spoleto and Perugia, returning by way of Todi, Amelia and Città Castellana.[115] His journey left behind tangible reminders of the papal presence. At Rieti, where he consecrated the churches of S. Eleuterio and S. Giovanni, he gave to both precious altar cloths, one decorated with lions, the other with leopards.[116] In Spoleto, where he dedicated an altar, he was attributed by his biographer with a small miracle.[117] A horse trough on which the city depended had dried up with serious consequences but, on the pope's arrival, an abundant spring began to flow and was known thereafter as the *fons papalis*. At Perugia he consecrated the high altar of the Duomo and at Todi, that of the church of S. Fortunato. For the decoration of all the altars, undertaken so personally, he obtained precious silken altar *pallia* and subtly worked covers.

At the Duomo of Città Castellana, the most spectacular cosmatesque portico, facing out towards the Via Flaminia, has been attributed to his patronage.[118] Art historians have seen this as a Roman triumphal arch, proclaiming as it does, its message of peace and goodwill: + GLORIA IN EXCELSIS DEO ET IN TERRA PAX HOMINIBVS BONEVOLVMTATIS LAVDAMVS TE ADORAMVS TE GLORI-FICAMVS TE GRATIAS AGIMVS +.[119] It has been suggested that the model was the antique arch of Gallienus,[120] used by the city of Rome in 1200 for the setting of the triumphal civic display of the key captured from the city of Viterbo.[121] A partly illegible

---

[114] *Gesta*, cols. cxcvi–cxcvii (1201–2), clxxxviii (1203).   [115] Ibid., cols. xxv–xxvi.
[116] Ibid., col. ccx.   [117] Ibid., cols. xxv–xxvi.
[118] P. Claussen, *Magistri Doctissimi Romani: die Römischen Marmorkünstler des Mittelalters, Corpus Cosmatorum*, I (Stuttgart, 1987), pp. 82–91.
[119] K. Noehles, 'Die Kunst der Cosmaten und die Idee der *Renovatio Romae*', *Festschrift Werner Hager*, eds. G. Fiensch and M. Imdahl, (Recklinghausen, 1966), pp. 17–37; H. Bloch, 'The new fascination with ancient Rome', in *Renaissance and renewal in the twelfth century*, eds. G. Constable and R. L. Benson (Oxford, 1982), pp. 615–36; E. Kitzinger, 'The arts as aspects of a Renaissance: Rome and Italy', ibid., pp. 637–70.
[120] Claussen, *Magistri Doctissimi Romani*, pp. 85–8 and Plate 105; S. G. MacCormack, *Art and ceremony in late antiquity* (Berkeley, 1981), pp. 32, 35 and Plate 10.
[121] Ciampi, *Cronache*, pp. 11–12; F. Cancellieri, *Le due nuove campane di Campidoglio* (Rome, 1806), p. 37.

inscription running along both sides of the portico could possibly tell us more.[122] Under the portico in the lunette above the right-hand doorway, a bearded Christ with a cruciform nimbus blesses with his right hand and holds a closed book in his left. The work, both portico and lunette, is signed by the Cosmati and dated 1210.[123] Claussen has suggested that on the portico of the Duomo at Terracina on the Via Appia to the south of the patrimony a similar inscription may well have matched that of Città Castellana.[124] Other gifts were given to the churches Innocent visited to north and south of the patrimony[125] – chasubles in red and purple, elaborately worked orphreys and a silver crozier to the Duomo of Anagni[126]; but of all these rich gifts Viterbo became the greatest beneficiary. There he gave to the churches of S. Lorenzo, S. Angelo de Spata, S. Sisto and S. Maria Nova not only the usual chasubles, orphreys and altar cloths but also a papal ring.[127]

Viterbo offered great advantages as a papal summer residence, not merely on account of the pleasant summer climate but also because of the space available to visitors.[128] As we know from the eyewitness account of William, abbot of the Cistercian abbey of Andres in Picardy, who journeyed there in June 1207, it could easily house all the *curiales* and papal chaplains as well as petitioners and pilgrims hoping to see the pope.[129] William asserts that the presence of the Curia and its hangers-on had increased Viterbo's normal population by as many as 40,000.[130] Even if this usually precise abbot did exaggerate somewhat, the fact remains that Viterbo was a large, well-developed town, with a rich hinterland, situated on the Via Cassia leading to Tuscany and Lombardy. The pope's presence there – 'as if he were in his own city'[131] necessitated the establishment of a stable chancery so that work could continue uninterrupted throughout the summer months.

---

[122] + INTRANTES---ASC----S--POTESA-VA-----RANTESSICETSALVA-OP ECAI---CEXAVD---. Transcribed 3 April 1991. Compare Claussen, *Magistri Doctissimi Romani*, p. 86 for a slightly different reading.

[123] + MAGISTER IACOBVS CIVIS ROMANVS CVM COSMA FILIO SVO + CARISIMO FECIT OHC OPVS ANNO DNI M C C X.

[124] Claussen, *Magistri Doctissimi Romani*, p. 88; Bianchini, *Storia di Terracina*, pp. 207–8.

[125] *Gesta*, cols. ccviii–ccx.   [126] Ibid., col. ccix.   [127] Ibid., cols. ccxxviii–ccxxix.

[128] 'Viterbo...una vera e grande città, non un "oppido", come erano le piccole citta del Lazio meridionale', Maccarrone, *Studi*, p. 58.   [129] William of Andres, *Chronicon*, pp. 737–8.

[130] Ibid., p. 737.   [131] 'In civitate propria manebat', Ibid., p. 737; Maccarrone, *Studi*, p. 61.

Whereas in 1207 the Chancery moved with Innocent when he visited Montefiascone for twelve days in August, by 1209, on his next visit, it was the pope who did the travelling while the Chancery stayed put in Viterbo.[132] By 1210, the city had what passed for a 'papal palace' and by that date, the two small and ancient ecclesiastical dependencies of Centocelle and Blera, had been transferred from Tuscania-Corneto to the bishopric of Viterbo.[133] Innocent thus combined his own preference for cooler summer places with the urgent need to create a political capital in territories likely to be contested by imperial forces. We also know, from the chance survival of uncensored remarks by papal chancery clerks, that the hard-pressed *curiales* did not care for such remote, stifling and mosquito-ridden towns as Subiaco where they stayed unwillingly throughout August and September 1202[134] or Segni where they endured three visits in 1201, 1212 and 1213.[135] While political events such as the troubles in Rome in the early years of his pontificate[136] or the incursions of Otto IV after 1209[137] limited or determined the extent and nature of the pope's itineration, Innocent used every opportunity at his disposal to show himself to the people of the patrimony for practical reasons, as well as for the customary crown-wearings. Wherever the pope had consecrated a church or dedicated an altar, he left behind a gift.[138] In whichever town he stayed, his patronage would benefit the citizens.

As he could not be everywhere at once, he needed a symbol as a reminder of the importance of the religion of the church in Rome, the foundation stone of 'Italia', and something which might help to suppress localism.[139] Innocent wished to unify his subjects throughout the patrimony by bringing them together in a particularly 'Roman' ceremony.[140] His success in this can be measured by the widespread veneration of images of the Saviour

---

[132] Ibid., pp. 58–9.   [133] *PL* 215. 1234; Ciampi, *Cronache*, p. 302.

[134] K. Hampe, 'Eine Schilderung des Sommeraufenthaltes der römischen Kurie unter Innocenz III in Subiaco 1202', *Historische Vierteljahrschrift* 8 (1905), 509–35.

[135] Potthast, 3727–3801; Van Dijk and Hazelden Walker, *Origins*, pp. 97–9.

[136] A. Luchaire, 'Innocent III et le peuple romain', *Revue Historique*, 81 (1903), 225–77.

[137] Lackner, 'Des Kirchenstaates', pp. 157–64.   [138] *Gesta*, cols. xxv–xxvi.

[139] *PL* 214. 377–8.

[140] W. Volbach, 'Il Cristo di Sutri e la venerazione del S. Salvatore nel Lazio', *Atti della Pontificia Accademia Romana di Archeologia. Rendiconti* 17 (1940–1), 97–127; B. M. Bolton, 'Advertise the message: images in Rome at the turn of the twelfth century', *Studies in Church History* 28 (1992), 117–30.

throughout the region, still perpetuated in Lazio even today.[141] The particular image which Innocent promoted was that in the *Sancta Sanctorum* or papal chapel of St Laurence at the Lateran, called by Gerald of Wales the *Uronica* and also known as the *Acheropita* or icon not made by human hand.[142] This venerable image was ritually processed through the streets of Rome on the night of 14 August, the Vigil of the Assumption, arriving early on the morning of 15 August at S. Maria Maggiore so that Christ could greet his mother on her special feast day.[143] In November 1207, when Innocent passed through Sutri, he rededicated the Duomo there to the Virgin of the Assumption and promoted the 'Roman' image of the Saviour in Majesty, a cruciform nimbus behind his head, seated on a throne with his right hand raised in blessing and holding in his left a closed book.[144] This image was identical to the Christ in the Lateran, although it is worth recording that Innocent later had the Roman image covered to the neck with a splendid silver cover to concentrate attention on the face.[145] Only one of the images in the patrimony is a direct copy in every sense. At S. Egidio at Palombara in Sabina, the fourteenth-century artist had only seen the covered image and so reproduced both cover and face as he had first seen them in Rome.[146] The image used in almost every small town in the region seems to have reproduced this particular Roman ceremony. Images of the Saviour on the Lateran model and associated with the Feast of the Assumption are known to have existed, not only at S. Maria Nova in Viterbo, right under Innocent's eye, but also at Trevignano, S. Andrea in Anagni, Velletri, Bracciano, Castel Sant'Elia at Nepi[147] and at Tivoli where the ceremony of *inchinata* – ritual bowing to each other – took place between Christ and his mother as recently as 1978.[148] All these many images were variants of the original Roman model of liturgical procession and possessed the same message.[149]

[141] E. Kitzinger, 'A Virgin's face: antiquarianism in twelfth-century art', *Art Bulletin* 62 (1980), 6–19.

[142] *Giraldus Cambrensis Opera*, eds., J. S. Brewer and J. F. Dimock, 8 vols., *RS*, (London, 1861–91), vol. IV, pp. 268–85; J. Wilpert, 'L'*acheropita* ossia l'immagine del Salvatore della Capella del *Sancta Sanctorum*', *L'Arte* 10, (1907), 159–77, 246–62, especially pp. 162–5.

[143] Volbach, 'Il Cristo di Sutri', p. 116.   [144] Ibid., p. 100.

[145] Wilpert, 'L'*Acheropita*', p. 174 and figure 9.

[146] Volbach, 'Il Cristo di Sutri', p. 114 and figure 11.   [147] Ibid., pp. 97–126.

[148] Kitzinger, 'A Virgin's face', p. 12, n. 46.   [149] Bolton, 'Advertise the Message', 125–8.

Marangoni in the eighteenth century believed that these processions were in the tradition of ancient imperial triumphal rites – based on the use of arches and marble sculpture and his views have been taken up with perhaps more enthusiasm than accuracy to show how, in the eighth century, the icon of Christ in Majesty replaced that of the Emperor.[150] Then it was associated with the idea of freedom from foreign usurpers.[151] Had not the *Liber Pontificalis* spelt out clearly how, in 752, Pope Stephen II had carried this image across the city of Rome on his own shoulders to gain divine intervention against the Lombards, themselves enemies of both liberty and religion?[152] Did this image bear similar associations of liberty through unity, this time against the 'tyrannical Germans'? Innocent, well-read in the *Liber Pontificalis*, would certainly have been aware of the image's history.[153]

Another unifying device was Innocent's apparent use of arches, antique and contemporary, as sites for the placing of a religious message. On two of the most important roads into the patrimony, the Via Appia to the south and the Via Flaminia to the north, at Terracina and Civita Castellana respectively, 'triumphal' arches have a most conspicuous position at the point of entry.[154] On the portico before each Duomo, the supremely 'Roman' cosmatesque decoration possibly reflects an anti-foreign emphasis. This Italian–Roman emphasis seems to have been a symbol of unity wherever it occurred. Each small town was thus a replica of Rome in this respect and a reinforcing message of one faith for 'Italia'.

In April 1216, Innocent set out on what was to be his final itineration throughout the patrimony with the intention of going north to settle a dispute between Pisa and Genoa. He hoped that this action would be both an example and a stimulus to those bishops subordinate to him in the Roman region. Already, Innocent had summoned the Fifth Crusade and legislated for it in

[150] G. Marangoni, *Istoria della Sancta Sanctorum* (Rome, 1747), p. 139; *Le Liber Censuum*, I, pp. 298–9; F. Gregorovius, *History of the city of Rome in the Middle Ages*, (A.D. 1200–1260), translated by A. Hamilton, vol. v (London, 1906), p. 14, n. 2; Compare S. MacCormack, 'Change and continuity in late antiquity, the ceremony of *Adventus*', *Historia* 21 (1972), 721–52; ibid., *Art and ceremony*, pp. 62–89.
[151] For a summary of these views, Volbach, 'Il Cristo di Sutri', pp. 121–6.
[152] *Liber Pontificalis*, ed. L. Duchesne, 3 vols. (Paris, 1886–92), I, p. 443.
[153] Van Dijk and Hazelden Walker, *Origins*, pp. 126–8.
[154] Figures 1 and 2. Claussen, *Magistri Doctissimi Romani*, figures 21, 22, 82, 99 and 105.

Ad Liberandum on 30 November 1215.[155] With this Crusade in mind, he wished Rome and the cities and towns of the patrimony to have a special and indeed 'peculiar' rôle.[156] It was part of his plan to make 'Italia' – middle Italy – the centre and pivotal force of the new crusade. For the very first time, crusaders from Rome and its surroundings were to be strongly encouraged to participate.[157] A ship and £30,000 were to be put at the disposal of these crusaders.[158] A further 3,000 silver marks which had come from the offerings of the faithful, personally given to the pope, would be passed on to the 'Italia' contingent. Finally, Innocent stated that he himself would travel in person to the south of Italy in June 1217 to bless the crusaders as they sailed away from Messina and Brindisi.[159] All he needed to do now was to encourage men and women alike to take the Cross. He hoped that his own preaching of the Cross would produce not only a great popular consensus – for crusading was, after all, a voluntary matter – but also that the efficacy of the appeal he preached would produce the manpower and finance which were so badly needed.[160] For a man of perhaps fifty-five, desperately affected by the heat, his proposal to travel the length of the peninsula in the height of summer, arousing popular religious enthusiasm as he went, was not without its own perils.[161]

The eyewitness account of Innocent's inspired preaching on Sunday 1 May 1216, during a torrential downpour, reveals the spontaneous, fascinating and truly evangelical aspect of the event.[162] By the end of the day, when Innocent was led away from the field in a triumphal procession, more than 2,000 men and many women had taken the Cross. Throughout the patrimony, his own bishops, like Innocent himself, had followed to the letter the instructions laid down in *Quia Maior*. In Bagnoreggio, for example, the bishop claimed for his diocese a very large number of crusaders.[163] From all the towns of the patrimony, therefore a definite Roman contingent emerged – a *magna turba*

---

[155] Riley-Smith, *The Crusades*, pp. 124–9.
[156] Macarrone, *Studi*, pp. 129–42.
[157] Ibid., pp. 137–8, especially n. 3.
[158] Riley-Smith, *The Crusades*, p. 126.
[159] Ibid., p. 125.
[160] Ibid., pp. 142–8.
[161] M. Petrucci, 'L'ultimo destino perugino di Innocenzo III', *Bollettino della deputazione di storia patria per l'Umbria* 64 (1967), 201–7.
[162] New York, Pierpont Morgan Library, M. 465, fo. 90 verso, printed in Maccarrone, *Studi*, pp. 8–9 and Plates I–II.
[163] Ibid., p. 138.

Romanorum.[164] In spite of everything which followed his untimely death on 16 July in Perugia, Innocent had brought together in unity, peace and concord the towns of the papal states in a common purpose.

[164] Ibid., p. 138, n. 3; *Lettres de Jacques de Vitry (1160/1170–1240) évêque de Saint-Jean-d'Acre*, R. B. C. Huygens, ed. (Leiden, 1960), p. 110, lines 227–32: 'novem vero naves cum domno Petro Hanibal et quibusdam aliis Romanis in ebdomada post festum sancti Bartholomei in portu Damaite applicuerunt.' Huygens suggests 22 September 1218 as the date of the letter.

—◆—

The medieval chapter of Armagh Cathedral

J. A. WATT

No historian of the medieval chapter of St Patrick's foundation at Armagh can echo the historian of the York chapter, for whom 'the evidence for both the internal administration of the late medieval Minster and for the careers of the members of the cathedral chapter is almost embarrassingly plentiful'.[1] Whereas for York superabundance of material has deterred investigators, for Armagh it is precisely the reverse that has been the deterrent. The possibility of writing a definitive history of the Armagh chapter had almost certainly disappeared by the first decades of the seventeenth century. In the aftermath of the plantation of Ulster, the Irish patent rolls recorded that the 'ancient records and charters concerning the dean and chapter of the Cathedral Church of Armagh have been lost, burned or defaced'.[2] Nevertheless the situation is far from hopeless. At the very time that that loss of evidence was being regretted, other types of Armagh documentation were being saved. It is material which allows the modern student to glimpse something of the history of the chapter, at least in its later medieval phase. An examination of this evidence, apparently the first approach to systematic study of the Armagh chapter, is here offered to honour a scholar, not the least of whose many-sided researches is his penetrating appreciation of the fascination and significance of the medieval cathedral and its institutions in medieval society, as well as the history of the Church in Celtic regions.

The survival of eight volumes of Armagh registers, covering

---

[1] R. B. Dobson, 'The later Middle Ages, 1215–1500' in G. E. Aylmer and R. Cant, eds., *A history of York Minster* (Oxford, 1977), p. 45.

[2] *Calendar of Patent rolls. Ireland, Charles I*, ed. J. Morrin (Dublin, 1864), n. 6 (1630).

unevenly and irregularly the period 1361–1546, allows the possibility of reconstructing something of the history of the Armagh chapter. The title 'register' is certainly misleading if it leads to the assumption that an Armagh register was 'a deliberately created working record of certain administrative acts by the bishop or his official and also containing copies of some incoming business'.[3] What can be said of the proper nature of the Armagh compilations at this stage when only one of them has been fully edited must be tentative. But it would seem that Quigley and Roberts, with their meticulous textual analysis of the register of Archbishop John Mey, have given us the key to the nature of the whole run of the registers.[4]

They see them as collections of medieval documents, but as the creation of the seventeenth century. At various points in his career, Archbishop James Ussher (1625–56) acquired different collections of Armagh material, some of them most likely already fragmentary, and had them bound under the name of what seemed the appropriate archbishop. He was not trying to reconstruct the pages of archiepiscopal registers which had been broken up. He was binding together, in rough chronological sequence, documents of different provenances. The editors of the Mey register think it best to regard it 'as the undifferentiated accumulation which underlies the distinct collections (for the most part now lost) whose existence has been argued on other grounds'. To a greater or lesser extent, then, generalising from their assessment of a single register, each of the other registers can be seen as bearing clear marks of similar accumulations. Each 'register' volume contains material from a variety of sources: court books, visitation records, formularies, notarial instruments, letter books, accounts, even fragments of original registers. In other words, the whole is a miscellany, a hotch-potch, an *indigesta moles*, indeed almost *chaos*. In the Mey register, its editors have found, 'there is a complete absence of any detectable principle or purpose, either of chronological arrangement or diplomatic category, in the entries on its folios'. And again, 'one of the most striking characteristics of Mey's Register is the large number of

[3] D. M. Smith, *Guide to bishops' registers of England and Wales* (London, 1981), p. ix.
[4] W. G. H. Quigley and E. F. D. Roberts, eds., *Registrum Iohannis Mey. The Register of John Mey Archbishop of Armagh, 1443–1456* (Belfast, 1972), pp. ix–xlii

cancellations, alterations and marginal or interlinear additions which the documents exhibit.'[5] *Mutatis mutandis*, the same features characterise the other collections which make up the registers. In all of them, there is displaced material: documents of one archbishop have been bound in a volume attributed to another. All in all, material that can be at best frustratingly incomplete and at worst, infuriatingly haphazard.

Nevertheless, if the registers as they have come to us with all their deficiencies and enigmas fail to provide any systematic record of diocesan and metropolitan administration, they are none the less a source *sans pareil* in Irish medieval ecclesiastical history; there is nothing remotely comparable from the other three ecclesiastical provinces of Ireland. As G. O. Sayles has rightly said, the registers, 'if we can continue to use a misleading descriptive term, constitute the largest single source of information for the history of the church in Ireland and should be subjected to an intensive examination'.[6]

Indeed they should. For despite their limitations (which we must understand in order the better to exploit them), they allow the reconstruction of the pattern of episcopal government, the framework within which the pastoral charge was exercised that would be impossible otherwise for any part of the late medieval Irish church. In particular, they have much to tell us, and certainly more than any other source, of how the church (in both its senses, as community of the faithful and as the clerical body), tried to come to terms with the ethnic and cultural division which so frequently saw Ireland divided by endemic hatred between the Irish and English nations. The registers (the title is too well-established to try to change it, even if there were an obvious, ready-made substitute) are uniquely informative on how the relationship between the *ecclesia inter Hibernicos* and the *ecclesia inter Anglicos* was, and was not, bridged.

It is through the registers that the usage of these formulae is known. They would appear to be already established technical terms by the time of the first register, that of Archbishop Milo

---

[5] The three quotations are, respectively, *Mey reg.*, pp. xlii, xxvi, xxxiii. 'Indigesta moles' (cf. Ovid, *Metamorphoses* 1.7) was first used of an episcopal register by A. H. Thompson, 'The registers of the archbishops of York', *Yorkshire Archaeological Journal* 22 (1936), 256.

[6] 'Ecclesiastical process and the parsonage of Stabannon in 1351' in *Scripta Diversa* (1982), p. 100.

Sweetman (1361–80).[7] The distinction between the two *ecclesiae* was the fundamental institutional reality whose existence conditioned every aspect of Armagh diocesan life, not least that of the chapter. It corresponded exactly to an administrative, judicial, political and physical division of the diocese along ethnic and cultural lines. The Irish part was composed of three deaneries. Two of them corresponded to an Irish political unit: Tullaghoge, the age-old inauguration site of the O'Neills in what is now County Tyrone and Orior (Erthir), O'Hanlon territory in modern County Armagh. The third was the city of Armagh itself, *civitas nostra* to the archbishops – but that did not make it anything but an Irish town. The portion *inter Anglicos* also comprised three deaneries, each centred on a colonial town: Drogheda, Ardee and Dundalk all in Louth, which was a medieval county. Also in this area lay the archbishops' manors of Dromiskin and Termonfeckin, the *temporalia* of the diocese. Termonfeckin was the archbishops' main residence, with St Peter's, in nearby Drogheda, often functioning as what a later age would call a pro-cathedral. The *ecclesia inter Anglicos* was expected to conform to the rules of English practice governing the relations of the clergy with the royal authority and the operation of the ecclesiastical courts. Its clergy sent proctors to the colonial parliament and paid the taxes it demanded. The *ecclesia inter Hibernicos*, outside the common law area, operated within its own framework of Irish law and custom. Clergy of English nationality did not hold benefices *inter Hibernicos*. In theory at least, Irish clergy ministering *inter Anglicos* were subject to screening which if successfully passed conceded by charter that the individual cleric, 'liberi sit status et anglice condicionis et ab omni servitute hibernicali liber et quietus'.[8]

The 'great church' of Armagh lay unambiguously *inter Hibernicos*. No document made the implications of that more strikingly than the archbishops' standard response to the colonial administration's writs that they instruct the dean and chapter of

[7] Trinity College, Dublin (hereafter TCD) MS 577/1 (transcript of the original); H. J. Lawlor, ed., *Calendar of the Register of Archbishop Sweteman. Proceedings of the Royal Irish Academy,* 39, Sect. C, no. 8, (1910–11), 213–310.

[8] The full text of one such charter, from which this quotation is taken, has been printed from the register of Archbishop Swayne (1418–39) in my '*Ecclesia inter Anglicos et inter Hibernicos*: Confrontation and coexistence in the medieval diocese and province of Armagh' in J. F. Lydon, ed., *The English in Ireland* (Dublin, 1984), pp. 48–9.

Armagh to send proctors to meetings of parliaments and great councils. These writs, routinely despatched year after year, received a routine reply: 'delivery of this writ to the dean and chapter of Armagh cannot be properly executed, just as similar writs in the past were not executed because the dean and chapter are pure Irish living *inter Hibernicos* to whom the king's council is not accustomed to reveal the confidential business of the council nor ought it to do so'.[9]

In the light of this evidence of distrust and suspicion of the Irish clergy, it is not surprising that it has often been assumed that the enmity between Irish and English clergy was such as to make an unbridgeable gulf between them. In which case, it would follow that the Anglo-Irish archbishops of Armagh restricted their presence, diocesan administration and pastoral charge to the *ecclesia inter Anglicos*, leaving the *ecclesia inter Hibernicos* virtually to its own devices. And since the cathedral and chapter of Armagh lay decisively *inter Hibernicos*, the conclusion seemed to be inescapable that 'the Primate himself probably knew little of what was being done by the dean and chapter in Armagh; and the dean and chapter very probably knew less and cared less as to what was being done by the Primate, his archdeacon and official and the rest of the English clergy within the English Pale'.[10]

The evidence of the earliest register, however, suggests that the reality of the relationship between Archbishop Sweetman and his chapter was somewhat more complex. There are entries showing plainly the archbishop officiating in his cathedral at Armagh making different sorts of decision in consultation with the chapter. The terminology used is especially revealing: dues are paid to him as he sits *in ecclesia sua cathedrali Ardmachana loco suo capitulari sedens pro tribunali*, with the relevant documentation witnessed by the dean *et ceteris residentibus de capitulo Ardmachano*;[11] Odo Mcdinim, a senior member of the chapter, whom Sweetman had appointed his proctor at the papal curia had his expenses allocated *de unanimi consensu et voluntate decani et capituli*;[12] the archbishop, *habito tractatione sufficienti capitulari*, grants an indulgence to those

---

[9] '...decanus et capitulum sunt meri Hibernici et inter Hibernicos conversantes quibus consilium regium nec consuevit nec decuit secreta consilia relevare', TCD MS 557/2, p. 359.
[10] A. Gwynn, *The medieval province of Armagh* (Dundalk, 1946), p. 83.
[11] TCD MS 557/1, p. 25; *Cal. Sweteman reg.*, no. 11.   [12] TCD MS 557/1, p. 174.

who contribute to the repair of Armagh cathedral, with the instrument authenticated by the seals of both archbishop and chapter;[13] Sweetman makes a rectory without cure of souls into a prebend *inter Hibernicos* in a document dated at Armagh *in loco capitulari*.[14]

These examples of the archbishop at work with his chapter encourage closer examination of the Sweetman register. Given the fragmentary nature of that document, it is to be expected that the information it yields will be of a spasmodic nature. There can be no possibility of any systematic analysis of the history of the chapter in Sweetman's time as archbishop because of the uneven coverage of that period in his register. Of the *c.* 250 entries it contains, over half are limited to the years 1365–7 only. For the years 1368 to the end of the pontificate there are only forty-three documents. Nevertheless, material concerning the chapter is sufficiently abundant, relatively speaking, to make it profitable to gather the scattered evidence together.

The evidence already cited showed the archbishop and chapter in harmony. It was not always so. In 1370, Sweetman threatened four canons with excommunication and deprivation of benefices for non-payment of dues.[15] In 1375, four others were summoned to appear before him in Armagh cathedral to answer charges of persistent non-residence.[16]

The register does not record either success or failure with these disciplinary measures. However, while it is clear that some canons defied their archbishop (the non-residents had been admonished frequently, without effect), there were others in the chapter who enjoyed his trust whom he employed regularly in the legal and administrative work of the diocese and province and whose placing in key positions he was in a position to assist.

One such was Odo Mcdinim.[17] He had already made his mark in Sweetman's service before his nomination as the archbishop's proctor to the papal court at Avignon. Sweetman took seriously his duty as metropolitan to conduct visitations of the suffragan sees of his province. Much of this work he delegated to commissaries – he told Urban V in 1367, when petitioning that he

[13] TCD MS 557/1, pp. 197–8.   [14] TCD MS 557/1, p. 198; *Cal. Sweteman reg.*, no. 150.
[15] *Cal. Sweteman reg.*, n. 109.   [16] TCD MS 557/1, p. 181; *Cal. Sweteman reg.*, no. 139.
[17] J. H. McGuckin, 'Aodh Mac Doimhin: clerical advancement in fourteenth-century Armagh', *Seanchas Ardmhacha* 11 (1983–4), 32–47.

should be allowed procurations as if he had conducted the visitation in person, that persistent plague and war had prevented him from fulfilling all his responsibilities in person.[18] In any case, the province was a large one (ten suffragan sees) and the cultural and political divide, if never an insuperable obstacle, was always a complication. Mcdinim had been chosen, along with his dean, to undertake on the archbishop's behalf visitation of the diocese of Derry in August 1365, and then to go on to repeat the operation in the neighbouring diocese of Raphoe.[19] His mission to Avignon in 1367 was to represent Sweetman in an important dispute concerning the Down diocese. The monastic chapter of Down and other Down clergy were contesting the archbishop's right as metropolitan to custody of the spiritualities of the see during vacancy.[20] Since the prior and Benedictine community of Downpatrick were considered of the *ecclesia inter Anglicos*, the choice of Mcdinim was all the more significant of the archbishop's confidence in him.

Later in the same year Mcdinim became chancellor of the Armagh chapter with considerable assistance from Sweetman. Asserting, as the law allowed, that the appointment of a new chancellor had devolved to him *per lapsum temporis*, Sweetman empowered the chapter to exercise this devolved authority and then confirmed their choice. This was Odo Mcdinim who was still at Avignon. The chapter petitioned the archbishop on his behalf. The chancellorship carried no revenue in spirituals and only a very small piece of land. On appointment as chancellor, Mcdinim would be required by canon law to give up the rectory he currently held. This made it doubtful whether he would accept the post. The chapter asked the archbishop to annex the rectory to the office of chancellor for the period of Mcdinim's life-time. This Sweetman did. When the chancellor-elect had inspected the relevant documents as authenticated jointly by archbishop and chapter, he accepted the promotion.[21]

---

[18] '...tota prouincia Ardmachana pro maiori parte tam in clero quam in populo destructa est precipue istis duobus annis iam proximis'. The document is dated 12 November 1367. TCD MS 557/1, p. 180; *Cal. Sweteman reg.*, no. 138.

[19] TCD MS 557/1, pp. 192–3; *Cal. Sweteman reg.*, no. 147.

[20] TCD MS 557/1, p. 124; *Cal. Sweteman reg.*, no. 93.

[21] TCD MS 557/1, pp. 229–32; *Cal. Sweteman reg.*, no. 179. The relevant canon law was *Decretales* 3.8.2: 'Cum uero prebendas ecclesie seu quilibet officia in aliqua ecclesia vacare contigerit, non diu maneant in suspenso, sed intra sex menses personis que digne administrare valeat,

In 1372 Mcdinim became dean. The later years of Sweetman's episcopate are but sparsely documented in the register. But Mcdinim appears just often enough to suggest that he had retained the archbishop's confidence as one of his leading advisers. In July 1373 he was assisting Sweetman in the negotiation of a treaty of peace between the Justiciar, Robert de Assheton, the head of the English colonial administration, with the gentry of Counties Louth and Meath on the one side and the local Gaelic leaders, McGuiness, McMahon and McDonald (*capitaneus Scottorum in Ultonia commorantium*) on the other.[22] And in 1379, at Mansfieldstown, *inter Anglicos* in co. Louth, he joined with Sweetman in decreeing canonical penalties for those who violated a royal *constitutio* ordering that a *grossa* of Scottish coinage should be valued at three English pence.[23]

Mcdinim was not the only senior member of the chapter on whose services Sweetman was able to rely. The name Peter Okerballan (Ua Cearbhalláin; O'Carolan), *magister* and chancellor, occurs in the register for the first time in February 1365.[24] Some three years later, with substantial support from his archbishop, he became dean of the chapter of Derry diocese. It was whilst serving in that capacity that Sweetman had an opportunity to give personal testimony of O'Carolan's value. In a letter to the bishop of Derry, he marvelled that the bishop ignored the advice of his dean, for 'if we could have him with us we would not want to do anything without his advice, just as we did not when he was in our service'.[25]

The register gives some details of some of the issues Sweetman had in mind. They were among the most taxing of Sweetman's episcopate – the disciplining of two scandalously immoral bishops.

conferantur. Si autem episcopus ubi ad eum spectat conferre distulerit, per capitulum ordinetur. Quod si ad capitulum pertinuerit, et infra prescriptum terminum hoc non fecerit, episcopus secundum Deum hoc cum religiosorum virorum consilio exequatur.'
[22] TCD MS 557/1, pp. 22–4; *Cal. Sweteman reg.*, no. 10.
[23] TCD MS 557/1, p. 332; *Cal. Sweteman reg.*, no. 254.
[24] *Cal. Sweteman reg.*, no. 173 (23 Feb. 1365).
[25] 'Mirari etiam non sufficimus quod non sequimini consilium dicti vestri decani in vestre ecclesie et vestris agendis pro bono vestro sine cuius consilio si eius presentians (*sic*) habere possemus nullum arduum facere vellemus sicut nec fecimus huiusque ipso penes nos existente et si premissa feceritis facilius de nobis imposterum gratiam habere poteritis.' TCD MS 557/1, p. 303.

One of these was Richard O'Reilly, bishop of Kilmore. His first mention in the register, from June 1366, is a citation for him to appear before his metropolitan for having ignored sentence of excommunication pronounced on him for incest and adultery. O'Reilly was cohabiting with his cousin, a married woman. The O'Reillys were the ruling family of Bréifne, a territory broadly coterminous with the diocese of Kilmore. Sweetman was trying to enlist the cooperation of Philip O'Reilly, king of Bréifne and the bishop's brother, Cathal, to deliver the citation and to nominate and support local clergy in the sequestration of the revenues of the diocese. O'Carolan was the foster-brother of Cathal O'Reilly's wife – this was a society where fosterage was the norm among the ruling classes. Sweetman might hope then that the personal connection between his chancellor and the O'Reillys might ease O'Carolan's official duties in Kilmore.

The first of these was laid on him in August 1366: he was to conduct, in the archbishop's name, a visitation of Kilmore, denounce its bishop throughout the diocese and oversee the sequestration process. The visitation was impeded by Bishop O'Reilly. With O'Carolan apparently reduced to ineffectiveness, Sweetman came to the diocese in person. O'Reilly submitted to him in November 1366 and begged for absolution. O'Carolan's name heads the list of witnesses to the lifting of the excommunication and suspension of the bishop and the definition of penalties to be imposed in case of relapse. He was then authorised, by now with the approval of the Kilmore clergy, to complete the interrupted visitation. O'Reilly did relapse and was again condemned. There were threats from Sweetman of delating him to the papal curia, with a view to his deposition. But O'Reilly was still bishop at the time of his death in 1369.[26] O'Carolan, by that time dean of Derry, does not appear to have been involved in these later stages of the case.

O'Carolan stood in for the archbishop on other visitations: for the ordinary visitation of Armagh *inter Hibernicos* in June 1367; for the metropolitical visitation of Down in October 1367, followed by that of Raphoe. The Down commission was likely to

[26] The texts need to be rearranged into their proper chronological sequence. Most are from the period 12 June 1366–21 Nov. 1366. *Cal. Sweteman reg.*, nos. 70, 71, 56, 57, 72–4, 120, 75, 69, 76–8, 121; no. 99 (1367?); no. 68 (15 Jan. 1368); no. 61 (28 Aug. 1369).

be delicate: the see was vacant and the archbishop's jurisdiction *sede vacante* was currently under challenge at Avignon, where Mcdinim was representing Sweetman and the rights of the church of Armagh. On another occasion, O'Carolan accompanied Sweetman when he conducted a visitation in person, that of the diocese of Meath (*inter Anglicos*) in January 1367.[27]

As with Mcdinim, Sweetman found it necessary to use his authority to provide O'Carolan with adequate finance, given the unresourced nature of the chancellorship and the rudimentary state of Armagh prebendal arrangements. Sweetman made Donaghhenry a prebend for O'Carolan and united it with the rectory of Derryloran, dispensing him also to hold other preferment along with them.[28] The assent of the chapter to this arrangement may be safely assumed, though no record of it happens to have survived. Its awareness of the need to finance the chancellorship is recorded when it wished to persuade Mcdinim to succeed O'Carolan. A canonry of Derry was one additional benefice which O'Carolan held. His promotion to the deanship of Derry, when disputed, received the strong backing of Sweetman.

The bishop of Derry was the other episcopal public sinner. He had been excommunicated *propter notorios concubinatus suos et adulteria*, which sentence he had long defied. The Derry chapter wished to make O'Carolan their dean, but with the bishop under excommunication, his confirmation of the election would be canonically invalid. They therefore turned to the metropolitan for confirmation and for rejection of the candidate the bishop had himself put forward. After going carefully through the appropriate procedure allowing the bishop to show cause why such confirmation should not be sanctioned, on the bishop's failure to appear, Sweetman confirmed the postulation of O'Carolan.[29]

---

[27] *Cal. Sweteman reg.*, nos. 222, 119, 241. The commissaries' instructions for the Raphoe visitation included: 'Principalitates de bonis episcopi predicti sic defuncti secundum antiquam legitime prescriptam ecclesie nostre Ardmachane et nobis debitas petendum, exigendum et recipiendum ad usum nostrum.' TCD MS 577/1, p. 154. [28] *Cal. Sweteman reg.*, no. 91.

[29] The chronology of the register documentation for this episode is confused because of the number of undated texts. I have suggested a chronological sequence in 'John Colton: Justiciar of Ireland (1382) and Archbishop of Armagh (1383–1404)' in J. Lydon, ed., *English and Ireland in the later Middle Ages* (Dublin, 1981), pp. 196–213 at 213 n. 26. The most informative single document of the series is *Cal. Sweteman reg.*, no. 185 (15 June 1367), the archbishop's finding in O'Carolan's favour, with a summary of the case. It is this document which refers to O'Carolan as 'filius naturalis et legitimus' of Donat the previous dean and to the bishop as 'notorius fornicator, concubinarius, adulterius' who had defied excommunication 'per annum et annos',

There was yet another obstacle to be surmounted for which the support of Sweetman was essential. The deceased dean was O'Carolan's father; the law prohibited such filial succession. So Sweetman granted a dispensation. On 31 July 1367 the bishop of Derry was informed that Peter O'Carolan was to be inducted as dean of Derry, his postulation thereto having been confirmed *iure deuolutionis* by the archbishop.[30] O'Carolan was able to establish himself in office. His final appearance in the register has him leading his chapter's defence of its rights against the alleged attacks of the bishop of Derry and seeking Sweetman's support therein.[31]

This concludes the search of the Sweetman register for material about the Armagh chapter. Considering the distribution in the register of entries of chapter interest, that for eight of the nineteen years there are no relevant entries and for five more only one, and that for only one year (1367) does the number of entries reach double figures, it has yielded a surprising amount of information: certainly enough to make it clear that the Irish canons of Armagh and their Anglo-Irish archbishop did not coexist in a state of mutual isolation and indifference to each other. And certainly enough to encourage further investigation into the material surviving from succeeding pontificates. Sweetman's register, the first in the Armagh series, is the obvious *terminus a quo* for such an investigation. The availability of an excellent modern edition of his register makes of Mey's period of office a very satisfactory *terminus ad quem*.

Sweetman's successor was an Englishman, John Colton, an academic (first Master of Gonville Hall, Cambridge, 1349–60); colonial administrator (treasurer in the Dublin administration, 1372–80; chancellor, 1380–3; justiciar, 1382); senior churchman in English Ireland (dean of St Patrick's cathedral, Dublin, 1374–83); archbishop of Armagh (1383–1404).[32] Unfortunately there is no register extant for his episcopate and Colton documents

---

TCD MS 557/1, pp. 333–7 at 336. The bishop was still in office in 1380 when in a letter to the dean of Armagh, Sweetman accused him of further crimes – simony, 'dilapidatio omnium bonorum sue ecclesie' and 'manifeste negligentie correctionis peccatorum', TCD MS 557/1, p. 29.

[30] *Cal. Sweteman reg.*, nos. 103, 104, (30, 31 Jan. 1367). The dispensation reads: '...dispensando cum ipso non obstante quod pater suus carnalis et legitimus immediate et ultimo extitit decanus ibidem'. TCD MS 557/1, p. 137.   [31] *Cal. Sweteman reg.*, no. 237 (14 Feb. 1368).

[32] Watt, 'John Colton'; C. N. L. Brooke, *A history of Gonville and Caius College* (Woodbridge, 1985), pp. 18–19.

in other registers are few. There is however evidence of other sorts to allow a glimpse of the cooperation between a prominent member of the Armagh chapter, one who was to become dean in the time of Colton's successor.

The canon was Thomas O'Loughran, member of a leading family of the church of Armagh *inter Hibernicos*. The detail of this family's relationship with their archbishops forms a highly instructive chapter in the realities of Armagh church life.[33] The record of Thomas's career begins in the papal registers in 1390 when Boniface IX granted him, as the son of a priest, dispensation to take holy orders. The pope noted that Thomas was 'a great combatant of schismatics in his diocese'.[34] The reference must be to opposition to the ambitions of one Thomas O'Colman, *lector sacre pagine* of the Armagh Franciscans who had persuaded Clement VII in Avignon to dispense him from illegitimacy so that 'he may freely accept the see of Armagh'.[35] There did exist at that time a little knot of episcopal supporters of the Avignon obedience in the Tuam province which presumably Clement VII was trying to build up. There is no evidence to suggest that the Clementinists developed any serious threat to the Roman line in either Gaelic or English Ireland. If O'Colman made any challenge to Colton's authority nothing is known of it. O'Loughran, like Mcdinim and O'Carolan before him, was to prove his worth as a bridge-builder across the ethnic divide of the Armagh diocese and province.

There is documentation to allow us to see something of Colton's rôle in two major public events: the first, in 1395, when Richard II in person received the fealties of the majority of the leading rulers of Gaelic Ireland; the second, in 1397, when Colton decided to make an emphatic assertion of his right, as metropolitan, to exercise *sede vacante* jurisdiction in the diocese of Derry. On each occasion, O'Loughran was one of his leading associates.

Richard II went to Ireland, the first visit by an English king since John in 1210, at least in part in response to prolonged complaints by the colonists about the decline of English authority in Ireland through the neglect of the home government. A pause

---

[33] Deserving more detailed investigation than I was able to give it in 'The papacy and Ireland in the fifteenth century' in R. B. Dobson, ed., *The church, politics and patronage in the fifteenth century*, (Gloucester, 1984), pp. 132–143 at 142–3. [34] *Cal. Papal letters*, IV, 340.
[35] *Cal. Papal letters*, IV, 206, 242.

in the Hundred Years War removed temporarily the distraction
which had done most to enfeeble royal power in Ireland and
allowed Richard to command the largest army ever to be
assembled in Ireland in the medieval period. He landed at
Waterford in October 1394 and after a brisk and successful
campaign in Leinster showed what that army was capable of.
Nevertheless, not all Gaelic Ireland was persuaded easily to
submit.[36] Such leading Irish kings as O'Connor, O'Brien and
MacCarthy, with their sub-kings wished to oppose Richard and
wanted O'Neill in Ulster to spearhead their defiance. O'Neill's
dilemma emerges clearly from the documents. With Richard had
come Roger Mortimer, earl of March and sixth earl of Ulster,
determined to restore his lost Irish lordship, lost especially to the
O'Neills. Backed by Richard's army, he might well succeed. But
O'Neill was also conscious of his leading position in Gaelic Ireland
– the English of co. Louth spoke of him as describing himself as
king of Ireland – and how he would lose face if he were to submit
tamely to the loss of lordship over his own subjects in his own
territories: 'we would be held to scorn by all the Irish and Scots'.

It was John Colton who emerged as his most influential adviser.
He persuaded O'Neill to summon an assembly of all the leading
Irish of Ulster to consider Colton's own recommendation of
submission to Richard. The hawks of Munster and Connacht
were listened to. But Colton's view prevailed: 'we prefer your
advice far above that of others', wrote O'Neill.[37]

Colton was with O'Neill senior (Niall Mór) as witness when he
swore liege homage to Richard on 19 January 1395 in the
Dominican house at Drogheda and swore a *concordia* with
Mortimer. He was likewise present with O'Neill's son (Niall
Óg), the *de facto* ruler, his father being aged, when he too swore
to be the faithful liege man of Richard and his heirs and
successors.[38]

Present too was Thomas O'Loughran. Canon of Armagh, he

---

[36] There is an excellent summary of 'Richard II and Ireland' in A. J. Otway-Ruthven, *A history of medieval Ireland* (1968), chapter 10. The notarial instruments recording the submissions of the Irish chiefs and letters sent to the king when in Ireland have been printed by E. Curtis, *Richard II in Ireland, 1394–5, and submissions of the Irish Chiefs* (Oxford, 1927). Some evaluation of this material so far as it touched Ulster, in my 'John Colton', pp. 202–4.

[37] Curtis, *Richard II*, Letter 21 (26 Feb. 1395).

[38] Curtis, *Richard II*, Instrument xxix (19 Jan. 1395).

had the trust of his archbishop; *clericus meus secretus* in O'Neill's own words, he had the trust of the O'Neills.[39] It was he who in Drogheda translated O'Neill's Irish into English for the benefit of Richard and the royal party, the only Gaelic Irishman to be named as interpreter in the notarial instruments which recorded the numerous submissions from all parts of Ireland.

Archbishop Colton and Thomas O'Loughran were in action together again in 1397. The see of Derry was vacant. Canonically, the metropolitan was custodian of its spiritualities and also, as the diocese lay outside the English law area, of its temporalities. Colton's *sede vacante* jurisdiction was being challenged by the dean and chapter of Derry. Colton set out to demonstrate, with all the legal force at his command, that during vacancy of the see he was its *iudex ordinarius* (in his chosen term) and to have the dean and chapter acknowledge that authority. It was not a metropolitan's visitation that he was undertaking but a vindication of another of the established rights and duties of the see of Armagh, custody of vacant suffragan sees. For this purpose he made certain that every exercise of those rights was carefully recorded in notarial instruments. Essentially he was acting as ordinary of the diocese of Derry. Richard Kenmore, the notary, produced the legal documentation testifying to Colton's use of those powers: in marriage disputes, institutions to benefices, visitation of an Augustinian abbey, reconsecration of churches and cemeteries, promulgation of canonical penalties for seizure of ecclesiastical lands. He was accompanied by clergy from both parts of his diocese: Thomas O'Loughran and Nicholas O'Loughran, abbot of the Armagh Augustinians, and Maurice O'Corry, dean of Armagh, were the clergy from Armagh *inter Hibernicos*. Unfortunately Kenmore's *publica instrumenta*, full though they are, do not record any distinctive individual contribution by these priests. We must therefore be content to acknowledge their presence with the archbishop as evidence of his trust in their support and cooperation, whatever difficulties the fact of an English archbishop and a native Irish chapter might at least in theory occasion.[40]

[39] Curtis, *Richard II, Letters* 4 (14 April 1395); 13 (undated).
[40] W. Reeves, ed., *Acts of Archbishop Colton in his metropolitan visitation of the diocese of Derry, A.D. MCCCXCVII, with a rental of the see estates at that time* (Dublin, 1850); Watt, 'John Colton', pp. 208–11.

The register of Nicholas Fleming (1404–16)[41] is of comparable length and nature to that of Sweetman: an invaluable hotch-potch of material apparently originating in different sources. It tends to be rather fuller for Armagh province than for the diocese.

Material concerning the chapter is mostly about what can be recognised as matters of routine: Thomas O'Loughran, now dean, has the *ex officio* responsibility of citing the chapter and the clergy of the other two deaneries *inter Hibernicos* to appear at Armagh cathedral for the archbishop's ordinary visitation; he, with the Anglo-Irish priest, John Dermot, is to act as the archbishop's commissary in the metropolitan visitation of Derry; he, with others, is commanded to denounce as excommunicate an O'Neill who had bound, stripped and robbed the bishop of Derry; he is the first witness to the recording in Armagh of a dispensation granted at the papal curia permitting the son of a priest to take holy orders and hold a benefice with cure of souls (he was declared *non esse paterne incontinencie imitatorem*); the dean and chapter exercise the Armagh *sede vacante* jurisdiction on Fleming's death in 1416.[42]

One important aspect of the relationship between archbishop and chapter particularly well-documented in the Fleming register is the routine granting of chapter assent to any transaction touching the lands of the see, especially those that lay *inter Hibernicos*, lands held *de herenacia*, in erenagh tenure. An erenagh (*airchinneach : herenacus*) was a tenant of church lands; an hereditary tenant, so one should think perhaps rather of erenagh lineages rather than individual landholders. Tenancy carried certain obligations: payment of customary rents and services, obedience to the church of Armagh, respect for the inalienability of the lands. It was apparently the practice for titles to erenaghies to be inspected at the archbishop's ordinary visitation. Any confirmations or changes required a charter granted by the archbishop *de unanimi assensu et voluntate* of the chapter and sealed by both prelate and chapter. The Fleming register contains a number of interesting specimens of these charters, some of which date back to the thirteenth century.[43]

---

[41] H. J. Lawlor (ed.), 'A calendar of the register of Archbishop Fleming', *Proceedings of the Royal Irish Academy* 30, Sect. C, no. 5, (1912–13), 94–190; TCD MS 557/2.
[42] *Cal. Fleming reg.*, nos. 10, 127, 58, 172, 254.
[43] *Cal. Fleming reg.*, nos. 22, 23, 29, 30, 32, 81, 179, 258.

One service expected of erenaghs was to provide for the expenses of the bishop as he travelled through his diocese. The notary Richard Kenmore provided as detailed an account of such services as could be desired when Archbishop Colton was availing himself of them on his way to Derry. The erenaghs provided all the necessaries of an over-night stay for the whole entourage and their horses and manned a security guard.[44] This type of service was the ecclesiastical equivalent of that which secular lords enjoyed from their tenants ('cuddies': *cuid oidhche*).

The church of Armagh had other sorts of hereditary tenants to which it granted charters in a joint action of archbishop and chapter. Sweetman's register recorded, *habito tractatione sufficienti capitulari*, that the archbishop granted to Cunlad Omolkall (O'Mulholland) and to all of his kin (*nacio*), exemption from any general interdict pronounced by the archbishop. This family was the hereditary tenant of the lands which went with the custody of the bell of St Patrick. It was the rôle of the tenant, custodian of the bell, to 'fast upon' or go on hunger strike against the archbishop's enemies, such as the oppressors of any of his tenants: the customary coercive fast of Gaelic society, combining commination with the ringing of the sacred bell. The exemption privilege was granted so long as the fast was practised and the authority of the bell was not exploited to give sanctuary to those under sentence of archiepiscopal excommunication.[45]

The miscellaneous nature of the contents of the Armagh registers is nowhere better illustrated than in the register of Archbishop John Swayne (1418–39). The second of its four sections is of no specifically Irish relevance; its documents relate in the main to the

[44] 'Tandem vero idem dominus Archiepiscopus cum sua comitiva ad villam de Ardstraha (Ardstraw) adveniens, vocatis vicario et herenacis ville predicte, eis mandavit ut de necessariis hominum et equorum, necnon de sufficienti vigilia pro corpore, bonis, et rebus ipsius Archiepiscopi et comitive sue, celeriter providerent. Qui, eius mandatis obedienter annuentes, panem, butyrum, lac, et carnes, focalia, stramina atque blada pro equis, umanque (Reeves suggested this was a Latin form of the Irish word for an oven) domui ubi homines et equi dicti domini Archiepiscopi inhospitati fuerunt, iuxta numerum hominum et equorum in domibus ipsis inhospitatorum, communibus sumptibus herenacorum et incolarum ipsius ville, apportari et ministrari fecerunt; et vigilias hominum per diversas partes ville predicte, et precipue circa domum ubi prefatus dominus Archiepiscopus inhospitabatur, cum magna diligentia statuerunt.' Reeves, *Acts of Archbishop Colton*, pp. 9–12.

[45] '...prout moris est jejunabit...'. The privilege is granted 'de unanimi voluntate et assensu decani et capituli nostri Ardmachani' and is to apply to Omolkall, his successors 'et omnibus de nacione sua', TCD MS 557/1, pp. 194–6; *Cal. Sweteman reg.*, no. 148.

proceedings of the council of Constance. Its fourth section is largely a collection of summonses to parliament and related civil documentation (and therefore concerning exclusively Armagh *inter Anglicos*). The third section consists apparently of the working papers of the archbishop's *officialis* and curator of wills (and therefore again, the material concerns matters *inter Anglicos*). The first section, a varied assemblage of episcopal *acta*, does contain information of chapter interest.

Some of this is of a nature by now familiar enough: charters granting land, including erenagh charters, with capitular assent, are one such feature. This assent is obtained even when land is granted *inter Anglicos*. There is a reminder, the more necessary perhaps when evidence of constructive relations between Irish and English churchmen is a primary objective, that animosity between the two nations could be a real obstacle to the fulfilment of canonical and pastoral obligations. In 1390, Archbishop Colton reported to the pope that he had been unable to make his visitation of Armagh chapter, city and diocese because of war between Irish and English.[46] In 1428, Archbishop Swayne is found taking action, at the request of the canons, against serious abuse of his office by Denis Occulean, the dean. The issue was custody and use of the common seal of the chapter. The dean had kept it in his sole custody for more than seven years and used it freely *preter et contra voluntatem capituli Admachani*. After frequent warnings, ignored by the dean, Swayne finally appointed the *officialis* of Armagh city, Eugene Olorkan, his commissary, to investigate. He found Occulean had misused the seal and that no authority was to be accorded any documents bearing this seal, a conclusion endorsed by Swayne with the result that the seal was invalidated.[47]

The most interesting chapter document in the Swayne register is that which shows the chapter engaged in one of its most important functions, that of electing an archbishop; the first register entry so to do.

What is recorded is in fact a second attempt to find a successor to Archbishop Fleming. The electors' first choice had been

[46] D. A. Chart, ed., *The Register of John Swayne Archbishop of Armagh and Primate of Ireland, 1418–1439* (Belfast, 1935), p. 16. Colton was asking for a dispensation from the visitatorial law (VI. 3.20.1) summarised in *glossa ordinaria*: 'Archiepiscopus volens prouinciam visitare, prius debet visitare ecclesiam, civitatem et diocesim propriam, clericos et laicos earundem.'
[47] *Cal. Swayne reg.*, pp. 91–3.

Richard Talbot, but he had preferred to accept Dublin which had become vacant after the death of Thomas Cranley in May 1417. With the death of Thomas O'Loughran, the deanship of Armagh being now vacant, the prior of the Culdees and the chancellor, acting in his place, summoned the electors to Armagh cathedral for 10 September 1417. All the electors are named. There are surprises in the list. The naming of the bishop of Meath and the abbot of the Cistercian monastery of Mellifont as electors is one of them. Another is the listing among the canons of the chapter of two Anglo-Irishmen from co. Lough: John Dermot, rector of St Mary's, Dublin and of St Columba's, Clonmore and John Taylor, vicar of St Nicholas's, Dundalk. This is the first time the registers have mentioned members of the chapter from the *ecclesia inter Anglicos*. Of the four Anglo-Irishmen (the bishop and the abbot being the other two), only John Dermot took a personal part in the election. The others were represented by proxies, as were two other canons.

After due observance of the canonical regulations, the eight electors present in person chose Robert Fitzhugh, the chancellor of St Patrick's Cathedral, Dublin. John Dermot and Philip MacEwen were then despatched to Dublin to obtain Fitzhugh's consent. Apparently in anticipation of it being given (it was), the result of the election was declared publicly to clergy and people. Then the Council of Constance, or the pope, should one have been elected, was asked to confirm the election.[48] In the event, Martin V preferred another John Swayne, who as a curial official had the advantage of being in the right place at the right time. Perhaps the final surprise of this documentation, depending on the preconceptions brought to the study of the Armagh situation, is the choice, twice, by a preponderantly Irish electoral body, of a churchman from 'the Englisshery'.

The editors of the register of Archbishop Mey (1443–56) have invited us to consider the possibility that it is 'a collection of miscellaneous notes and drafts by William Somerwell in his various capacities as notary and registrar preparatory to the production of instruments and their enregistration where appropriate'.[49] Somerwell, a Bristol man, practised as a notary in Drogheda and officiated as Armagh registrar in the period

[48] *Cal. Swayne reg.*, pp. 32–4. [49] *Mey reg.*, p. xli. For Somerwell's career, pp. xliii–iv.

broadly from 1429 to 58, was ordained priest in Ireland and acquired various benefices *inter Anglicos*. He was a canon of Armagh for at least sixteen years. His papers provide documentation about the chapter somewhat more plentifully than other registers. It was a succession of disputes involving Mey and the chapter which produced this spurt of notarial activity.

One of these concerned that chapter dignitary, third in rank after the dean and chancellor, whom the registers refer to variously as *prior communitatis capituli Ardmachani* or *prior Colideorum*. The *Colidei* were the later medieval successors of the Céile Dé ('servants of God': Culdees), first mentioned as existing in Armagh in the tenth century. Any uncertainty about their precise canonical status and ecclesiastical function in the fifteenth century is removed by a case extensively reported by Somerwell.

In 1430, the Culdees elected a new prior, Donald Okellachan, a canon of the chapter, and sent him as was established practice to his archbishop for confirmation. In granting this, Archbishop Swayne referred to his suitability for the office which he described as *tamquam in loco precentoris*. The prior then was precentor under another name. Swayne went on to add that *per antiqua tempora* priors had held benefices with cure of souls, so Okellachan could continue to hold with the priorate the perpetual vicariate of the parish church of Tynan.

Some twelve years later, however, Okellachan fell victim to the Rome-running, benefice-seeking which so plagued the fifteenth-century Irish church. A priest of the Clogher diocese challenged Okellachan's right to the Tynan benefice on the grounds that the priorate was a cure of souls and its possession incompatible with that of another with cure. When the case was referred to judges-delegate in Armagh, they found for the challenger. Okellachan of course appealed and eventually the case was delegated to Mey and the Augustinian abbot of SS Peter and Paul, Armagh. Adequate testimony being given that the priorate was simply *nudum officium non curatum*, and thus tenable with Tynan, the decision went to Okellachan. The case had taken about four years to reach settlement.

As well as clarifying the capitular rôle of the prior, the documentation of the case clarified the position of the Culdees themselves. They were described in a letter of Nicholas V, though doubtless his information came initially from Armagh, as a college of secular priests, known *vulgariter* as the *colidei* of the church of Armagh. There is no suggestion anywhere in the registers that these priests were members of the chapter though the association of college and chapter was close. With their prior functioning as precentor, there is little difficulty in concluding that their rôle in the cathedral church was liturgical.[50]

Another cleric to be exposed to the perils of Rome-running was the long-serving dean of the chapter, Denis Occulean. His title to his office had been challenged at the papal curia by Charles Omellan. The details of the challenge are obscure because of absence of evidence from Rome. But Omellan's case had not been upheld and Archbishop Prene had been instructed from Rome to command obedience to Occulean. Omellan, however, had considerable local support: a significant part of the chapter itself and of senior clergy *inter Hibernicos* as well as the bishops of Clogher and Kilmore. Prene, faithful to the duty laid on him by the pope, showered excommunications on those who persisted in acknowledging Omellan as lawful dean.[51] They included the bishop of Clogher, the chancellor, the prior of the Culdees, the official of Armagh city and the abbot of SS Peter and Paul, Armagh. The problem seems to have solved itself with the deaths of both Occulean and Prene in 1443. Throughout the vacancy following on Prene's death, Omellan acted as dean apparently without challenge to his right so to do and continued as dean throughout Mey's pontificate and beyond.

Nevertheless, Omellan's relationship with Mey was not a happy one. The archbishop found it necessary to reprimand him severely for serious usurpation of the jurisdiction of the Armagh *officialis*, threatening him with deprivation if he persisted. Omellan failed to pay procurations. He was unchaste. In July 1455 he was absolved from penalties incurred for *lapsus carnis*, and other offences, Omellan having promised *vite mundicia*. However, repentance did not last long. In November 1455 Omellan's name

[50] W. Reeves, *The Culdees of the British Islands as they appear in history with an appendix of evidences* (Dublin, 1864). Reeves collected all the references to the Armagh Culdees from the register originals and published them, pp. 98–104, with evaluation, pp. 11–19. The most important single source is now available in full in *Mey reg.*, n. 129, pp. 106–28.
[51] *Mey reg.*, nos. 1, 2, 20, 27.

occurred on a long list of clergy *inter Hibernicos* excommunicated for non-payment of procurations. More seriously, his non-observance of celibacy continued. Henry O'Neill was asked to take him into custody, so that what spiritual penalties failed to accomplish – Omellan had been *publice sepe ac sepius et sepissime solemniter denunciatus* – might be brought about by *corporalis...severitas discipline*.[52] There is nothing in the registers to suggest that any arrest took place. Omellan continued in office; he was a survivor.

Between the July absolution and the November reiteration of canonical penalties, Omellan had played an important rôle in resolving a major dispute in which all the church of Armagh *inter Hibernicos* was embroiled. At issue was the treatment of the archbishop, his church and his tenants by the O'Neills. In July 1449, having ignored repeated warnings that they should maintain a concord theoretically in force, Owen O'Neill, his sons and his client rulers were excommunicated and their lands interdicted. Essentially, their offences were two: violent occupation of church lands with resultant oppression of their tenants; and impeding the archbishop's access to his city and diocese for visitation and other official purposes, an insult to the cross of St Patrick, Mey asserted, unknown since the days of the saint himself. Mey gave this account to the lord-lieutenant, Richard, duke of York:

when we were redy bound to oure sayd visytassy we were lett by Oneyll ys sonnes, so that we mowe no3t frely to passe as for this tyme to oure sayd vysytassy, and so for the said letting and undewe occupying of oure chyrche londes divers iniuryes and excessiz to us and oures, we have made processe and opynly accused Oneyll his sones and his subiectys all gylty yn thes partee and included hem and all Oneyll lordshipp and peres under generall interdiccion under certaynd fourm, as yn oure processe ther uppon more pleynner apperech, of the which we opynly and with all solempnite dyd execucion yn the market of Dundalk an Moneday now last passed.[53]

By early August 1449 peace with O'Neill's sons had been achieved on their undertaking to cease the practices complained of. The absence of any record of a similar undertaking by the father is almost certainly an accident of document survival. But the peace was short-lived, if indeed it was ever implemented. By the end of 1451, Mey was repeating the same charges, complaining

[52] *Mey reg.*, nos. 132, 334, 320, 323.   [53] *Mey reg.*, n. 168. 'Oure processe' is n. 167.

bitterly of broken oaths, of O'Neill accepting an annual *stipendium* from the archbishop and then failing to honour its obligations. The usual penalties of excommunication and interdict were threatened. The register is silent as to whether on this occasion Mey did carry out his threat. But a mandate of 11 November 1454 instructed all the clergy *inter Hibernicos* to promulgate sentences of excommunication on Owen O'Neill, his wife, his eldest son Henry, four more sons, three grandsons and many other kinsmen and subjects. Their territories were interdicted. The charges were those already well-formulated from earlier years.[54]

This time, however, there were better prospects for peace since the O'Neills had need of the archbishop's services. There was to be a transfer of the Ulster kingship from father to son. There is some reason for thinking that Owen, despite his advanced years, had to be compelled to stand down. If this were the case, all the more reason why the authority of the *coarb* or successor of St Patrick should help to validate the new ruler's succession. Archbishop Mey was present at Henry O'Neill's inauguration at the traditional Tullahoge site in July 1455. Shortly thereafter, in a great assembly of clergy and laity gathered in the monastery of SS Peter and Paul in Armagh city, Mey confirmed Henry as *sue nacionis capitaneus*, the term used habitually by the colonial administration for Irish rulers. The relevant memorandum in the register has Henry O'Neill making the remarkable assertion that 'his election and institution to his temporal lordship pertained to his lord primate'.[55]

After such a conciliatory statement, owing more to expediency than established tradition, it is hardly surprising to find Henry O'Neill coming to terms with the church of Armagh. Both parties agreed to the appointment of four mediators who were to draw up the form of the agreement. They were four senior members of the chapter: Charles Omellan, the dean; David MacDewyn, the treasurer (a fourth chapter dignitary making its first appearance in the Prene and Mey registers), who had been involved in the 1449 agreement; James Leche, prominent in the judicial work of the diocese *inter Anglicos*; Art MacCathmhail, a canon for over ten years, dean of Tullahoge since 1449, a specialist

[54] *Mey reg.*, nos. 178, 222, 343.
[55] Cf. my 'Ecclesia inter Anglicos et inter Hibernicos' (n. 8 above), pp. 53–5.

in both canon and Irish law (he was *officialis* of Tullahoge and brehon of O'Neill). In substance, the agreed concord is much the same as those of 1449 and 1451.[56] But with the array of legal expertise represented by the four canon-mediators, it is not surprising to find it spelled out with a degree of detailed precision absent from the earlier documentation.

There were two general principles for O'Neill to observe, the conventional basics of ecclesiastical thinking about any lay power: respect for the liberty of the church and the affording of protection to the spiritual power. These generalities were then elaborated in the specifics of the particular situation. The lands of the archbishop, of the church of Armagh, of the canons, *Colidei*, the nuns and all their tenants were to be preserved from all disturbance and molestation. No sort of servitude must be imposed on the clergy or tenants of church lands and O'Neill was to defend them against any attackers. O'Neill must assist the archbishop's officials to collect his dues. There must be no impeding of the archbishop or any of his staff, clerical or lay, who are engaged in visitation or other ecclesiastical business; they must be facilitated in exercising their jurisdiction and collecting anything due to them. O'Neill was to swear faithful service and all goodwill (*favor*) to the archbishop and the church of Armagh and all its clergy, religious and tenantry. If he observed his oath he would be paid an annual *pencio*, revocable for non-observance of his obligations. He was allowed, at his own request, to commute this money payment into donations of quality cloth for his own dress and for that of his wife.

The treaty may or may not have been invariably respected by O'Neill. But he could never claim that the church of Armagh – archbishop and chapter – had not made clear what it expected of him.

It was the Swayne register, as has already been noticed, which made known for the first time that the chapter included Anglo-Irishmen among its members. The Mey register adds further information about this important aspect of chapter membership.

That the English-born notary William Somerwell was a canon of Armagh has already been mentioned. The negotiations leading

---

[56] Full text, with commentary, printed by K. Simms, 'The Concordat between Primate John Mey and Henry O'Neill (1455)', *Archivium Hibernicum* 34 (1976–7), 71–82.

up to the peace with O'Neill in 1455 highlighted the importance of another canon from the other side of the ethnic divide, James Leche. In addition, there is frequent reference in the Mey register to John Leche, a canon since at least 1443 who, like his brother James, functioned as *officialis* of the archbishop's court and as curator of wills *inter Anglicos*. That these three were full members of the chapter, though not resident in Armagh, seems clear from the citation to the election of a new canon and discussion of capitular business which they received from the dean and the other resident canons in May 1452 and their reply, referring to themselves as *concanonici et fratres vestri*. But there was also another sort of Anglo-Irish canon, which might well have been an innovation of Mey's, the canon *ad extra* or one who enjoyed the title canon but not full membership of the chapter with participation in its business. Mey promoted the perpetual vicar of St Peter's, Drogheda, Henry Paton, to such a titular canonry in October 1454. When, however, the following year, he ventured further and appointed William Corre, perpetual vicar of St Mary's, Ardee to a full canonry, he provoked the opposition of the chapter. They complained that Mey created canons without their consent and despite their resistance and collated to benefices touching such appointments without consulting them. The canons were also opposed to his intention to abolish certain prebends in the deanery of Tullahoge which Archbishop Swayne had created to alleviate poverty. Mey claimed that these changes had been abused. They were proposing to appeal to Rome against such prejudice to their church, themselves and their successors.[57]

The chapter did not proceed with this appeal. How the respective claims of archbishop and chapter in this dispute were reconciled can no longer be reconstructed in its entirety. But it is known that Mey made one important clarification which amounted to a concession. In November 1455, he acknowledged that election to its membership belonged by ancient, established and laudable custom to the chapter itself, that his promotions of Paton and Corre were only *ad extra*, having no validity *ad infra*, that is to say, as to the entitlement of a choir stall and place in the chapter.[58] Examination of the nationality of canons in the period covered by this essay makes it clear that there was no question of

[57] *Mey reg.*, nos. 265, 266, 358, 378, 365.   [58] *Mey reg.*, no. 348.

the existence then of that 'English half of the chapter' said to administer the diocese *inter Anglicos*.[59] The chapter remained of essentially Irish composition with the occasional addition of a small number of Anglo-Irish, some *ad infra*, some *ad extra*.

This survey, conducted through six pontificates and five registers, has covered a period of just about a century. It is time to stand back from the detail and attempt some general conclusions. These can be grouped under two headings: one, the internal history of the chapter, concerning its composition and function; the other concerned with its relationship with its archbishop – the most important of its external relationships and the aspect of chapter life for which the registers supply the most evidence.

The Armagh chapter was never a large body: twelve canons would seem to have been its optimum size. It had four dignitaries: dean, chancellor, precentor (who was also prior of the college of secular priests attached to the cathedral known commonly as Culdees) the treasurer (a late arrival, probably towards mid-fifteenth century). The archdeacon who functioned principally but not wholly exclusively *inter Anglicos* was not a member of the chapter.[60]

It was composed preponderantly of Gaelic Irishmen. It did not fall under the control of any one ecclesiastical lineage or group of lineages, always a danger given the close kinship structure of Irish society and the prevalence of clerical marriage. When all the names of canons mentioned in the registers are examined, they do show a certain recurrence of family names. But not to the extent of suggesting the chapter was any sort of closed shop. When the names of canons mentioned in the Sweetman register, at the beginning of our period, are compared with those in the Mey register, at its end, only one name (O'Loughran) is common to both lists. The chapter was not averse to allowing membership of a small number of non-resident Anglo-Irish canons. Such could help to provide necessary and useful liaisons between the two parts of the diocese, between chapter and archbishop, between the church of Armagh and the Dublin colonial administration. But

[59] A Gwynn and R. N. Hadcock, *Medieval Religious Houses Ireland* (London, 1970), p. 60.
[60] A. Lynch, 'The archdeacons of Armagh 1417–71', *Journal of the County Louth Archaeological and Historical Society* 19 (1979), 218–26.

the chapter was not prepared to allow an archbishop to override its autonomy in the creation of canons as Mey found. Titular canons, from *inter Anglicos*, seem to have been a new feature introduced by Mey.

As to the chapter's functions, the registers are at their most uninformative: with only two exceptions, nothing on electoral processes and very little on *sede vacante* jurisdiction. The term *opus Dei* does not seem to appear anywhere in the registers. There is next to nothing on upkeep of the cathedral itself.

We should not expect the relationship between the chapter and its archbishops to be altogether uncomplicated, for ease in such relationships was not always the general experience. Of fifteenth-century England, it has been said: '...above them (the chapter and its dignitaries) in a very special, delicately adjusted and frequently contested relationship which varied from cathedral to cathedral, stood the pastor of the mother church of the diocese, the bishop himself'.[61] The particular circumstances of Ulster called for especial delicacy of adjustment.

The registers show, on balance, the adjustment to be more evident than contestation. Such conflict as happened to get recorded, most importantly from the Prene and Mey period (the deanship of the wayward Charles Omellan and the chapter's threat to appeal to Rome against Mey's alleged lack of consultation in appointments), seems to have been resolved fairly quickly, without excessive acrimony or lasting damage to the mutual relationship.

The delicacy in the adjustment came from a blending of different influences: respect for the traditions, rights and dignity of St Patrick's see of Armagh, respect for the canon law of the universal Church and a realistic appreciation of the interplay of the respective interests of both chapter and archbishop.

There were certain routine procedures, it is suggested, that kept chapter and archbishop in fairly regular contact. Though the register references are occasional, it can be said with some confidence that the ordinary visitation of the diocese *inter Hibernicos*, which included visitation of the dean and chapter and of the Culdees, was never allowed to lapse into desuetude. All the prelates of this period conducted such visitations, sometimes by

[61] E. F. Jacob, *The fifteenth century 1399–1458* (Oxford, 1961), p. 290.

delegation, more often in person. Visitation might bring disciplinary actions against some canons but records of what actually happened on visitation are sparse indeed and make it impossible to assess how frequently this was required. Visitation was an occasion for the archbishop to collect procurations and tithes from the clergy of the Irish deaneries and such rights as 'the true successor of St Patrick' was entitled, like *primogenita pecudum*,[62] and rents from erenagh lands. Canons of the chapter were often his revenue agents. Titles to erenagh lands as indeed all property and financial business touching the church of Armagh were discussed *capitulariter*, with the chapter's assent a necessary part of any decision.

There pertained to the archbishop what might be called a residual power to be exercised when the ordinary procedures for one reason or another had failed: circumstances where a dispensation would resolve a difficulty, intervention to end untoward delay in filling a vacancy, abuse of office, benefice adjustments to alleviate poverty are instances which have been encountered in the registers. Sometimes it was the archbishop himself who drew on this reserve of authority; sometimes it was exercised at the request of the chapter.

All occasions of contact, routine and discretionary, added up to one thing: the chapter was the archbishops' *entrée* into the Gaelic Irish world and its *ecclesia inter Hibernicos*, the world of Culdees, erenaghs, brehons, kingship inaugurations, fosterage, the world in which the hunger-strike fortified by the toll of a sacred bell was a canonical penalty. The chapter could and did provide men to be relied upon for trustworthy assistance in that area of the pastoral charge where help was most needed by prelates of different nationality.

[62] *Mey reg.*, no. 377.

Religious cultural production

The murals in the nave of
St Albans Abbey

PAUL BINSKI

In process of time, Masses grew round the abbeys as ivy grows round a
tree, yet no man dared or even wished to lay his axe to the root
(G. G. Coulton, *Five Centuries of Religion*)

My contribution to this volume honouring Christopher Brooke
is intended to shed a little light on the history of some English
medieval wall paintings, those dating from the thirteenth and
fourteenth centuries in the nave of St Albans Abbey. The St
Albans murals illustrate several aspects of the relationship between
art, audience, religious sentiment and church design, appropriate
both to the chosen theme of this volume, and to the work of its
dedicatee.[1] The issue the St Albans paintings raises is specifically
this: what was the relationship between lay and monastic use of
abbey churches, especially with respect to the naves of Benedictine
abbeys?[2] In my opinion this question remains comparatively

I am most grateful to John Blair, Walter Cahn, Suzanne Lewis and Christopher Norton for
offering their comments on this paper, dedicated to C. N. L. B. with warmest affection and thanks.

[1] See especially C. N. L. Brooke, 'Religious sentiment and church design in the later Middle
Ages' in *Medieval church and society: collected essays* (London, 1971), pp. 162–82; R. and C.
Brooke, *Popular religion in the Middle Ages: western Europe 1000–1300* (London, 1984).

[2] The principal texts on the thirteenth-century murals at St Albans are: W. Page, 'The St Albans
school of painting, mural and miniature: part I, mural painting', *Archaeologia* 2nd ser. 8 (58)
(1902), 275–92; W. R. Lethaby, 'English primitives – I', *Burlington Magazine* 29 (1916),
189–96; E. W. Tristram, *English medieval wall painting: the thirteenth century* (Oxford, 1950), pp.
317ff., also pp. 497–501 (500 for bibliography) and pls. 161–9; E. Roberts, *A guide to the
medieval murals in St Albans Abbey* (Friends of St Albans Abbey, 1971). Supplementary
literature is given in later notes. In the following discussion I have also used the following
primary sources: (1) Matthew Paris and Thomas Walsingham, *Gesta Abbatum monasterii sancti
Albani*, ed. H. R. Luard, RS (London, 1867), (cf. W. Wats, ed., *Matthaei Paris monachi
Albanensis...viginti trium abbatum S. Albani vitae* (London, 1683); (2) J. Amundesham, *Annales
Monasterii S. Albani*, ed. H. R. Luard, RS, (London 1870), (esp. Appendix C, 'De picturis et
imaginibus (etc.)', pp. 418–30, and Appendix D, 'De altaribus (etc.)', pp. 431–50; cf. the
English translation with extensive notes by R. Lloyd, *An account of the altars, monuments, &*

neglected in art-historical and liturgical discussions and so far as St Albans is concerned the neglect is especially striking in view of the unique extent of artistic survivals there, whose existence begs exactly this question. St Albans' paintings serve also to remind us that the past can be dull and its products over-sentimentalised. It was the Victorian and Edwardian tradition, that of Page, James, Lethaby and Tristram, even Knowles, that lauded (with the same slack hyperbole as St Albans' medieval historians) its great 'school' of painters and illuminators, its most famous alumni being Walter of Colchester, *pictor et sculptor incomparabilis* and Matthew Paris, *pictor peroptimus*; a 'school' to parry those with which the newly discovered Italian 'primitive' painters had in the nineteenth century been endowed.[3]

This is not the place for polemic, however. Most authorities agree that the idea of a school of artists of high calibre at St Albans now seems increasingly improbable. It is scarcely borne out by the murals found in the nave in the nineteenth century.[4] Epithets such as 'primitive', hidebound by the standards of the classical tradition, no longer warrant serious critical response. Yet issues of quality and patronage remain central to our historical awareness: the truth about the nave paintings in one of England's grandest yet architecturally most uneven churches is that they are not schooled, but are rather haphazard and average in quality, less interesting

---

tombs, existing A.D. 1428 in Saint Alban's Abbey (St Albans, 1873); also the St Albans Book of Benefactors, BL Cotton MS Nero D. vii, printed in part in *Monasticon*, II, pp. 217ff.

[3] For the 'school' of St Albans, see Page, 'St Albans school', 278; also W. R. Lethaby, 'English primitives – v', *Burlington Magazine* 31 (1917), 45–52; M. R. James, *La Estoire de Seint Aedward le Rei* (Roxburghe Club, Oxford, 1920); 'The drawings of Matthew Paris', *Walpole Society* 14 (1925–6), 1–26; D. Knowles, *The religious orders in England*, I (Cambridge, 1948), pp. 296–7 (Walter of Colchester cited as 'the most gifted English artist and craftsman of his day'); Tristram, *English medieval wall painting*, pp. 317ff. Recent studies are more circumspect: R. Vaughan, *Matthew Paris* (Cambridge, 1958), pp. 205ff.; G. Henderson, 'Studies in English manuscript illumination', *Journal of the Warburg and Courtauld Institutes* 30 (1967), 71–137, esp. 71–85; W. Cahn, 'St Albans and the channel style in England', in *The year 1200: a symposium* (Metropolitan Museum of Art, New York, 1975), pp. 187–223; N. J. Morgan, *Early gothic manuscripts (I) 1190–1250* (A survey of manuscripts illuminated in the British Isles, IV) (Oxford, 1982), pp. 30–1; R. M. Thompson, *Manuscripts from St Albans Abbey 1066–1235* (Woodbridge, 1982); B. Golding, 'Wealth and artistic patronage at twelfth-century St Albans', in *Art and patronage in the English Romanesque*, eds. S. Macready and F. H. Thompson, Society of Antiquaries Occasional Papers, n.s., VIII (London, 1986), 107–117; S. Lewis, *The Art of Matthew Paris in the Chronica Majora* (Berkeley, 1987), pp. 418–27; P. Binski, 'Reflections on "La Estoire de Seint Aedward le Rei"', in *Journal of Medieval History* 16 (1990), 333–50. For the words of praise see the discussion of Walter of Colchester and Matthew Paris in Henderson, 'Studies', 74–5.

[4] The murals were uncovered from whitewash in 1862, Page, 'St Albans school', 282.

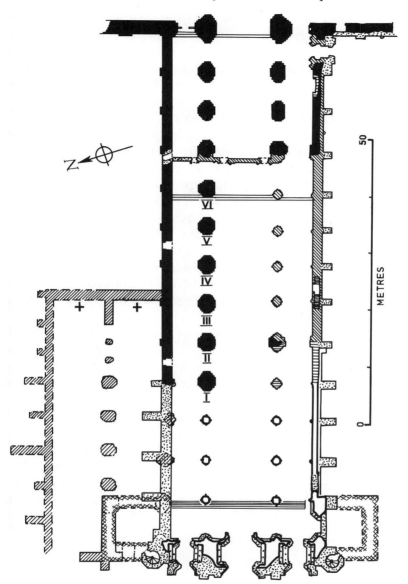

Plan of nave of St Albans Abbey (after VCH), showing locations of murals
I–VI on the north side (J. Blair)

from the point of view of conventional style than from that of function and reception. In themselves they are ordinary: but it is not wholly in themselves that they should be judged. Entering the nave of the abbey church (Plate 2 and plan), and having mounted the steps at its west end, we see to our left, along the piers of the north arcade, a set of murals done mostly in the usual Gothic secco technique, each of which depicts in two stages the Crucifixion above and a subject, usually Marian, below (plates 3, 5, 7–9). On each of the inner faces of the piers are grand but loosely executed murals of saints – Thomas of Canterbury and Christopher are immediately recognisable.[5] These crowded images are not works remotely comparable to the achievements of contemporary Benedictine art at Westminster Abbey, nor even lesser establishments like the Priory of Horsham St Faith in Norfolk: the faded, ochreous reds, blacks and whites proclaim a utilitarian art carefully eschewing the most expensive colours, an art as much of the parish church as of high Benedictine patronage.[6] And that is the issue at stake: who had them painted, and for whose attention were they executed?

Let us first consider the physical evidence. The nave murals (I will not be considering those in the transept and presbytery, and in the vicinity of the shrine)[7] adorn the blunt rectangular piers of abbot Paul of Caen's late eleventh-century church which survived the thirteenth- and fourteenth-century rebuildings of the nave which lent to it its present lopsided aspect.[8] Abbot Paul's church – the church which Matthew Paris knew – was dedicated in 1115, and comprised a long western limb of ten bays enclosing the choir, surpassing in scale the transepts and eastern limb with their seven-apsed termination.[9] Abbot de Cella (1195–1214), employ-

---

[5] Fuller descriptions may be found in Tristram, *English medieval wall painting*, pp. 497ff.; VCH, *Herts.*, II (London, 1908), 505–6; Roberts, *Medieval murals in St Albans Abbey*, passim.

[6] For Horsham St Faith, see *Age of Chivalry, Art in Plantagenet England 1200–1400*, eds. J. Alexander and P. Binski (Royal Academy, London, 1987), 313, no. 263.

[7] E. Roberts, 'The St William of York mural in St Albans Abbey and Opus Anglicanum', *Burlington Magazine* 110 (1968), 236–41; E. Roberts, *The St William of York Mural, and the altar of the relics in St Albans Abbey*, Herts. Local History Council, occasional paper no. 6, (London and Chichester, 1979).

[8] For the architectural history of the church I am indebted mostly to VCH, *Herts.* II, 483ff.; RCHM, England, *Inventory of the historical monuments in Hertfordshire* (London, 1911), 177–88; N. Pevsner and P. Metcalf, *The cathedrals of England: southern England* (Harmondsworth, 1985), pp. 245ff.

[9] Recent observations on the Romanesque church include C. N. L. Brooke, 'St Albans: the great abbey church', in *Cathedral and city, St Albans ancient and modern*, ed. R. Runcie (London,

Plate 2. St Albans Abbey, nave arcade, north side, showing (to left) junction of eleventh and thirteenth-century work

ing a legacy from his predecessor Warin, took it upon himself to demolish the west front of Paul's church and to re-erect a new one three bays further westwards, so extending the nave in the new Gothic style but leaving the choir and presbytery intact (plan).[10] This was a reversal of the more usual procedure at this date, exemplified shortly before at Canterbury Cathedral, of rebuilding the choir and presbytery of great churches before the nave. De Cella, who appears to have been most remarkable for being able to recite the entire Psalter from memory in any order, was an otherwise impractical man 'shunning the solicitude of Martha' whose scheme quickly foundered.[11] Matthew Paris in the *Gesta Abbatum* also castigates John's master mason, a man whom Matthew is unlikely to have known, for sharp practice.[12]

1977), pp. 43–70; D. Kahn, 'Recent discoveries of Romanesque sculpture at St Albans', in *Studies in medieval sculpture*, ed. F. H. Thompson, Society of Antiquaries Occasional Papers, n.s., III (London, 1983), 71–89; J. Bony, *French gothic architecture of the twelfth & thirteenth centuries* (Berkeley, 1983), p. 55.

[10] For the thirteenth- and fourteenth-century rebuildings of the west front and nave, *Gesta Abbatum*, I, 215, 218–20; II, 361–2; in addition to the VCH, and RCHM, see also L. F. Rushbrook Williams, *History of the abbey of St Alban* (London, 1917), pp. 86ff.

[11] *Gesta Abbatum*, I, 232; D. Knowles, C. N. L. Brooke, V.C.M. London, *The heads of religious houses: England and Wales, 940–1216* (Cambridge, 1972), p. 67.

[12] *Gesta Abbatum*, I, 218: the master, Hugh de Goldclif, was *vir quidem fallax et falsidicus, sed artifex praeelectus*. Matthew, according to Vaughan, I, was professed in 1217 and must have

The *Gesta Abbatum*, taken up with its reprimand of abbatial gullibility, is imprecise as to the exact pace of work on the west front and nave, but indicates that William de Trumpington (1214–35), evidently desirous of completing this and other domestic projects, finished the new extension around the tenth year of his abbacy (*c.* 1224).[13] There is room for debate as to who built what in the years 1195–*c.* 1224, and in what order, but the VCH proposal seems to be the one most consonant with the evidence.[14] Construction appears to have proceeded eastwards from the west facade, four Gothic bays being built on the north, five on the south. Evidence for this order may be found in changes in the design of the arcade's elevation apparent as the work progressed eastwards: the marble vault shafts and the corresponding details in the stringcourse found in the western bays were eradicated, the capitals of the piers were altered, and a new type of oculus inserted into the triforium arches. A plan to provide the nave with a sexpartite vault had thus been abandoned, placing the easternmost part of the nave extension latest in date. The plan to vault was abandoned after the setting of the north side string course, indicating that the latest work done on the nave was that in the fourth and fifth bays on the south side. When this decision was taken is unclear: possibly under de Cella, but more probably under his more worldly and businesslike successor William, and so after 1214 St Albans did not have much luck with vaults. Later in the thirteenth century, perhaps with bitter memories of the failure of the earlier more ambitious scheme, a wooden vault was erected in the presbytery when it too was eventually remodelled.[15]

been relying on a tradition about the first master mason, who evidently departed before 1200. See X. Muratova, 'Vir quidem fallax et falsidicus, sed artifex praeelectus: remarques sur l'image sociale et littéraire de l'artiste au Moyen Age', in *Artistes, artisans et production artistique au moyen age*, ed. X. Barral i Altet, 1 (Paris, 1986), pp. 53–72.

[13] The span of about ten years (*circiter decem annis*) of William's abbacy is mentioned in the account of Abbot de Cella's difficulties with the west front: *Gesta Abbatum*, 1, 219 and 281 for the completion.

[14] W. Page, 'On some recent discoveries in the Abbey church of St Alban', *Archaeologia* 56 (1899), 21–6, and plan, pl. II, attributes the work at the east end of the nave to de Cella, for example; RCHM, *Herts.*, 181, attributes most of the nave arcade to de Cella; cf. VCH, *Herts.*, II, 501ff.; Pevsner and Metcalf, *Cathedrals of England*, pp. 250–1.

[15] See J. Bony, *The English decorated style: Gothic architecture transformed 1250–1350* (Oxford, 1979), pp. 22, 41, 77 n. 5: the wooden vault with attached shields dates to *c.* 1285.

Plate 3. Nave mural I under junction of eleventh- and thirteenth-century
work: Virgin and Child (below); Crucifixion (above), *c.* 1230

William decided to consolidate the decaying appearance of the remainder of the church in two ways. According to the *Gesta Abbatum* he had certain windows in the aisles and transepts redesigned, partly for the better illumination of altars: surviving examples of his work with dogtooth ornament are in the south choir ambulatory and west wall of the south transept.[16] William, according to Matthew Paris, illuminated the church, and its altars, with a beneficial new light so that it appeared to be renewed (*ita ut ecclesia, novi beneficio luminis illustrata, videretur quasi renovata*). He also had the church further brightened by having its brick and flint structure newly rendered or whitewashed.[17]

Two conclusions and one hypothesis spring from these records. The conclusions are, first, that the paintings in the nave are highly unlikely to predate the completion of building work on the nave extension; and second (and there are many pieces of corroborating evidence for this in the *Gesta Abbatum*), that it was principally under Abbot William that substantial steps were taken in this period to redecorate and re-equip the church. The hypothesis is that if the record that the church was whitewashed under Abbot William can (as I suppose) be taken to refer to its interior and not its exterior, it too would be pertinent to the decoration of the nave.

To illustrate these thoughts, we should begin with the first mural, on the fourth pier from the west end under the junction of the eleventh and thirteenth-century work (plate 3). The junction is unhappy in appearance, since it was decided to retain the masonry of the lower part of the west face of the pier and set the shafts and capitals of the new work upon it: it smacks of rushed or compromised work. Presumably this suture was in building, or at least surrounded by building work, in the period between Abbot John's accession in 1214 and his completion of the extension in *c.* 1224, since it was just at this stage that the vault was abandoned. The Crucifixion mural is directly beneath the junction in question,

[16] *Gesta Abbatum*, I, 281.
[17] Ibid., 281, 285; 287: ...*muros ecclesiae in magna parte, quos longaevus squalor pulveris deturpaverat, dealbavit (etc.)*. I am grateful to Dr Christopher Norton and Professor Peter Fergusson for discussing this reference with me. Matthew's association of illumination with renovation is conventional, see J. Gage, 'Gothic glass: two aspects of a Dionysian aesthetic', *Art History* 5, no. 1 (1982), 36–58, 39ff.

and this has prompted the idea that the mural predates the Gothic work and that the pier was reverentially cut down to receive the new work only so far as not to disturb the old painting.[18] This nonsense ignores the usual medieval practice of not showing the slightest hesitation in dispensing with old paintings. The mural in question should by almost every medieval standard post-date the completion of building work hereabouts. William probably undertook to whitewash the church only after these building operations were completed and the appearance of the remainder of the church was decided upon, tasks improbable before the last ten years of his abbacy, 1225–35.

William's whitewashing, in keeping with medieval practice, included the red and blue-grey ornamental work visible on the piers and arches in the nave (plate 2), choir and transepts.[19] A painted censing angel over the arch leading from the south transept to the presbytery aisle, also executed in this campaign, anticipates the sculpted imagery of the transept terminals at Westminster Abbey of the 1250s. An important point to note is that the first nave mural, stylistically the earliest of the set, is coeval with this decorative work.[20] Unlike it, the five other pier paintings were executed over William's masonry patterning and so are palimpsests (e.g. mural v, plate 9). The decorative work was executed on damp plaster so bonding the pigments more firmly, whereas the later superimposed paintings were done purely in secco technique. The first nave painting is thus earlier than, or more probably contemporary with, the larger decorative scheme since it has the same technique. Its contemporaneity is demonstrated by the fact that the censing angel in the south transept is obviously by the same team which did the angels censing the seated Virgin Mary in the first nave painting. This campaign, including the first nave Crucifixion and Mariola, embraced the

[18] E.g. J. C. and C. A. Buckler, *A history of the architecture of the abbey church of St Alban* (London, 1847), pp. 103–4; Pevsner and Metcalf, *Cathedrals of England*, p. 250.
[19] This decorative work is thus not Romanesque; cf. Page, 'St Albans School', 277 and pl. xvii.
[20] Here I follow W. R. Lethaby, 'English primitives – II', *Burlington Magazine* 29 (1916), 281–9, 289. His date for the mural, after *c.* 1225, is to my mind correct; that of Tristram, *English medieval wall painting*, p. 325 (*c.* 1215) is too early; also R. Lloyd, 'The wall-paintings in St Alban's Abbey', *Archaeological Journal*, 39 (1882), 164–70, at 164.

Plate 4. Virgin and Child, Glazier Psalter, London, *c.* 1220–30 (New York, Pierpont Morgan Library MS 25, fo. 2) (photo: Pierpont Morgan Library)

bulk of the church's redecoration and should have been done during William's abbacy after the completion of the Gothic extension, and I suggest that it was done about 1230.

What of the other paintings? While we cannot establish the absolute dates of the wall paintings by their style alone, their relative chronology is apparent and more important for our discussion. The remaining murals on the west faces of the piers (but not the saints which face into the nave) bear witness to the progress of run-of-the-mill English wall painting over the next seventy or so years. Far from having been done at one time, their style indicates a gradual process of accretion in a strict west-to-east order after *c.* 1230, followed in turn by the addition of the saints at some point in the first half of the fourteenth century. This observation is not new: Lethaby, with typical astuteness, made it first, and got the order of work (west–east) right.[21]

The changes in idiom are gradual but symptomatic. The first mural, *c.* 1230, with its old-fashioned four-nail crucifix and dark flesh underpainting (plate 3), represents a sub-Byzantine style common in Benedictine circles (paintings and illuminations for Winchester, Westminster and St Albans) in the period between the late twelfth century and *c.* 1230, and appears in its enthroned Virgin Mary to be related to London work of the 1220s such as the identically profiled Virgin and Child in the Glazier Psalter (New York, Pierpont Morgan Library, Glazier MS 25, fo. 2) (plate 4).[22] Murals II–VI were done over the masonry patterning coeval with mural I, and so date to after *c.* 1230. Mural II (plate 5) mostly repeats the imagery of I, but bears comparison with the idiom of line drawings from Matthew Paris's circle of the period 1240–60, notably the Virgin and Child in BL Royal MS 2. B. VI, fo. 12v, the Psalter of John of Dalling (datable after 1246) (plate 6).[23] This is the only striking analogy to be found with manuscript illumination conducted in this period at St Albans.

Murals III and IV with their flatter simpler profiles and garment

[21] Lethaby, 'English primitives – I', 190; cf. Page, 'St Albans School', 282, who proposes the reverse order.

[22] I refer especially to the thirteenth-century murals in the Holy Sepulchre Chapel at Winchester Cathedral, dated by Park *c.* 1220: D. Park, 'The wall paintings of the Holy Sepulchre Chapel', in *Medieval art and architecture at Winchester Cathedral*, British Archaeological Association Conference Transactions 6 (1983), 38–62, 47–8; also to the later Winchester Bible styles represented by the Westminster Abbey Psalter BL Royal MS 2 A. xxii and the St Albans Glossed Gospels at Trinity College, Cambridge, MS B.5.3, see Thompson, 72; Morgan, nos. 2, 3 and no. 50 for the Glazier MS.

[23] Morgan, no. 86; Lewis, *Matthew Paris*, pp. 425–6, pl. VI. The mural seems to have been retouched in the fourteenth century. W. R. Lethaby, 'English primitives – VI', *Burlington Magazine* 31 (1917), 97–8, suggests a date of *c.* 1250.

Plate 5. Nave mural II: Virgin and Child (below); Crucifixion (above),
c. 1240–60

formations correspond to developments in English painting of the
third quarter of the century (plates 7, 8). These paintings, which
replace seated Virgins with Annunciation scenes (to Mary and

(perhaps) to Zacharias respectively) are roughly contemporary with the grandiose image of Christ in Majesty holding His blood in a chalice, facing the high altar on the east face of the east crossing arch (painted over in the fifteenth century).[24] Last in date is mural v (plate 9), technically the finest of the set, which reverts to a formal presentation of the Virgin, this time crowned and sitting with Christ, with a curvaceous Crucifixion above, in an idiom inconceivable at this level of patronage before *c.* 1280–90 and doubtless dating to the turn of the century, 1290–1310.[25] A sixth mural requires comment: the faint remains on the top of the sixth painted pier of a half-length Christ Pantocrator with outstretched arms, under a trefoil arch (plate 10) with intercessory inscriptions on banderoles formerly held by two figures beneath, of indeterminate thirteenth-century date but, like murals II–V, palimpsest and so later than mural I.[26]

The paintings were thus done at roughly ten- to twenty-year intervals: *c.* 1230, *c.* 1240–60, *c.* 1250–75 and *c.* 1290–1310. They were followed, lastly, by the altogether grosser images of saints on the south faces of the piers: Christopher, Thomas of Canterbury, Citha and a pair of figures often identified as St Edward and St John, but (since the left-hand figure has neither shoes, crown nor

---

[24] I have been unable to establish from ground level whether the presbytery mural was executed before or after the insertion of the wooden vault in the 1280s: it appears that the top of the composition, and the lateral pinnacles of its side aedicules, have been cut off by the vault's wall rib and that the mural is earlier. The relationship of this mural to the remodelling of the presbytery begun in 1257 (which it may either predate or be part of) has not to my knowledge been clarified either: see Matthew Paris, *Chronica Majora*, ed. H. R. Luard, RS, v (London, 1880), 608; VCH, *Herts.*, II, 486, 497–8; Tristram, *English medieval wall painting*, 329 and pl. 167. The central image of Christ is similar to that in a St Albans manuscript datable *c.* 1247–58, BL Cotton MS Junius D. vii, fo. 60v, see James, 'Matthew Paris', 26 and pl. xxx; Morgan, no. 91 (cf. also no. 45); Lewis, *Matthew Paris*, 138, 139 fig. 76, 390, 419–20, 425. There had been a substantial Romanesque painting over the altar, *Gesta Abbatum*, I, 60.

[25] Evidence for such a date includes the elegant painted vinescroll running along the capital over the Cross, and on the flat vertical expanses to either side of the convex surface of the pier: cf. also Lethaby, 'English Primitives – I', 190; Tristram, *English medieval wall painting*, 327. The south-west angle of this pier retains the shadow of a smaller version of this same type of composition, also a palimpsest.

[26] A small reproduction of this painting in a better state of preservation may be seen oddly transposed to the westernmost pier in J. C. and C. A. Buckler, *A history of the architecture of the abbey church of St Alban* (London, 1847), pp. 103–4 and fig. Cf. C. E. Keyser, *A list of buildings in Great Britain ... having mural and other painted decorations* (London, 1883), pp. 214–7, at 214. The figures beneath evidently prayed for the community, to judge by the word *collegiu[m]* which is just legible on the pier. The composition at the top of the pier is reminiscent of the pantocrator set under a trefoil arch in the Holy Sepulchre Chapel at Winchester, *c.* 1220, Park, 'Wall paintings', pl. xvi b.

Plate 6. Virgin and Child, Psalter of John of Dalling (British Library Royal MS 2. B. VI, fo. 12v), 1246–60 (photo: British Library)

beard, common attributes of Edward) perhaps more probably Alban and Amphibalus. These paintings, datable to the 1320s or 1330s, are accompanied by traces of small supplicant figures (plate 11) and votive inscriptions which lend to them a decidedly more popular flavour.[27]

Neither Lethaby nor his disciple Tristram made anything of the chronological order they observed in the nave paintings of St Albans. I believe we can and should go a little further, since the issue of chronology is connected to that of function.

While the possibility remains that the paintings had some votive rôle, the single most plausible and widely accepted account of their function is that they were intended to accompany altars set against the nave piers.[28] Each painting, with its two-tiered structure, represents in effect a rood placed upon a beam over a statuesque Marian figure, a smaller counterpart to the grander exalted carved and painted roods by now common in the midst of Benedictine churches, and also over their high altars.[29] Contemporary examples of the coupling of the Virgin Mary's image with the Crucifixion are plentiful.[30] The two-tier format of these murals is also one with numerous counterparts in other media, as for example in the cases of the odd prefatory illumination to genesis in the contemporary Bible of William of Devon (plate 12) and a small English ivory panel at Liverpool.[31] By now St Albans

[27] Tristram, *English medieval wall painting*, p. 328, is incorrect in ascribing these works to the late thirteenth century; cf. also the large figures of saints painted high on the choir walls, also (*pace* Tristram) certainly of fourteenth-century date, ibid., p. 326, pl. 164. St Christopher is prayed to by a small coifed layman with '[...]mey richard' on his prayer scroll (ill. 10). There is a similar (female) figure on the west face of the next pier, turned towards St Christopher on the south face. Under the pair of saints (?Alban and Amphibalus) is a two-line text in fifteenth-century script: ' + P[riez] pu[r lalmes de] Willelme iadis bal... e iohanne sa femme e pur lalme Will...', for William Toode and his wife, bailiff of St Albans in the 1420s: transcription of Lloyd, *Altars, monuments & tombs*, pp. 49–50, 60–2. Such grandiose nave paintings are rare: one comparable example, of St Christopher, is at the west end of the nave at Rochester Cathedral.

[28] Buckler, *History*, p. 103; Page, 'Abbey church of St Alban', 281; VCH, *Herts.*, II, 505; Tristram, *English medieval wall painting*, p. 325; Roberts, 'St Albans Abbey', 7; Brooke, 'St Albans: the great abbey church', 56. The suggestion of Lloyd, *Altars, monuments & tombs*, p. 63, that the murals were stational is improbable in the light of their periodic execution.

[29] The literature is extensive: for England, see A. Vallance, *English church screens* (London, 1936), pp. 1–12, and *Greater English church screens* (London, 1947), pp. 1–12; also R. Haussherr, 'Triumphkreuzgruppen der Stauferzeit', in *Die Zeit der Staufer*, v, eds. R. Haussherr, C. Vaterlein (Stuttgart, 1979), 131–68 for European examples.

[30] E.g. the Hedingham obituary roll (BL Egerton MS 2849), *c.* 1226–30; Morgan, no. 56 (fig. 202); cf. Lethaby, 'English primitives – I', 190–95.

[31] For the Bible of William of Devon, BL Royal MS I. D. I, see N. J. Morgan, *Early Gothic manu-*

had at least four rood beams, and it is striking that it is principally during William's abbacy that we hear about the renewal and addition of great roods in the church as well as their association with images of the Virgin Mary, indicating a heightened awareness of the rôle of such imagery.[32]

The disposition of the paintings on the piers is curious, however, since they are comparatively high up off the ground, their lowest edge well above the reasonable level for an altar *mensa* (plate 2). Conceivably the blank spaces immediately below the lower images were occupied by another art form which the Benedictines in this period had a substantial rôle in developing: the painted wooden retable, of which some of the earliest known examples are cited under John de Cella's abbacy in the *Gesta Abbatum*.[33] In the nave, then, we have substantial evidence for the more ambitious altar-arrangements springing up in the thirteenth century as a whole, including, we may add, the structure erected around the high altar by Walter of Colchester which, from its description in the *Gesta Abbatum*, is likely to have been an embryonic reredos.[34]

Is there corroborative evidence for the location of altars at these points in the nave? Certainly little from the fabric of the church

scripts (*II*) *1250–1285* (London, 1988), no. 159; P. Brieger, *English art 1216–1307* (Oxford, 1968), p. 157; M. H. Longhurst, *English ivories* (London, 1926), p. 102, no. 54, pl. 43.

[32] William had constructed a new rood screen in the nave and moved St Amphibalus' relics beneath it; the old ('leaning') rood was moved from the nave to the north transept where it was displayed with an old statue of the Virgin Mary. Additionally the old beam over the high altar which, like those formerly at Christ Church and St Augustine's Canterbury displayed not the Cross but Christ in Majesty, was replaced and shifted to the south transept and joined by a statue of the Virgin; *Gesta Abbatum*, I, 281–2, 287; Vallance, *Greater English church screens*, pp. 89–90; W. H. St John Hope, 'English altars from illuminated manuscripts', *Alcuin Club Collections* I (1899), pl. ix. One is reminded of the multiple displays of crucifixion imagery in Franciscan churches, notably the upper church of S. Francesco at Assisi.

[33] *Gesta Abbatum*, I, 232–3: the passage appears to refer both to frontals (as on the high altar) and retable–frontal combinations. I am preparing a separate study of the early development, context and audience of such altarpieces in England.

[34] Ibid., 283: *quasdam structuras nobilissimas circa majus altare construxit, cum quadam trabe, historiam Sancti Albani repraesentate, quae totam illam artificiosam machinam supereminet.* The linking of the *artificiosa machina* to the beam implies a reredos-like arrangement. Cf. the 'apparatus' erected in the early fourteenth century around the high altar of Meaux Abbey, see D. Park, 'Cistercian wall and panel painting', in *Cistercian art and architecture in the British Isles*, eds. C. Norton and D. Park (Cambridge, 1986), pp. 181–210, 209. The early history of such reredoses is largely unwritten: cf. C. Wilson, 'The Neville screen', in *Art and architecture at Durham Cathedral*, British Archaeological Association Conference Transactions 3 (1980), 90–104, and P. Binski, 'What was the Westminster retable?', *Journal of the British Archaeological Association* 140 (1987), 152–74, 168–9.

Plate 7. Nave mural III: Annunciation to the Virgin Mary (below);
Crucifixion (above), *c.* 1250–75

itself: signs of the attachment of *mensae*, altar blocks or piscinae in this place are unforthcoming, and the plinths of the piers appear to remain undisturbed. We have nothing to compare with the solid stone altars and tiled floors in the nave of Rievaulx Abbey. But this cannot detain us, since there is documentary evidence that altars were attached to the corresponding piers at the east end of the nave on the south side: three were dedicated here during the abbacy of Michael Mentmore (1335–49) after the rebuilding of the nave arcade.[35] Of these altars there is no physical trace, although there remains, on the fifth pier from the west on the south side, a crude and faint painted image of the Virgin Mary clearly once associated with the altar known as 'St Mary at the pillar' in the fifteenth century.[36] The paintings on the opposite, north, side of the nave are grander but entirely comparable works which present every sign of having had a similar function.

The next step in the argument is to propose that, since the murals on the north side were added sequentially from west to east, their corresponding altars were also added in the same sequential manner. This is hard to demonstrate without recourse to the commonsense argument that if the decoration of the altars was a separate process from their erection and dedication (and that is inherently unlikely, since such wall paintings cannot have represented a donation of inhibiting expense), the observable orderly sequence of decoration is inexplicable. Why begin at the west and work eastwards? Such a pattern would be odd, if not absolutely impossible, if the altars were to be used by monks, since, as we shall see presently, the west end of the nave was used quite as much by layfolk.

This then brings us to the matter of the use of the proposed altars. More altars means more masses; we have here admirable relics of what Coulton somewhat unsympathetically called the

[35] The altars are described (*Gesta Abbatum*, II, 362) as being *in australi parte ecclesiae de novo aedificata*, and were dedicated to the Virgin Mary, St Thomas and SS. Oswyn, Benedict and others, with accompanying images. Amundesham specifies that these altars were later (after 1401) moved up against the rood screen, Lloyd, *Altars, monuments & tombs*, pp. 18, 59, after Amundesham, I, 448.

[36] E. W. Tristram, *English wall painting of the fourteenth century* (London, 1955), 69, 132; for the altar, see Lloyd, *Altars, monuments & tombs*, 14, 15, 17, 18, 48, following Amundesham, I, 442–3.

Plate 8. Nave mural IV: Annunciation to Zacharias? (below); Crucifixion
(above), *c.* 1250–75

medieval 'Mass machine'.[37] But were the monks performing masses in the nave? Certainly the growth of private monastic and conventual mass obligation and performance in the Middle Ages is so well documented that it could provide *prima facie* evidence that St Albans Abbey ought to have been bursting at its monastic seams with altars.[38] Yet quantifying the impact of this trend is not always easy. Since St Albans was exempt from episcopal visitation (I must admit that I have not checked the Lincoln diocesan records for ordinations at the abbey) the proportion of monastic ordinations at St Albans in the critical period is hard to estimate. The size of the community, roughly calculable, provides a guide of sorts. St Albans, like most Benedictine abbeys, saw its greatest period of expansion in the twelfth and early thirteenth centuries. In fact its population seems to have peaked relatively late, rising rapidly from about fifty in the late twelfth century to 100 (perhaps a few more) in the early thirteenth century, a rise which prompted statutory limitations on the population and the construction of new accommodation. The community had returned to something like its late twelfth-century size by 1349.[39]

Even if the proportion of priests remained stable, the doubling of the community's size is likely to have posed a practical problem for the convenient performance of daily masses by each monk-priest by the early thirteenth century. St Albans, a church wedded in design and constitutions to Lanfranc's reforms, had no crypt and functionless galleries, pressing mass-performance and the location of altars into the restricted space at the church's east end,

[37] G. G. Coulton, *Five centuries of religion*, I (repr. New York, 1979), pp. 100ff., 126.

[38] Ibid., pp. 124ff. and III, pp. 65–86, also Brooke, 'St Albans, the great Abbey church', p. 56. The literature is extensive, but see especially J. A. Jungmann, *The Mass of the Roman Rite: its origins and development*, I (repr. Westminster MD, 1986), 74–141, 212–223; O. Nussbaum, *Kloster, Priestermonch und Privatmesse*, Theophaneia, Beiträge zur Religions- und Kirchengeschichte des Altertums, 14 (Bonn, 1961), passim.

[39] D. Knowles and R. N. Hadcock, *Medieval religious houses, England and Wales* (London, 1971), pp. 74–5; J. C. Russell, 'The clerical population of medieval England', *Traditio* 11 (1944) 177–212, 185–90. In 1199–1200 John de Cella ordained that the number of monks was not to exceed 100 (excepting those of high rank); he also rebuilt the refectory and began work on a new dormitory, completed by Abbot William: *Gesta Abbatum*, I, 220, 234, 280. A continuing expansion of numbers under William is indicated by the remark, ibid., 288, that beds additional to those provided by the new dormitory had to be supplied over St Cuthbert's Chapel, dedicated by John of Ardfert before 1225. Williams, *History of the Abbey of St Alban*, pp. 165–6 notes that forty-seven out of a total of fifty-six died in the Black Death.

principally the transepts or, theoretically at least, into the nave.[40]
The demographic pressures on Paul of Caen's buildings were
compounded by ritualistic ones, since in the early thirteenth
century we also hear of an amplification of some of St Albans'
liturgies, especially of that of the Virgin Mary. Under abbots de
Cella and Trumpington there are corresponding signs of attempts
to order and rationalise services (largely in line with cuts in liturgy
made later at the General Chapters in 1249, 1277 and 1279).[41]
Despite this pruning of a fast-growing plant, the need was soon
felt entirely to remodel the east end of the church, the presbytery
being reshaped in the years after 1257 in such a way as to boost its
processional space, the Lady Mass finally housed eastwards in its
own building in the early fourteenth century.[42] The peak in
numbers in the early thirteenth century certainly seems also to
have coincided with the extension of the nave, but whether these
were causally related is obscure: commonplace ambition may
have been as much a consideration as the newer need to house
longer processions comfortably, and the inclination to lengthen
naves of this type was anyway pre-Gothic.[43]

But what we cannot be sure of is the use to which the nave was
put to supplement the monastic working space of the church. The
liturgical use of this part of the church is almost entirely
undocumented, and there is remarkably little circumstantial

---

[40] *The monastic constitutions of Lanfranc*, ed. D. Knowles (London, 1951); Brooke, 'St Albans: the
great abbey church', 46; the most recent and useful liturgical study is A. W. Klukas, '*Altaria
Superiora*: the function and significance of the tribune-chapel in Anglo-Norman Romanesque', unpublished Ph.D. diss., University of Pittsburgh, 1978, I, 290ff., II, 338ff., 429; see
also A. W. Klukas, 'The architectural implications of the *Decreta Lanfranci*', *Anglo-Norman
Studies* 6 (1984), 136–71.

[41] This took the form either of restricting the number of collects said at private and conventual
masses, *Gesta Abbatum*, I, 235, II, 101–2 (in the latter case to allay tedium – *ut sublatio taedii*), or
of planning services in such a way as to avoid either collisions or bringing the monks into the
view of women, ibid., I, 293.

[42] See above, n. 24; for the Lady Chapel, *Gesta Abbatum*, II, 114–15 (completed *c.* 1310–20); VCH,
Herts., II, 488–9. N. Coldstream, 'Cui Bono? The saint, the clergy and the new work at St
Albans', in *Medieval architecture and its intellectual context, studies in honour of Peter Kidson*, eds. E.
Fernie and P. Crossley (London, 1990), pp. 143–9, argues that this extension was related to
liturgical considerations, not the shrine, and I am inclined to agree.

[43] J. P. McAleer, 'Particularly English? Screen façades of the type of Salisbury and Wells
Cathedrals', *Journal of the British Archaeological Association* 141 (1988), 124–58, 140–2 and fig. 11
has recently commented on the vogue for constructing wider west fronts in this period; the
tendency to extend in length naves (at for example St Albans' cells of Binham and
Wymondham) was, however, older: F. H. Fairweather, 'Additions to the plans of Norman
priory churches in Norfolk', *A supplement to Blomefield's Norfolk*, ed. C. Ingleby (London,
1929), p. 337.

Plate 9. Nave mural v: Coronation of the Virgin (below); Crucifixion
(above), *c.* 1290–1310

evidence to suggest that it had important monastic uses, a more general feature of churches belonging liturgically to the so-called 'Bec-Lanfranc' group including notably Christchurch, Canterbury, Westminster, Durham and St Albans.[44] Moreover, unless the proportion of ordinations increased markedly from the 1230s on, the addition of altars to the nave seems to have coincided with a period of demographic stagnation or decline at St Albans, and not a marked increase.

It is therefore worth pondering whether the process we have observed at work in the nave was exclusively internal to the monastic house. By the thirteenth century it becomes sufficiently common for documents to record the existence of (presumably somewhat more long standing) lay rights of access and use in the naves of Benedictine and other regular churches, for us to think that the St Albans nave altars were in part, if not demonstrably wholly, for the use of secular priests. Layfolk gained ingress to three parts of the church at St Albans: the north transept, the eastern ambulatory and Lady Chapel, and the nave, its north nave and choir aisle giving the townsfolk access to the north transept, and retaining images (a Trinity painted on the west face of one of the choir piers) aimed at passing layfolk. By the late fourteenth century the nave and north transept had altars associated with lay confraternities; but even under abbot William it is recorded that the transept was used for the display of images for the 'edification and worldly consolation of lay people' (*ad laicorum et omnium illuc adventantium aedificationem et consolationem saecularium*) – specifically (and the nave murals should be recalled) the Crucifixion and Virgin Mary.[45] That exactly this type of straightforward

---

[44] Klukas, '*Altaria Superioria*', 344. The *Gesta Abbatum*, II, 128–9 notes that in 1323 a monk was celebrating at St Amphibalus's altar at the east end of the nave (itself within an iron enclosure), when the nearby south arcade collapsed.

[45] *Gesta Abbatum*, I, 287; Lloyd, *Altars, monuments & tombs*, pp. 17, 20ff. after Amundesham, I, 446 (cf. 418ff.); VCH, *Herts.* II, 500. The north transept possessed a confraternity at its altar of the Holy Trinity numbering 200 men and women, the nave a confraternity (most likely a guild) of St Alban at the altar of St Mary at the pillar. Both were short lived, ibid., 480. The history of the edifying imagery in the north transept (Lloyd, *Altars, monuments & tombs*, pp. 20–3, 66–7, after Amundesham, I, 418–21) deserves our attention for another reason. According to Amundesham the twelfth-century leaning rood in the transept near the public path (*prope viam publicam situatam*) was accompanied by a set of odd didactic images pertaining to the mystery of Christ's Passion and Resurrection. Of these only a fifteenth-century mural of Doubting Thomas (i.e. the history of the Resurrection) remains. The other items consisted of two columns with bases and capitals (or turrets), denoting love of God and love of one's neighbour,

imagery was conceived as an appropriately simple devotional stimulus for laypeople at Mass is demonstrated by an early fourteenth-century English illuminated tract on the Mass somewhat in the tradition of the Lay Folk's Mass Book, beginning 'Ceo qe vous deuez fere e penser a chascon point de la Messe' (Paris, BN MS fr. 13342) which, at the moment of the *Christe eleyson* (fo. 45v) admonishes the people to think of the humility of Christ's incarnation and birth, the gentleness of his life and death and the sweetness of his Resurrection and Ascension, in terms of an image of the seated Virgin and Child, Crucifixion and Resurrection.[46]

The murals are thus in no sense inappropriate to the religious life of laypeople. For our purposes the interesting art-historical point is how hard it is to ascertain from the iconography of such paintings alone whether their character is lay or monastic: strictly it is both, since we are now in a period when laypeople have begun more generally to appropriate to themselves types of devotion formerly of monastic origin, in which images played an important part. It is, after all, Matthew Paris who, in the *Historia Anglorum* (BL Royal MS 14. C. VII, fo. 6), depicts himself as a tonsured figure grovelling at the feet of a seated Virgin Mary in type much like those in the nave murals of his abbey. Who is to say that this is not a fully monastic picture?

What applies to the content of the murals applies also to the space they occupy, since it too demonstrates the probability that in areas of monastic churches like the nave there was a substantial overlap of lay and conventual functions which tended as the Middle Ages progressed increasingly to favour the laity. Lay use of

the columns and turrets themselves depicting the *Arma Christi* and other Passion material. The base and capital of the first column signified Humility and Charity respectively, and of the second Virtue and Honour. Amundesham, ibid., 420 observes: '*Et notandum quod ab humilitate per Columnam Amoris Dei et proximi ad Turrim Caritatis pertingitur, per virtutes etiam et rectitudinem vitae ad Turrim Honoris pervenitur ... et de honore, qui juxta Philosophum [sc. Theophrastus] praemium virtutis dinoscitur*' (my underlining). The didactic intention and architectonic presentation of this subject-matter is reminiscent of earlier mendicant schemata of the sort in the Psalter of Robert de Lisle (BL Arundel MS 83 pt II). But it reminds us far more clearly of the imagery of Dr Caius' sixteenth-century Renaissance gateways marking the passage through the college (Humility-Virtue-Honour) at Gonville and Caius College, Cambridge, which represent a more purely humanistic interpretation of such fifteenth-century monastic moralisation: C. N. L. Brooke, *A history of Gonville and Caius College* (Woodbridge, 1985), pp. 65–6.

[46] F. Wormald, 'Some pictures of the Mass in an English XIVth century manuscript', *Walpole Society* 41 (1966–8), 39–45, 41 and pl. 38.

Plate 10. Nave mural VI, detail: Christ Pantocrator, after *c.* 1230.

St Albans' nave, eastern ambulatory and Lady Chapel is demonstrated by the burial patterns that had established themselves in the church by the early fifteenth century, monastic burials being concentrated in the eastern limbs of the church and before the

273

Holy Cross altar, but with extensive lay burials in the nave proper.[47] There are also incidental and scarcely surprising references to layfolk gathering in the church, principally the nave, to hear Masses.[48] Most importantly, in the early twelfth century the decision had already been taken to build a parochial chapel, dedicated to St Andrew, on the north side of the nave's western end. This chapel was enlarged by abbots de Cella and Trumpington as part of the project to extend the monastic nave, and the chapel was again enlarged in the fifteenth century. The building abutted directly onto the north nave aisle, being joined to it for at least part of its history by an arcade as well as doors providing layfolk with physical and visual access to the western end of the nave.[49]

The provision from an early date of a parochial chapel off the nave at St Albans raises the much wider question, which cannot possibly be considered here, of the relationship of lay and monastic use of twelfth and thirteenth-century monastic churches, to earlier Anglo-Saxon minster complexes catering both for monks and layfolk.[50] So far as ascertaining the function of the nave murals is concerned, we should stress that the earliest of the murals, commissioned c. 1230 apparently as part of Abbot William's tidying-up of the building and its liturgy, fell immediately next to the junction of the parochial chapel and the north nave aisle. Is it likely that altars for private monastic masses would have been pushed so far westwards as to fall within the orbit of the parishioners? Probably not: this altar, with its mural, was located more for the parish's convenience, yet sufficiently far from the choir to isolate the conventual masses from parochial disturbance. The provision by the monastic authorities of a conveniently placed lay altar with suitably simple edifying subject-matter may be comparable to events at Dunstable Priory in the same period where, in 1219, the burgesses of the city were allowed an altar (*altare parochie*) in the north nave aisle dedicated to St John the

[47] Lloyd, *Altars, monuments & tombs*, pp. 5–9 after Amundesham, I, 431–50.
[48] *Gesta Abbatum*, II, 128: 'Nam cum orandi causa, ac Missas audiendi, in ecclesia affuiset virorum ac mulierum multitudo copiosa' (*ecclesia* in this context clearly means the nave, in keeping with older tradition, see Klukas, 'Altaria Superiora', II, 458).
[49] Page, 'Recent discoveries', 21–6; VCH, Herts., II, 487, 503, 504, 510.
[50] I have benefited from discussing this complex issue with Dr John Blair, who has important observations to make on this question in 'St Frideswide's Monastery: problems and possibilities', *Oxoniensia* 53 (1988), 225–8.

Baptist.[51] Later disputes at Dunstable inform us that the nave was so arranged as to permit access to it by secular chaplains serving the parishioners, without obstructing monastic processions in the nave. St Albans' lateral nave altars appear to represent much the same phenomenon, catering for monastic liturgy in their location between the nave piers.

We arrive then at the conclusion that the murals and altars in the nave could perfectly well have been intended for lay not monastic use. Whether such altars were associated with chantry foundations, guilds or other fraternities from the early thirteenth century, and whether they could have been used for private monastic masses too, is unknown. What is apparent is that the nave of the church was on the whole being consolidated as a non-monastic and increasingly autonomous space. By the middle of the fourteenth century it was cut off from the choir by a new screen, possessed its own rood, its own parochial altars and indeed its own shrine, that of St Amphibalus, translated before 1225 from the east end to the site of the Holy Cross altar.[52] In the first half of the fourteenth century, most likely during the 1320s and 1330s, a time of poor relations between monastery and town reflecting the growing economic aggressiveness of the borough,[53] the parish appears to have further consolidated its appropriation of the nave by painting the southern faces of the north piers with hagiographical images. These murals, purely votive in character, are precisely the type of image near which layfolk sought in their wills to be buried, images and burials located in public thoroughfares to attract prayer.[54] A late medieval pattern of close but independent coexistence of monks and townsfolk, by no means restricted to St Albans, and elsewhere not always peaceful, was established.

By about 1400 the pressures which had conditioned the decoration of the nave in the thirteenth century were clearly spent. The altars seem to have contracted in number. Some gravitated to the stone rood screen erected across the east end of

[51] *Annales prioratus de Dunstaplia*, in *Annales Monastici*, ed. H. R. Luard, RS, III (London, 1866), p. 56; VCH, *Beds.*, III, 365; Vallance, *Greater English church screens*, pp. 21–2.

[52] For the screen and translation of St Amphibalus, *Gesta Abbatum*, I, 281–2, cf. also ibid., II, 129.

[53] *Gesta Abbatum*, II, 149ff., 216ff.; VCH, *Herts.*, II, 477–80.

[54] So great a problem did lay burial become in the nave that it had to be repaved in the later fourteenth century: BL Cotton Nero MS D. vii, fo. 23; VCH, *Herts.*, II, 487.

Plate 11. Kneeling male figure with banderole, facing St Christopher, south side of fourth pier from west end of nave, north side

Plate 12. Prologue to Genesis, Bible of William of Devon (British Library
Royal MS I. D. I, fo. 4v) (photo: British Library)

the nave in the middle of the fourteenth century. Others were
replaced by sculpted saints standing on brackets, as in the case of
the earliest nave painting which had thrust through it a corbel for
the support of an image of St Richard, standing by the entrance to
St Andrew's chapel.[55] So far as we know there are no fifteenth-
century paintings in the nave. This practical ebb-and-flow is not
incompatible with the view that the nave remained as it were
urbanised, a town-hall space.[56] The great screens cutting across
the nave and behind the high altar in the presbytery, seem to have
answered, in a grand and explicit fashion, to a complex of older
practical and devotional developments which, among other
things, increasingly isolated the monks.[57] In this period too the
abbot's household retreated into a well-stocked and self-sufficient
household capable of lavish entertainment in rooms of kingly
form.[58] St Albans seems never to have suffered from the explosive
disagreements about territory between monks and laity seen later
at Rochester, or Waltham, or at its own daughter house,
Wymondham.[59] None the less the developments we have
considered anticipated and perhaps to some extent eased the
transition of this once great Benedictine abbey to a humbler rôle,
after the Dissolution: to that of a parish church.[60]

[55] For St Richard, see Lloyd, *Altars, monuments & tombs*, p. 15 after Amundesham, I, 444.
[56] Brooke, 'St Albans: the great abbey church', 53ff.
[57] Brooke, 'Religious sentiment', 179ff.; 'St Albans: the great abbey church', 54; see also
Vallance, *Greater English church screens*, pp. 21–2, 91, 94, 102, 119, 121, 129.
[58] I refer to the guest hall constructed in the mid-thirteenth century which, owing to its two-
storied design, was likened by Matthew Paris (*Gesta Abbatum*, I, 314) to a royal palace; cf. also
ibid., II, 194; *Chronica Majora*, VI, 202. The separation of abbatial and conventual revenues from
the twelfth century is discussed by Golding, 'Wealth and artistic patronage', 113–14; it was
true also of Westminster Abbey, see B. Harvey, *Westminster Abbey and its estates in the Middle
Ages* (Oxford, 1977), 85–91.
[59] For Wymondham, where a dispute erupted in the thirteenth century and continued into the
fifteenth, see F. Blomefield, *An essay towards a topographical history of the county of Norfolk*, I
(Fersfield, 1739), pp. 729–30; H. Harrod, 'Some particulars relating to the history of the abbey
church of Wymondham in Norfolk', *Archaeologia* 43 (1871), 264–72; Vallance, *Greater English
Church screens*, pp. 21, 129.
[60] The church was handed over to the mayor and burgesses in 1553, VCH, *Herts.*, II, 488.

The annals of Bermondsey, Southwark and Merton

MARTIN BRETT

When Christopher Brooke came to write his magisterial history of London, his account of the city histories for the twelfth century was necessarily brief, for there was very little to say. There seem to be no substantial narratives composed in the city or its immediate neighbourhood before the works of Ralph of Diceto, the dean of St Paul's, put together about the turn of the century. Even these are surprisingly casual in their treatment of the affairs of the city and cathedral before the author's own time.[1]

The most striking silence is that of the monks of the great royal abbey of Westminster, uniquely well-placed to know and celebrate the deeds of their royal patrons. Edward the Confessor of course kept them busy enough; they worked over his life again and again. Yet there seem to have been no chronicles for the later kings written there before the fourteenth century, for none survives, and it is unlikely that we have lost much. At any rate, Flete, their fifteenth-century historian, has no information of substance which might have come from such a source. The

I have discussed these and related problems with Christopher Brooke at intervals over many years. It would have been a much better paper had I been free to consult him. I owe a special debt of gratitude to Dr V. I. Flint of the University of Auckland, who read an earlier draft and improved it greatly; she bears no responsibility for the argument or the errors.

[1] C. N. L. Brooke, assisted by G. Keir, *London 800–1216: the shaping of a city* (London, 1975), pp. 83–5. It is remarkable that Diceto does not record the great fires of 1087 (Anglo-Saxon Chronicle s.a.), 1132/3 or 1135 (below, Appendix), particularly since those of 1087 and 1135 are said to have done very serious damage to his cathedral. Nor does he provide a complete succession to the see of London (as against Canterbury). There are no entries for the death of Bishop William and succession of Hugh in 1075, the death of Maurice in 1107, or the death of Robert de Sigillo in 1150 in the *Abbreviationes* or *Ymagines*. There is of course much of importance for the history of London in chronicles written elsewhere.

comparison with St Denis at Paris, sometimes not without force, here breaks down completely.[2]

The Augustinian house at Aldgate, founded by Queen Matilda in 1107/8, does not contribute much more. Some precious local narrative is incorporated in its cartulary, but again very little in the way of wider historical record survives until the last years of the medieval city.[3]

The only other possibly early material which remains is found in a thin scatter of short entries found in the later annals of other houses in and near London. The annals of Southwark, Bermondsey and Merton priories, all surviving in thirteenth-century manuscripts or later, certainly do have something to contribute, but they are far from easy to use, or even to understand. The purpose of this paper is to sketch the relationship between their texts, and to try to isolate their more valuable elements.

The Annals of Southwark are found in BL Cotton Faustina A viii, fos. 121–146v. They are written in one hand to 1207; from then on a series of possibly near-contemporary hands carries the narrative to 1240. A second copy in the Bodleian, written in one hand c. 1300, reflects the Faustina text faithfully to its end, but continues to 1306 from other sources. Although this is not entirely a copy of the Faustina version for the common text, both descend from a single archetype.[4]

---

[2] In general E. M. Hallam, 'Royal burial and the cult of kingship in France and England 1060–1330', *Journal of Medieval History* 8 (1982), 359–80; E. Mason, 'Westminster abbey and the monarchy', *Journal of Ecclesiastical History* 41 (1990), 199–216; Flete, *History of Westminster abbey (to 1386)* ed. J. Armitage Robinson (Cambridge, 1909); A. Gransden, *Historical writing in England c. 500 to c. 1307* (London, 1974), pp. 61–2, 420ff.; A. Gransden *Historical writing in England c. 1307 to the early sixteenth century* (London, 1982), pp. 105ff., 393ff.

[3] Brooke, *London*, p. 85, esp. n. 2; *The cartulary of Holy Trinity Aldgate*, ed. G. A. J. Hodgett (London Record Soc. VII, 1971) nos. 1–30, 1072–3, Appendix pp. 223–35. Though copied in the fifteenth century, the last text may have been composed much earlier, possibly even under Henry III.

[4] The Southwark annals are largely unprinted, except for the passages reproduced by M. Tyson in 'The annals of Southwark and Merton', *Surrey Archaeological Collections* 35 (1926), who discusses the Cotton manuscript at 25–6, and prints a number of the annals before 1207 in his discussion, as well as many more after 1207. Some further extracts are in MGH Scriptores xxvii, 430–2. Gransden, *Historical Writing c.500–c.1307*, pp. 332–3 summarises the literature on their later influence (though earlier scholars did not distinguish between Southwark and its sources). The character of the copy of the Southwark annals in Oxford, Bodl. Library MS Rawlinson B. 177 was defined by N. Denholm-Young in 'The Winchester-Hyde chronicle' (reprinted from *EHR* 49 (1934) 85–93 in his *Collected Papers* (Cardiff, 1969), pp. 236–44, esp. p. 242). Although the Rawlinson copy shares the more obvious faults of the Faustina MS and adds a few of its own, there are occasional better readings which are not necessarily mere corrections by the scribe of B. The clearest is under 1176 where Rawlinson reads 'cancellato',

It has long been known that the Annals of Southwark as far as 1208 were an important source for Liebermann's *Annales Wintonienses deperditi*, which lie behind the later annals of Winchester, Hyde and Waverley. Their earliest form is best represented by BL Cotton Vespasian E iv. This shares almost every eccentricity of the Faustina copy,[5] but there are enough small differences to show that the Vespasian annals were not taken from either of the surviving Southwark copies; another, possibly earlier, version seems to lie behind them.[6]

At first sight the character of the Faustina copy of the Southwark annals suggests that we are dealing with an original compilation, written up at short intervals. However, many years ago Tyson compared the passages from 1207–40 with those in a set of Merton annals, written in several thirteenth-century hands in Cambridge, Corpus Christi College 59, fos. 158v–180 (there is a clear change of hand in 1207 here too, though at a different point in the annal).[7] He was able to show that both derived

rightly, where Faustina and the Vespasian annals (below n. 5) have 'cancellario'. There is a curious case in the Appendix below under 1180–1, where the two copies follow different versions of an annal.

[5] The Vespasian annals in their surviving form were compiled in the later thirteenth century. From their beginning to 1202 they were almost wholly transcribed in the early fourteenth century *Annals of Worcester*, ed. by H. R. Luard in *Annales monastici* (5 vols. RS London, 1864–9), IV, pp. 355–90. He printed the Vespasian passages in small type. Liebermann set out the evidence for supposing the Vespasian annals to represent part of a lost set of annals of Winchester, and printed those entries which Luard omitted, in F. Liebermann, *Ungedruckte Anglo-Normannische Geschichtsquellen* (Strassburg, 1879) [*UANG*] pp. 173–202. Denholm-Young (above, n. 4) used Bodl. MS Bodley 91, a copy unknown to either Luard or Liebermann, to refine the argument, and to suggest that the first home of the annals was Hyde, rather than Winchester cathedral. See too Gransden, *Historical writing, c.500–c.1307*, esp. p. 333.

[6] Under 1072 (*Ann. mon.* IV, p. 372) the Vespasian annals end: 'Gelu magnum et glacies ualida a kal' Nouembris usque in medio Aprilis'. The passage does not occur in either MS of the Southwark annals, but does appear (under 1076) in both the annals of Bermondsey (in *Ann. mon.* IV p. 425) and the annals of Merton, discussed below. The account of the death of Rufus (*Ann. mon.* IV, p. 373) is much closer to Merton than Southwark. The account of the dedication of St Albans in 1116 is found as in *Ann. mon.* IV, p. 376 in *Berm.* p. 432 and Merton fo. 162ra (in both cases s.a. 1114) but not Southwark. Under 1195 (*Ann. mon.* IV, p. 388) the bishop of Bangor's name is given as Alan; again the name is not in the Southwark copies but is in Merton. In both MSS of the Southwark annals (and in Merton) the sum raised by John's tax of a thirteenth in 1207 is left blank; in Vespasian (*UANG*, p. 185) it is given as a hundred thousand marks. These trivia could be explained by subsequent annotation of Vespasian (or rather Vespasian's immediate source), but it is tempting to suppose that the original Winchester annals used a version of the Southwark annals which ended in 1208 or so, after which they do not seem to have borrowed from them again.

[7] For the manuscript see Tyson, 'The annals of Southwark and Merton', 34–6, though I place its script rather earlier than he does. M. L. Colker, 'Latin texts concerning Gilbert, founder of Merton priory', *Studia monastica* 12 (1970), 249n., 257n., 261n., 270n., notices a few entries from

independently from a common source, and a good one.[8] If so, of course, the Southwark annals as we have them cannot be original, and the palaeographical break at 1207 may not be of much significance.

A comparison of the texts of Merton and Southwark between 1066 and 1207 tends to show that Tyson's conclusion also holds good for much of the earlier material, though there are important differences between them. The most obvious is that the Merton annals begin at 1066, while those of Southwark begin with Christ's birth. The Merton annals for the period before the reign of Henry II are very much fuller, and a number of duplicate entries show clearly that they depend on more than one source. There are for instance no less than four reports of the death of Henry the young king, though this is the result of copying two reports twice.

Nevertheless the two sets are clearly closely related well before 1207. The annals for 1187 and 1196 show something of the character of the connection:

1187

Southwark fo. 135va	Merton fo. 166va
Hoc anno crux Domini capta est a paganis. Rex quoque captus est episcopus Acon et multi alii cum Templariis et Hospital[ar]ibus. Ierusalem quoque capta est. Mater ecclesia Cicestre et tota ciuitas combusta est xiii kalendas Nouembr'	Hoc anno crux Domini capta est in bello a Saracenis iii kal' Iulii et abducta. Rex quoque captus est cum multis et occisi multi cum Templariis et Hospitalariis. Ierusalem capta est ii non' Octobr' et Acchon et omnes fere munitiones terre. Mater ecclesia Cicestrie et tota ciuitas igne combusta est xiii kal' Nouembr'.

the Merton annals. The Latin text is otherwise largely unprinted except for the passages used by Tyson and Petit-Dutaillis (below n. 98). Those which deal with the internal affairs of the priory are translated in A. Heales, *The records of Merton Priory* (London, 1898).

[8] Tyson, 'The annals of Southwark and Merton', *passim*. This is a remarkable piece of work; in many respects what follows is no more than an effort to work out the implications of Tyson's suggestions in more detail.

1196

Ann. Southwark fo. 137ra

Hoc anno consecratus est
Iohannes decanus
Rotomagensis in episcopum
Wigornensem xiii
kl' Nouemb'. Eodem anno
Willelmus filius Osberti
cognomine A la barbe de
London' viii id' Aprilis
suspensus et cum eo ix ex
sociis eius. Eodem anno
factus est uentus uehemens a
mane usque ad horam
nonam iii non' Nouembr'.

Ann. Merton fo. 168rb

Hoc anno Willelmus filius
Osberti cognomento
odlalabarde London'
suspensus fuit viii id' Aprilis
et cum eo nouem ex sociis
eius. Iohannes de
Constancia decanus
Rothomagensis consecratus
est in episcopum
Wygorniensem xiii kl'
Nouembris. Ventus
uehemens factus est a mane
usque ad horam nonam.

In both cases the texts are clearly related, but each has detail omitted by the other. Such examples could be multiplied at length. The natural conclusion is that before 1207, as after it, both have a common source from which they abbreviate independently. The overlap is much less close before the reign of Henry II, but there are still some convergences. Under 1066 both sets of annals include a short verse on the appearance of Halley's comet, and the same explanation of its significance. The occasional agreement of the two texts between 1066 and 1155 is unlikely to be a matter of chance.

One striking characteristic of the Merton annals is also a source of some confusion. From 1068 until 1093 the year date is often followed by the date of Easter, as in the elaborate form of the entry for 1083:

Anno Domini MLXXXIII. A Pasch'. v id' Aprilis. Obiit Matildis regina [etc][9]

The Dominical letter only appears occasionally, but with it or without it there is obvious room for misunderstanding what is being dated. In fact there is other good evidence that Queen Matilda died in November.[10] After 1093 Merton abandons the use

---

[9] Merton fo. 159va; it recurs in *Berm.* p. 426.   [10] Anglo-Saxon Chronicle s.a. 1083.

of these Easter dates, though there are some oddities under 1163 and 1171 which might suggest that its source still had them.[11]

In the Southwark annals elaborate forms of these Easter dates first occur with some regularity from 1209 onwards, long after Merton had abandoned them,[12] but one instructive case suggests that they did stand in its source well before that. Under 1155 the only entry is:

Henricus secundus rex Anglie duxit exercitum ad Tolosam *ii id' Aprilis*

This expedition, as is well known, took place in 1159; Southwark's error must have been made easier by the absence of any entry for 1156–8. Easter fell on 12 April in 1159, but the day has no apparent significance in the conduct of the expedition. The entry is most easily explained if we suppose that Southwark took it from a set of annals similar to Merton's source. The surviving Merton annals have the same entry but under 1159, and without any reference to 12 April.[13]

It is natural to speculate on the origin of the shared source. As one would expect, both sets of annals have a number of entries on the history of their own houses, but neither shows any obvious interest in the other until 1198, when the Southwark annals record the succession at Merton, as they do again in 1218 and 1222; in 1223 the Merton annals enter the succession to Southwark, and in each case the entry is in the same form in both sets of annals.[14] The

---

[11] Under 1163 Merton fo. 164rb places the duel of Robert of Montfort and Henry of Essex at Reading on 8 April, which was Easter Day, 162 (Southwark has the same entry but without the day). P. M. Barnes, 'The Anstey case' in *A medieval miscellany for Doris Mary Stenton* (PRS NS 36 (1962) for 1960) p. 21 places the trial on 31 March, though it was clearly prolonged. It is most unlikely, however, that a judicial duel would be held on a great feast of the church. Under 1171 Merton fo. 164vb gives the day of Henry of Winchester's death as 27 March (vi kl' Aprilis). Henry died on 8/9 August (v/vi id' Augusti), according to J. Le Neve, *Fasti ecclesiae Anglicanae 1066–1300* (rev. ed. by D. E. Greenway, London 1968–91) II.85. Easter fell on 28 March (v kl' Aprilis). Merton could here depend either on a slight error from a source with an Easter date or on a more substantial muddle in the transmission.

[12] Tyson, 'The annals of Southwark and Merton', 45–6. They appear erratically after that date. For a particularly elaborate example see fo. 142vb:

  1224. Litera dominicali F, ciclo ix, anno bissextili, Dominica beate resurrectionis xviii kl' Maii, die scilicet Sanctorum Tiburcii et Val[eriani].

[13] Southwark fo. 134rb. The false date for the Toulouse expedition (without the day) reappears in the Vespasian annals (*Ann. mon.* IV, p. 380). Another possible trace of an Easter date in the earlier section of Southwark occurs under 1164 (for 1163) in the appendix below, with its note.

[14] See the appendix below s.a. 1198, 1218 and Merton fo. 174ra, Southwark fo. 142va, s.a. 1222: 'Obiit Thomas octauus prior de Merton' cui successit dominus Egidius de Burn', et in stallo positus a domino P. Winton' episcopo honorifice viii kl' Nouembris'; Merton fo. 174rb,

Merton annals have only two other references to other houses which might suggest their place of origin; one is a bare mention of the death of the abbot of Hyde under 1171,[15] the other a note of the consecration of Dunstable priory under 1214.[16]

With the Southwark annals the case is different. From the outset they have a clear secondary focus. From 910 to 1189 the annals regularly report on the affairs of Cluny and the Cluniac priory of Bermondsey. Under 910, 926, 943, 954, 964, 992 and 1048 they enter the succession to Cluny.[17] Under 1088 they record the death of Prior Geoffrey of La Charité (Bermondsey's mother house), and under 22 July 1089 the arrival of the monks at Bermondsey.[18] Under 1094 they record the death of Ailwin, Bermondsey's founder, under 1119 the day of the death of the first prior and the appointment of the next, under 1120 the rapid succession of two more, and there is a similar note under 1134. So far the annals record every known prior of Bermondsey; the more shadowy figures of the later twelfth century do not appear until 1189, where a small group of manifest interpolations includes the passage:

Eodem anno recessit Henricus prior Bermund 'et factus est abbas Glaston' ad festum S. Michaelis. Cui successit Ricardus Normannus in die S. Nicholai.[19]

Southwark fo. 142vb s.a. 1223: 'Hoc anno obiit Robertus prior ecclesie sancte Marie de Suthwerk' xiiii kl' Maii, cui successit Humfridus kl' Maii.'

[15] Merton fo. 164vb: 'Item obiit Saledus abbas de Hyda' (D. Knowles, C. N. L. Brooke and V. C. M. London, *The heads of religious houses in England and Wales 940–1216*, (Cambridge, 1972), p. 82); cf. Denholm-Young (above, n. 4), p. 238.

[16] Merton fo. 172ra (Tyson, 'The annals of Southwark and Merton', 48–9): 'Item hoc anno dedicata est ecclesia sancti Petri de Dunstaple a domino Hugone Lincolin' episcopo xv kl' Nouembris'. Compare the Dunstable annals (*Ann. mon.* III, p. 42) s.a. 1213, but in a section where the years are one out.

[17] These entries correspond largely with those of the annals of 'Fécamp' (below n. 18) but are often fuller.

[18] The entry: 'Monachi Bermund' uenerunt in Angliam' or something like it occurs in several other annals, notably the 'Annales Fiscannenses'. These all lack Bermondsey's day, which cannot plausibly be interpreted as a confusion with any date for Easter near 1089. The annals of 'Fécamp', for the complex tradition of which see L. Delisle, *Histoire litteraire de France* 32 (1898), 205–9 and P. Meyer, 'Notice sur le manuscrit Ii. 6.24 de la bibliothèque de l'Université de Cambridge' *Notices et extraits des manuscrits de la Bibliothèque Nationale* 32 (2) (1888), 37–81, contain a number of annals suggesting that they spent some time in England during the twelfth century. From 910 until at least 1185 they show some agreement with the annals of Bermondsey and Southwark, though not exclusively with either. For the text see the paper of Meyer, P. Labbe, *Novae bibliothecae manuscriptorum librorum* (Paris, 1657) I, pp. 325–8 and *Recueil des historiens de France* 12, 776–7; 18, 353–4; 23, 466–7.

[19] Southwark fo. 136ra. These passages, on the election of several bishops (which occurred on 15–16 September) and on Bermondsey, are clearly interpolated, since they divide an account of the coronation of Richard I on 3 September (found in related form in Merton fos. 166vb–167ra) from an account of the massacre of the Jews of London which followed

'Recessit' is a curious word to use outside the house involved. It is likely that the passage was drafted in Bermondsey, and that other intervening entries have been edited out by the Southwark compiler.[20]

The Bermondsey entries in the annals of Southwark also appear in the annals of Bermondsey proper. These survive only in a fifteenth-century copy, from which Luard printed them with all his customary accuracy, and they have enjoyed little esteem. Brooke describes them memorably as: 'among the most unreliable of such records; but they occasionally deviate into accuracy'.[21] Their distinctive contribution is a mass of details on the acquisition of estates by the house under dates the compiler thought appropriate. Recent scholars have rarely agreed with him, and it seems clear that he was working by the light of nature from the archives of his house long after the event, and very probably no earlier than the fifteenth century. Rose Graham, in a celebrated paper, showed that the record of the succession of the priors of Bermondsey from the thirteenth century cannot be squared with what we know from other, and earlier, sources.[22] However, the succession of priors up to 1221 presents few problems, and can often be confirmed elsewhere. There is a clear likelihood that the annalist had a better source for the earlier period than he had for the later.[23] It seems a modest speculation that the annals of Southwark also contain much of an early form of the annals of Bermondsey.[24]

The existing Bermondsey text is clearly composite. It is not difficult to peel away the notes of benefactions to the priory and some very general observations on the history of the church at large, such as one might find in any universal history between the thirteenth century and the fifteenth. What then remains is a

immediately on it. This begins 'Nocte sequenti facta est strages...'. Compare the Appendix below s.a. 1189.

[20] Compare the form which recurs regularly in the Bermondsey annals proper (discussed below) in comparable cases, e.g. s.a. 1148, 1157, 1161, in the Appendix below.

[21] Brooke, *London*, p. 110.

[22] Rose Graham, *English ecclesiastical studies* (London, 1929), pp. 91–124, esp. 93, 97–100, 121–4; Knowles, Brooke and London, *Heads*, pp. 6, 114–16.

[23] The succession only becomes wholly improbable in 1221–3 (*Berm.* p. 455), where two priors are said to have died or left their office in 1221, three in 1222, and two more in 1223. There is certainly serious confusion under 1186 (appendix below, s.a.), but this may be the product of a later addition. Compare Knowles, Brooke and London, *Heads*, pp. 115–16.

[24] As already suggested by Tyson, 'The annals of Southwark and Merton', 29–30.

substantial deposit of entries on other houses of Cluniac observance in England,[25] and a number of more general annals clearly related to those of Merton and Southwark. There are fewer of these general annals in the Bermondsey annals than in either of the other two, but the verbal connection is often very close. The annal for 1172 for instance is virtually identical in all three. Elsewhere the relationship is more complex, with Bermondsey agreeing now with one, now with the other. In the earlier sections Bermondsey is close to the Merton annals, sometimes abbreviating, sometimes providing more than Merton from the ultimate source.[26] As the Southwark annals become fuller Bermondsey shares more with them.

Again examples give the clearest idea of their interconnection. In the Bermondsey entries that follow, passages shared with Southwark are in italics, with Merton underlined:

1099. <u>Hoc anno fluctus marinus per Tamensem ascendit et uillas multas cum hominibus mersit</u>. Et hoc anno *Ierusalem capta est a* Francis. Hoc etiam anno *apud Fynchamstede in Berwykschire quoddam stagnum fluxit sanguine.*

1194. <u>*Hoc anno Ricardus rex Anglie liberatus est a potestate Henrici imperatoris Alemannie ii nonas Februarii*</u>, et <u>*iii id' Martii apud Sandwiche*</u> applicuit et <u>*feria quarto post*</u> [scilicet xvii kl' Aprilis *add.* Merton] <u>*apud Londoniam cum magno apparatu receptus est.*</u>

[*Here Merton, largely agreeing with Southwark, adds*:] Post eodem anno, scilicet xv kl' Maii coronatus est apud Winton'. Post iiii id' Maii transfretauit in Normanniam.]

Et eodem anno *ii nonas Iunii* hora uespertina <u>*subito choruscationes*</u> et <u>*tonitrua terribilia audita sunt.*</u>[27]

Relationships of this kind become more complex as the entries in Merton and Southwark become longer. They end in 1222–3.[28]

---

[25] E.g. s.a. 1094–5, 1097, 1104, 1106–7, 1114, 1148, 1154, 1164, 1179.

[26] The annal for 1070 in Bermondsey and Merton is based on something very close to *Radulfi de Diceto decani Lundeniensis opera historica*, ed. W. Stubbs (2 vols. RS, London, 1876), I, p. 201, and each includes passages from it which the other omits. Similarly the annal for 1091 in both derives ultimately from William of Malmesbury's *Gesta Regum* (ed. W. Stubbs, RS, 1887–9) II, p. 374 (para. 323), and each is sometimes nearer the source than the other. Merton and Bermondsey share a distinctive double entry for 1149 and 1151 (Appendix below), which suggests a very close relation here.

[27] Compare also the entries for 1114, 1132, 1149, 1192, 1194 in the Appendix below.

[28] The entry for 1222 in *Berm.* p. 455: '...tertio id' Martii – orbem fecit' is clearly found in Merton fo. 174ra and Southwark fo. 142va (where it is a marginal addition in a small hand). Under 1223 Bermondsey has the less distinctive 'rex Ierusalem uenit in Angliam', also in Merton and Southwark.

From then onwards the slight general history in the Bermondsey annals bears no relation to that in Merton or Southwark.

Another illustration of this family relationship can be found in the appearance of a number of unexplained day dates in the Bermondsey annals between 1067 and 1138. Again many of these are Easter dates. While those in the Merton and Southwark annals appear for the most part at the beginning of the annal, at Bermondsey they often occur in the middle of the entry, making for yet more confusion.[29] They do not coincide closely with those of the Merton annals, and do not reappear in the thirteenth century as they do at Southwark. They go some way to confirm the existence, and something more of the character, of the source common to all three.

So far I believe it can be shown that the three sets of annals share such a common source from 1066, and that they do so independently. It follows that obscurities in one form may legitimately be resolved by consulting the others, and that passages common to two of the three almost certainly stood in their source. When one assembles these agreed passages, the archetype proves a good deal more substantial than any one of the surviving copies. Each of these copies omitted a good deal, and it is quite likely that certain passages from the archetype are preserved in only one of them.

The Merton and Southwark annals show they share one source until 1240. Since the Bermondsey annals agree with them only as far as 1223, it is possible that one form of the common source did not extend much further. If this is the case, there lies beneath the confused and misleading surface of the Bermondsey text a witness of considerable importance. The inclusion of a little Southwark information in Merton, and a good deal of Bermondsey matter in Southwark, might suggest that the point of departure of the archetype was Bermondsey. Whether or not this is the case, it is still clear that all the most distinctive local information found in the archetype deals with London, and constitutes a valuable addition to our slender knowledge. The material annals are printed in an appendix below.

Luard's edition of the Bermondsey annals throws more light on

[29] E.g. s.a. 1067, 1070, 1075–6, 1083, 1089, 1094, 1103, 1115, 1124, 1131, 1135, 1138.

the enquiry, for he printed a number of passages in small type to show the parallels with the so-called 'Matthew of Westminster', the *Flores Historiarum*. The earliest form of Book II, the relevant section, seems to have been compiled by Matthew Paris at St Albans in 1250–5.[30] For Luard there was nothing improbable in a fifteenth-century compiler using the *Flores*, but the evidence we have examined so far makes it most unlikely that the three sets of annals depend on them. In fact when Luard turned to editing the *Chronica Maiora* of Paris he adopted the opposite view, possibly without realising it, for he noted that Paris had enlarged his Wendover source with a number of passages from the Annals of Southwark.[31] Some of these seem to have passed from Paris into the *Flores*, but the *Flores* also include a number of passages from a similar source which were not used in Paris.[32]

There is something approaching proof that Paris was using a set of annals very like the London archetype. Under 1178 Paris has the entry: 'Nix maxima et diuturna; animalia maritima inuoluta sunt fluctibus; sol passus est eclipsim sexto id' Ianuarii.'[33] The ultimate source is represented by Diceto I 424, recording the floods on 'vi idus Ianuarii' and Diceto I 427, noting the eclipse on 'id' Septembris'. Southwark and Merton place the two passages side by side, in a form which makes the confusion of date very simple, while it is inexplicable from Diceto alone.[34]

[30] For the composition of the *Flores historiarum*, ed. H. R. Luard (3 vols. RS, 1890), see R. Vaughan, *Matthew Paris* (Cambridge, 1958) pp. 92–103; Gransden, *Historical writing*, pp. 357 n. 7, 366–7, and the literature cited there. The later continuations of the *Flores* are irrelevant for this purpose. A systematic comparison of the St Albans versions with the other sets of annals would require collation of London, BL Cotton MS Vespasian A 20, fos. 77–108, another compilation by Paris containing independent versions of much of the shared matter. See Vaughan, *Matthew Paris*, pp. 41, 103–8.

[31] *Matthaei Parisiensis monachi sancti Albani chronica maiora*, ed. H. R. Luard (7 vols. RS, London, 1872–83) II, pp. xxxvii–l. Luard occasionally cites a parallel from 'Gervase, ed. Leland', but this is a ghost text. *The historical works of Gervase of Canterbury*, ed. W. Stubbs (RS, London, 1879–80) II, pp. ix–x showed that John Leland's so-called edition of Gervase in his *Collectanea* I (1770), p. 257ff. was based on notes from Cambridge, Trinity College MS R.5.41 (James no. 729). For the period after 1066 in which the convergences occur the Trinity manuscript depends on the *Flores*, and is a derivative, not a source, for the St Albans chronicles.

[32] Those which could be identified in the annals of Southwark were printed by Luard in large type and identified in the margin. Naturally he did not identify the source of passages found in Merton or Bermondsey in the same way. Vaughan, *Matthew Paris*, pp. 103–9 discusses the problem, showing that Southwark as we have it cannot have been the source.

[33] *Chronica maiora*, II, p. 301; *Flores*, II, p. 89 is slightly fuller.

[34] Merton fo. 165vb, Southwark fo. 135rb: 'Nix maxima. In maritimis – inuoluta sunt aquilone flante vi id' Ianuarii. Sol passus est eclipsim id' Septembris.' They are both here much nearer Diceto.

Paris indeed seems to refer directly to these annals. Under 1074, he notices that while his ultimate source for the passage, the Anglo-Saxon Chronicle, says that Queen Edith died on 2 November, 'alius historiographus' gives the date of her death as 'v id. Aprilis' [9 April, which was Easter Day, 1075].[35] This seems to be a direct reference to the annal for 1075 in the annals of Merton and Bermondsey (but not Southwark), cited above. This is only one among many confusions created by the intrusion of the date of Easter into the narrative, for such misunderstood dates recur constantly in the Paris/Flores text between 1073 and 1132, more frequently even than in the annals of Bermondsey.[36]

The connection between the Chronica Maiora, the Flores and the London annals, indicated by these curious errors, is substantial, if not entirely straightforward. If the Easter dates are a mark of the common source, then St Albans preserved a good deal more of them than any of the other versions, or indeed any combination of them. Examination of the shared annals confirms this view.

On all counts it is clear that something like Southwark was an important source, as Luard had already recognised.[37] Remarkably, the entry on the fire which destroyed part of London and Southwark, including the priory church, in 1212, is rather fuller in Paris than it is in the annals of Southwark proper,[38] while the Flores include the succession of Prior Richard of Southwark under 1202, which is not in Southwark at all, though it could be inferred from it.[39]

However, the focus of the St Albans chronicles is less clear than this might suggest. Paris also includes a note of the appointment of the first prior of Merton in 1117 which is not even in the Merton annals.[40] Paris includes a further distinctive Merton entry

[35] Chronica maiora, II, p. 13n.
[36] E.g. Flores under 1071; 1073; 1075–7 (with Merton); 1083 (with Merton, cf. above n. 9); 1087 (date is for Easter 1086); 1089 (death of Lanfranc, but blundered on any view); 1094–5; 1099; 1104; 1107–11; 1113–15; 1119–21; 1123–7. The entry for 1132 is another probable case, discussed in the appendix below. Chronica maiora includes some material taken from these annals but not incorporated in the Flores. This may include (II, p. 132) another relic of an Easter date added to Torigni's account under 1106. Tinchebrai is dated 'viii kl' Maii' [24 April] but the battle was fought in September (Orderic Vitalis, The ecclesiastical history ed. M. Chibnall, Oxford Medieval Texts (Oxford, 1968–81), VI, p. 89n.; Flores, II, pp. 38–9; Merton fo. 161vb). Easter 1106 fell on 'viii kl' Aprilis' [25 March]. [37] Above n. 32.
[38] Compare Chronica maiora, II, p. 536 with the entry from Southwark in the appendix below.
[39] Flores, II, p. 126; cf. Knowles, Brooke and London, Heads, p. 184.
[40] Appendix below, s.a. 1117.

under 1125, which is also in the Merton annals (but not those of
Southwark or Bermondsey).[41] The *Flores* contribute two further
pieces of local information from the Merton annals under 1167
and 1176 which are not in Paris or the annals of Southwark.[42] The
Merton copy of the *Flores* also includes one piece of Bermondsey
information which is not in Southwark; strikingly it is not in the
surviving Bermondsey annals either.[43]

If one turns from the purely local information from Merton
and Southwark in the St Albans histories to additions dealing with
larger matters, the picture is largely the same. Though Paris has a
number of entries found in Southwark but not in Merton,[44] there
are a considerable number too which are found in Merton but not
in Southwark.[45] The same holds good for the *Flores*.[46] There are
other cases where the St Albans texts are closer to Bermondsey
than either Southwark or Merton. They have some entries
otherwise peculiar to Bermondsey.

Under 1094 Paris runs:

Id' Aprilis episcopatus de Theofordia translatus est Norewicum ab
Hereberto Losenge.

The passage, apart from the day, may derive ultimately from
William of Malmesbury, but appears almost exactly as here in

---

[41] Appendix below, s.a. 1125. [42] Appendix below, s.a. 1167, 1177.
[43] Appendix below, s.a. 1115.
[44] For example the coming of Lanzo to Lewes (1077), the foundation of Bermondsey (1089), the
death of Aldwin of Bermondsey (1094), and entries under 1099, 1104, 1106, 1117, 1120, 1121,
1131, 1140, 1176, 1179, 1198 (details of the storms). In one or two cases the substance is also in
the annals of Merton, but the form is unmistakably that of the Southwark annals. In each case
where the entry concerns Bermondsey it also occurs in Southwark.
[45] For example, under 1076 (*Chronica maiora*, II, p. 16, *Flores*, II, p. 9, in Merton and
Bermondsey), 1100 (*Chronica maiora*, II, p. 115, *Flores*, II, p. 34 independently, where the
passage on a well of blood, ultimately from Malmesbury's *Gesta Regum*, is more or less as in
Merton, while Southwark is very slight, and the mistaken note on Archbishop Thomas at
the coronation of Henry I is in Bermondsey and Merton, but is absent from Southwark),
1107 (*Chronica maiora*, II, p. 134, *Flores*, II, p. 40, foundation of Aldgate, in Merton and
Bermondsey but not Southwark), 1135 (*Chronica maiora*, II, p. 163, *Flores*, II, p. 58, burning
of St Pauls, with Merton and Bermondsey against Southwark, printed below in Appendix),
1144 (*Chronica maiora*, II, p. 177, *Flores* II, p. 65, death of Geoffrey de Mandeville with
Merton against Bermondsey and Southwark, see Appendix), 1148 (*Chronica maiora*, II, p. 183,
Floresm II, p. 67, translation of St Erkenwald, see Appendix), 1150 (*Chronica maiora*, II, p. 184)
freezing of the Thames, in Merton and Bermondsey (though under 1149) against
Southwark (see appendix), 1214 (*Chronica maiora*, II, p. 584 [largely duplicating II, p. 573
from Wendover], *Flores*, II, p. 151), death of Bishop Gilbert of Rochester, with Merton against
Bermondsey and Southwark.
[46] For example, *Flores*, II, p. 11 (death of Queen Matilda, s.a. 1083, where Paris is distinct); II,
pp. 16–17 (death of the Conqueror); below Appendix s.a. 1132, 1141.

Bermondsey.[47] The one difference is that Bermondsey gives 'v id' Aprilis' [9 April], and Easter 1094 was on 9 April; it is most improbable that Bermondsey's annal was a later addition from the *Flores*.

Paris and the annals of Bermondsey have very similar accounts of the translation of Edward the Confessor, Paris under 1163, Bermondsey under 1164, but adding the day, 13 October. Paris has the year right, and Bermondsey's day is correct. It is conceivable that the reports are independent, but borrowing from a common source seems far more probable.[48] The likelihood is much increased by other passages where the St Albans texts agree with Bermondsey against Southwark and Merton, as under 1124:

Bermondsey	*Flores* II, 50	Southwark fo. 133va
Hoc anno viii id' Aprilis [*Easter Day*] sol similis noue lune apparuit. Et eodem anno obiit Kalixtus papa secundus. Successit Honorius secundus.	viii id' April. Obiit Calixtus papa, successit Honorius. Sol similis visus est noue lune.	Sol similis noue lune. Obiit Calixtus papa ii. Successit Honorius.

There is a rather similar case under 1147:

Bermondsey	*Flores* II, 66	Southwark fo. 134ra
Hoc anno motio regum et iter agentium in Ierusalem vii kl' Nouembris.[49]	Motio imperatoris et regis et multorum iter agentium in Ierusalem.	Hoc anno facta est motio euntium Ierusalem.

Though the information is slight in each case, the relation between St Albans and Bermondsey is closer than that between St Albans and either Merton or Southwark.[50]

The demonstration of these elusive relationships involves the comparison of a number of similarly banal entries, but there is a

---

[47] *Chronica maiora*, II, p. 35, *Flores*, II, 26, *Berm*, p. 428; cf. Malmesbury, *Gesta regum*, II, 386.

[48] Below, Appendix s.a. 1163. *Flores*, II, p. 78 is more remote.

[49] This date is unexplained; it does not seem to represent a mistaken version of any date for Easter 1145–9.

[50] Merton has nothing under 1124, and under 1125 a long entry (fo. 162rb) beginning: 'Hoc anno Honorius Romane ecclesie clxvii presidet'; what follows has nothing in common with Bermondsey. Under 1147 (fo. 163va) it reads: 'Hoc anno mouerunt apud Ierusalem.'

point of importance to establish. Unless one supposes that Paris had several versions of these London annals to hand, taking additions now from one, now from another, then there was at St Albans by 1250[51] a version of the common source which contained more than any single surviving copy. The hypothesis that Bermondsey, Southwark and Merton are partial representatives of a larger original is confirmed by the existence of a fourth witness which conforms entirely to none of the others, but partly to each of them. St Albans seems to have used this lost text up to 1217, but not later.[52]

So far I have tried to show that a single source lies behind the annals of Southwark, Merton and Bermondsey, and behind the additions made by Matthew Paris to Wendover's chronicle in the *Chronica* and the *Flores*. Paris abandons it in 1217, Bermondsey in 1222–3, though this does not prove that any version of the source necessarily ended in either year. It is also possible that the compilation was first made at Bermondsey, though subsequently enlarged at Southwark and Merton, and that Paris used a version of this enlargement.

To conjure up a lost source from such scattered materials is never a comfortable business, but the conclusion finds some confirmation in a fifth text, the historical narrative at the beginning of the *Liber de antiquis legibus* of London, written under Edward I.[53] Until 1135 this is little more than an abbreviation of William of Malmesbury, but its character then changes entirely. The death of Henry I and succession of Stephen are reported more or less in the words of Merton, and from then until 1213 there is very little of substance which is not in Merton.[54] However it is clear that the Merton annals as we have them cannot be the source of these passages, for there are a number of small details which are

---

[51] For the date at which Paris was working on the *Chronica* to 1250 see Vaughan, *Matthew Paris*, pp. 49–61.   [52] See below, Appendix s.a. 1218 and its note.

[53] Largely printed by T. Stapledon in *De antiquis legibus liber. Cronica maiorum et uicecomitum Londoniarum* (Camden Soc. [Orig. Series] 1846), pp. 179–205, esp. 196ff. See further Gransden, *Historical writing*, I pp. 508–17, Brooke, *London*, pp. 375–6.

[54] The only substantial pieces of distinct information which I notice in the *Liber* which cannot be found in the Merton annals in these years occur in 1164 (p. 198), where Archbishop Thomas is said to have been exiled 'et omnis parentela sua expulsus est ab Anglia per preceptum regis', and under 1188 and 1189 (p. 199): 'pace firmata inter eos, cruces susceperunt apud Gisortium' (not in either Merton or Southwark) and 'in parliamento de Beauesiu' (where Southwark and Merton have 'Bonsmolins'). Most of the other variants are either trivial or require no independent source of information.

found only in Southwark. Further, in 1214, 1215 and 1216, the *Liber* has a great deal more detail on the military operations of the year than are found in Merton, but seems to be abbreviating a source very close to Southwark. On the other hand the *Liber* and Merton contain part of a passage also found in Diceto, but the *Liber* has more of it than Merton does, while Southwark has nothing at all.[55]

Unless the *Liber* had two very similar sources, turning from one to the other more or less at random, it provides further evidence of a set of annals near London which was neither the surviving text of Southwark nor Merton, though close to both. The brief section of the *Liber* from 1225 to the end is quite unlike either Merton or Southwark, again suggesting that the common source ended soon after 1224.

It would be a hazardous enterprise to try to reconstruct this underlying source in all its details. In general one might proceed on the assumption that distinctive passages found in any two of the five texts, Southwark, Merton, Bermondsey, St Albans and the *Liber*, once stood in the source at some point in its life, but such a principle is not easy to apply. It is in the nature of annals to import odd entries from other sources, often well after their original composition, so that one can easily be deceived by isolated convergences. There is a thin scatter of the entries we have been considering in annals which have not been discussed here at all.[56] St Albans at least clearly knew many of the sources from which the annals were constructed, as well as the annals themselves, so passages from the ultimate source may have arrived independently in both.

Even with all these qualifications, one can say something of the materials out of which this underlying source was put together. In the earlier sections Merton, Bermondsey and St Albans establish

[55] For examples of the agreement of the *Liber* with Merton see e.g. p. 198 s.a. 1185 'pro auxilia a rege postulando ad succurrendum terram sanctam' with Merton fo. 166rb against Southwark (which has a much abbreviated version). For evidence that Merton is not the unique source see e.g. *Liber*, p. 197 (s.a. 1139) 'filia...regis Henrici' with Diceto, I, p. 253 (MS B) against Merton (Southwark has nothing here). The entry under 1180 'ut annum eundem annum benignitatis – imminere diebus' is fuller, and nearer Diceto, I, p. 436, than Merton, and again Southwark has nothing.

[56] See for instance the next note, and the notes under the years 1114, 1132, 1140, 1141, 1148–9, 1176, 1180, 1212, 1215 in the appendix below. Tyson, 'The annals of Southwark and Merton', 30–1, 37 has some discussion of the connection of Merton and Southwark with the Waverley annals.

the use of William of Malmesbury's *Gesta regum*. From 1066 to 1180 the most substantial source appears to be Diceto in his *Abbreviationes* and *Ymagines*. From 1066 to 1179 the parallels between the complex of London annals and Ralph recur year after year, most obviously in the Merton annals, but far from exclusively so. There remain two minor problems concerned with Diceto.

In the first place the London annals sometimes seem to be nearer Diceto's source than to Diceto himself, and to cite passages from it which Diceto omits. For example, under 1077 Merton, Bermondsey and the *Flores* have the entry:

xvi kalend' Maii [Easter Day, *om. Berm.*]. Dominica Palmarum circa horam sextam sereno celo stella apparuit.[57]

This is not in Diceto, though it is in Sigebert and Torigni, Diceto's source. Similarly, the translation of St Nicholas to Bari under 1087 in the *Flores* and Merton adds to Diceto's brief entry the note by Sigebert:

Facta est autem hec translatio anno DCCXLV a depositione sancti Nicholai.[58]

Such oddities may be explained by the annals having consulted Torigni directly, as well as Diceto, for his text was widely used in twelfth-century England.[59]

Secondly, the connection between the annals and Diceto ends abruptly in 1179. This is very curious; Diceto after that date contains material indistinguishable from that the annalists had exploited so vigorously before, and there is no reason to believe that any version of the *Ymagines* ever ended so early.[60] Even more to the point, the connection ends with a passage in Diceto which seems to require some explanation. After describing the remarkable harvest of 1179 Diceto observes:

Euentu tali satis debes esse commonitus aliquid aliud subitum, insperatum, insolitum, tuis forsan imminere diebus.[61]

---

[57] *Flores*, II, p. 9, (*Chronica maiora*, II, p. 16); *Berm.* p. 425; Merton fo. 159va. Cf. Sigebert in MGH Scriptores, VI, 363. It also occurs in the Annals of Waverley, *Ann. mon.* II, p. 193.
[58] Compare *Flores* [MS E], II, p. 18 (*Chronica maiora*, II, p. 18), Merton fo. 160rb and Sigebert 366, with Diceto, I, p. 211. There is another case under 1086 (*sic*) where Merton fo. 160ra, *Flores*, II, p. 13 (*Chronica maiora*, II, p. 19) and Sigebert, 365 agree against Diceto, I, p. 211.
[59] E.g. by Wendover and the Annals of Waverley (*Ann. mon.*, II, p. 238).
[60] Diceto, II, pp. viii–xvi; Gransden, *Historical writing*, I, pp. 230–6.
[61] Diceto, I, p. 436.

Although the passage is quoted as it stands in the annals of Merton and in the *Liber de antiquis legibus*,[62] it is difficult to imagine that such a passage could have been first written long after the events to which it refers. If the author knew what was portended, he would presumably have told us; if this is Diceto writing ten years or more after the event, with no clear idea of its significance, it is hard to see why he should have written in this way. It is in fact inherently improbable that Diceto composed the annals from 1163 (where his version of Torigny abandoned him) up to his own time from his own recollection alone, apart from the few passages of known origin. That he used lost sources for some of his annals is thoroughly likely on general principles. It seems quite possible that the London annals preserve a shadow of one of these sources up to 1179.

The conclusion which I suggest then is that there was once a set of London annals, possibly based on materials collected at Bermondsey, which ended *c.* 1225, but was subsequently continued by the source of Southwark and Merton until 1240. This is also attested by the works of Paris in the 1240s and by the *Liber de antiquis legibus* under Edward I. At the end of the thirteenth century the same work played an important part in the formation of the annals of Waverley and Hyde. Among its sources may have been material also known to Diceto, but incompletely preserved in his pages.

If the case is made out, it contributes a little to the study of a fairly arid branch of historical scholarship in the thirteenth century. It also suggests, more importantly, that a small number of annals on the history of London found scattered in later sources deserve rather more credit than is at first apparent.

APPENDIX

SELECT ANNALS ON THE HISTORY OF LONDON 1089–1218

The text below is based on Merton, or Southwark if the passage does not occur in Merton. Where it occurs in neither, the orthography is a modification of the printed texts. The text notes refer only to substantive variants, and ignore

[62] Merton fo. 166ra; *Liber*, p. 198; cf. above n. 55.

variations of word order. The commentary deals only with the transmission of the material, not its substance. The selection ends where the distinctive London annals are only found in Southwark and Merton. It includes all annals directly bearing on the history of London or on the internal history of Bermondsey, Southwark or Merton. It omits references confined to the consecration of prelates or celebration of councils at Westminster, where they have no direct bearing on the history of the city. I use these conventions:

B = Bermondsey (in Luard's edition)

F = *Flores* II (in Luard's edition). Manchester, Chetham's Library MS 6712 (Mun.A.6.89), is partly in the hand of Paris [Fa]; Eton College, MS 123, a copy made at Merton, possibly from a Westminster archetype, contains early material from St Albans not included in Fa [Fe]. A Merton scribe added further notes on the succession of priors, subsequently partly erased [Fe *mg.*].[63]

L = *Liber* in Stapledon's edition (from 1135)

M = Annals of Merton (Cambridge, Corpus Christi Coll. MS 59, fos. 159va–180ra)

P = Paris, *Chronica Maiora* (in Luard's edition)

S = Annals of Southwark (London, BL Cotton MS Faustina A viii fos. 121–146v [sa]); also Bodl. MS Rawlinson B 177, fos. 208–216 [sb]

V = BL Cotton MS Vespasian E iv fos. 153–201, ed. Luard in *Ann. Mon.* iv, 355–492 for the passages shared with the later annals of Worcester. Liebermann in *UANG*, 182–202 printed the small number of annals in Vespasian which do not appear in Worcester.

1089 (SFPV) xi kl' Augusti[a] monachi Bermund'[b] uenerunt in Angliam.[64]
    [a] xi – Aug' sv; Eodem anno P; *om.* F [b] uocante Lanfranco *add.* F

    (B) Hoc anno littera dominicalis G xvi kl' Maii [*Easter Day*, 1088] luna currente per vii Petreus, Ricardus, Osbertus et Vmbaldus, monachi de Caritate, uenerunt Bermundeseye. Et Petreus factus est prior ex ordinatione prioris de Caritate.

1091 (SF) [xvi kl' Nouembris feria vi] uentus uehemens[a] percussit Lundoniam,[b] [turres et edificia cum arboribus fructiferis concutiens *add.* F].[65]

    MB here have the much fuller account of the storms from Malmesbury, Gesta regum II.374–5, *but B inserts* 'feria vi', *which is not in Malmesbury.*

---

[63] In general, *Flores*, I, pp. xv–xvi, lii; Vaughan, *Matthew Paris*, pp. 92–103; Gransden, *Historical writing*, I, pp. 356–7, 377–8, 456–63; N. R. Ker, *Medieval manuscripts in British Libraries* II (1977), 740–1, III (1983), pp. 348–50.

[64] Compare Annals of 'Fécamp' (above n. 18) s.a. 1090: 'Hoc anno uenerunt monachi de Caritate ad Bermundeseiam.'

[65] The 'Annales meridionales' in *UANG*, p. 46, and the Annals of Waverley in *Ann. mon.*, II, p. 202, have an internally inconsistent version of this entry, placing it on 'vi kl' Nouembris, feria vi'. 27 October 1091 was not a Friday, 17 October was.

ᵃ et dampnosus *add.* ꜰ ᵇ Sb *originally had the whole entry under* 1090, *but subsequently altered it.*

1094 (ꜱʙᴘꜰ) Obiit Alwinus fundator Bermund' [littera dominicalis ᴀ vi id' Aprilis (*Easter Day*) *add.* ʙ].

1106 (ꜱʙꜰᴘᴠ) Hic constitutus est ordo canonicorum in ecclesia sancte Marie de Suthewer'ᵃ
ᵃ in eecl. – Suth. ꜱʙꜰᴠ (Londoniis *add.* ꜰ); Saresbirie ᴘ

1107 (ᴍʙꜰᴘ) Hoc annoᵃ Normannus prior fundauit ecclesiam sancte Trinitatisᵇ London' in religioneᶜ [auctoritate Matildis regine Anglie *add.* ᴍ]
ᵃ Hoc anno ᴍʙ; xviii kl' Maii [*Easter Day*] ꜰ; *om.* ᴘ ᵇ sancte Trinitatis ᴍ; Christi ʙꜰᴘ ᶜ religione ᴍꜰ; religione sacra ʙ; sub ordineque sancti Augustini canonicos collocauit ᴘ

1114 (ᴍꜱʙꜰᴘ) Hoc annoᵃ Tamisia exsiccata est et mare decemᵇ miliariis duobus diebusᶜ [siccatum est *add.* ᴍ].⁶⁶
ᵃ Hoc anno ᴍʙ; *om.* ꜱ; Quarto kl' Aprilis [*Easter Day*] ꜰᴘ ᵇ mare decem ᴍʙ; mare per duodecim ꜰᴘ; maxim' ꜱ ᶜ duobus diebus ᴍʙꜱꜰ; per duos dies ᴘ
(ᴠ) Tamisia exciccata est per duos dies.

1115 (ꜰᴇ) Obiit Lofstan domesman et iacet apud Bermudeseye.⁶⁷

1117 (ꜰᴘ) Robertus prior cum paucis fratribus locumᵃ Meretonam primo inhabitareᵇ cepit.
ᵃ locum ꜰ; *om.* ᴘ ᵇ inhab. ꜰ; hab. ᴘ
(ᴠ) Robertus prioratum Mertonii primus suscepit.⁶⁸
(ꜱᴀ *mg.*) Incepit dom[us] de Merton'
(ʙ) Et hoc anno crux sancti Saluatoris inuenta est prope Thamisiam.⁶⁹

1118 (ʙ) Et eodem anno miraculose uirtute sancte crucis liberatur Willelmus comes Moritonie de turri Londonie.

1119 (ꜱʙꜰᴘ) iiii id' Ianuariiᵃ obiit Petrus primus prior Bermund'. Successit Herebrannusᵇ.
ᵃ iiii id' Ianuarii ꜱ; iiii id' Iunii ʙ; *om.* ꜰᴘ (ᴘ *places under* 1118) ᵇ Succ. Her. *om.* ꜰᴘ

1120 (ꜱʙ) Obiit Herebrandus. [prior Bermundeseye, cui *add.* ʙ] Successit Petrus et postea Walterius.

⁶⁶ *Radulphi de Coggeshall Chronicum Anglicanum*, ed. J. Stevenson (RS London, 1875), p. 7 and the Annals of Winchester (*Ann. mon.*, ɪɪ, p. 44) date versions of this 'vi id' Octobris'.
⁶⁷ Brooke, *London*, pp. 246–7, 372.
⁶⁸ Cf. Annals of Winchester and Waverley (*Ann. mon.*, ɪɪ, pp. 45, 216).
⁶⁹ This and the next annal are treated with the utmost scepticism by Graham (above n. 22), pp. 108–9, possibly justly.

1125   (M)   Hoc anno obiit Gilebertus uicecomes fundator ecclesie sancte Marie de Meritona vii kl' Augusti.[70]

       (F)   Obiit quoque Gilebertus fundator Meretonie

1130   (SF)   viii id' Ianuarii[a] obiit Algodus primus prior sancte Marie de Suthewer'. Successit Algarus.

       [a] viii id. Ian. s; *om.* F

1132   (MBF)   Hoc anno Londonia pene tota combusta est de igne Gileberti Beket[a] [iii id' Aprilis *add.* BF[71]].

       [a] de igne – Becket MB; *om.* F

       (P)   (*s.a. 1132*) Londonia pro maxima parte combusta est.[72]

       (SV)   (*s.a. 1130*) Lundonia tota combusta est extra unam wardam et dimidiam.

       (S)   Obiit Algarus prior secundus viii kl' Nouembris sancte Marie de Suthwerk. Successit Varinus.

1134   (SB)   Obiit Walterius prior de Bermund'. Successit Clarembaldus.

1135   (MBLFP)   Hoc anno[a] ecclesia sancti Pauli London' combusta est de illo[b] igne qui accensus est ad pontem London'[c] et perrexit usque ad sanctum Clementem[d] ecclesiam Danorum.

       [a] Hoc anno ML; eodem anno BPF [b] illo *om.* PF [c] Lond. *om.* P [d] S. Clementem MBL; *om.* PF

       (S)   xiii kl' Iunii[a] ecclesia sancti Pauli combusta.

       [a] Iunii sa; Iulii sb

       (V)   Eodem anno combusta est ecclesia sancti Pauli Londoniis.

1140   (MSFP)   [a] Hoc anno in Lundonia[b] Albericus de Ver occisus est id' Maii.[73]

       [a] Paris (*II.174*) *places this under* 1140, *though with several other entries belonging under* 1141 [b] in Lundonia SF; Londoniis P; *om.* M

       (B)   Hoc anno Willemus comes Moritonii uenit Bermundeseye et suscepit habitum monachalem.

1141   (ML)   Tunc imperatrix a Londoniensibus [ii kl' Maii *add.* M] et ab omni

---

[70] Compare Colker, 'Latin texts' (above n. 7), 261.

[71] Easter Day 1132 fell on 'iv id' Aprilis'.

[72] The date of the fire is obscure. Apart from sv (which are here dislocated, with another long entry for 1133 under 1130), the London annals seem to agree on 1132. *The Chronicle of John of Worcester, 1118–1140*, ed. J. R. R. Weaver (Oxford, 1908), pp. 36–37 seems to put it under 1133. For further discussion see J. C. Russell, 'The date of Henry I's charter to London', reprinted from *Dargan historical essays* no. 4 (1952) in *Twelfth-century studies* (New York, 1978), pp. 94ff.; Brooke, *London*, p. 212 n. 4. The Winchester Annals (*Ann. mon.*, II, p. 49) have 'Londonia tota combusta est', s.a. 1131, but all the entries are here one year out; 1132 is intended.

[73] Compare Coggeshall, *Chronicum*, p. 11: 'Comes Albericus de Ver a ciuibus Londonie peremptus est.'

pene gente Anglorum suscepta est in dominam, exceptis Kentensibus. Set tamen[a] a London' expulsa est in die sancti Iohannis baptiste [proximo sequenti *add.* L].

ML *agree largely with* Diceto 1,254n. (ms. B), *as far as* 'expulsa est'. SVB *lack any account of the arrival of the Empress in London, or her departure.*
[a] tamen M; tandem L

(F)   Ciuitas Londoniarum reddita est imperatrici, sed cito post fugata est inde, scilicet viii kl' Iulii.

(MLF)   Postea statim in eadem estate obsessa est turris London' a Londoniensibus, quam Willelmus de Mandauilla tenebat et firmauerat.[74]

(P)   Galfridus de Mandauilla firmauit turrim Londoniensem. (*Under 1140 again*)

(MF)   Captus est etiam Robertus Lond' episcopus vi non' Iulii[a] apud Fuleham a Galfrido de Mandauilla id' Nouembris[b].[75]

[a] vi non. Iulii M; *om.* F [b] id. Nou. M; ix kl' Iulii F. F *has whole entry under 1142.*

1142   (S)   Obiit Warinus prior tertius sancte Marie de Suthwer' ii kl' Martii[a]. Successit Gregorius.
[a] Martii sa; Aprilis *corr. from* Maii sb

1143   (MLV)   **Rex Stephanus cepit Galfridum de Mandauilla in curia sua** apud sanctum Albanum post festum sancti Michaelis. **Qui ut liberaretur reddidit turrim London' et castella sua**[b]. Ipse uero postea in Aduentu Domini fecit castellum ecclesiam [sancti Benedicti *add.* M] de Romeseya.

The passages in bold type are also in Diceto I, 255. Torigni (Diceto's source) i, 230 also adds 'apud sanctum Albanum'. V *lacks* in curia sua — Michaelis *and* Ipse uero — Romeseya. [b] et castella sua ML; et omnia oppida sua V

1144   (MFP)   Obit Galfridus de Mandauilla xviii kl' Octobris [et sepultus est apud templum London' *add.* M]

1148   (MBFPL)   Anno eodem [facta est *add.* B] translatio sancti Erkenwaldi [Lond' *add.* M] episcopi xviii kl' Decembris[a] [apud sanctum Paulum Londiniarum *add.* BL].[76]

[74] F. *Nicholai Triveti Annales*, ed. T. Hog (English Historical Society, 1845) p. 13 here has a passage loosely related to M, agreeing that the empress was expelled on the feast of St John, but placing her reception on 'xi kl' Maii'.
[75] Compare Coggeshall, *Chronicum*, p. 12, a very brief entry. J. H. Round, *Geoffrey de Mandeville* (London, 1892), pp. 117–18 discusses a version of this entry which he knew only from Trivet, *Annales*, p. 13: 'Robertum civitatis episcopum ... cepit apud maneuum suum de Fulham'. Here and elsewhere (e.g. pp. 11–12, 16–17, 196–7, 201) Trivet shows some contact with the London annals, particularly with the forms represented by M and L, but rewrites his sources too freely to allow exact analysis. M's November date is bewildering; it may perhaps refer to a subsequent entry which was later omitted.
[76] Compare Diceto, I, 267 n.; Coggeshall, *Chronicum*, p. 12.

^a Decmbris MBFP; Octobris L

(B)   Recessit Clarembaldus prior de Bermundeseye cum duodecim monachis, et factus fuit primus abbas de Feuersham, cui successit Robertus Blesensis.

1149   (MBPFL)   Hyemps maxima^a a iiii^b id' Decembris^c usque ad xi^d kl' Martii. Et Tamisia sic gelata^e est ut pede et equo transiretur^f.⁷⁷

^a Hyemps maxima MBL (cf. Diceto I, 291 ; Hoc. anno gelu cepit PF (*both s.a. 1150*)
^b iiii MBPF viii L ^c et durauit *add.* FL; durans *add.* P ^d xi MBPF x L ^e gelata MBP; congelata L; ingelata F ^f transiretur MBP; transfretetur L; et quadrigis etiam oneratis transmeabilis redderetur F; *cf. s.a.* 1151 *for* MB

(S)   (*s.a. 1150*) Tamisia congelata fuit.

1150   (MFe)   Hoc anno obiit [dominus *add.* M] Robertus primus prior [Meriton' *add.* M], [cui successit Robertus *add.* Fe].

(Fe *mg.*) Obiit Robertus primus prior, cui successit Robertus pridie non' Ianuarii, anno prioratus sue ...⁷⁸

(S)   xiii kl' Februarii obiit Gregorius prior de Suthewer'. Successit Radulfus.

1151   (MB)   Anno eodem a tercio^a id' Decembris usque xi kl' Martii Tamisia sic ingelatur ut pede et equo transiretur. Et nix maxima a Natali Domini usque ad Purificationem [beate Marie *add.* B] iacuit^b.

^a tercia M: quarto B^b *cf. s.a.* 1149

1154   (S)   vi id' Martii obiit Radulfus prior de Suthewer'. Successit Ricardus.

1155   (B)   Hoc anno recessit Robertus prior de Bermundseye.

1156   (B)   Hoc anno successit Rogerius prior de Bermundeseye post annum recessionis Roberti predicti, et factus est prior idem Rogerius xvi kl' Maii anno reuoluto.

1157   (B)   Hoc anno recessit Rogerius prior de Bermundeseye xii kl' Martii, et factus est abbas apud sanctum Audoenum. Successit dompnus Adam viii id' Iunii.

1160   (M)   Hoc anno dedit Gozo uinitarius London' redditum lx solidorum ecclesie Meriton'.

1161   (M)   Hoc anno capella infirmarie Meriton' dedicata est.

(B)   Hoc anno xvi kl' Maii [*Easter Day*] recessit Adam prior de Bermundeseie, et factus est abbas apud Euesham. Cui successit dompnus Gaufridus prior.

---

⁷⁷ Compare Coggeshall, *Chronicum*, p. 13, beginning: 'Hoc tempore gelare cepit' (the year is uncertain); Annals of Winchester in *Ann. mon.*, II, p. 54 (s.a. 1150).
⁷⁸ Colker, 'Latin texts', (above n. 7), 264 makes it clear that Prior Robert died on 'ii non' Ianuarii'.

1163 (M) Hoc anno perrexit dominus Willelmus de sancto Aucon' ad Bedefordiam.[79]

(B) Hoc etiam anno recessit Gaufridus prior de Bermundeseye, cui successit Petrus.

(BP) [a]Eodem anno translatum est corpus gloriosi et uere sancti regis Edwardi[b] ab eodem sancto Thoma[c], presente eodem rege Henrico, tertio id' Octobris[d].[80]

[a] Under 1164 B [b] gloriosi et uere sancti regis Edwardi B; sancti regis et confessoris Edwardi apud Westmonasterium P [c] ab eodem sancto Thoma B; a beato Thoma Cantuariensi archiepiscopo P [d] tertio id' Octobris B; qui hoc procurauerat P

1164 (S) Electio et translatio Gileberti Foliot episcopi Hereford' ad episcopum Lundon' ix kl' Aprilis [Easter Day 1163[81]].

1166 (B) Hoc anno recessit dompnus Petrus prior de Bermundeseye, cui successit dompnus Raynoldus.

1167 (MFaFe mg.) Obiit Robertus secundus prior [ecclesie de add. M] Meriton'. [Successit illi Willelmus ii non' Augusti anno prioratus sui xvii add. Fe mg.]

(B) Hoc anno recessit dompnus Raynoldus prior de Bermundeseye. Cui successit dompnus Rogerius.

(M) Ecclesia de Kingeston dedicata est.

1173 (M) Hoc anno obiit domnus Teoldus subprior.

1174 (M) Hoc anno altare sancti Iohannis baptiste dedicatum est a Frogero Sagiensi episcopo vi kl' Martii. Obiit Radulfus de Cahaines.

1175 (B) Hoc anno recessit Rogerius prior de Bermundeseye et factus est abbas apud Abendone. Cui successit Robertus de Bethleem.

1176 (MS) Hoc anno pons lapideus London' inceptus est a Petro capellano de Kolechierche[a].[82]

[a] At foot of leaf, referred here by a pen stroke sa; in text sb

(B) Hoc anno recessit Robertus prior de Bermundeseye. Successit ei Werricus.

[79] Presumably the William prior of Newnham recorded from 1166 or earlier to c. 1170 in Knowles, Brooke and London, Heads, p. 177.
[80] See particularly Herbert of Bosham in Materials for the history of Thomas Becket, ed. J. C. Robertson (7 vols. RS, 1875–85) III, pp. 260–1. The accounts in the Annals of Winchester, Waverley and Worcester (Ann. mon. II, p. 57, 238; IV, p. 380) are quite distinct.
[81] Gilbert's translation took place on 6 March 1163; he was enthroned on 28 April (Fasti (above n. 11), I, 2).
[82] Also in the Annals of Waverley (Ann. mon. II, p. 240); it may, therefore, have stood in the ancestor of V (above n. 5), though it is not in the surviving copy. In general see Brooke, London, pp. 109–10.

Annals of Bermondsey, Southwark, Merton

1177 (MFaFe*mg*.)ª Hoc anno obiit Willelmus tercius prior Meriton'ᵇ
(M) vi kl' Martii et Stephanus quartus successit.
(Fe *mg*.) xi kl' Martii anno prioratus xi. [Successit?] Stephanus quartus qui obiit eodem anno, cui successit Robertus quintus.
ª Fa *s.a. 1176* ᵇ Mer. *om.* Fe *mg*.

1178 (B) Hoc anno recessit Werricus prior de Bermundeseye et factus est abbas de Feuersham. Successit dompnus Bertrannus.

1179 (MSP) Obiit Ricardus de Lucy [episcopus Wintoniensis *add.* P, *in error*]

1180 (Msb) Noua moneta currit in Anglia post baseleres circa festum sancti Martini.⁸³
(SaB) (s.a. 1181) In isto anno mutata est moneta die sancti Martini.
F: Moneta in Anglia renouatur (s.a. 1180)
PL: Noua moneta in Anglia [facta est *add.* P] (*Paris II.315, s.a. 1180, but compare II.317 s.a. 1181 from Diceto*)

1184 (B) Hoc anno obiit Bertrannus prior de Bermundeseie, cui successit Constantinus uel Constantius.

1186 (B) Et eodem anno obiit Constantius uel Constantinus prior de Bermundeseye, cui successit Henricus de Soliaco. Obiit Henricus, cui successit Adam. Et eodem anno obiit Adam, cui successit Henricus.⁸⁴

1189 (MSBVFL) Ricardus...coronatusª est apud Westmonasteriumᵇ a Baldewino Cantuar' archiepiscopo iii non' Septembris.
ª coronatus MSVL; consecratus B; coronatur F ᵇapud Westmonasterium MBVFL (eodem anno *add.* M, die dominica *add.* V); *om.* S
(MSVFL) Nocte sequenti facta estª strages Iudeorum in London'ᵇ et domus eorum ex magna parte igne consumpte sunt.⁸⁵
ª maxima *add.* L ᵇ et domus – sunt *om.* F
(SB) Eodem anno recessit Henricus prior Bermund' et factus est abbas Glaston' ad festum sancti Michelis. Cui successit Ricardus Norm' in die sancti Nicholaiª.⁸⁶
ª episcopi *add.* B

1190 (S) Obiit bone memorie Valerianus prior de Sudwerk' kl' Aprilis, cui successit Willelmus de Oxoneford'.

1192 (M) Hoc anno turris ecclesie sancti Iohannis baptiste de Croydene percussa ex magna parte diruta est.

⁸³ The Annals of Waverley (*Ann. mon.* II, p. 242) have the same sentence under this year, preceded by: 'Henricus secundus rex mutauit monetam ad festum sancti Martini', so apparently conflating both versions. For 1180 as the correct year see W. L. Warren, *Henry II* (London, 1973), p. 265.
⁸⁴ The passage 'Obiit Henricus – successit Henricus' seems to be a mistaken addition; compare Knowles, Brooke and London, *Heads*, pp. 115–16.
⁸⁵ Compare Annals of Winchester (*Ann. mon.* II, p. 63). ⁸⁶ See above n. 19.

303

(MSBV) Henricus[a] abbas Glaston' [quondam prior de Bermundeseye *add.* B] consecratus est in episcopum Wygornien' ii id' Decembris, et cum eo episcopus Landaf'[b] a domino Huberto Cantuar' archiepiscopo.
  [a] Henricus MBV; *om.* S [b] et cum — Landaf' MS; *om.* B; et cum — archiepiscopo *om.* V

1194 (MSBVL) iii id' Martii apud Sandwiz applicuit[a] rex Ricardus, post feria iiii[b] [scilicet xvii kl' Aprilis *add.* M] cum magno apparatu apud Lond' receptus est.
  [a] applicuit MBVL; *om.* S [b] feria iiii MSBL; in octauis Pasche regni diadema suscipiens V

(ML) [In Kalendario *add.* L] Dies mala fuit quando Ricardus rex Anglie[a] fuit coronatus, dies mala quando suscepit crucem, dies mala quando exiuit de terra sua [uersus terram sanctam *add.* L], dies mala quando captus fuit in Allemannia, dies mala quando liberatus est.[87]
  [a] Ric. rex Anglie M; iste rex L

(MSL) Post eodem anno scilicet[a] xv kl' Maii coronatus est apud Winton'. Post[b] iiii id' Maii[c] transfretauit in Normanniam.[88]
  [a] Postea eodem anno sc. M; rex de quo mentio fit S; Et postea V; Postea idem rex L [b] Post M; Postea S; Et postea V; et L [c] Maii MS; eiusdem mensis L; ii non' Iunii V

(M) Anno eodem dedicata sunt altaria sancti Stephani et sancti Nicholai a domino Godefrido Winton' episcopo viii id' Nouembris.

1195 (MBPS) Hoc anno obiit Henricus [de Solini *add.* M] episcopus Wygorn' [quondam prior de Bermundeseye *add.* B].

1196 (MSLV) Hoc anno Willelmus filius Osberti cognomine a la barbe de London'[a] suspensus fuit viii id' Aprilis[b] et cum eo nouem ex sociis eius.
  [a] cognomine a la barbe de London' S; cognomento Odlalabarde London' M; cognominatus cum barba per procurationem Londoniensium L; cognomine a la barbe...aput Londonias patibulo V [b] viii id' Aprilis MSL; *om.* V

1197 (M) Hoc anno uti cepimus primo nostro nouo sigillo argenteo iii id' Decembris. Villa de Tappelawe empta est. Altare sancte crucis dedicatum est ii kl' Nouembris a domino Roberto episcopo de Bangor.

1198 (MS) Hoc anno obiit Ricardus sextus[a] prior sante Marie de[b] Meriton' kl' Aprilis. Cui successit eodem anno[c] Walterus septimus prior Meriton'[d] [et in sede sua collocatus est xvi kl' Iunii, scilicet in die Pentechostes *add.* M]

---

[87] Compare the marginal note to the Annals of Waverley (*Ann. mon.* II, p. 249n.).
[88] V's false date stems from a misunderstanding of its source. The rest of the annal in SB runs: 'ii non' Iunii postea [*om.* B] hora uespertina subito coruscationes et tonitrua horribilia [terribilia B] audita sunt'. M has: 'Audita sunt tonitrua horribilia et subito uise sunt coruscationes ii non' Iunii'.

ª sextus MSb; *om.* sa; ᵇ sancte Marie de S; *om.* M ᶜ eodem anno MSb; *om.* sa
ᵈ Meriton' MSb; *om.* sa

(Fe *mg.*)　Obiit Ricardus sextus prior. Successit Walterus septimus.

1201　(B)　Hoc anno obiit Ricardus Northam prior de Bermundeseye, cui successit Hugo.

1203　(S)　Hoc anno obiit Willelmus de Oxeneford prior sancte Marie de Suthwerk' iiii id' Nouembris.
　　　(V)　Obiit Willelmus de Oxeneford prior de Suwerke
　　　(F)　Willelmus de Oxonia prior Suwerch obiit, cui successit Ricardus de sancta Mildretha (s.a. 1202)

1205　(SV)　Eodem anno obiit Ricardus de sancta Mildrida [non' Ianuarii *add.* s] prior [ecclesie sancte Marie *add.* s] de Suthwer', [cui successit Willelmus filius Samari *add.* s].
　　　(Annals of Waverley, *Ann. mon.* II. 256–7) Obiit Petrus de Cole-chirche qui inchoauit pontem lapideum Londoniensem, et sepultus est in capella super pontem.[89]

1206　(B)　Et hoc anno facta est translatio dompni Petreii, primi prioris istius loci, v id' Iunii a domino Bernardo quondam Raguensi archiepiscopo, qui cum rege Ricardo in Angliam uenit, a quo etiam custodiam episcopatus Carduliensis ecclesie suscepit. Ipse etiam archiepiscopus sequenti festo sancti Barnabe apostoli dedicauit altare matutinale in honore perpetue uirginis Marie et omnium sanctorum. Item eodem anno id' Iulii auditum est tonitruum apud Bermundeseye tante molis quod quidam ibi presentes tam de Gallie quam Burgundie necnon et Auernie regionibus oriundi testati sunt se nunquam tam terribile tonitruum audisse. Et eodem anno rediit Iohannes rex Anglie de Pictauia.

1207　(F)　Eodem anno imperator Otho uenit in Angliam, in cuius aduentu tota ciuitas Londonie induit sollempnitatem, palliis et aliis ornamentis circumornata.[90]
　　　(B)　Hoc anno Otho imperator Romanorum in Angliam transuectus est.

1208　(B)　Et hoc anno inundate sunt terre de Bermundeseye per fluxum Thamisie.

1209　(M)　Item hoc anno Iohannes recepit homagia liberorum hominum per totam Angliam et fidelitatem aliorum per suos balliuos recipi precepit apud Noctingeham et apud Wodestok. Et apud Marlebergiam fecit uenire fere omnes Londonienses ad faciendam sibi fidelitatem.

---

[89] Compare above, s.a. 1176; this is an addition at the foot of the leaf.
[90] Either misplaced or written later, since Otto was not crowned until 1209.

1212 (MSFP)[91]   Hoc anno combusta est ecclesia sancte Marie de Suthwerk' et pons London'[a] inter tres columpnas[b] et capella super pontem combusta est et omnes domus site super pontem[c], et magna[d] pars de Suthwerk'

[a] et pons London' MSP; *om.* F   [b] inter tres columpnas SFP; ecclesie *add.* FE; *om.* M   [c] et omnes domus site super pontem S; et omnis domus super pontem P; et omnia edificia que super ipsum pontem stabant, et pons nimis deterioratus est F; *om.* M   [d] magna MS; maxima F

(MS)   et maxima pars in London', [scilicet a ponte London' usque ad turrim et usque ad Vinetariam *add.* M],

(F)   combusta est, et ex illo igne Thamisiam transiliente combusta est maxima pars Londoniarum, uidelicet tam ciuitatis quam suburbii cum uiris et mulieribus et paruulis,

(P)   (super pontem cum magna parte ciuitatis et parte uille de Suwerc) igne Tamisiam transiliente, perieruntque multi (circiter mille) homines cum mulieribus et pueris,

(V)   Item magna pars Londoniarum scilicet Suwerke cum capella sancti Thome et ecclesia sancte Marie canonicorum cum omnibus eiusdem dom[ib]us exceptis refectoriis combustum est.

(MSFP)   in nocte translationis sancti Benedicti abbatis vii id' Iulii[a].

[a] vii id' Iulii S; sc. v id' Iulii F; *om.* MP

(SB)   Hoc anno inceptum est fossatum a Londoniensibus extra muros London' id' Octobris.[92]

---

[91]   The Bermondsey version of these events (*Berm.*, p. 451) is seriously dislocated. Under 1207 it has:
   Et eodem anno combusta fuit ecclesia beate Marie canonicorum de Southwerk et magna pars Londonie et Southwerk. Quo anno canonici eiusdem eccleie fundauerunt quoddam hospitale in fundo eorum proprio prope prioratum, ubi celebrauerunt diuina usquequo idem prioratus de nouo fuit reparatus ...
Under 1209 it has:
   Hoc anno fuit fundatio arche pointis Londonie, et reparatio prioratus ecclesie sancte Marie de Ouereye post combustionem que fuit in tertio anno precedente.
While the chronicle of the mayors of London in *Liber*, p. 3 s.a. 1212: 'Hoc anno fuit uehemens ignis de Suthwerk et combussit ecclesiam sancte Marie, et pontem cum capella, et maximam partem ciuitatis' might depend on some version of the London annals, there is much other evidence to confirm that the fire occurred in 1212, e.g. the Annals of Waverley, Tewkesbury and Worcester, (*Ann. mon.* I, p. 60, II, p. 268, IV, p. 400, here interrelated but clearly independent of the London annals), the Annals of Bury (*UANG*, pp. 153–4), the Barnwell chronicler in *Memoriale fratris Walteri de Coventria*, ed. W. Stubbs (RS no. [58] 1872–3) II, pp. 205–6. It seems to follow that the two Bermondsey entries, if they contain any early information, are to be placed under 1212 and 1214. Alternatively, the first half of the annal for 1209 (to 'Londonie') was rightly entered in the source, and refers to early work on the bridge, not its repair, while the rest of 1209 and all 1207 were entered later under the wrong years.

[92]   S has this under 1212; B, here dislocated (see previous note), places it under 1213; the Annals of Dunstable, more or less contemporary, give an independent account under 1211, though its years are here one out, and 1212 seems to be intended (*Ann. mon.* III, p. 34). The fourteenth-century 'Annales Londonienses' edited by Stubbs in *Chronicles of the reigns of Edward I and Edward II* (RS no. [76] 1882–3) I, p. 15 are in general based on the *Flores*, but here agree largely with S, placing the digging of the ditch 'a Londoniensibus circa muros suos' immediately after the fire, though both entries are under 1213.

(MSF)   Obiit Henricus maior London' xiii kl' Octobris[a].[93]

[a] xiii – Oct. MS; *om.* F

1213   (P)   Per idem tempus rex Iohannes arguens Robertum filium Walteri proditionis et rebellionis sternere fecit castrum Bainardi Londoniis in crastino sancti Hylarii, per manus Londoniensium, scilicet die lune.[94]

(MS)   Hoc anno Iohannes rex Anglie congregauit fere exercitum[a] totius Anglie apud Lond' in die lune ante festum apostolorum Philippi et Iacobi, scilicet iii kl' Maii. Qui statim fecit eos uenire apud Doueram in sequenti ebdomada cum omni apparatu armorum[b], de quibus quosdam domi remisit, quosdam secum retinuit apud Doueram [usque ad Pentechost' *add.* S].

[a] congregauit fere exercitum M; congregato exercitu fere S   [b] apud Lond' – apparatu armorum M; uenit apud Doueram iii kl' Maii S

(L)   Rex, congregato exercitu fere totius Anglie et Londoniensibus, uenit apud Doueriam iii kl' Maii...

(MSFB)   Hoc anno applicuit dominus Stephanus Cantuarien' archiepiscopus [vii id' Iulii *add.* M[95]] apud Doueram et cum eo dominus Willelmus London' episcopus et dominus Eustachius Elyensis episcopus et dominus Hugo Lincolien' episcopus.

(M)   Et postea uenerunt apud Meretonam kl' Augusti et ibi hospitati sunt dominus Stephanus Cant', dominus Eustachius Elyen' et dominus H. Lincolnien' et inde perrexerunt Geldeford'.

1214   (MSBL)   Hoc anno relaxatum est interdictum generale[a] in ecclesia sancti Pauli London' a domino Eustachio Elyensi episcopo[b] in die sanctorum Processi et Martiniani,

[a] int. gen. MSB; predictum int. L   [b] a domino – episcopo MSB; *om.* L

(F)   Die uero Iouis in crastino sanctorum Processi et Martiniani, scilicet v non' Iulii, relaxatur generale interdictum Anglicane ecclesie... apud sanctum Paulum Lundoniis.

(MSBL)   presentibus domino Nicholao apostolice sedis legato et domino Stephano Cantuar' archiepiscopo [et domino Egidio Herefordensi episcopo et domino Iocelino Bathon' episcopo *add.* M] et multis aliis.

(MSBFL)   Quod interdictum durauit[a] per totam Angliam per sex annos continuos et xiiii ebdomadas et tres[b] dies.

[a] durauit MSFL; durauerat B   [b] tres MSBL; duobus F

1215   (MSL)   Hoc anno Iohannes rex Anglie crucesignatus est a domino

---

[93] Compare *Liber*, p. 3, Brooke, *London*, p. 376.

[94] Compare the Annals of Dunstable in *Ann. mon.* III, p. 35; *Flores II*, 143–4.

[95] Wendover (in *Chronica maiora*, II, p. 550) gives 16 July; it is not necessarily preferable (*Acta Stephani Langton*, ed. K. Major, Canterbury and York Society I, 1950, p. 164). The Annals of Worcester in *Ann. mon.* IV, p. 402 (but not V) agree with M.

Willelmo London' episcopo in ecclesia sancti Pauli iiii non' Martii, et
cum eo comes Cestrie et comes de Ferreres[a] et Ricardus de Marisco
[regis cancellario *add.* s] et multi alii[b]. Et fuit in illa die capud ieiunii[c].[96]

[a] et comes *and a lacuna add.* s [b] cum eo – alii MS; quamplures magnates Anglie L
  [c] Et – ieiunii M; in caput reiunii s; in capite quadragesima tunc temporis L

(V) Iohannes rex suscepit crucem in eclesia sancti Pauli Londoniis a
Willemo eiusdem sedis episcopo, sc. feria iiii in capite ieiunii.

(MSL) Hoc anno capta[a] est ciuitas Lond' a[b] baronibus norrensibus xvi
kl' Iulii[c] in die dominica circa[d] horam primam, nullo resistente nec
ictum opponente. Qui barones cum Lundoniensibus confederati promiserunt[e] se nullam pacem facturos cum rege Iohanne[f] sine assensu
utriusque partis.[97]

[a] capta MS; reddita L [b] a MS; *om.* L [c] Iulii MS; Iunii L [d] circa MS; ante L [e] promiserunt
  MS; sunt et iurati L [f] Iohanne MS; *om.* L

1216 (MS)[98] Item ipse dominus Ludouicus in die Iouis ebdomade
Pentechostes fuit[a] London', et ibi cum magna processione in ecclesiam
sancti Pauli receptus est. Et in feria sexta proxima[b] recepit homagia
ciuium et baronum apud Westmonasterium.

[a] fuit M; uenit s [b] Et in feria – proxima M; ibique s

(L) (Ludowycus) die Iouis in ebdomada Pentecostes uenit Londoniis et
ibi cum magna processione in ecclesia sancti Pauli receptus est. Et in
crastino barones et ciues Londoniarum fecerunt ei homagium apud
Westmonasterium.

(M) Et ipse eadem die recepit homagia ciuium Londonien' in cimiterio
sancti Pauli, Roberto filio Walteri primo illud faciente, deinde Willelmo
Hardel maiore London' et multis aliis.

(SL) Die lune post festum sancte Margarete mouit Ludouicus cum
magno exercitu[a] apud Doueram, qui ibi moratus est per xv ebdomadas
in obsidend' dicti castelli[b]. Venit apud Lameiham die Veneris ante
festum sancti Leonardi, [scilicet non' Nouembris *add.* s]. Qui in die
sancti leonardi obsedit turrim Lond'[c] et reddita est ei eodem die[d] hora
uespertina.[99]

[a] mouit – exercitu s; duxit magnum exercitum L [b] qui ibi – castelli s; et moram
  fecit in obsessione dicti castri per xv septimanas sed nichil acquisiuit. Sed
  recessit et L [c] Qui in – Lond' M; et in festo sancti Leonardi L [d] eodem die M;
  turris Londoniarum in L

1217 (MS) Facta est pax firma inter Henricum regem Anglie et dominum
Lodowicum per dominum Gualonem legatum

[96] F here adds to the account of Paris: 'cum eo multi magnates iiii non' Martii'.
[97] The passage 'confederati – partis' also appears in the Annals of Waverley (*Ann. mon.* II, p. 283).
[98] The whole account in M from here to 'die dominica sequenti' below under 1218 is printed in
    C. Petit-Dutaillis, *Etude sur la vie et le règne de Louis VIII 1187–1226*, Bibl. de l'Ecole des hautes
    études, 101, (Paris, 1894) pp. 513–15, and by Tyson.
[99] Compare Waverley (*Ann. mon.* II, pp. 285–6).

(M)   in quadam insula[100] extra Kingestone feria tertia ante exaltationem sancte crucis et in uigilia exaltacionis absolutus est dominus Lodowicus a domino legato in eadem insula et multi alii de magnatibus Francie. Item uenit dominus Gualo legatus apud Meriton' dominica post exaltacionem sancte crucis, et ibi receptus cum magna processione et sollempni. Fecit moram usque ad diem sabbati. In die lune post aduentum domini legati uenerunt apud Meriton' fere magnates tocius Anglie, scilicet dominus Lodowicus et socii sui, comes Britannie, comes de Cneuers, Rob' Drus, et alii multi de Francia. De Anglia episcopi plures et regina Anglie et comites et barones et milites multi, et firmata est pax inter dominum Henricum regem et Lodowicum. Item in die sancti Mauritii uenit dominus Lodowicus apud Meriton' et iniuncta est ei penitencia a penitenciario domini legati. Qui statim post reddidit turrim London' domino Petro Winton' episcopo, et recessit a London' in sabato proximo, et dominus legatus conduxit eum usque ad mare. Dominus autem legatus uenit London' feria vi ante festum apostolorum Simonis et Iude, et dominus Henricus rex uenit London' die dominica sequenti.

(B)   Facta est pax inter Henricum regem et Lodouicum apud Kyngestone iii id' Septembris.

(F)   Conuenientibus igitur in unum Gualone legato cum episcopis et clero et populo, Willelmo Marescallo rectore regis et regni tunc existente, de pace tractatum diligentem habuerunt in quadam insula satis uicina uille de Kingestune, et formata est et facta pax inter regem et Lodouicum in uigilia exaltacionis sancte crucis, ipso prius a sententia excommunicationis ... solempniter absoluto.

(L)   iii id' Septembris facta est pax inter predictum regem Henricum et predictum Lodewycum apud Kingestonam per dominum Gallonem, legatum domini pape, existente ibidem et congregato per preceptum domini regis maximo exercitu militum et liberorum tenentium ab omni parte totius Anglie, qui omnes fuerunt crucesignati in pectore per eundem legatum eundi super predictum Lodewycum et Londonienses et complices eorum. Ipse uero Lodewycus et milites sui qui ibidem presentes fuerunt, eodem die fuerunt absoluti. ... Postea ix kl' Octobris uenerunt apud Mertonam dominus legatus, dominus Lodewycus, et omnes fere magnates Anglie, comes Britannie, et multi alii de Francia, ubi firmata est pax inter ipsos. ... Post hoc dictus Lodewycus uenit Londoniis, capiens licentiam a Londoniensibus et a boro, qui ei adheserunt, et transfretauit in patriam suam. Et sciendum quod predictus Lodewycus, quando reuersus fuit in patriam suam, mera liberalitate sua transmisit mille libras sterlingorum Londoniensibus quas ipsi ei accomodauerant.

---

[100] *Chronica maiora*, III, p. 30 adds 'in quadam insula' to Wendover's account of the treaty. Compare the summary account in the *Flores*.

(s) (Gualonem legatum) apud Kingestun' iii id' Septembris, existente ibi exercitu fere tocius Anglie, et absolutus est a predicto legato, et multi alii tam de maioribus quam minoribus Francie et terre anglicane. Venerunt apud Merton dominus legatus, Lodouicus et omnes fere magnates Anglie, comes Britannie et alii multi de Francia. Et ibi firmata est pax inter dominum Henricum regem Anglie et Lodouicum. Postea uero rediit Lond' Lodouicus cum suis, et accepta licencia, deductus est cum episcopis et comitibus et baronibus ix kl' Octobris ad mare, sicque rediens in terram suam pax et concordia facta est in terra nostra.

1218 (MS) Walterus prior Meriton' septimus factus est monachus apud Cartusiam. Successit Thomas iii id' Nouembris.

(s) Obiit Martinus quondam prior ecclesie sancte Marie de Suthwerk canonicus Meriton' iii id' Iunii. Cui successit Robertus prior de Oseneia scilicet kl' Septembris.

---◆◇◆---

Citizens and chantries in late medieval York

BARRIE DOBSON

It is now a quarter of a century since Christopher Brooke drew our attention to 'one of the most notable revolutions in our history: the development of the idea of privacy, of the notion that some parts of our life at least should not be exposed to public gaze'.[1] As Brooke went on to locate that 'revolution' quite firmly in the later Middle Ages, his perception may offer some consolation to those recent historians of the fourteenth and fifteenth-century English church who – despite the comparative wealth of documentation at their disposal – are so often at a loss when trying to assess the spiritual attitudes of that period with any certainty. Obviously enough, the more 'private' an individual's religion the more it is liable to be highly resistant even to the most pertinacious historian; and it is equally of the essence of such interiorised devotion that it will often be more notable for its diverse than its common features. Despite such familiar difficulties, it has undoubtedly been one of Christopher Brooke's most significant contributions to medieval studies in recent years to stimulate the present remarkable and unprecedented interest in 'popular' as opposed to a more institutionalised religion.[2] Moreover, and of more relevance to the purposes of this paper, it was also Brooke who once argued that the late medieval transformation towards a more private worship – and a more compartmentalised church design – was founded on an increasing

---

[1] C. Brooke, *Medieval church and society: collected essays* (London, 1971), p. 178.

[2] R. and C. Brooke, *Popular religion in the Middle Ages* (London, 1984), although primarily concerned with the period between 1000 and 1300, is itself the most obvious example. Recent research upon late medieval English religious beliefs and practices is well represented in the lengthy bibliographies of C. Harper-Bill, *The pre-Reformation church in England, 1400–1530* (London, 1989) and R. N. Swanson, *Church and society in late medieval England* (Oxford, 1989).

emphasis upon 'the personal nature of the Eucharist as an individual approach by the priest to the central mysteries of the Church'.[3] Might it even be that the now much vaunted 'rise of the private life' in western Christendom during the centuries immediately before the Reformation owed its genesis less to the increased availability of a more materially comfortable environment than to a new religious sensibility within the parish church?

Fortunately enough, that difficult and perhaps even insoluble question raises problems too vast to be the subject of this essay; but it is a question, nevertheless, which immediately redirects attention to the crucial rôle of the chantry as the most widespread institutional expression of late medieval society's most powerful personal religious aspirations. Partly for that very reason no doubt, the English chantry foundations of the fourteenth and fifteenth centuries have attracted greater, and more sympathetic, attention during the last twenty than in the previous two hundred years. In retrospect the late Miss K. L. Wood-Legh's remarkable conspectus of perpetual chantry foundations in England and Scotland already seems less the definitive study it appeared to be on its publication in 1965 than a pioneering venture into largely uncharted seas.[4] Nor can there be any doubt that the late medieval chantry continues to pose formidable problems of analysis. As Dr Clive Burgess and others have recently shown, it will never be possible to appreciate the complex rôle of the perpetual chantry at all adequately until it has been placed – no easy matter – within the context of the even more diversified, and much less firmly documented, world of the anniversary, the obit and other forms of temporary provision for masses on behalf of the deceased.[5] More prosaically, the correct enumeration and

---

[3] Brooke, *Medieval church and society*, p. 181, anticipating several arguments in J. Bossy's influential article on 'The Mass as a social institution', *Past and Present* 100 (1983), 29–61.

[4] K. L. Wood-Legh, *Perpetual chantries in Britain* (Cambridge, 1965). For the single most detailed reassessment of the issues – in one particular but important locality – since the appearance of Miss Wood-Legh's book see C. Burgess, 'Chantries in fifteenth-century Bristol' (Oxford University, History D. Phil. thesis, 1981) and the same author's '"For the increase of divine service": chantries in the parish in late medieval Bristol', *Journal of Ecclesiastical History* 36 (1985), 46–65.

[5] C. Burgess, 'A service for the dead: the form and function of the anniversary in late medieval Bristol', *Transactions of Bristol and Gloucestershire Archaeological Society* 105 (1987), 183–21. The remarkable range of masses and prayers for the dead available to the late medieval citizen is perhaps the most important revelation of N. P. Tanner, *The church in late medieval Norwich, 1370–1532*, Pontifical Institute of Medieval Studies, Studies and Texts 66 (1984), 91–110.

identification of both perpetual chantries and their founders now appears to be by no means as simple an exercise as it once seemed. Nearly all attempts to estimate the numbers of chantries in English towns and counties are notoriously bedevilled by the fact that the two most important sources at the historian's disposal (testamentary bequests on the one hand and royal licences to amortise rents or property to a perpetual chantry establishment on the other) frequently emerge as declarations of intent rather than proofs of creation. In those rare cases where a chantry's foundation documents survive in their entirety, the processes of endowment are so often revealed in such tortuous complexity that one must assume that few such institutions were ever achieved without considerable expenditure of effort and often many changes of plan.[6] A display of hesitation and even of perplexity as to whether the testator's desire to create a chantry would ever be fulfilled at all is indeed a remarkably common feature of late medieval wills themselves. More nerve-wracking still was the possibility that one's perpetual chantry might prove not to be perpetual. It may indeed have been this anxiety in particular which did more than anything else to induce among the parishioners of late medieval England the radical conviction that 'the clergy could (and should) lawfully be subject to lay control'.[7]

Such at least were the closing words of Miss K. L. Wood-Legh's own survey of the perpetual chantries in Britain a generation ago; and for that considerable scholar the propensity of the chantry to generate lay activity within the very structure of the established church was perhaps the single most redeeming feature of an institution otherwise – so she believed – not readily reconcilable with the message of the New Testament.[8] The primary purpose of this paper is to reconsider that proposition in the case of only one English town but in the light of a somewhat remarkable

---

[6] *The cartulary of the Wakebridge chantries at Crich*, ed. A. Saltman (Derbyshire Archaeological Society, Record Series, VI, 1976) provides perhaps the best documented example, a *locus classicus* indeed, of the regular – and sometimes irregular – procedures to which the founder of a perpetual chantry was so often compelled to resort.

[7] Wood-Legh, *Perpetual chantries*, p. 314; cf. pp. 125–9.

[8] Ibid., p. 312. Miss Wood-Legh's highly representative distaste for the 'endless multiplication of mechanically performed masses' was even more pronounced in her earlier studies of the late medieval chantry, e.g. in *Studies in English church life under Edward III* (Cambridge, 1934) and 'Some aspects of the history of chantries in the later Middle Ages', *TRHS*, 4th ser. 28 (1946), 47–60.

collection of forty-one original deeds and other documents which
relate to various chantries founded in the city of York during no
less than two centuries, between 1321 and 1528.[9] These records,
surviving as they do neither in the York Dean and Chapter
Library nor among the archiepiscopal muniments in the Borthwick Institute of Historical Research but rather within the
official archives of the city of York, are in themselves an indirect
testimony to a late medieval urban community's close supervision
of several of the chantries, and their chaplains, in its midst. The
complex web of perpetual and other chantries in the parish
churches, religious houses and cathedral of medieval York have
received only a very limited amount of attention since they were
obliterated forever in 1548; and a detailed analysis of these much
neglected documents must await the full-scale study which those
chantries so self-evidently deserve.[10] Here it may suffice only to
observe that this was a city and cathedral so committed to the
concept of the perpetual chantry that it came to house more such
institutions (at least 140) than any provincial town in fifteenth-
century England. Whether or not most late medieval Englishmen
and Englishwomen would have accepted the York mayor and
council's self-interested claim that their city was and always had
been '*nomee la secounde citee du Roialme et la Chaumbre de Roy*', no
one at all could have disagreed with Roger Burton, its distinguished Common Clerk, when he observed in the late 1430s
that this was 'the chief place of all the north'.[11] No doubt the
intricate skeins of chantry foundation and maintenance in this

---

[9] York City Archives [hereafter cited as YCA], G. 70, nos. 1–40. YCA, G. 70, no. 13, recording
Thomas Duraunt's foundation of a chantry at the parish church of St Crux in 1340, is a copy
of YCA, G. 70, no. 12; but YCA, G. 70, no. 38 in fact comprises two quite distinct documents
(one of 1485 and one of 1386) relating to the Acastre family's perpetual chantry in All Saints,
Pavement. A few of the items in this collection have been known to previous scholars; but their
full importance was first made properly apparent when a typescript calendar of them all
(available in the City Archive Office) was prepared by Mrs Joyce W. Percy, then York City
Archivist, at some time in the early 1960s.

[10] For a brief and somewhat premature attempt to establish the general patterns of chantry
foundation in the city, to which this present paper is in part a sequel, see R. B. Dobson, 'The
foundation of perpetual chantries by the citizens of medieval York', *Studies in Church History*
4 (1967), 22–38. On the dramatic consequences of the dissolution of all the York chantries
in April 1548, see especially D. M. Palliser, *The Reformation in York, 1534–1553* (Borthwick
Papers, no. 40, Borthwick Institute of Historical Research (hereafter cited as BIHR), 1971),
22–5.

[11] YCA, D. 1 (Freemen's Register), fo. 348; *York Memorandum Book BY*, ed. J. W. Percy (Surtees
Society 186, 1973), p. 124; cf. R. Davies, *The state swords of the York corporation* (Yorkshire
Philosophical Society Annual Report 1868), pp. 27–32.

'chief place', all in all more fully documented than in the case of any other English town, were often *sui generis*; but when those skeins are finally unravelled, there can be no doubt at all that they should bear directly upon the wider issues raised by Christopher Brooke and Miss Wood-Legh.

Meanwhile the survival at York of these forty-one charters, indentures, quit-claims and letters of presentation must be seen as an unexpected bonus in the case of a city and church already well provided with an abundance of late medieval registers, accounts and wills, if not of parish records.[12] Why they should survive at all is something of a mystery: for in most cases there can have been no practical reason for their preservation in the civic council offices on Ouse Bridge for more than a decade or two after the dissolution of all the chantries concerned in the 1530s and 1540s. It is equally surprising, given the liability of the York civic muniments as a whole to damage by neglect or even by occasional immersion under the waters of the River Ouse, that these chantry documents are generally in a very good and legible state of preservation.[13] None of the items in the series seems to have been produced by notaries; and the great majority take the form of tripartite indentures, of which the mayor and council's copy is of course the one to survive. In the case of the most important documents, the lists of witnesses are long and highly varied, often throwing new light on the identities of chantry chaplains, prominent citizens and civic office-holders in York. Almost all the indentures and other deeds were authenticated by seals; and it is striking, if not entirely unexpected, that from the early fourteenth century onwards not only the richer merchants of York but also its more obscure residents and chantry priests had personal seals at their disposal. These seals sometimes survive, most interestingly perhaps in the case of a letter of March 1518 presenting a chaplain to Adam de Banke's chantry at St Nicholas's altar in All Saints, North Street: this document still preserves the separate seals of the

---

[12] The only pre-Reformation churchwardens' accounts to survive at York are those for 1518–28 from St Michael, Spurriergate; see York Minster Library, MS. Add. 220/2; *Records of early English drama: York*, ed. A. F. Johnston and M. Rogerson, 2 vols. (Toronto, 1979), I, pp. xxxvii–xxxix; D. M. Smith, *A guide to the archive collections of the Borthwick Institute of Historical Research*, Borthwick Texts and Calendars: Records of the Northern Province, I (York, 1973), pp. 39–40.

[13] YCA, K. 100; W. Giles, *Catalogue of the Charters, House Books, etc., belonging to the Corporation of York* (York, 1909).

rector and four of the parishioners of that church. On the other hand, and not too surprisingly, the royal seals attached to original letters patent among the collection are now invariably missing.[14] Copies of a few of these items naturally survive elsewhere, notably Robert Holme, Jr's important new ordinances of 14 February 1428 for his father's impressive chantry in St Anne's Chapel on Foss Bridge, ordinances which were also registered in one of the city's contemporary official 'memorandum books'.[15] However, it seems clear that on the whole the Common Clerk of York was under no compulsion to have these chantry deeds copied laboriously into his city's registers: this no doubt is the chief reason why the originals were – and are – themselves preserved.

As already implied, the forty-one documents in question are of very diverse genres and varied contents. The only common denominator is that they all relate to chantry foundations in which the mayor and council of the city of York had been assigned a direct or reversionary supervisorial rôle. As already mentioned, the documents range in date from 1321 to 1518; and in one or two cases the relevance of the transaction in question to a chantry, although certainly present, is not immediately apparent.[16] Four items actually relate to an obit rather than to a perpetual chantry foundation. All of these are of a comparatively late date and involved religious houses rather than parish churches in the city: they are accordingly of most interest as illustrations of the extraordinary variety of ways in which desire for vicarious intercession could be satisfied in a large medieval town as well as of the increasing tendency for potential founders to see the mayor and commonalty of York as the most reliable guarantors that their very different religious aspirations would come to fruition. Accordingly in December 1466 the prominent York merchant and ex-mayor, Thomas Nelson, only established his elaborate obit at Holy Trinity Priory, Micklegate ('in consideration of a certain sum of money and of the great window at the east end of the choir

---

[14] YCA, G. 70, nos. 9, 10, 25, 28.

[15] YCA, G. 70, no. 35; copied in *York Memorandum Book BY*, 149–51.

[16] E.g. a quitclaim of January 1406 whereby two parish chaplains released a tenement in Jubbergate to Thomas de Holme, possibly to support one of the several Holme chantries in the city (YCA, G. 70, no. 26; 'Some early civic wills of York', ed. R. B. Cook, *Associated Architectural Societies Reports and Papers* 28, part II (1906), 840–71.

newly glazed by him'), on condition that the mayor and commonalty could distrain on the prior and chapter there if the due services lapsed for more than forty successive days.[17] A very similar precaution was taken by William Butler of Selby (in January 1465) and John Gillyot, Jr, alderman of York (in April 1489) when they founded their respective obits within the Franciscan and Carmelite friaries of the city. The two stray documents which record these endowments suggest, almost certainly correctly, that the number of temporary chantry and other pious foundations made within the houses of mendicant friars have been unduly neglected by recent historians of the English town; and it is more revealing still that it was to Gillyot, albeit a member of one of the city's most notable merchant families, that the White Friars of York looked for the re-plenishment of their stock of ecclesiastical vestments ('three copes, one chasuble and two tunicles of black chamlet cloth adorned with the letters J and G joined together in Venetian gold').[18] However, it may be an even more instructive comment on the increasing reliance of the religious orders of the north upon the services of the local laity that in 1514 it was the most prestigious civic fraternity in the city, the Corpus Christi Guild, which undertook to found and administer an important obit in the Chapel of St Thomas Becket outside Micklegate Bar on behalf of a monastic superior, Thomas Tanfelde, prior of Thorneholme in Lincolnshire.[19]

With one important exception, however, all the other original chantry documents preserved within the York civic archives relate not only to perpetual foundations but to foundations made by members of the city's mercantile élite within one or other of its two civic chapels or its forty parish churches.[20] Such a conclusion

[17] YCA, G. 70, no. 37; cf. BIHR, Probate Register, 5, fo. 212.

[18] YCA, G. 70, nos. 36, 39. Between the death of his father in 1484 and his own demise in 1509, Sir John Gillyot was in many ways 'the most conspicuous person in York of his time': see *Testamenta Eboracensia: a selection of wills from the registry at York*, ed. J. Raine and others, Surtees Society, vols. 4, 30, 45, 53, 79, 106 (1836–1902), v, 12–17.

[19] YCA, G. 70, no. 40. Prior Tanfelde had been admitted to the fraternity of the York Corpus Christi Guild in 1497: see *The register of the Corpus Christi guild in the city of York*, ed. R. H. Skaife, Surtees Society, 57 (1872), p. 143.

[20] The civic jurors who in 1428 assessed the value of York's parish churches, *in civitate predicta et in suburbiis eiusdem*, estimated their total number at 39: see *York Memorandum Book*, ed. M. Sellers, Surtees Society, 120, 125 (1911–14), II, 131–4; but cf. VCH, *City of York* (1961), 365–7.

is hardly surprising given the well-known propensity of the richer – and no doubt poorer – inhabitants of the late medieval town to direct their most urgent spiritual needs and ambitions towards the church of the parish wherein they resided. Although at least sixty perpetual chantries seem to have been in existence within York Minster at one point or another during the fourteenth and fifteenth centuries, very few indeed were ever founded by the citizens as opposed to the canons of York. More precisely, of the eight such Minster chantries established between 1400 and 1500 (during a century when the pace of such foundations in the cathedral, as in the city's parish churches, had much slackened), the only one to be founded by an individual member of the laity was that established at the altar of St Stephen by Thomas Lord Scrope of Masham in 1459.[21] For the great majority of the citizens of York, whose attitudes towards the great cathedral in their midst were often ambivalent to a degree, neither burial nor (much less) the creation of a chantry in the Minster was ever a practical or indeed a particularly looked-for possibility.[22] Even the lavish bequest of £400 made in September 1396 by Robert Holme, Sr, perhaps the richest of all York merchants in the prosperous 1390s, failed to ensure a chantry to perpetuate his name in the cathedral church of St Peter.[23] The citizens of York entered the metropolitan church of St Peter for a multiplicity of purposes in the later Middle Ages but hardly ever to observe masses being sung for the souls of their ancestors.

All the more impressive within this context is the exception mentioned above, namely the success of the powerful civic guild

[21] *Yorkshire Chantry Surveys* (hereafter cited as *YCS*), ed. W. Page. Surtees Society, 91–2, (1892–3), I, 25; II, 440–1. This elaborate Scrope chantry (for two chaplains) was apparently the single most lavish such foundation in fifteenth-century York: it is well discussed in S. E. McManaway, 'Some aspects of the foundation of perpetual chantries in York Minster' (University of York, MA in Medieval Studies thesis, 1981), pp. 95–9.
[22] However the wealthier inhabitants of the city and their wives were perhaps slightly more likely to aspire to interment in the nave or aisles of York Minster than is implied in Dobson, 'Perpetual chantries', 25–6. For some examples from the early fifteenth century, see BIHR, Probate Registers, 2, fo. 153; 3, fos. 60, 287, 606, 613.
[23] The perpetual chantry eventually founded to pray for Holme's soul in Holy Trinity, Goodramgate, was undoubtedly more spacious and more responsive to the wishes of his descendants than would have been the case in the Minster: see RCHM, *An Inventory of the Historical Monuments in the City of York*, v, *The Central Area* (1981), p. 5; BIHR, Probate Register, 1, fo. 102; Cook, 'Civic wills', *Associated Architectural Societies Reports and Papers* 28 (1906), 853–7.

of St Christopher in coming to terms with the dean and chapter
in order to found (on 13 December 1426) a perpetual chantry of
one chaplain at the altar of St Christopher in York Minster.[24] This
particular foundation, unique in York but not of course in the
country, can be interpreted in many ways, most persuasively
perhaps as the intrusion of what was essentially a civic institution
into the *ecclesia matrix* of northern England. Although the
successive chaplains were naturally to be presented to, and
admitted by, the dean and chapter, they were first selected by the
master of St Christopher's Guild and its eight longest-serving
aldermen. During vacancies, the goods and muniments of the
chantry were to revert to the custody of the guild itself; and the
ordinances of 1426 leave no doubt at all that neglect of his duties
on the part of the chaplain would lead rapidly to his removal from
office – and on the initiative of the guild rather than the cathedral
clergy at that. More strikingly still perhaps, the chaplain serving St
Christopher's altar was specifically instructed to achieve a high
degree of proficiency in both grammar and song, a requirement
very rarely encountered in the other Minster chantry ordinations
of the later Middle Ages.[25] No doubt only a civic fraternity with
the remarkable influence of St Christopher's Guild (largely
responsible, amidst much else, for the construction of the present
York City Common Hall or Guildhall between 1446 and 1459)
could have been capable of founding a Minster chantry of such a
distinctive type; but in doing so they had undoubtedly helped to
create a lay enclave within the greatest concentration of clergy in
northern England.[26] Perhaps to make that development even
more explicit, it seems that the area around the chantry of St
Christopher's Guild occasionally became an informal citizens'
preserve within the Minster. It was in close proximity to this
cathedral chantry, the only one ever recorded at St Christopher's
altar, that the mayor and aldermen not infrequently held meetings

[24] YCA, G. 70, no. 33. The then new guild of St Christopher had projected a two-chaplain
chantry in the Minster as long ago as 1396 (*CPR, 1391–96*, pp. 711, 716; cf. *YCS*, I, 20–1; II,
448–9).
[25] YCA, G. 70, no. 33; McManaway, 'Perpetual chantries in York Minster', pp. 85–7.
[26] A. Raine, *Mediaeval York: a topographical survey based on original sources* (London, 1955), pp.
134–40. The guild of St Christopher (later united with that of St George) was one of the most
influential if most mysterious fraternities in fifteenth-century York: it was also wealthy enough
to sustain one or perhaps even two maisons dieu: see VCH, *Yorkshire*, III (1913), p. 365; E.
White, *The St Christopher and St George Guild of York* (Borthwick Paper, no. 72, York, 1987).

to conduct their own highly worldly business, 'beyng togadder in counsaill behynd Saint Christopher'.[27]

A much more obvious locale in which to have observed the mayor and council of late medieval York in heated debate was their 'Counsell Chambre apon Ouse Bridge', the effective centre of urban self-government in the city until the mid–eighteenth century. Although the early history of that famous bridge and of the shops and many other buildings constructed upon it remains problematic to a degree, it seems probable that the capacious late Romanesque chapel of St William built near the north-west end of the bridge preceded the appearance of a council chamber on an immediately adjacent site.[28] However, there was already a civic prison on Ouse Bridge by the end of the thirteenth century; and from that date to the Reformation there could never be any doubt that in effect St William's Chapel was synonymous with 'the chapel of the community of York', whose council chamber was literally next door.[29] Nowhere in York, and hardly anywhere in England, can a civic chapel have been more exposed to the close and direct scrutiny of the urban authorities; and nowhere perhaps is it easier to demonstrate the subordination of the ideal of the chantry to the attitudes and interests of a mayor and council. In the first place, it can hardly be a coincidence that within the short space of ten years between 1321 and 1331, at the very height of the fashion for chantry foundation in the city, a chapel which had apparently previously held no perpetual chantries at all came to house no less than four. The very first document to survive within the collection of chantry deeds in the York city archives is indeed the formal licence issued by the mayor and commonalty in January 1321 to enable the appointment of a suitable chaplain to celebrate for the soul of Robert of Wistow in St William's chapel.[30] During the following year, the executors of Roger de

[27] York Civic Records, ed. A. Raine (Yorkshire Archaeological Society, Record Series, xcviii–cxix, 1939–53), II, 14; and for the location of the chantry in the south aisle of the Minster nave see E. Gee, 'The topography of altars, chantries and shrines in York Minster', Antiquaries Journal 64 (1984), 347.

[28] RCHM, Inventory of York, III, South-West of the Ouse (1972), pp. 48–50; Raine, Mediaeval York, pp. 207–22.

[29] VCH, York, 515–16; York City Chamberlains' Accounts, 1396–1500, ed. R. B. Dobson, Surtees Society, 192 (1980), pp. xxi–xxii, xxviii.

[30] YCA, G. 70, no. 1. Wistow's chantry survived within St William's chapel until its dissolution in 1536 (York Civic Records, IV, 144).

Mar, late rector of the parish church of Whixley and succentor of York Minster, endowed another chantry at the altar of St Eligius in the same chapel; and in 1328 and 1331 respectively yet two further chantries were established at St William's College in the spiritual interests of Richard le Toller, a positively prolific founder of chantries in the city, and of the chaplain John Fourbour and his benefactors.[31]

Not one of these four Ouse Bridge chantries was particularly well endowed, and none of their chaplains could expect an annual income much in excess of five or six marks. Nevertheless within a few years, and almost certainly as a result of deliberate policy rather than of the vagaries of individual benefaction, the mayor and council had equipped themselves and their city with a team of chaplains, of *oratores*, directly at their service. The value of this *équipe* for the spiritual as well as economic welfare of the mayor and council's administration of the city was to survive until the eve of the Reformation. Personal animosities within so tightly knit a group of chantry chaplains were naturally not always easy to avoid; and in 1499 the city council found it necessary to reiterate the customary admonition that the four priests should be at 'good, quiete, peciable and honest conversacion' with one another while eating their meals in common within the hall at St William's Chapel.[32] Their chantries and *camerae* were subject to regular aldermanic visitation; and the hours at which these chaplains recited or sang their masses were also often subjected to detailed regulation in order to suit the convenience of councillors attending meetings and of other inhabitants of the town crossing the bridge on their daily business.[33] In such and many other ways the chantry chaplains of St William's Chapel could be left in no doubt at all that it was to their services for the living as much as to their prayers for the dead that they owed their prominent position as perhaps the best known and most exposed chantry chaplains in the city.

Only slightly more secluded were the priests who after 1412 came to serve the three chantries located in the chapel of St Anne

---

[31] YCA, G. 70, nos. 2, 5, 8. For a fifth chantry founded in St William's Chapel, to pray for the prominent fourteenth-century Selby family, see *York Memorandum Book*, I, 24–5; II, 51–2.

[32] *York Civic Records*, II, 141; cf. Raine, *Mediaeval York*, pp. 215–16.

[33] *York Civic Records*, III, 18; cf. IV, 166.

on the city's second most important bridge, over the little river Foss. Almost a century after the mayor and council's deliberate sponsorship of perpetual chantries on Ouse Bridge, their successors took a conscious decision to increase yet again the number of chantry chaplains in the service of the city. According to Richard II's charter of 11 February 1393 which authorised the citizens to purchase lands worth £100 *per annum* to maintain the bridges of Ouse and Foss, the latter was then so fragile 'that it cannot survive for long without major reconstruction and repairs'. From the very outset of these repairs, however, one of the primary motives of the civic government was to build a new chapel on the enlarged Foss Bridge, a chapel quite specifically constructed to house altars at which masses could be said for the souls of the royal family and for the mayor and citizens of the town.[34] To that extent St Anne's Chapel on Foss Bridge was even more obviously a civic chantry chapel than was that of St William on Ouse Bridge, a fact more or less explicitly recognised by the dean and chapter of York cathedral when they licensed the mayor and citizens to celebrate *tres missas peculiares* there in November 1424.[35]

As the three perpetual chantries created in the new St Anne's Chapel were initially brought into existence by an act of civic corporate will, it is therefore hardly surprising that their foundation deeds figure prominently among the original deeds in the city's archives. These deeds make it abundantly clear that in the early fifteenth century there was still no shortage of York citizens eager to respond to the civic appeal to establish chantries on Foss Bridge. As early as 1412, the executors of the late Alan de Hamerton, a prominent York merchant, had amassed enough lands, tenements and rents to support a chantry chaplain there at a stipend of £5 a year.[36] Much more impressive was the 'great

---

[34] *York Memorandum Book*, I, 143–5; cf. II, 72. The foundation of a chantry on a newly completed or repaired bridge naturally enhanced the pious significance of both causes; and it may not be altogether coincidental that the St Anne's Chapel chantries at York were established only a few years after the endowment of the celebrated chapel of St Mary on Wakefield Bridge by Edmund, Duke of York, in 1398: see *Yorkshire Chantry Surveys*, II, 312–14; G. H. Cook, *Mediaeval chantries and chantry chapels* (London, 1947), pp. 44–5.

[35] BIHR, Reg. 5A (Sede Vacante Register, 1299–1554), fol. 388v; *Fabric Rolls of York Minster*, ed. J. Raine, Surtees Society, 35, (1859), p. 238.

[36] YCA, G. 70, no. 30. By 1431–2 at latest, the chaplain of the Hamerton chantry had been provided with a full set of vestments (*York Memorandum Book*, I, 236).

beneficence of Nicholas Blackburn, senior, former Admiral of the King of England and Mayor of York (in 1412–13)'. As John Leland noticed on his visits to York over a century later, Blackburn was probably the most prominent of all lay founders of chantries in late medieval York; and in view of his various other projects, for instance his double chantry foundation at the York Dominican convent, it is remarkable to discover that in December 1424 he was able to assign various messuages and tenements as well as no less than 340 marks in cash to support a chaplain at the high altar of St Anne's Chapel.[37] Quite as ambitious was the third and last chantry in the Foss Bridge chapel, established in February 1428 by yet another York mercer and ex-mayor (1413–14), Robert Holme, Jr. In this case Holme's initial financial grant to the mayor and commonalty was no less than 500 marks, more than enough to provide the chaplain appointed to pray for his and his family's souls with the generous (by York city standards) stipend of ten marks *per annum*.[38] All three of these 'prests of Fossebrygg' survived to the 1530s, receiving their stipends from the York city chamberlains and usually living in houses rented from the city's wardens of Foss Bridge.[39] Once again the chaplains in question were expected to act as a team, cooperating in acts of common worship wherever possible: Robert Holme specifically founded his own chantry on the assumption that 'the number of priests, clerks and other ecclesiastical ministers' in St Anne's Chapel would increase to the extent that his own chaplain 'should attend personally, wearing a surplice and singing'.[40] How far these ambitions were fully achieved is by no means easy to know; but there can be no doubt that St Anne's Chapel was the most impressive – and most characteristic – new 'prayer house' of early fifteenth-century York. Located only a few yards from the great and then new hall of the York mercers (now Merchant Adventurers) in Fossgate, this chapel on Foss Bridge was also a memorial to the golden age of the city's overseas *mercatores*. Few architectural disasters in the history of the city are more to be

---

[37] YCA, G. 70, nos. 31, 32; cf. John Leland, *Itinerary*, ed. L. Toulmin Smith (1906–10), V, 144.
[38] YCA, G. 70, nos. 34, 35: the advowson of this chantry remained in the hands of the Holme family until the early sixteenth century (James Torre, 'Antiquities of the city of York', York Minster Library, fo. 745).
[39] *York Chamberlains' Accounts*, 13–14, 23, 32, 62, 74, 92–3, 109, 125, 151; *York Civic Records*, III, 174.   [40] YCA, G. 70, no. 35.

lamented by the medieval historian than the gradual dismantling of St Anne's Chapel in the reign of Elizabeth, with the ultimate result that now 'so far as is known not one stone of it has survived'.[41]

The two bridge chapels of late medieval York accordingly provided the mayor and commonalty with a unique and eagerly seized opportunity to control and manage not only the occasional isolated perpetual chantry but also what amounted to a couple of separate and substantial ecclesiastical establishments. In the parish churches of the city the mayor and aldermen naturally had to step a little more cautiously. Nevertheless, the twenty-five original deeds within the York city archives which relate to the foundation of perpetual chantries in those churches altogether confirm a prevailing general impression that the latter were all subjected to meticulous and at times almost obsessive lay control.[42] Naturally enough, it is the wishes of the benefactor, his executors and no doubt their advisers, which loom largest in the documents themselves. Thus in 1395 the chaplain of Robert Holme, Sr's elaborate chantry foundation at Holy Trinity, Goodramgate, was required to assemble with six other chaplains on the day of the founder's obit to say the Placebo and Dirige 'with music', a ceremony to be followed by the singing of a Requiem Mass on the following day.[43] An even more informative example of posthumously minute control on the part of the deceased is provided by the perpetual chantry founded at All Saints, North Street, in November 1411 to celebrate for the soul of the recently deceased dyer, Adam de Banke, mayor of the city in 1405. Not only did Banke's executors require the chaplains of this new chantry to reside continuously and to refrain from celebrating pecuniary masses outside the church: they also prescribed his duties and financial commitments on the anniversary of the founder's death in scrupulous detail. Once again cooperation with the other members of the parish clergy ('wearing a surplice, to sing the canonical hours and parochial masses on every Sunday and festival with the other chaplains, clerks and ministers of that church') was essential. More significantly still, it was to be the mayor of York

[41] RCHM, York, v, 104; Raine, Mediaeval York, pp. 69–70.
[42] Cf. Wood-Legh, Perpetual chantries, pp. 65–92; C. Burgess, '"By quick and by dead": wills and pious provision in late medieval Bristol', EHR 102 (1987), 837–58.
[43] YCA, G. 70, no. 24.

or his deputy who conferred the chantry on presentation by the
rector and four senior parishioners; and it was also the mayor who
had the responsibility of removing criminal, incontinent or
mutilated chaplains.[44] Few founders of perpetual chantries in
York's parish churches were quite as precisely exacting as were the
executors of Adam de Banke; but the majority of the York
townsmen certainly did envisage the possibility of direct and
speedy intervention by the mayor and commonalty either against
a negligent chaplain or against those holders of urban tenements
who failed to make their due rent payments towards the
sustenance of the chantries in the city.[45]

In the case of several York chantries, moreover, the mayor and
corporation had direct responsibility for that sustenance themselves. All the surviving civic chamberlains' accounts of the
fifteenth century systematically record the payment of annual
stipends to a group of chaplains who derived all or most of their
income from the city government itself. Among these *salaria
capellanorum* were the £5 6s 8d and £4 2s od paid to the two
chaplains respectively serving the chantries of Adam de Banke
and John Catton in All Saints, North Street; and the chaplains
entrusted with commemorating the souls of Alan Hamerton,
Nicholas Blackburn and Robert Holme at St Anne's Chapel, Foss
Bridge, similarly received annual stipends from the city chamber
at the rates of £5, £5 6s 8d and £6 13s 4d. The chantry chaplains
located at St William's Chapel on Ouse Bridge received most of
their income directly from the wardens of that bridge but also
received a supplementary payment of £2 a year for their daily
celebration of Our Lady's Mass in that chapel.[46] In these and
several other cases the mayor and council of York were
accordingly directly responsible for the financial survival as well
as the disciplinary supervision of perpetual chantries in the city.
The various foundation deeds surviving in the York civic archives
make it sufficiently clear that when rents and tenements were
delivered to the city government as an endowment for a new
chantry these were added to the revenues of the wardens of the
two bridges; but when the founder of a perpetual chantry
preferred to deliver a large initial cash endowment to the mayor

[44] Ibid., no. 27.   [45] Ibid., nos. 4, 5, 8, 11, 14, 15, 21, 22, 30, 32.
[46] *York Chamberlains' Accounts*, 13–14, 23, 32, 62, 73–4, 92–3, 136–7, 168–9, 184–5, 202.

and commonalty this too was invested in real property. Of the
500 marks provided by Robert Holme, Jr, in 1428 to endow his
chantry in St Anne's Chapel, it is recorded that the city council
invested 100 marks in buying a tenement in Coney Street which
thereafter produced a net annual rent of six marks.[47] In such and
many other ways, the city government of York (like all founders
and sponsors of perpetual chantries in late medieval English
towns) became entangled in complicated speculation within the
highly volatile urban property market. Indeed one of the more
common if paradoxical results of the growth of perpetual
chantries in late medieval towns was a reduction in the size of the
parish cemetery. The now celebrated timber-framed Our Lady
Row (Nos. 60–72 Goodramgate, originally built in 1316) is only
one of many York examples of a phenomenon which still deserves
more study at a national level – the erection of two or three-
storeyed *domos rentales* on the street fronts of urban churchyards in
a deliberate attempt to provide rents to endow and support
chantries.[48] To the extent that the main trend in fourteenth- and
fifteenth-century property development in the English town was
towards increasing institutional ownership of urban tenements,
the impact of the perpetual chantry foundation on that trend
would also clearly warrant more urgent attention than it has ever
received.

Not that it will ever be easy to assess the no doubt volatile
economic fortunes of the York perpetual chantries – and their
chaplains – in anything but a highly impressionistic manner. Even
in the case of the chantries directly financed and administered by
the mayor and council, the fact that their endowments were
usually absorbed within the city chamber's total sources of
revenue makes it impossible now to determine whether problems
of insolvency were occasional or perennial. However, there can
be little doubt that financial security was generally much easier to
achieve in the fourteenth century, when rent values in the city
often remained remarkably buoyant, than during the increasingly

[47] YCA, G. 70, no. 34 (the context makes it clear that the mayor and council regarded an annual
return of more than five per cent on invested capital perfectly satisfactory); see *York
Chamberlains' Accounts*, pp. xxxv–xxxvi.
[48] RCHM, *York*, v, lix. The endowment of chantries by means of rent charges on newly built
housing is one of the main themes of S. Rees-Jones, 'Property, tenure and rents: some aspects
of the topography and economy of medieval York' (University of York, D. Phil. thesis, 1987).

difficult years for urban landlords which began to affect York soon after the creation of the Foss Bridge chantries in the 1420s.[49] Waning confidence among York's townsmen about the prospects of sustaining a perpetual chantry's resources into the future still seems the most probable explanation for what came to be a sharply declining pace of chantry foundation in the city as a whole.

In very general terms (and according to a pattern fully confirmed by the surviving original chantry documents preserved in the city archives) enthusiasm among the inhabitants of York for the foundation of perpetual chantries began comparatively late and declined comparatively early. Only three or four such chantries are known to have been founded within the city's parish churches before 1300. By contrast, almost forty perpetual chantries were created in the first half of the fourteenth century, at what was unquestionably the climacteric period of fervour for such institutions; and between 1350 and 1400, during a period when perpetual chantry foundation was still occasionally within the means of York craftsmen as well as merchants, the number of new chantries was still over twenty. During the three decades between 1400 and 1430, in some ways an 'Indian Summer' of urban prosperity at York, twelve new perpetual chantries were founded in the city. However, from that date until the total suppression of the 1540s, there were only nine new perpetual chantry foundations at York, one by a Yorkshire knight (Sir Ralph Bulmer at St Michael le Belfrey in 1472) and all the others by a small handful of the city's mercantile and aldermanic élite.[50] So pronounced a fall in the number of new perpetual chantries is almost certainly less the consequence of declining respect for the ideal of the private mass than an index of the gradual contraction of the number of sizeable mercantile fortunes in the fifteenth-century city. At all social levels within the town, it is evident that chantries and their chaplains were still highly valued: as late as

---

[49] J. N. Bartlett, 'The expansion and decline of York in the later Middle Ages', *Economic History Review*, 2nd ser., 12 (1959), 28–32; Rees-Jones, 'Property, tenure and rents', passim; P. J. P. Goldberg, 'Mortality and economic change in the Diocese of York, 1390–1514', *Northern History* 24 (1988), 38–55.

[50] These numerical estimates, based on royal licences for alienation in mortmain and the chantry commissioners' certificates of 1548 as well as references in York records, are unlikely to be absolutely complete: see Dobson, 'Foundation of perpetual chantries', 32–3; H. Swanson, *Medieval artisans* (Oxford, 1989), p. 159.

1503, to take only one example, 'the parochianz of Saynt Nicholas in Mekilgate putt in a bill of peticion for the reformacion of a chaunterie in the said Kyrke called Eschton chaunterie'.[51] On this occasion, as so often in the past and future, it was the mayor and commonalty who were required to come to the rescue; and as yet there were few visible signs of any erosion in their commitment to the chantries under their official or informal care. It was only as late as 1536, when they were under increasing pressure from 'great dett' and 'great ruyne and decay', that the civic council finally accepted the financially inevitable and secured from parliament that abrupt suppression of seven of the city's chantries which now seems so clear a portent of the universal *dénouement* a dozen years later.[52]

In many ways of course the mayor and commonalty of a city like York never had any alternative but to be heavily involved in the remarkable spate of late medieval perpetual chantry foundations within their midst. As the collection of foundation deeds in the York city archives once again makes abundantly clear, most of the men who established such chantries were themselves ex-mayors and aldermen of the city, predestined to believe that the civic council they had once served would be the most reliable custodian or supervisor of their spiritual foundations. Nor were the responsibilities incurred by that council without some very real compensations for itself. Above all perhaps, the mayor and aldermen — as well as prominent parishioners in each city church — were provided with the possibilities of patronage. That last, and highly prized, commodity was not otherwise immediately available even to the most substantial inhabitants of a medieval town; and there can be little doubt that the ability to influence the appointment of chantry and other chaplains in the city's parish churches did more than anything to bind town's laity and clergy personally together. Indeed it seems to emerge from the York evidence that one of the motives for the establishment of a chantry

---

[51] *York Civic Records*, II, 190–1. It has been properly pointed out by Dr Jennifer I. Kermode that during the fifteenth century more bequests were made to augment existing chantries than to create new ones: see her 'The merchants of three northern towns', in *Profession, vocation and culture in later medieval England: essays dedicated to the memory of A. R. Myers*, ed. C. H. Clough (Liverpool, 1982), pp. 24–5.

[52] *York Civic Records*, IV, 144; A. G. Dickens, 'A municipal dissolution of chantries, 1536', *Yorkshire Archaeological Journal* 36 (1944–7), 164–73.

at all was a testator's wish to safeguard the future of a priest who had served him long and faithfully as chaplain and confessor. In 1340, for example, Thomas Duraunt founded a perpetual chantry at the church of St Crux and appointed John de Grayngham as its first chaplain, on the express understanding that he was to be under no obligation to celebrate mass or attend matins and vespers in the church 'as long as he remains in the said Thomas's company'.[53] Nearly a century later, in 1435, John Turnour, the priest appointed by Richard Russell to serve his new chantry in St John's, Hungate, was so close an intimate of this ex-mayor that he went on to act as one of his executors and also received a bequest in Russell's will (to sing masses of course) of no less than seventy marks.[54]

Nor is future research at all likely to confirm that such chantry chaplains were quite so obscure, impoverished and isolated figures as is traditionally assumed. At York at least, an increasing proportion of these priests left wills which bear witness not only to their collections of vestments and service books but also to specialist skills which enhanced their status and value in the eyes of their parishioners.[55] In 1492 the city council authorised William Insklyff, chaplain of Robert Holme's chantry on Foss Bridge, 'to fynysche and make up two books, that is to say a masse book and a cowcher' despite the opposition of the company of city textwriters. More surprisingly perhaps, William Duffield, chaplain of St Thomas's chantry at All Saints, Pavement, in 1433, was in possession of several of the books once owned by the late Archbishop Thomas de Corbridge (1299–1304); while less serious volumes, including works of history and even a mysterious 'Balletboke', could be found among the goods of other fifteenth-century chantry priests of the city.[56] The contribution of the chantry priests both to the extension of literacy and the distribution of charity in the city is likely to have been as important as it is usually obscure; but it was more important still

---

[53] YCA. G. 70, no. 12.

[54] BIHR, Probate Register, 3, fos. 439–40; *Testamenta Eboracensia*, II, 52–7.

[55] See, e.g., *Testamenta Eboracensia*, I, 73, 146, 196; II, 178, 184, 202, 268, 275; III, 94; IV, 41. Cf. the comparatively favourable judgement of P. Mackie on 'Chaplains on the diocese of York, 1480–1530: the testamentary evidence', *Yorkshire Archaeological Journal* 58 (1986), 123–33.

[56] *York Civic Records*, II, 78; *York Chamberlains' Accounts*, pp. 178, 185, 191, 202; *Testamenta Eboracensia*, II, 87–8, 213; cf. Mackie, 'Chaplains in diocese of York', 126–7.

that they were expected by the laymen of York to integrate themselves for acts of common worship into the teams of parish clergy (comprising at least an average of six or seven in each of the forty town churches) which lay at the heart of whatever popular religion in the city actually was.[57] With such numbers of priests (and private and communal masses) at their disposal, most citizens of York presumably never felt that they were in danger of suffering from serious spiritual neglect as they contemplated their progress into the next world. When, on a famous and often cited occasion in 1388, Mayor William Selby made his controversial declaration that 'the chantry priests and other stipendiary clergy of this city and its suburbs are the special orators of the citizens, their patrons and their masters', he was not in fact being at all economical with the truth.[58]

The laymen of late fifteenth-century York were accordingly not without many spiritual and other rewards for the serious financial cares imposed upon them by the scores of perpetual and other chantries within the city. However, the perpetual chantry was then – as it remains in retrospect – a highly ambiguous institution. It is a good deal easier to demonstrate that the mayor and council of York were strenuous in their endeavours to preserve chantries at a respectable spiritual level than to prove that they were always or often successful in doing so. Most arduous of their responsibilities perhaps, especially in a system of 'urban self-government by amateurs', were those presented by the complex legal, administrative and disciplinary problems which clustered round every chantry in the city.[59] A close perusal of the original foundation deeds which have provided the basis for this paper leaves one with the cumulative impression that in order for the founder of a chantry to secure some remission of purgatorial pains in the next world, his family, his descendants, his executors and

[57] J. A. Hoeppner Moran, *The growth of English schooling, 1340–1548: learning, literacy and laicization in pre-Reformation York diocese* (Princeton, New Jersey, 1985), pp. 83–90; M. Rubin, *Charity and community in medieval Cambridge* (Cambridge, 1987), pp. 184–92. That there were approximately 260 parish chaplains in fifteenth-century York is established by a reference to bequests of 4d to each of them in the will (4 September 1436) of Thomas Bracebridge: BIHR, York Probate Register, 3, fo. 488; Dobson, 'Perpetual chantries of York', 37–8.

[58] *York Memorandum Book*, II, 19; cf. P. Heath, 'Between reform and Reformation: the English Church in the fourteenth and fifteenth centuries', *Journal of Ecclesiastical History* 41 (1990), 675 ('One aspect which emerges clearly from all these studies is the growing experience shared by laymen and women of proprietorship over the church or clergy').

[59] See especially Wood-Legh, *Perpetual chantries*, pp. 155–81 ('Chantries and the towns').

the mayor and council were often forced to undergo many purgatorial hours on his behalf in the earthly city he had left behind him. By a paradox fundamental at most levels of the medieval Christian church, the quest for one's personal salvation might all too easily add to the worldly care of one's neighbours and descendants. More paradoxically still perhaps, enthusiasm for the private chantry made the parish churches of York and elsewhere less secluded, more vibrant with diverse religious activity, than they had ever been. As Christopher Brooke pointed out in the book cited at the very beginning of this paper, 'the bustle of chantry priests and the singing of chantry masses helped to make large churches resemble vast mausolea'.[60]

However, for modern travellers in quest of the personalised religion of the fifteenth-century city, the primary objectives of pilgrimage are to be found less in the major mausoleum of York Minster than in parish churches like St Michael's, Spurriergate (the tomb of Sir Richard York), Holy Trinity, Goodramgate (the memorial brass of Mayor Thomas Danby) and All Saints, North Street (the Nicholas Blackburn window).[61] It is in such churches that even now one may occasionally encounter battered memorials to the religious proclivities of York citizens who once hoped to be remembered – and not just by the historian – for ever. Perhaps a greater reward yet may await those who visit the still surviving, if now almost totally stripped and denuded, chantry chapel of St James, founded by the powerful Holme family next to the south aisle of the nave of Holy Trinity, Goodramgate: only there perhaps in late twentieth-century York may it be possible physically to recapture what the appeal of a perpetual chantry could once have been.[62] If so, how appropriate that six hundred years ago this was exactly the church and chapel in which Robert Holme, Sr, envisaged the frequent presence of twenty-five chaplains, not only to intercede for his own soul but also 'so that divine worship through them may be there increased'.[63] The

---

[60] Brooke, *Popular religion in the Middle Ages*, p. 110.

[61] RCHM, *York*, III, 7, 18–19; v, 7; VCH, *York*, 370, 385.

[62] The arms of the Holme family are still visible on a shield near the entrance to this chantry chapel. Its interior is lit (much to the confusion of several architectural historians in the past and even the present) by two re-used reticulated windows of the early fourteenth century inserted into the later outer wall (RHMC, *York*, v, 6–7; and see above, n. 23).

[63] BIHR, Probate Register, 3, fos. 100v–103v; Cook, 'Early civic wills', *Associated Architectural Societies Reports and Papers* 28 (1906), 20–1.

perpetual chantries of the late medieval English town are not always easy to defend or justify; but at the least they present the most ambitious — and most costly — attempts ever made to reconcile and even merge the different spiritual needs of church and city at a deeply personal level.

A bibliography of Christopher Brooke

General editor 1959–87, with V. H. Galbraith and Sir Roger Mynors and subsequently D. E. Greenway and M. Winterbottom, of *Nelson's Medieval Texts* (from 1966, *Oxford Medieval Texts*).

General editor, with D. Mack Smith, *Nelson's History of England* 1960–74.

General editor, Thames and Hudson's *Library of Medieval Civilisation* 1971–2.

General editor, Thames and Hudson's *Currents in the History of Culture and Ideas* 1974.

General editor, Cambridge University Press' *A history of the University of Cambridge* 1988–.

BOOKS

1 Introduction (with M. Postan) and glossary to *The Book of William Morton, Almoner of Peterborough Monastery (1448–67)*, ed. W. T. Mellows and P. I. King (Northamptonshire Record Society, 1954).

2 Introduction, notes and appendices to *The letters of John of Salisbury, I, Early letters*, ed. W. J. Millor and H. E. Butler (Edinburgh: Nelson's Medieval Texts, 1955; now repr. Oxford Medieval Texts 1986). The same, and translation, in *II, Later letters* (Oxford Medieval Texts, 1979, ed. with W. J. Millor).

3 (With M. Postan) *Carte Nativorum: a Peterborough Abbey cartulary of the fourteenth century* (Northamptonshire Record Society, 1960).

4 *From Alfred to Henry III, 871–1272* (Nelson's History of England, II, Edinburgh, 1961).

5 *The Saxon and Norman kings* (London, Batsford, 1963; 2nd edn 1978).

6 *Europe in the central Middle Ages* (General History of Europe, III, London: Longmans, 1964). Also in French and Spanish translation. 2nd edn, with three additional chapters, 1987.

7 (With A. Morey) *Gilbert Foliot and his letters* (Cambridge University Press, 1965).

8 (With A. Morey) *The letters and charters of Gilbert Foliot … Bishop of London (1163–87)* (Cambridge University Press, 1967).

9 *The twelfth century Renaissance* (London: Thames and Hudson, 1969). Also in Portuguese translation.

10 *Medieval church and society* (London: Sidgwick and Jackson, 1971): reprinted and other essays.

11 *The structure of medieval society* (London: Thames and Hudson, 1971; expanded reprint of chapter in *The flowering of the Middle Ages*, ed. J. Evans, (London: Thames and Hudson, 1966, repr. 1985), pp. 11–40. Also in Dutch translation.

12 (With D. Knowles and V. C. M. London) *The heads of religious houses, England and Wales, 940–1216* (Cambridge University Press, 1972).

13 (With Wim Swaan) *The monastic world 1000–1300* (London: Elek, 1974). Also in Dutch, French and German translations.

14 (With Mrs G. Keir) *London 800–1216: the shaping of a city* (A History of London, ed. F. Sheppard, vol. II, London: Secker and Warburg, 1975).

15 (Editor, with D. E. Luscombe, G. H. Martin and D. M. Owen), *Church and government in the Middle Ages: essays presented to C. R. Cheney* (Cambridge University Press, 1976).

16 (Editor, with D. Whitelock and M. Brett) *Councils and Synods with other documents relating to the English Church I, 871–1204* (2 parts) (Oxford: Clarendon Press, 1981).

17 (Editor, with B. H. I. H. Stewart, J. G. Pollard and T. R. Volk) *Studies in numismatic method presented to Philip Grierson* (Cambridge University Press, 1983).

18 (Editor, with M. R. James and Sir Roger Mynors) Walter Map, *De nugis curialium* (Oxford Medieval Texts, 1983).

19 (With R. Brooke) *Popular religion in the Middle Ages: western Europe, 1000–1300* (London: Thames and Hudson, 1984).

20 *A history of Gonville and Caius College* (Woodbridge: Boydell and Brewer, 1985).

21 *The church and the Welsh border in the central Middle Ages* (Woodbridge: Boydell and Brewer, 1986): reprinted papers.

22 (With Roger Highfield and Wim Swaan) *Oxford and Cambridge* (Cambridge University Press, 1988).

23 (With D. E. Luscombe), revised edn of D. Knowles, *Evolution of medieval thought* (London: Longmans, 1988).

24 *The medieval idea of marriage* (Oxford University Press, 1989).

25 (With M. Brett and M. Winterbottom), revised edn of Hugh the Chanter, *The history of the church of York 1066–1217*, ed. and trans. C. Johnson, (Oxford Medieval Texts, 1990).

26 (Editor and part-author, with Abbot Aelred Sillem, D. E. Luscombe and R. Lovatt) *David Knowles remembered* (Cambridge University Press, 1991).

Bibliography

27 *A history of the University of Cambridge, IV: 1870–1990* (Cambridge University Press, forthcoming 1992).

ARTICLES AND LECTURES

Note: Those articles marked with an asterisk are reprinted in *Medieval church and society* (List of Books no. 10), those with a ¶ in *The Church and the Welsh border in the central Middle Ages* (List of Books no. 21).

1 (With Z. N. Brooke) 'Hereford cathedral dignitaries in the twelfth century', *Cambridge Historical Journal* 8, no. 1 (1944), 1–21, with supplement in no. 3 (1946) 179–85.

2 (With Z. N. Brooke) 'Henry II, Duke of Normandy and Aquitaine', *English Historical Review* 61 (1946), 81–9.

3 (With A. Morey) 'The Cerne letters of Gilbert Foliot and the legation of Imar of Tusculum', *English Historical Review* 63 (1948), 523–7.

4 'The Canterbury forgeries and their author', *Downside Review* 68 (1950), 462–76; 69 (1951), 210–31.

5 (With P. Grierson) 'Round halfpennies of Henry I', *British Numismatic Journal* 26 (1951), 286–9.

6 'The Composition of the chapter of St Paul's 1086–1163', *Cambridge Historical Journal* 10 no. 2 (1951), 111–32.

⋆7 'Gregorian Reform in action: clerical marriage in England, 1050–1200', *Cambridge Historical Journal* 12, no. 1 (1956), 1–21, appendix in no. 2 (1956), 187–8. Also repr. in *Change in medieval society*, ed. S. Thrupp (New York, 1964), pp. 49–71.

8 'The Deans of St Paul's, c. 1090–1499', *Bulletin of the Institute of Historical Research* 29 (1956), 231–44.

⋆9 *The dullness of the past: an inaugural lecture* (Liverpool, 1957).

10 'The earliest times to 1485', in *A history of St Paul's cathedral*, ed. W. R. Matthews and W. M. Atkins (London, 1957), pp. 1–99, 361–5.

11 'Canons of English church councils in the early decretal collections', *Traditio* 13 (1957), 471–80.

¶12 'The archbishops of St David's, Llandaff and Caerleon-on-Usk', in N. K. Chadwick et al., *Studies in the early British church* (Cambridge, 1958), pp. 201–42.

13 *The Investiture disputes* (Historical Association pamphlet, 1958, repr. 1966).

14 'Episcopal charters for Wix priory', in *Medieval miscellany for Doris Mary Stenton*, ed. P. Barnes and C. F. Slade (PRS, London, 1962), pp. 45–63.

¶15 'St Peter of Gloucester and St Cadoc of Llancarfan' in N. K. Chadwick et al., *Celt and Saxon* (Cambridge, 1963), pp. 258–322.

16 'The church of the Middle Ages, 1000–1500', in *The layman in Christian history*, ed. S. C. Neill and H. R. Weber (London, 1963), pp. 111–34.

⋆17 'Problems of the church historian', in *Studies in Church History* 1 (1964), 1–19.

Bibliography

¶18 'The church and the Welsh border in the tenth and eleventh century', *Journal of the Flintshire Historical Society* 21 (1964), 32–45.

★19 'St Dominic and his first biographer', *Transactions of the Royal Historical Society* 5th Series, 17 (1967), 23–40.

★20 'Religious sentiment and church design in the later Middle Ages', *Bulletin of the John Rylands Library* 50 (1967), 13–33.

21 'Archbishop Lanfranc, the English bishops and the Council of London of 1075', *Studia Gratiana* 12 (1967): *Collectanea Stephan Kuttner*, II, 39–60.

★22 'Approaches to medieval forgery', *Journal of the Society of Archivists* 3 (1958), 377–86.

23 *Time, the Archsatirist* (Inaugural Lecture, Westfield College, London, 1968).

★24 'Heresy and religious sentiment: 1000–1250', *Bulletin of the Institute of Historical Research* 41 (1968), 115–31.

25 'The missionary at home: the church in the towns 1000–1250', *Studies in Church History* 6 (1970), 59–83 (Presidential Address, Ecclesiastical History Society).

26 'The teaching of diplomatic', *Journal of the Society of Archivists* 4 (1970), 1–9.

27 'Historical writing in England between 850 and 1150', *La Storiografia Altomedievale: Settimane di Studio del Centro italiano di Studi sull'Alto Medioevo* 17 (1970), 233–47.

28 'Princes and kings as patrons of monasteries: Normandy and England', in *Il Monachesimo e la riforma ecclesiastica (1049–1122)*, Miscellanea del Centro di Studi Medioevali 6 (Milan, 1971), 125–52.

29 (With M. D. Knowles and A. J. Duggan) 'Henry II's supplement to the Constitutions of Clarendon', *English Historical Review* 87 (1972), 757–71.

30 'Lambeth and London in the eleventh and twelfth centuries', *Report of the Friends of Lambeth Palace Library for 1972* (1973), 11–23.

31 (With G. Keir and S. Reynolds) 'Henry I's charter for the city of London', *Journal of the Society of Archivists* 4 (1973), 558–78.

32 (With R. H. Pinder Wilson) 'The reliquary of St Petroc and the ivories of Norman Sicily', *Archaeologia* 104 (1973), 261–305.

33 'The ecclesiastical geography of medieval towns', in *Miscellanea Historiae Ecclesiasticae* 5 (*Colloque de Varsovie, 27–29 October 1971*) (Louvain, 1974), 15–31.

34 'David Knowles', *Proceedings of the British Academy* 51 (1975), 439–77; also shorter memoirs in *Peterhouse 1975–6*, pp. 39–44; *Studies in Church History* 12 (1975), ix–xii.

¶35 'Geoffrey of Monmouth as a historian', in *Church and government* (List of Books no. 14), 77–91.

36 'The medieval town as an ecclesiastical centre', in *European towns, their archaeology and early history*, ed. M. W. Barley (London, 1977), pp. 459–74.

37 'St Albans: the great abbey church', in *Cathedral and city, St Albans ancient and modern*, ed. R. Runcie (London, 1977), pp. 43–70.

38 (With R. M. T. Hill) 'From 627 until the early thirteenth century', in *A history of York Minster*, ed. G. E. Aylmer and R. Cant (Oxford, 1977), pp. 1–43.

39 (With R. B. Brooke) 'I vescovi di Inghilterra e Normandia nel secolo XI: contrasti' in *Le istituzioni ecclesiastiche della 'societas christiana' dei secali XI–XII: Diocesi, pievi e parrocchie*, Miscellanea del Centro di Studi Medioevali 8 (Milan, 1977), 536–45.

40 *Marriage in Christian history: an inaugural lecture* (Cambridge University Press, 1978).

41 'Alcuin', *49th Annual Report of the Friends of York Minster* (1978), 13–24.

42 '"Both small and great beasts": an introductory study' in *Medieval women*, presented to Professor Rosalind M. T. Hill, *Studies in Church History, Subsidia* 1 (1978), 1–13.

43 (With R. B. Brooke) 'St Clare' in *Medieval women*, presented to Professor Rosalind M. T. Hill, *Studies in Church History, Subsidia* 1 (1978), 275–87.

44 'Joan Evans', *Antiquaries Journal* 58 (1978), 9–12.

45 'The Normans as cathedral builders', in reprint of R. Willis, *Architectural History of Winchester Cathedral* (Friends of Winchester Cathedral, 1980), pp. 83–98.

46 'Charles Clay', *Proceedings of the British Academy* 64 (1980), 311–40; repr. *Yorkshire Archaeological Journal* 52 (1980), 1–18.

47 'Aspects of marriage law in the eleventh and twelfth centuries' in *Proceedings of the Fifth International Congress of Medieval Canon Law, Salamanca, 1976*, ed. S. Kuttner et al. (Vatican City, 1980), pp. 333–44.

48 'Marriage and society in the central Middle Ages', in *Marriage and Society: studies in the social history of marriage*, ed. R. B. Outhwaite (London, 1981), pp. 17–34.

49 'Anniversary address' as President of the Society of Antiquaries, in *Antiquaries Journal* 62 (1982), 1–12; 63 (1983), 1–10 and 64 (1984), 1–9.

50 'Rural ecclesiastical institutions in England. The search for their origins', *Cristianizzazione ed organizzazione ecclesiastica delle campagne nell'alto medioevo: espansione e resistenze: Settimane di Studio del Centro italiano di studi sull'Alto medioevo* 28 (1982 for 1980), 685–711.

51 'Aspetti del matrimonio e della famiglia nel mondo di Santa Caterina e di San Bernardo' in *Atti del Simposio Internazionale Cateriniano-Bernardiniano (Siena, 1980)*, ed. D. Maffei and P. Nardi (Siena, 1982), 877–89.

52 'Cristianità e regni in Inghilterra', in *La Cristianità dei Secoli XI e XII IN OCCIDENTE: Coscienza e Strutture di una Società*: Miscellanea del Centro di Studi Medioevali 10, (Milan, 1983), 45–66.

53 (With Catherine Hall) 'The Masters of Gonville Hall', *The Caian* 1983, 43–50.

54 'John of Salisbury and his world', in *The World of John of Salisbury*, ed. M. Wilks, *Studies in Church History, Subsidia*, 3 (Oxford, 1984), 1–20.

55 'The churches of medieval Cambridge', in *History, society and the churches: essays in honour of Owen Chadwick*, ed. D. Beales and G. Best (Cambridge, 1985), pp. 49–76.

56 'The archdeacon and the Norman Conquest', in *Tradition and change: essays in honour of Marjorie Chibnall*, ed. D. Greenway, C. Holdsworth and J. Sayers (Cambridge, 1985), pp. 1–19.

57 'Monk and canon: some patterns in the religious life of the twelfth century', *Studies in Church History* 22 (1985), 109–29.

58 'On the archives of a school and a college' (review article), *Journal of Ecclesiastical History* 37 (1986), 303–8.

59 'St Bernard, the patrons and monastic planning', in *Cistercian art and architecture in the British Isles*, ed. C. Norton and D. Park (Cambridge, 1986), pp. 11–23.

60 'Allocating rooms in the sixteenth century', *The Caian* 1987, pp. 56–67.

61 (With V. Ortenberg) 'The birth of Queen Margaret of Anjou', *Historical Research* 61 (1988), 357–8.

62 (With J. M. Horn and N. L. Ramsay) 'A canon's residence in the eighteenth century: the case of Thomas Gooch', *Journal of Ecclesiastical History* 39 (1988), 545–56.

63 'Christopher Robert Cheney', *Proceedings of the British Academy* 73 (1989), 425–46.

64 'Priest, deacon and layman, from St Peter Damian to St Francis', *Studies in Church History* 26 (1989), 65–85.

65 'The University Chancellor' and Appendix 1, 'Chancellors of the University of Cambridge, *c.* 1415–1535', and Appendix 2 (with R. Rex, S. Thompson and M. Underwood) 'Fisher's career and itinerary, *c.* 1469–1535', in *Humanism, Reform and the Reformation: the career of Bishop John Fisher*, ed. B. Bradshaw and E. Duffy (Cambridge, 1989), pp. 47–66, 233–4, 235–49.

66 'King David I of Scotland as a connoisseur of the religious Orders', in *Mediaevalia Christiana, xie–xiiie siècles: Hommage à Raymonde Foreville*, ed. C. Viola (Paris, 1989), pp. 320–34.

67 'The central Middle Ages: 800–1270', in *The British Atlas of Historic Towns*, iii, *The city of London from prehistoric times to c. 1520*, ed. M. D. Lobel (Oxford, 1989), pp. 30–41.

68 'Reflections on late medieval cults and devotions', in *Essays in honor of Edward B. King*, ed. R. Benson et al. (Sewanee (Ten.), 1991), pp. 33–45.

69 'Cambridge and the antiquaries, 1500–1840', *Proceedings of the Cambridge Antiquarian Society* 79 (1991 for 1990), 1–14.

70 'Chaucer's parson and Edmund Gonville: contrasting roles of fourteenth-century incumbents', in *Studies in clergy and ministry in medieval England*, ed. D. M. Smith (York, 1991), pp. 1–19.

Index

Index

Armagh, cathedral chapter
Anglo-Irish elements, 221–3, 229–32
  canons, 236–7, 241–3
  ecclesia inter Anglicos, 221–2, 225, 226, 228,
    235, 236, 240, 243–4 *passim*
  inter Hibernicos, 221–3, 225, 227, 230, 232,
    233, 238–40 *passim*, 244, 245
Culdees, 237–8
  political involvement, 226, 230–1, 235, 243
  registers, 219–21, 223ff, 229, 234, 236, 240,
    241, 243–5
  relations with archbishops
    disciplinary rights, 227–9, 232, 238–9
    dues, 223, 224–6
    election, 236
    and Ulster kingship, 231–2, 239–41
artifacts, cultural, 18
Ashburton
  churchwardens' accounts, 7
Ashkenaz, 111
Assheton, Robert de, 226
assarting, 137
Assumption, Vigil of, 215
Augustine of Hippo, St, 32, 42, 43, 46
Augustinian order
  Aldgate, 280
  Armagh, 232, 237, 238, 240
Autun, 163
Auvergne, 159
Ava of Aquitaine, 151
Avendauth, Iohannes, *see* Ibn Dawud
Averroes, 52, 53
Avicenna, 52
Avignon, 10, 11
  visitations, 224, 225, 228

Baer, Yitzhak, 113
Bagnoreggio, 217
Bailey, Mark, 17
Bakhtin, Mikhail, 18
baking, 119–20, 167
Balearic Islands, 112, 113, 117
Banke, Adam de, 315, 324–5
Barcelona, 115, 120
Barnwell Priory, 63
Bassingbourn, 14
Bath and Wells, diocese, 194
Battle, monks of, 192
'Bec-Lanfranc' group, 269
Bede, 180
beeswax, 143
bells, 12, 181, 192, 234
  Toral, 123
Benedict XI, Pope, 105
Benedictine order, 268
  Armagh, 225

art, 249, 252, 257, 259, 263, 263
  Cambridge, 59–60
  use of nave, 249, 271
Bennaggero, march of, 136
Berengar of Ivrea, 133
Bermondsey priory
  annals, 286ff
  comparisons, 285–7
  shared source, 288ff, 293–4, 296
  texts, 297ff
Bernhard, Bishop of Halbertstadt, 131
Berzé, house of, 157, 170
Beverley, 13
Bible, 204
  Hebrew, 38–9
  of William of Devon, 263
Billung, Hermann, 132
Black Death, 17
Blackburn, Nicholas, 323, 325, 331
Blangernon family, 15
Blera, 214
Boethius, 49, 50, 51
Bohemia
  silver, 142
Boniface VIII, Pope, 98, 100–3, 105, 109
Boniface IX, 230
Bonifaz, Pedro, 109
books, 329, of Hours, 18, 22
Boso, priest, 148
Brabançons, 164
Bracciano, 215
Brackmann, Albert, 129, 132, 133, 146
Brame, land, 69–70
Brancion, lady of, 170
Brandenburg, diocese, 131, 133, 142
bread tax, 119
brehons, 241, 245
Bréifne, 227
Bremen, 131
bridge chantries, *see* Foss Bridge; Ouse
  Bridge
Britnell, Richard, 16
Briviesca, archdeaconry, 99
Brooke, Christopher, 109, 129, 249
  medieval studies, 3, 311, 315, 331
  Cambridge, 60
  London, 173, 185, 279, 286
  bibliography, 333–8
Bulmer, Sir Ralph, 327
burgenses, 157–9, 166
Burgess, Clive, 312
Burgos, cathedral chapter
  and Dominican friars, 83ff, 106–7
  burial rights, disputes, 84–7, 88–91, 104
  harassment, 93ff, 104–5
  property, 85–6, 96–8, 102–4, 108

DATE DUE

JAN 21 96			
AUG 21 96			